2014

INSANITY AND DIVINITY

How close is spirituality to psychosis?

Covering the interrelation of psychosis and spirituality from a number of angles, *Insanity and Divinity* will generate dialogue and discussion, aid critical reflection and stimulate creative approaches to clinical work for those interested in the connections between religious studies, psychoanalysis, anthropology and hagiography.

Bringing together an international range of contributors and covering many different types of religious experience, this book presents its theme in three parts:

- psychoanalysis, belief and mysticism
- anthropology, history and hagiography
- psychology, psychosis and religious experience.

Each section includes discussion of the hinterland between madness and religious experience from the perspective of a number of religions, autobiographical accounts of those who have experienced a psychosis in which spirituality played a key part and a comprehensive review of the position of psychology research into the meaning and function of spirituality in relation to the psychoses.

Insightful, enlightening and wide-ranging, *Insanity and Divinity* is ideal for clinicians, academics and chaplains working in clinical settings.

John Gale is a former Benedictine monk who later trained as a psychotherapist and is now CEO of the charity Community Housing and Therapy. He is particularly interested in the interface between philosophy, spirituality and psychoanalysis.

Michael Robson is the Director of Studies in Divinity at St Edmund's College, Cambridge. He is the author of a number of books and editor of *The Cambridge Companion to Francis of Assisi*.

Georgia Rapsomatioti is a community mental health advocate who previously worked at Community Housing and Therapy as deputy manager at Lexham House and senior therapist at Highams Lodge. She has an interest in Lacanian psychoanalysis, trauma and psychosis.

The Book Series of the International Society for
Psychological and Social Approaches to Psychosis
Series editors: Brian Martindale and Alison Summers

ISPS (The International Society for Psychological and Social Approaches to Psychosis) has a history stretching back more than fifty years during which it has witnessed the relentless pursuit of biological explanations for psychosis. The tide has been turning in recent years and there is a welcome international resurgence of interest in a range of psychological factors that have considerable explanatory power and therapeutic possibilities. Governments, professional groups, people with personal experience of psychosis and family members are increasingly expecting interventions that involve more talking and listening. Many now regard practitioners skilled in psychological therapies as an essential component of the care of people with psychosis.

ISPS is a global society. It aims to promote psychological and social approaches both to understanding and to treating psychosis. It also aims to bring together different perspectives on these issues. ISPS is composed of individuals, networks and institutional members from a wide range of backgrounds and is especially concerned that those with personal experience of psychosis and their family members are fully involved in our activities alongside practitioners and researchers, and that all benefit from this. Our members recognise the potential humanitarian and therapeutic potential of skilled psychological understanding and therapy in the field of psychosis and ISPS embraces a wide spectrum of approaches from psychodynamic, systemic, cognitive, and arts therapies to the need-adapted approaches, family and group therapies and residential therapeutic communities.

We are also most interested in establishing meaningful dialogue with those practitioners and researchers who are more familiar with biological-based approaches. There is increasing empirical evidence for the interaction of genes and biology with the emotional and social environment, and there are important examples of such interactions in the fields of trauma, attachment relationships in the family and in social settings and with professionals.

ISPS activities include regular international and national conferences, newsletters and email discussion groups. Routledge has recognised the importance of our field in publishing both the book series and the ISPS journal: *Psychosis – Psychological, Social and Integrative Approaches* with the two complementing one another. The book series started in 2004 and by 2012 had 15 volumes with several more in preparation. A wide range of topics are covered and we hope this reflects some success in our aim of bringing together a rich range of perspectives.

The book series is intended as a resource for a broad range of mental health professionals as well as those developing and implementing policy and people whose interest in psychosis is at a personal level. We aim for rigorous academic standards and at the same time accessibility to a wide range of readers, and for the books to promote the ideas of clinicians and researchers who may be well known in some countries but not so familiar in others. Our overall intention is to encourage the dissemination of existing knowledge and ideas, promote productive debate, and encourage more research in a most important field whose secrets certainly do not all reside in the neurosciences.

For more information about ISPS, email isps@isps.org or visit our website, www.isps.org.

For more information about the journal *Psychosis* visit www.isps.org/index.php/publications/journal

MODELS OF MADNESS: PSYCHOLOGICAL, SOCIAL AND BIOLOGICAL APPROACHES TO SCHIZOPHRENIA
First edition
Edited by John Read, Loren R. Mosher & Richard P. Bentall

PSYCHOSES: AN INTEGRATIVE PERSPECTIVE
Edited by Johan Cullberg

EVOLVING PSYCHOSIS: DIFFERENT STAGES, DIFFERENT TREATMENTS
Edited by Jan Olav Johanessen, Brian V. Martindale & Johan Cullberg

FAMILY AND MULTI-FAMILY WORK WITH PSYCHOSIS: A GUIDE FOR PROFESSIONALS
Gerd-Ragna Block Thorsen, Trond Gronnestad & Anne Lise Oxenvad

EXPERIENCES OF MENTAL HEALTH IN-PATIENT CARE: NARRATIVES FROM SERVICE USERS, CARERS AND PROFESSIONALS
Edited by Mark Hardcastle, David Kennard, Sheila Grandison & Leonard Fagin

PSYCHOTHERAPIES FOR THE PSYCHOSES: THEORETICAL, CULTURAL, AND CLINICAL INTEGRATION
Edited by John Gleeson, Eión Killackey & Helen Krstev

SURVIVING, EXISTING, OR LIVING: PHASE-SPECIFIC
THERAPY FOR SEVERE PSYCHOSIS
Pamela Fuller

MODELS OF MADNESS: PSYCHOLOGICAL, SOCIAL AND
BIOLOGICAL APPROACHES TO PSYCHOSIS
Second edition
Edited by John Read & Jacqui Dillon

INSANITY AND DIVINITY

Studies in psychosis and spirituality

Edited by
John Gale, Michael Robson and
Georgia Rapsomatioti

Routledge
Taylor & Francis Group

LONDON AND NEW YORK

First published 2014
by Routledge
27 Church Road, Hove, East Sussex BN3 2FA

Simultaneously published in the USA and Canada
by Routledge
711 Third Avenue, New York, NY 10017

Routledge is an imprint of the Taylor & Francis Group, an informa business

British Library Cataloguing in Publication Data
A catalogue record for this book is available from the British Library

Library of Congress Cataloging in Publication Data
   Insanity and divinity : studies in psychosis and spirituality/edited
by John Gale, Michael Robson, and Georgia Rapsomatioti.
     pages cm
1. Psychoses—Etiology.   2. Mental illness—Religious aspects.
3. Psychiatry and religion.   4. Spirituality—Psychological aspects.
I. John, Gale.   II. Robson, Michael J. P., 1946-   III. Rapsomatioti,
Georgia.
RC512.I45 2013
616.89—dc23
                                                        2012049618

ISBN: 978-0-415-60861-9 (hbk)
ISBN: 978-0-415-60862-6 (pbk)
ISBN: 978-0-203-69424-4 (ebk)

Typeset in Garamond
by RefineCatch Limited, Bungay, Suffolk, UK

Printed and bound by CPI Group (UK) Ltd, Croydon, CR0 4YY

This book is dedicated to Dom Aelred Baker osb who first introduced me to patristic studies almost forty years ago. His erudition and guidance has been an inspiration to me ever since. And it is to his continued encouragement, enthusiasm and kindness that I owe so much.

–John Gale

CONTENTS

ABOUT THE EDITORS

John Gale is CEO of Community Housing and Therapy (CHT), which specialises in therapeutic communities for the psychotherapy of the psychoses. Formerly a Benedictine monk, he was director of studies and lectured in philosophy and church history. After leaving the priesthood, he trained as a psychotherapist and has worked in therapeutic communities in the voluntary sector for over twenty years. He was the clinical director of CHT before being appointed to his present post in 1999. He is a board member of ISPS UK and of the Consortium of Therapeutic Communities, President of the International Network of Democratic Therapeutic Communities and sits on the advisory panel of the Community of Communities programme at the Royal College of Psychiatrists. He was development editor and deputy editor of the journal *Therapeutic Communities* for seven years and is currently a member of its international editorial advisory group, and was a member of the International Advisory Committee of the 11th World Congress of the World Association for Psychosocial Rehabilitation. He regularly speaks at conferences, has contributed to books and has published articles in academic journals. He is particularly interested in the interface between philosophy, spirituality and psychoanalysis.

Michael Robson was until very recently Dean and Fellow of St Edmund's College, Cambridge. Dr Robson is Honorary Visiting Fellow in the Borthwick Institute of Historical Research, University of York, 1999/2000. He is the Associate Editor of *Franciscan Studies* and was a member of the international council of the *Revue d'histoire ecclésiastique* for a number of years. He is the author of a number of books on St Francis of Assisi and has published seventeen monographs on medieval history and theology. He is currently editing the *Companion to Francis of Assisi*, which is to be published by Cambridge University Press.

Georgia Rapsomatioti is a psychologist who studied at Panteion University Athens and for a Master's degree in psychoanalysis under the supervision of

Dr Dany Nobus at Brunel University. She is a member of the British Psychological Society and the Hellenic Psychological Society. Georgia trained in psychoanalysis at the New Lacanian School in Athens and her Master's dissertation was on Lacan's concept of the Real of sexuality in psychosis. She has worked in a variety of clinical settings in Greece and the UK. Her particular interest is in a Lacanian psychoanalytic approach to the treatment of the psychoses.

ABOUT THE CONTRIBUTORS

Rodney Bomford, formerly Vicar of Camberwell, and author of *The Symmetry of God*

Audrey Cantlie Visiting Reader at the Department of Anthropology and Sociology, School of Oriental and African Studies, University of London

Christopher MacKenna Director of the Guild of Health and of St Marylebone Healing and Counselling Centre

Josè Mannu Psychiatrist and Psychoanalyst, Director of the Therapeutic Community ASLRMB, Rome

Satish Reddy Psychiatrist and Psychoanalyst, New York

Human-Friedrich Unterrainer Psychologist and Senior Lecturer at Karl-Franzens-Universität, Graz, Austria

Gary Winship Associate Professor at School of Education, and Senior Fellow, Institute of Mental Health, University of Nottingham

FOREWORD

Things fall apart; the centre cannot hold;
Mere anarchy is loosed upon the world,
The blood-dimmed tide is loosed, and everywhere
The ceremony of innocence is drowned;
The best lack all conviction, while the worst
Are full of passionate intensity.

Surely some revelation is at hand;
Surely the Second Coming is at hand.
The Second Coming! Hardly are those words out
When a vast image out of Spiritus Mundi
Troubles my sight . . .
And what rough beast, its hour come round at last,
Slouches towards Bethlehem to be born?

(Yeats 2000: 158–9)

Spiritus mundi or 'the spirit of the world' refers to Yeats' belief that each human mind is linked to a collective intelligence. Perhaps the second coming will be a collective effort. The collective effort here from Gale, Robson and Rapsomatioti and colleagues is the hard toil of academics, clinicians and service users who have together worked up a wide-ranging and searching interrogation of the merging discourses of divinity and insanity. In particular, psychoanalytic intelligence is brought to bear on a topic often illusive and controversial. And it is timely – timely because psychoanalysis can cast cool beams of light across the domains of cultural and religious diversity which all too easily end in polemical and alarmist fights. Audrey Cantlie's (Chapter 4) enthralling anthropological field observations attest to the complex and diverse weft and warp of spiritual belief and practice in West Bengal, and she tells us in the end that, if it is madness, then it is not as we know it.

Spirituality is not easily decoupled from religion, and perhaps nor should it be. MacKenna's (Chapter 3) exploration of Jung's midlife psychotic collapse draws attention to the centripetal force of religion in the emergence of our understanding of spirituality. As MacKenna tells us, Jung (1976) felt as if his thoughts circled round God like the planets round the sun. Religion can be a tricky business for practitioners working in mental health settings with people suffering from psychosis. There is an illuminating account where the author tells us that, in a vision, Jesus appeared to her. Later she felt as though she had to kill the devil. And, in another first-hand account of a psychotic breakdown, the author describes an experience of what was felt to be revelatory visions that led her to think that she might indeed be the next messiah. These accounts might feel familiar to many who have worked in acute psychiatry. The oldest mental hospital in the world, the Bethlehem is, of course, named after the birthplace of Jesus of Nazareth, and many who have worked on the frontline will have met a number of messiahs along the way.

That the oldest mental health asylum in the world is named after the spiritual birthplace of Christianity is of note, though somewhat contradictory when we consider that the idea of 'spirit possession' is included in the ICD-10 and DSM-IV classifications. But, as Human-Friedrich Unterrainer reminds us in Chapter 11, the empirical evidence is sparse when it comes to determining whether religious and spiritual ideas are causal in psychosis or curative. It is probably fair to say that people who work in psychiatry tend towards atheism. Having said that, at his memorial service over the summer of 2011, I discovered that one of my enduring mentors, the late Murray Jackson – a psychoanalyst and consultant psychiatrist at the Maudsley Hopsital (Jackson 2001; Jackson & Williams 1994) – latterly described himself as a Christian atheist. The vicar who conducted the memorial service told the gathered family, friends and colleagues that some of us might be surprised that the service was being held in a church. But here it was: Murray had attended the church in Wimbledon whenever he could and he was happy to align himself in the end to his Christian roots. Murray had begun as a Jungian, and though he became most closely associated with the deepening of Bion's work in particular, perhaps in the end, like Jung, he turned a full circle, returning to some proximity with his spiritual roots.

The theoretical seam that joins madness, spirituality and psychoanalysis are key corner elements which thread together in *Insanity and Divinity*. As John Gale's (Chapter 1) Lacanian-inspired etymological investigations of the linguistic interleave of madness and spirituality show, scholars have been seeking out the language with which to articulate the psychotic experience – that is, what it is of itself and how words can penetrate the space that enfolds it. We may find sympathy in Lacan's transcendentalism, but we know Freud to be less keen. As Josè Mannu highlights in Chapter 2, Freud's own account was that he had a 'completely negative attitude to religion, in any form or however attenuated' (Meng and Freud 1963: 110). Freud's perspective on religion took devastating shape in 1927 in *The Future of an Illusion* and his sentiments were deepened by the time he wrote *Civilisation and its Discontents* (1930), where he described religion and drugs as the two great evils that were the bane of mankind. Freud offered a cultural diagnosis of despair about mankind that situated man's compulsion to hold on to the illusion that some great overseer could save us from ourselves, that this was ultimately self-defeating. Religion was a non-scientific hyperbole of consolation, albeit with lyrical doctrines, but in the end he was sure that we would be better off with fact rather than fiction. But here's the thing. As Mannu irrefutably demonstrates, Freud kept coming back to religion again and again. From tackling a new way of dream-telling (the Joseph of the Bible) from the outset in *The Interpretation of Dreams* (1900) to *Totem and Taboo* (1910), *The Future of an Illusion* (1927), *Civilisation and Its Discontents* (1930), and then finally in his dying preoccupation with *Moses and Monotheism* (1938), Freud couldn't get away from religion. There is a compelling case that the treasured Bible that Freud's father gave to him when Freud was 35 years old was never really very far from his side. Indeed, we might say that at each major biographical juncture he kept coming back – religion was the oxygen that ignited his clinical fire. Mannu takes us through the body of Freud's best-known writings, and highlights the considerable and enduring depth of influence of religious thought that carved out Freud's oppositional theorising.

Of course, there is a difference between religious spirituality as a psychic event and the ecclesiastical institutionalisation of religion as a social practice. It would indeed be the latter that concerned Freud, while the former he arguably overlooked. This book may well be a jolt for some practitioners who work within the frame of their own faith. Good counselling and psychotherapy trainings expect practitioners to work out their prejudices, their cultural blind spots, how their own sexuality, ethnicity or upbringing impinges on practice and so forth. And so the debate in this book takes us towards an intriguing core essence of experience: the valley of the soul, as Del Nevo (2008) calls it, where ideas about spirituality are unfolded and exercised. And we can see here that the valley of the soul across cultures has some intriguing manifestations.

As an item of core curriculum development on an increasing number of training courses in counselling, psychotherapy and mental health, spirituality occupies a left-of-centre position in the preparation of practitioners. Spirituality here is given a refreshing outside-in perspective, in a long trajectory of philosophy – a discourse of the Other – which helpfully gives context to the idea of a personal spiritual or divine core.

So this idea of spirit outwith is the key. It is not so much spirit in the sky, but rather spirit on the street corner. The story of Francis of Assisi's descent, told eloquently by Michael Robson in Chapter 5 – from the largesse of youthful finery and wealth, to his apparent madness as a poor beggar on the streets – might be a motif for the predicament we face today in a world driven by the madness of capitalism. Francis would probably approve of the camp outside St Paul's Cathedral in London, where we saw a rousing protest against the folly of unequal wealth. The direct action of a group of spirited activists has received support in some quarters of the Church of England. But elsewhere on the streets, and in the community, old Christian churches seem on the wane. Yet it is not so unusual to see churches transformed into properties, pubs, theatres or clubs, and also mental health services.

We are more exposed to the multiplicity of religions than ever before, especially in schools. Hindu, Jewish and Muslim festivals are celebrated alongside Christian ones. Actually, the idea of religious icons standing alongside each other – Christ alongside several-headed Hindu goddesses – might diminish religious zeal in the long run. The inclusivity of a range of religious beliefs was notable in Barack Obama's inaugural address, where he referred to many faiths and even mentioned non-believers, too. While I might prefer the idea of a network of gods battling among themselves for authority, and especially the domestic warfare that is the marriage of Zeus and Hera, as a template for working out the transactions of the good society, the question remains: How are we are going to reconcile a world which exists under the reign of multi-monotheisms? Once it was only Athena who was perceived to have the power to trample a city in one blow; now a human has the power of the gods. Heidegger thought that only a god could save us now, but perhaps it will be a network of divinities that will prevail.

The second coming must be a concerted effort. And here, in *Insanity and Divinity*, there is an ebullient concert of spiritualities. If mental health service providers and practitioners are to be among the new guardians of spirituality, then we should be careful that new psychiatric 'churches' do not become centres of pharmaceutical reverence, places of ceremonial chemistry, as Szasz (1974) has warned us. There are new revelations to hand which can shake the tree of medical certainty. 'Our sights have been troubled', yes, but does the centre hold? The lion-human beast in Yeats' poem may be the emphasis on biology and the brain. As Nina Coltart (1993) says, we've been slouching towards Bethlehem for a while and our hopelessness and suffering needs to be countered by some clear thinking. A theory of spiritual crisis in psychosis, rather than an approach which begins by assuming biological imbalance, tracks one of many new directions and gives an intriguing vista for debates. Gale, his fellow editors and contributing colleagues have furnished a hugely erudite book that keeps its pace up throughout – there's no slouching here. In the end, whatever the contestations, there is a discourse that sets us on a journey to reframe old philosophic and practice givens. The challenge of working with people with psychosis can shift with new insights.

Gary Winship

References

Coltart, N. (1993). *Slouching Towards Bethlehem*. London: Free Association Books.
Del Nevo, M. (2008). *The Valley Way of Soul, Melancholy, Poetry and Soul Making*. New South Wales: St Paul's Publications.
Jackson, M. and Willams, P. (1994). *Unimaginable Storms*. London: Karnac Books.
Jackson, M. (2001). *Weathering the Storms: psychotherapy for psychosis*. London: Karnac.

Jung, C.G. (1976). *Letters*, vol. 2, *1951–1961,* ed. G. Adler and A. Jaffé, trans. R.F.C. Hull. London: Routledge and Kegan Paul.

Meng, H. and Freud, E.L. (eds) (1963). *Psychoanalysis and Faith. The Letters of Sigmund Freud and Oskar Pfister.* New York: Basic Books.

Szasz, T. (1974). *Ceremonial Chemistry. The Ritual Persecution of Drugs, Addicts and Pushers.* London: Routledge and Kegan Paul.

Yeats, W.B. (2000). *The Poems,* ed. D. Albright. London: Everyman's Library.

PREFACE

The history of madness, as it has been called, is so closely interwoven with that of religious life and thought that tracing and deciphering the points of connection and dissimilarity between the two needs little or no justification (Quétel 2012).[1] Spiritualities, as we encounter them within their various historical expressions,[2] whether in ritual or practice, or in texts – be they scriptural, hagiographical or mystical – are inextricably intertwined with beliefs, modes of perception, certainties and doubt, as well as with heterogeneous notions of transcendence. As such they are embedded in what we may call, to avoid circumlocutions, the symbolic, and thus language is as crucial to our understanding of spirituality as it is to psychosis. So much so that the French psychoanalyst Jacques Lacan thought that it was principally language that distinguished madness from mysticism. A point he illustrated by comparing the writings of Daniel Schreber to those of John of the Cross (Lacan 1993). To say this is to indicate a limit to symbolisation, a frontier that is expressed in an elliptical obscurity that characterises both mystic speech and the language of psychosis. Such a limit, of course, resonates with the possibility of its transgression (Oedipus).

Spirituality and psychosis

Although a number of books and articles have been published on the subject of spirituality and mental ill health, it is usually approached from the angle of healthcare or psychology[3] and in terms of diagnostic categories (e.g. psychosis,[4] substance misuse), different patient groups (children and adolescents, people with an intellectual disability, the elderly) and clinical responses (how to assess the spiritual needs of patients; spiritual care and psychotherapy). In addition, there is in the literature some discussion of the more fundamental question of the relationship between religion, religious experience and spirituality. Arguably, within this genre, attempts to define spirituality and its relationship to religion, understanding of the philosophical discourse underlying spirituality and issues concerning its context and historical perspective – familiar territory both to biblical scholars and theologians – are less frequently addressed. However, these issues are crucial to the notion of spirituality, whether we are discussing it in terms of religious belief – religion being the medium, as it were, through which spirituality is frequently experienced and elucidated – or the more general, postmodern conception in which it is not anchored to a traditional, culturally rooted form of theism. The situation where this is brought most visibly to the surface is in the case of psychosis, as it confronts us with the question of where belief stands in relation to rationality and thus in relation to sanity.

Psychoanalysis and the study of religious phenomenology

The exception to this overly pastoral, pragmatic approach is found in psychoanalytic studies of religion which have, over the years, thrown up a number of more academic works which deal with the history of religious phenomenology and its philosophical and historical foundations. The more erudite studies focus on the foundations of psychoanalysis in its relation to religious belief (Ricoeur 1970), particularly the influence on Freud of the Jewish mystical tradition (Ostow 1982). But with the exception of two recent studies, both published in 2012 and which deserve particular mention, these all appeared some years ago. The first of these recent works is by Delphine Renard and is an analysis of the essential proximity between the Jewish tradition and psychoanalysis based on a close reading of the four discourses of Lacan. The second, by Gérard Guillerault, is a study of the Catholicism of Françoise Dolto. However, neither of these books directly discuss the related theme of psychosis.

The studies in this present volume explore, sometimes from an oblique angle, various facets of that inward turn associated equally with psychoanalysis and spirituality. In so doing they bring together issues concerning the interrelation of psychosis and religious experience from a variety of fields, including the neighbouring intellectual landscapes of philosophy, psychoanalysis, anthropology and hagiography. This broad approach, which in itself resonates to some extent with Freud's own method of elucidation (*Aufklärung*),[5] inevitably hints at the hidden symmetry between these various discourses.[6] However, darkness inevitably appears, as Nägele (2007) puts it, at the sutures where radically heterogeneous processes interlace. This is what Derrida (1967) describes as an enigmatic conjuncture that resists unification. Yet it is precisely at this complex, though nevertheless quite intelligible, point that any serious work must begin.[7] Such an approach goes back a long way, beyond the Sophists, to philosophers like Heraclitus. It is an approach in which myth is subjected to a rationalism that is not necessarily hostile to spirituality.[8] Xenophanes, a deeply religious man, had said that if oxen could paint, they would paint gods that looked like oxen.[9] Thus, he writes that mortals think their gods are born, have clothes, speech and bodies;[10] that Ethiopians think their gods have stub noses and are black; that Thracians see them with blue eyes and red hair,[11] as the different races see the gods having their own characteristics. By a *reductio ad absurdum*, he concludes, animals would do the same. That is to say, Xenophanes understood the essential relativity of religious ideas and used this insight to drain off any residue of anthropomorphism from his conception of the divine (Jaeger 1947) while remaining responsive to the numinous. What Freud added to this was the notion that the gods were made not just in man's own image but in the image of the imaginary or ideal father. Psychoanalysis maintains that the complex concept of the father has great bearing, not only on our relationship to the Other – which is always elsewhere – but also to psychic structure in general and specifically to psychosis. Such an approach privileges analogy and biography. And this includes the terrain of *Krankengeschichten* (histories or stories of illness; what we would call case studies) which, as Freud himself realised, function more like novellas than science.[12] De Certeau comments shrewdly that psychoanalytic biography works from within, eroding and dismantling historical encomiums in much the same way as the mysticism of the sixteenth and seventeenth century did in relation to the religious institution (de Certeau 2006). In this sense, as critique, psychoanalytic biography functions to dissolve hagiography.

The languages of interiority, conversion and psychosis

The structure of this volume is that of a triptych. Part 1 depicts the languages of interiority as they allude to what has largely been, starting out with Freud's own works, a suppressed transcendence. Here we cannot but fail to be reminded of Dennis Klein's shrewd observation that, from its beginning in 1902 until 1906, all seventeen members of the original group of psychoanalysts were Jews (Klein 1981), even if we demur at reading psychoanalysis merely as a dissimulated form of Hassidism (Bakan 1958). As we now know, Freud was deeply suspicious of Jung, even prior to their break in 1912, precisely because he was not a Jew. The latter's subsequent breakdown, which has generally been referred to as his *Auseinandersetzung mit dem Unbewußten* (confrontation with the unconscious) resulted in his rejection of the Lutheranism of his father, as he recalled a childhood dream of a temple containing a giant ritual phallus (Bishop 2008). Yet, despite his Christian formation, and although his narrative is impregnated with patristic and scholastic references, it fell not to the Protestant pastor's son Jung, but to Jacques Lacan, more than to any other analyst, to reveal this Freudian distortion by punctuating his seminars with references to Paul, Luther and Pascal and, more particularly, to mystical writers including Hadewijch of Antwerp, Meister Eckhart and Angelus Silesius.[13] Yet, even in its encounter with Buddhism, Lacanian space is filled with a Catholic concern, its appearance corresponding to the extraordinary growth in interest in Eastern religion in the West, since the Second World War.[14] Zen, with its intentional attempts to express spiritual truths in a non-logical, non-rational way, came as an enormous liberation to many who felt intellectually constrained and restricted by the dominant orthodoxy of the time. It meant discovering that the Buddha is not what the effigies in the temple lead one to expect, 'for there is no longer any image, and consequently nothing to see, no one to see it, and a Void in which no image is even conceivable. "The true seeing," said Shen Hui, "is when there is no seeing"' (Rice 1972: 82). Indeed, the relationship between the visible (the ritual; the relic; the symptom) and the invisible (the gods; the heavens; the mind; the unconscious) is itself emblematic of that terrain into which psychoanalysis and the sacred are inserted.

It is the eye, in the act of seeing, that links the first to the second panel of the triptych. Jean Paris (1965) sees in Giotto's painting, *Stigmata of St Francis,* in the Louvre, a complex interplay of connections between the wounds in Francis' hands, feet and side, and the Christ figure which hovers above him.[15] Their eyes are fixed upon one another, rays of light come from Christ's wounds and somehow represent the invisible gaze that links them. Through an analysis of these connections, Paris articulates an understanding of the power of the gaze and its relation to the function of the stigmata. Schreber had spoken of being penetrated by divine rays, in a way reminiscent of Giotto's depiction of Francis, which 'serve mainly to inflict damage on the body' while in a dissociated state of ecstasy (Schreber 2000: 141). Some of these rays Schreber describes as impure, others as pure. The pure rays, he says, build up or mend the damage. Here we find traces of the specular image in the fragmented body of the saint, which becomes an exemplum of the constituted nature and irreparable fragility of identity, and this includes sexuality, which in both hagiographical and psychoanalytic discourse becomes a 'privileged ideogram' (Brown 1991: 230). This echoes a stanza from John of the Cross: 'Your gaze was on my eyes imprinted so, That it effeminized (*me adamabas*) . . . On me you well may gaze' (Campbell 1972: 23). In this epitome of the imaginary, where manifold personal mythologies intertwine to give birth to the ego, the subject's relation to himself is made manifest ambiguously both as symptom and as *bios,* lifestyle. This dual disclosure amounts to what we might call an enunciation of the trajectories of conversion, in which the body is made to pay the price for having access to the symbolic (de Certeau 2006). This confrontation with all that lies below the threshold of the visible (Foucault 1994) is played out equally in asceticism and in psychosis, and here Augustine, Krishna, Nicholas of Cusa, Francis of Assisi, Arjuna, Teresa of Avila and John of the Cross, and an assortment of sadhus, devotees of the Tantra, make an appearance. That this is no mere excursus is clear from an examination of Freud's own interests. For he had corresponded at length with Romain Rolland about Indian mysticism and in 1931, on the occasion of his seventy-fifth birthday, the Indian Psychoanalytical Society presented him with a small ivory statue of the god Vishnu. Freud put it on his desk (Vaidyanathan and Kripal 1999).

It is the psychoses more directly that forms the third panel in the triptych. Reviewing the well-authenticated examples of religious madness and hysteria – including its associated abnormal physical phenomena as it had been discussed in James (1902), Underhill (1911), Delacroix (1908) and Starbuck (1899) – Butler (1951) questions whether it is possible to distinguish a genuine mysticism from 'morbid pathological conditions' (Butler 1951: 192). His conclusion is an interesting one. First, he says that in both cases – that of madness and that of mysticism – the phenomena (visions, voices, trances, etc.) may be identical and can therefore only be of secondary interest. Second, that in both cases the *visio* (literally, 'what is seen' – the vision, and the mode of organising the visible) and hallucinations spring from the unconscious.[16] That is to say, they are written in a language we have forgotten how to read. And third, that it is only in the effect these experiences have on the life of the person that we are able to distinguish madness from mysticism. Citing numerous examples, Butler (1951) demonstrates that, whether or not we consider the descriptions the mystics give of their spiritual experiences as illusory or as intimations of divinity, they lived vigorous, powerful and coherent lives.[17] Here, in this third section of the book we encounter some of our contemporaries who, like Jung, have been through periods in which they have been enveloped in their own suffering and struggle with sanity.

Our interest in publishing these papers is not in order to present a neat doctrinal edifice but rather, to some extent, to subvert the allure of the simulacrum, of systematic explanations and false architectures by indicating the ambiguities, disjunction and contradictions that lie behind these varied intellectual dialects. For this reason the introductions to each part of the book do not attempt to recapitulate everything the authors say or even to synthesise their arguments. The latter approach, though no doubt somewhat more respectful of the intelligence of the reader than the former, would still confer on the contributions an imaginary conclusion rather than the intimation of a further opening. Our approach tries to avoid settling into the resemblance between psychosis and spirituality by the imposition of any such *méconnaissance* (parody) of cohesion or solution to what is articulated in the variegated corpus of the text, but rather to punctuate the illusion of mastery or an easy understanding, by gesturing towards new, sometimes tangential, directions of thought.[18] Some of the chapters, while lucid, are rather more dense than others and come with a sediment of notes and references. However, taken together, these studies – precisely because they form a catena that transverses a number of discourses – show that it is in psychosis that the question of where religious belief and experience stand in relation to sanity is brought most forcefully to the surface.

John Gale

Notes

1 See Foucault (1961). Quétel discusses the curious etymology of the French word *folie* (madness), which has its origins in Late Latin and from which the word *fou* (fool, imbecile) derives. These are difficult words to translate into English, as their sense ranges from folly to mental illness and madness, and from idiot to insane.

2 The background literature on the interface between spirituality and culture is vast but particular mention should be made of Michel de Certeau (1987), *La Faiblesse de croire* (Paris: Éditions du Seuil – see esp. pp. 41–65).

3 The best example of this is J. Swinton (2001), *Spirituality in Mental Health Care: Rediscovering a Forgotten Dimension* (London: Jessica Kingsley Publications), on which most other recent studies depend. Swinton's research emerged from his background in nursing and healthcare chaplaincy.

4 One book which addresses the specific relationship between psychosis and spirituality is I. Clarke (2001), *Psychosis and Spirituality. Exploring the new frontier* (London: Whurr Publishers). Clarke begins with the premise that psychosis and spirituality could be said to share a mode of perception that is different from that familiar to the empirical sciences. A number of contributors then discuss this issue, which Clarke then ties together within a broadly cognitive model of psychology. There is, however, only a very limited engagement with the history of spirituality or psychoanalytic approaches and for this very reason one reviewer comments astutely that such things 'would require another book'; see T. Smiley (2003), *Psychologist* 16(1): 36.

5 Freud was a man of letters or to use Lacan's phrase, 'an encyclopaedia of the arts and muses' (Lacan 2006: 434) and his oeuvres abound with references to the classics, to anthropology, art, literature and religion. Jung and Lacan were no less well read. Lacan, with an erratic brilliance, in his seminars, evidenced the same broad literary tradition by including incursions into philosophy, history, literature, anthropology and mysticism – all of which he regarded as essential in the training of analysts. See J. Lacan (2006), The Instance of the Letter in the Unconscious or Reason Since Freud. In *Écrits*, trans. B. Fink, in collaboration with H. Fink and R. Grigg (New York and London: W. W. Norton and Co), p. 432.

6 Knowledge in any sphere is culture-bound and disparate discourses may seem at first to have little in common and even less possibility of finding common ground for purposes of communication. This has led postmodern thought to cast doubt on the possibility of meaningful dialogue and communication between cultures, however broadly or narrowly culture is defined. Yet, it is precisely because all discourses share a common grounding in language that synthesis and cross-fertilisation has frequently occurred in the history of ideas.

7 Psychoanalysis, philosophy and theology, as any other discourse, need specialised languages and it would not be possible to conceptualise discussions of psychopathology or religious belief and experience without resorting to terms and usages which belong to those disciplines.

8 This is not intended as an endorsement of Nestle's view but rather to see that reason adheres to the foundations that myth has laid for it as both myth and reason are narratives which aim to describe the world. See W. Nestle (1942), *Vom Mythos zum Logos. Die Selbstenlfaltung des griechischen Denken vom Homer bis auf die Sophistik und Sokrates* (Stuttgart: Alfred Kröner Verlag) and R. Buxton (ed.) (1999), *From Myth to Reason? Studies in the Development of Greek Thought* (Oxford: Oxford University Press).

9 *all ei cheiras echon boes (hippoi t') ēe leontes ē grapsai cheiressi kai erga telein haper andres, hippoi men th' hippoisi boes de te bousin homoias kai (ke) theōn ideas egraphon kai sōmat*

epoioun toiauth oion per kautoi demas eichon (hekastoi), Xen. fr. 15. See H. Diels (1906), *Die Fragmente der Vorsokratiker. Griechisch und Deutsch* (Berlin: Weidmannsche Buchhandlung), vol. 1, p. 49.

10 *all hoi brotoi dokeousi gennasthai theous, tēn spheterēn d'esthēta echein phōnēn te demas te.* Xen. fr. 14. Diels, ibid.

11 *Aithiopes te (theous spheterous) simous melanas te Thrēikes te glaukous kai purrous (phasi pelesthai)*. Xen. fr. 16. Diels, ibid.

12 The psychoanalytic interest in biography (including autobiography) dates back to its earliest days. Fliess had criticised Freud over it and the latter was well aware how unscientific his case studies seemed – see P. Gay (2006), *Freud. A Life for Our Time* (London: Max), esp. pp. 89–90.

13 By resituating the place of religious discourse within psychoanalysis, Lacan opened his seminars to an influx of young Jesuits. These included Louis Biernaert, François Roustang, Denis Vasse and Michel de Certeau. On the latter, see J. Ahearne (1995), *Michel de Certeau. Interpretation and its Other* (Stanford, CA: Stanford University Press) and the more recent assessment by Cecilia Padvalskis (2010), Recorrido por sus Multiples Pertenencias. *Revista Teologia* 47(102): 189–207.

14 In French, Swami Abhishiktananda (Henri Le Saux) and Jules Monchanin began to write on a Christian approach to Hinduism and Jean-Marie Déchanet on yoga from the mid-1950s. Cf. M.-F. Euverte, F. Jacquin, J.-G. Gelineau, P. Massein, X. Perrin and R. Williamson (2012), *Henri Le Saux. Moine de Kergonan* (Paris: Éditions Parole et Silence). The first edition of Déchanet's *La Voie du Silence* was published by Desclée de Brouwer in Paris in 1956. By the 1960s, interest in the East had become more widespread in Catholic circles and a number of writers published on the interface between Christian and Eastern spirituality, including, from 1961, Thomas Merton, who began to publish books on Zen Buddhism, which were almost immediately translated into French. Some books on the subject in English slightly predate the war, the first being A. W. Watts (1936). *The Spirit of Zen* (London: Murray). Although Bede Griffiths' autobiography *The Golden String* was not published until 1954, the author had begun by studying the *Upanishads* and other Eastern texts in 1946. Du Boulay cites an article he wrote on Lao Tzu entitled 'Integration' and published in *Pax* as early as November 1938. Here he described Lao Tzu as having a profound mystical intuition. See S. du Boulay (1998), *Beyond the Darkness: A Biography of Bede Griffiths* 276 n.13 (London: Rider); and B. Griffiths (1954), *The Golden String* (London: Harvill Press).

15 Deleuze and Guattari (1980) also comment on Giotto's depiction of the stigmata of Francis but follow more closely Sartre's reading of the notion of the gaze, in which paranoia – being seen by the Other – takes centre stage. Cf. G. Deleuze and F. Guattari (1980). *Mille Plateaux: Capitalisme et schizophrénie II*. Paris: Editions de Minuit; J.-P. Sartre (1956) *Being and Nothingness. An Essay on Phenomenological Ontology*, trans. A.M. Seridan Smith (New York: Vintage Books).

16 The term hallucination (from Greek *aluō* , Latin *alucinari* – to wander in mind, to be ill at ease, troubled, distraught) was coined by Esquirol in 1817 to cover non-visual as well as visual illusions. Cf. É. Esquirol (1838), *Traités des maladies mentales considérées sous le rapport médicale, hygiénique et médico-légal*, 2 Vols. Paris: J.-B. Bailliere.

17 In his comprehensive and masterly study (first published in 1908) of Catherine of Genoa – one of the 'mothers' that dominate and help denote the subversive character of the mysticism of the period – von Hügel had reached practically the same conclusion. Basing his discussion on Pierre Janet's work under Charcot at the Salpêtrière, von Hügel concluded that, while many of Catherine's hysteriform

phenomena appear to be identical to the symptoms of hysteria, what differentiates her state from morbidity is that her personality is not disintegrated. Cf. von Hügel (1961), *The Mystical Element of Religion as Studied in Saint Catherine of Genoa and her Friends*, 2 vols (London: J. M. Dent and Sons Ltd) (see esp. vol. 2, pp. 3–61). Gay (op. cit.) is surprisingly reticent in his comments on Freud's dependence on Janet's ideas. See P. Janet (1893), *État Mental des Hystériques. Les Stigmates Mentaux* (Paris: Rueff).

18 *Méconnaissance*, literally 'misunderstanding' or 'misrecognition' in English, is the word Lacan uses to indicate, amongst other things, the way understanding always includes a denial of some kind.

References

Bakan, D. (1958). *Sigmund Freud and the Jewish Mystical Tradition*. Princeton, NJ: D. Van Nostrand.

Bishop, P. (2008). *Analytical Psychology and German Classical Aesthetics: Goethe, Schiller, and Jung*, vol. 1. London and New York: Routledge.

Brown, P. (1991). *The Body and Society: Men, Women and Sexual Renunciation in Early Christianity*. London: Faber and Faber.

Butler, C. (1951). *Western Mysticism*. Dublin: Arrow Books.

Campbell, R. (trans.) (1972). *The Poems of St John of the Cross. The Spanish Text with a Translation*. London: Harvell Press.

de Certeau, M. (2006). *Heterologies. Discourse on the Other*, trans. B. Massumi. Minneapolis/London: University of Minnesota Press.

Delacroix, H. (1908). *Études d'Histoire et de psychologie du Mysticisme: Les Grands Mystiques Chrétiens*. Paris: Alcan.

Derrida, J. (1967). La Parole Soufflée. In *L'Écriture et la Différence*, pp. 253–292. Paris: Seuil.

Foucault, M. (1961). *Histoire de la Folie*. Paris: Librairie Plon.

Foucault, M. (1994). *The Birth of the Clinic. An Archeology of Medical Perception. Discource of the Other*. Minneapolis and London: University of Minnesota Press.

Guillerault, G. (2012). *Françoise Dolto: la foi dans le désir*. Paris: Éditions du Cerf.

Jaeger, W. (1947). *The Theology of the Early Greek Philosophers*. Oxford: Clarendon Press.

James, W. (1902). *Varieties of Religious Experience: A Study in Human Nature*. London: Longmans Green.

Klein, D. (1981). *Jewish Origins of the Psychoanalytic Movement*. New York: Praeger.

Lacan, J. (1993). *The Psychoses. The Seminar of Jacques Lacan Book III 1955–1956*, trans. R. Grigg. London: Routledge.

Lacan, J. (2006). *Écrits*, trans. B. Fink. New York and London: W.W. Norton and Company.

Nägele, R. (2007). Introduction. In *Hölderlin and the Question of the Father*, ed. and trans. L. Carson (pp. ix–xxxiv). Victoria: ELS Editions.

Ostow, M. (1982). *Judaism and Psychoanalysis*. New York: KTAV Publishing Inc.

Paris, J. (1965). *L'Espace et le Regard*. Paris: Seuil.

Quétel, C. (2012). *Histoire de la folie de l'antiquité à nos jours*. Paris: Éditions Tallandier.

Renard, D. (2012). *Judaïsme et psychoanalyse. Les 'discours' de Lacan*. Paris: Éditions du Cerf.

Rice, E. (1972). *The Man in the Sycamore Tree: The Good Times and Hard Life of Thomas Merton*. New York: Harcourt Brace Jovanovich.

Ricoeur, P. (1970). *Freud and Philosophy. An Essay on Interpretation*. New Haven, CT: Yale University Press.

Schreber, D.P. (2000). *Memoirs of My Nervous Illness*, ed. and trans. I. Macalpine and R.A. Hunter. New York: New York Review of Books.

Starbuck, E.D. (1899). *Psychology of Religion*. London: Walter Scott Ltd.

Underhill, E. (1911). *Mysticism: A Study of the Nature and Development of Man's Spiritual Consciousness*. New York: E. P. Dutton and Co.

Vaidyanathan, T.G. and Kripal, J.J. (1999). *Vishnu on Freud's Desk. A Reader in Psychoanalysis and Hinduism*. Oxford: Oxford University Press.

ACKNOWLEDGEMENTS

I should like to express my sincere thanks to all who have contributed to these studies and assisted me. There have been many who have helped both directly and indirectly, particularly Ivan Ward at the Freud museum in Hampstead, whose assistance in gathering contributors was of inestimable value. I wish also to thank my fellow editors – Dr Michael Robson, erstwhile Dean of St Edmund's College Cambridge and Georgia Rapsomatioti – all those who have contributed chapters and Dr Laurence Errington who compiled the index. I should also like to thank the Reverend Alban McCoy of Fisher House, Cambridge, for kindly reading an earlier draft of Chapter 1 and for making a number of useful suggestions. Although no sub-editor has been officially appointed, Miriam Nuñez and Ekaterina Kalistratova have in fact done more than an editor could reasonably expect of any colleague with that title.

To my great regret Dr Samir Mahmoud had to leave Cambridge at the eleventh hour and return to Lebanon to be near his family, due to the violence that erupted there, before being able to complete his chapter on Sufism and psychoanalysis. His untimely departure has left a considerable lacuna as unfortunately I was unable to find another contribution from an Islamic perspective.

This volume was originally planned as long ago as 2007, when the series editor, Dr Brian Martindale, suggested it after I had arranged a conference on the subject of spirituality and psychosis. I am deeply grateful to him for his kindness in including this volume in the ISPS series, as well as to Professor Stephen Trenchard and Robert Dowler MBE, the chairmen of the boards of trustees of ISPS (UK) and of Community Housing and Therapy respectively, with whom I have had the good fortune to work. My thanks are also due to the staff at Routledge, particularly for their long suffering in agreeing to numerous extensions to the deadline for the submission of the final manuscript. And last, but by no means least, to my wife, to whose continual encouragement and support I owe so much.

I am, of course, alone responsible for any errors.

John Gale

Part 1

PSYCHOANALYSIS, BELIEF AND MYSTICISM

No more than Freud does Lacan underestimate the religious belief to which he does not adhere. What can be done today with this weighty history, if one rejects giving the illusion of repressing it? The West has for three centuries been concerned with the question of what to do about the Other.

(Michel de Certeau 2006: 60)

INTRODUCTION TO PART 1

Fragments of madness and delusion

John Gale

Psychoanalysis and the psychoses

Although a well-established distinction between neurosis and psychosis is found even in Freud's earliest texts – for example, in his correspondence with Fliess – psychoanalysis has not developed as complex or extensive a system of classification of mental disorders as has psychiatry. This is because its interests have been narrower and directed principally towards the distinction between the clinical structures of the perversions, the neuroses and the psychoses.

> Within . . . [the psychoses] psycho-analysis has tried to define differ-ent structures: on the one hand, paranoia (including, in a rather general way, delusional conditions) and schizophrenia; on the other, melancholia and mania. Fundamentally, psycho-analysis sees the common denominator of the psychoses as lying in a primary distur-bance of the libidinal relation to reality; the majority of manifest symptoms, and particularly delusional construction, are accordingly treated as secondary attempts to restore the link with objects.
>
> (Laplanche and Pontalis 1980: 370)

Psychoanalytic approaches to psychosis abound, the most notable probably being those of Bion (1967), Fromm-Reichmann (1960), Giovacchinin (1979), Klein (1930, 1948, 1975), Lacan (1993), Lucas (1992, 2009), O'Shaughnessy (1992), Rosenfeld (1966), Segal (1957), Sohn (1985) and Yorke (1991).[1] These have oscillated in their self-understanding but almost without excep-tion argue for an alternative or at least an addition to biological psychiatry. While much has been written of the increasing value of pharmacological treatments for the psychoses within the conceptual model of a medical illness, it is equally well documented that biological and genetic explanations do not exclude other factors that may have a role to play in the onset and develop-ment of psychosis (Andreasen 1999; Cullberg 2006; De Waelhens and

Ver Eecke 2001; Hartmann et al. 1984; Kendler and Diehl 1993; Mortensen et al. 1999; Mosher, Gosden and Beder 2004; Tienari 1992).

Freud and the web of belief

Freud's interest in religion was something that persisted throughout his life. He considered religion – all religion, including Judaism and Christianity – an illusion. With the publication of *Moses and Monotheism* in 1939, he characterised Christianity as the most severe kind of illusion, 'blending into the madness of delusion' (Gay 2006: 644).

Freud was familiar with the work of the biblical scholar Wellhausen whose analysis of the structural problem of Genesis and the dating of the Pentateuch, published in 1883 and 1885 respectively, had completely transformed Old Testament studies.[2] Wellhausen's work was continued by a series of other scholars[3] and was generally accepted in Germany by the time Freud came to write *Moses and Monotheism*, the first third of which appeared in German in *Imago* and in English in the *International Journal of Psycho-Analysis*. However, for an historical foundation to his thesis Freud relied not on the firm scholarship of Wellhausen but on a monograph published in 1922 by Ernst Sellin entitled *Mose und seine Bedeutung für die israelitisch-jüdische Religionsgeschichte*. He could not have made a worse choice. Freud had originally planned the book as an historical novel and Peter Gay suggests that he would have done well to have kept to his original plan. Sellin's argument, which was founded on dubious textual emendations, had not been well received by biblical scholars. But Freud took Sellin's thesis to an extreme and added to it a series of suppositions which, as is widely known, were unanimously rejected or ignored by biblical scholars, historians of religion and anthropologists alike (e.g. Albright 1957; Hyatt 1940; Wallace 1983). This was not because they were shocked or offended by his attack on religion – although it did inspire reactions of that kind as well – but because it was devoid of serious historical method and because of the way he used historical data, much of which was doubtful, basing his arguments on ethnological assumptions that were already outdated. Neither did Freud's earlier study of the foundations of religion in *Totem and Taboo* (Freud SE 1913) stand the test of time. Based on the work of the semitic scholar Robertson Smith, it contrasted primitive religion and rationality. Freud concluded that totemism was akin to neurosis (Wallace 1983). From its publication, anthropologists demonstrated its inadequacy and implausibility (Gay 2006) and later on the whole concept of totemism itself came to be seen as a mirage, an idea which leads nowhere (Wilcken 2010). Like hysteria, which emerged possibly not by coincidence around the same time, totemism was destined to vanish from the intellectual horizon within less than a hundred years.

The only real surviving interest in Freud's study of religion lies in the light it throws on his own psychological struggle with his father and with Jewish identity – something he could not shake off by not being religious – a point that is brought out clearly by Yerushalmi (1991) in his authoritative book, *Freud's Moses*.

Psychosis and the scars of the fall

The body, unlike the physical organism, is constructed, 'carved up and made visible by language' (Apollon, Bergeron and Cantin 2002). That is to say, our conception of the body is built up through the complex structure of signifiers that together combine to give us our understanding of what a body is. This imaginary construction is partly made up from the way we see ourselves in the mirror, our understanding of the way others look at us and the things they say about how we look. Thus, the act of seeing – what in French is known as *le regard* (the gaze or, more generally, perception itself) – looking at and being looked at, is integral to the formation of the mental image of body. The power of the eyes is an important theme in many Greek texts, as the gaze was thought to create an opening through which the soul could be reached. Thus Xenophon warns that the young, when they are the object of desire, are more dangerous than scorpions for they do not need to come into contact, like an insect, to inject their poison but can drive a person mad merely with a look (Xen. *Mem.* I. iii.12–13). Similarly, it was in the force of sexual desire that Augustine saw the 'stigmata [literally, the scars] of the Fall' (Foucault 1985: 138). Psychoanalysis shares with religion this conviction that appearances, which set desire in motion, are deceptive. They masquerade as something they are not and lure us into a mere semblance of the truth.

It was Jung who, in 1908, in the library of the Berghölzli, drew Freud's attention to Schreber's autobiographical account of his psychosis, which he had referred to the year before in his study of *dementia praecox*. Jung was arguably always more interested in madness than Freud but over the next few years the two great men were to discuss Schreber's memoires frequently (McGuire 1974). When Freud read the case he was already preoccupied with paranoia and here was a baroque example, liberally peppered with neologisms.

Jung had been studying the Schreber text since it first appeared in 1903 under the title *Denkwürdigkeiten eines Nervenkranken*. In 1911, three years after he had first read the book, Freud wrote up his study of the Schreber case, masterfully, suggesting that the cause of Schreber's psychosis was a crisis of sexuality (Freud SE 1911). Although Jung disagreed strongly, there is an interesting comparison to be made between the case of Schreber and that of one of Jung's famous patients, Emile Schwyzer (1862–1931). Like Schreber, there was a strongly religious component to his psychosis. Schwyzer, whom Jung began treating in 1901, had believed himself to be God and like Schreber had bizarre sexual delusions. In Schreber's theory of the universe, his messianic calling demanded that he transform himself into a woman. Schwyzer saw himself as the object of interest to perverse fashionable ladies, who visited him dressed as men in order to confuse him. Schwyzer felt an obligation to distribute his semen, since otherwise the world would perish, and believed he was able to determine the weather. When asked how he did this, he replied that the sun had a gigantic phallus, and if he looked at it with eyes half shut and moved his head from side to side he could make the phallus move, and that was where the wind came from and, by extension, the weather (Bair 2004). The sun also featured in Schreber's delusions. The similarity between Schreber and Schwyzer was not missed on Jung's one-time patient and later gifted research assistant, Johann Honegger. Honegger, having at Jung's bidding recorded Schwyzer's delusional speech verbatim and collected his drawings, presented an analysis of the material at the 2nd International Psychoanalytic Congress in Nuremberg in March 1910. The paper was not well received and soon afterwards Honegger became psychotic himself and tragically committed suicide.

Notes

1 With the exception of Lacan, these approaches have been usefully summarised by R. Lucas (2001), Managing psychotic patients in a day hospital setting, *Psychosis (madness)*, ed. P. Williams, pp. 65–77, London: Institute of Psycho-Analysis. See also A.-L. Silver, B. Koehler and B. Karon (2004), Psychodynamic psychotherapy of schizophrenia. Its history and development, *Models of Madness*, ed. J. Read, L.R. Mosher and R. Bentall, pp. 209–22, London and New York: Routledge.

2 Julius Wellhausen (1844–1918) was a notable biblical critic and orientalist. He was professor of Old Testament studies at Greifswald and later professor in semitics at Marburg and Göttingen. In many ways he followed the lead of E. Reuss and devoted most of his life to 'higher' criticism, as it was known; that is, the critical study of the literary methods and sources used by the Old Testament authors, in distinction to textual or 'lower' criticism. In later years he devoted himself to the critical study of the New Testament and upheld the priority of Mark over Q, its composite nature and its original Aramaic form, although he made no attempt to illustrate his observations of Aramaic construction or usage from available sources. Nevertheless, many of his conjectures were, in the learned opinion of Matthew Black, brilliant. See M. Black (1957), *An Aramaic Approach to the Gospels and Acts*, Oxford: Clarendon Press. Wellhausen's philological analysis of texts laid down many of the lines for the later development of *Formgeschichte* or 'form criticism', which attempts to assess the historicity of texts by a study of their structure. See J. Wellhausen (1878), *Die Geschichte Israels,* Berlin: Reimer, and (1885) *Die Komposition des Hexateuchs und der historischen Bücher des Alten Testaments*, Berlin: G. Reimer.

3 Notably by K. Budde (1850–1935) at Strassburg and Marburg; by C.F. Burney (1868–1925), by G.B. Gray (1865–1922) at Oxford, and C.C. Torrey, and later A.J. Wensinck, who emphasised the Aramaic background of the Gospels. For a good summary, see Black (1957), pp 1–12.

Abbreviation

Xen. *Mem.* Xenophon. *Memorabilia. Oeconomicus. Symposium. Apologia*, trans. E.C. Marchant and O.J. Todd (1997). Loeb Classical Library 168. Cambridge, MA and London: Harvard University Press.

Bibliography

Albright, W.F. (1957). *From the Stone Age to Christianity. Monotheism and the Historical Process*. Baltimore, MD: Johns Hopkins University Press.

Andreasen, N.C. (1999). Understanding the causes of schizophrenia. *New England Journal of Medicine* 340(8): 645–7.

Apollon, W., Bergeron, D. and Cantin, L. (2002). *After Lacan. Clinical Practice and the Subject of the Unconscious*, ed. R. Hughes and K.R. Malone. Albany: State University of New York Press.

Bair, D. (2004). *Jung. A Biography*. London: Little Brown and Company.

Bion, W. (1967). *Second Thoughts: Selected Papers on Psychoanalysis*. London: Maresfield Library.

Cullberg, J. (2006). *Psychoses*. London and New York: Routledge.

de Certeau, M. (1986). *Histoire et psychanalyse entre science et fiction*. Paris: Gallimard.

De Waelhens, A. and Ver Eecke, W. (2001). *Phenomenology and Lacan on Schizophrenia, after the Decade of the Brain*. Leuven: Leuven University Press.

Foucault, M. (1985). *The Use of Pleasure. The History of Sexuality* , vol. 2, trans. R. Hurley. Harmondsworth: Penguin.

Freud, S. (1911). *The Case of Schreber*. In *The Standard Edition of the Complete Psychological Works of Sigmund Freud*, vol. 12, ed. and trans. J. Strachey. London: Hogarth Press/ Institute of Psycho-Analysis.

Freud, S. (1913). *Totem and Taboo*. In *The Standard Edition of the Complete Psychological Works of Sigmund Freud,* vol. 12, ed. and trans. J. Strachey. London: Hogarth Press/ Institute of Psycho-Analysis.

Fromm-Reichmann, F. (1960). *Principles of Intensive Psychotherapy*. Chicago: University of Chicago Press.

Gay, P. (2006). *Freud. A Life for Our Time*. London: Max.

Giovacchinin, P.L. (1979). *The Treatment of Primitive Mental States*. New York and London: Jason Aronson.

Hartmann, E., Milofsky, E. Vaillant, G., Oldfield, M., Falke, R. and Ducey, C. (1984). Vulnerability to schizophrenia. *Archives of General Psychiatry* 41(11): 1050–6.

Hyatt, J.P. (1940). Freud on Moses and the genesis of monotheism. *Journal of Bible and Religion* 8(2): 85–88.

Kendler, K.S. and Diehl, S.R. (1993). The genetics of schizophrenia: A current genetic-epidemiological perspective. *Schizophrenia Bulletin* 19(2): 261–85.

Klein, M. (1930). The psychotherapy of the psychoses. *British Journal of Medical Psychology* 10: 242–4.

Klein, M. (1948). *Contributions to Psychoanalysis 1931–1945*. London: Hogarth Press.

Klein, M. (1975). *Envy and Gratitude*. New York: Free Press.

Lacan, J. (1993). *The Psychoses. The Seminar of Jacques Lacan Book III 1955–1956*, trans. R. Grigg. London: Routledge.

Laplanche, J. and Pontalis, J.-B. (1980). *The Language of Psycho-Analysis,* trans. D. Nicholson-Smith. London: Hogarth Press/Institute of Psycho-Analysis.

Lucas, R. (1992). The psychotic personality: A psychoanalytical theory and its application in clinical practices. *Psychoanalytic Psychotherapy* 6(1): 3–17.

Lucas, R. (2009). *The Psychotic Wavelength. A Psychoanalytic Perspective for Psychiatry*. London: Routledge/Institute of Psycho-Analysis.

Mortensen, P.B., Pedersen, C.B., Westergaard, T., Wohlfahrt, J., Ewald, H., Mors, O., Andersen, P.K. and Melbye, M. (1999). Effects of family history and place and season of birth on the risk of schizophrenia. *New England Journal of Medicine* 340(8): 603–8.

Mosher, L.R., Gosden, R. and Beder, S. (2004). Drug companies and schizophrenia: Unbridled capitalism meets madness. In *Models of Madness*, ed. J. Read, L.R. Mosher and R.P. Bentall, pp. 115–30. London and New York: Routledge.

McGuire, W. (Ed.) (1974). *The Freud/Jung Letters: The Correspondence Between Sigmund Freud and C.G. Jung*, trans. R. Manheim and R.F.C. Hull. Princeton: Princeton University Press.

O'Shaughnessy, E. (1992). Psychosis: Not thinking in a bizarre world. In *Clinical Lectures on Klein and Bion*, ed. R. Anderson, pp. 89–101. London: Routledge.

Rosenfeld, H. (1966). *Psychotic States: A Psycho-analytical Approach*. New York: International University Press.

Segal, H. (1957). Notes on symbol formation. *International Journal of Psycho-Analysis* 38: 391–7.

Sohn, L. (1985). Narcissistic organisation, projective identifications and the formation of the identificate. *International Journal of Psycho-Analysis* 66: 201–14.

Tienari, P. (1992). Interaction between genetic vulnerability and rearing environment. In *Psychotherapy of Schizophrenia: Facilitating and Obstructive Factors*, ed. A. Werbart and J. Cullberg. Oslo: Scandinavian University Press.

Wallace, E.R. (1983). *Freud and Anthropology: A History and Reappraisal*. New York: International Universities Press.

Wilcken, P. (2010). *Claude Lévi-Strauss. The Poet in the Laboratory*. London: Bloomsbury.

Yerushalmi, Y.H. (1991). *Freud's Moses: Judaism Terminable and Interminable*. New Haven and London: Yale University Press.

Yorke, C. (1991). Freud's 'On Narcissism: a teaching text'. *Freud's 'On Narcissism: an introduction'*, ed. J. Sandler, pp. 35–53. Yale: Yale University Press.

1

FROM BEYOND SPEECH TO NON-INSCRIPTION

Spirit and psyche in the philosophy of psychoanalysis

John Gale

An ambiguous archaeology

The origins of the words spirituality and psychosis reveal, perhaps surprisingly, that they are closely connected, indeed, overlapping terms. Our English word spirituality, as the French *esprit* and the Spanish *espiritu*, is derived from the Latin *spiritus*. The original sense of *spiritus* is breathing or breath. This root is retained in English in words like respiration. From taking in breath, it is a short journey to an auspicious flow of ideas, as we find it in Cicero, where, citing Ennius, the father of Roman poetry, he calls the poet holy (*sanctos*), because he is infused with divine inspiration '*et quasi divino quodam spiritu inflari*' (Cic. *Pro Archia* 18). It is this word *spiritus* that Jerome used in the Vulgate to translate the Greek term *pneuma*, a word we first find used by Anaximenes to mean air or wind (Kirk et al. 1984; Liddell and Scott 1863).[1] A sense which preserved in our word pneumatic. It is only what we would expect when we are told that Anaximenes had said the air was god (Cic. *De Nat. De.* I, 10.26).[2] According to Theophrastus, the same conclusion was drawn by Diogenes of Apollonia (floruit 425 BCE), who said that the air within us is 'a small portion of the god' (Theoph. *De Sen.* 42).[3] Later, we find Herodotus using the word in his *Historia*. In Plato, Pythagoras and Empedocles we find the word *daemon* being used sometimes interchangeably with *theos* (god), as a divine element in man and sometimes to describe something like a guardian angel (Guthrie 1962), sometimes an evil spirit (Dodds 1951). Although the precise definition of the terms *daimon* and *daimonios* is vague in antiquity, by the second century CE virtually everyone, whether pagan, Jew or Christian, believed in the existence of intermediary beings 'whether he called them *daemons*, angels or simply spirits (*pneumata*)' (Dodds 1965: 38). When the spirit possessed someone, his speech would be considered either prophetic or demonic, depending, perhaps, on whether one agreed with him or not. In general, illness – and this included mental illness – was thought to be the result of the agency of malevolent *pneumata* (spirits). Here we begin to see the ambiguous connection between matters spiritual and madness.

In the Septuagint, which was already being compiled during the period when Diogenes wrote, the word *pneuma* was used to translate the Hebrew *ruah*. For biblical authors, the fact that the wind cannot be seen but that its effects are visible whether in a rustling of the leaves or in a sandstorm made it a transparent image of the divine. But through a multitude of lexical mutations, *ruah* also came to signify a kind of emptiness (cf. Micah 2.11). In this sense, spirituality might indicate the fundamental lack which belongs to the structure of understanding – something within experience itself that cannot be unravelled (Lacan 1993).

Patristic writers saw, in biblical history, a gradual unfolding of the notion of the spirit from an instrument of divine action, both in the natural world and in human psychology, to its literal personification as the Holy Spirit and its identification with the divine itself. Thus in Old English *gást* (god) becomes the Holy Ghost (Burton 2007). Paradoxically, this development corresponded to a suppression of the *pneumatikoi* (also known as *prophetai*, *entheoi* and *ekstatikoi*), those previously thought to be possessed by the spirit and who acted as spokesmen for the supernatural (Fascher 1927). By time Augustine came to write his treatise *De Trinitate*, the Holy Spirit, although retaining its status as an element within the triadic structure of the absolute Other, had 'outlived his primitive function' (Dodds 1965: 67).[4] From the middle of the third century we find we find exorcism of evil spirits, a task originally associated with the *prophetai*, being discharged by the clergy (Eus. *Hist. Eccl.* 6.43.11). With Spirit as a third term in the divinity, transforming the dual relationship between the Father and the Son, Christian spirituality came to bear the characteristics not just of a radical alterity, but also one that reflected the Oedipal structure (Deleuze and Guattari 1983). With this, a further indicator of the proximity of spirituality to the structure of psychosis becomes apparent (Lacan 1993).[5]

We find a further nuance in the distinction between *pneuma* and *gramma* (letter) as we come across it, for example, in Origen (Crouzel 1960). Here the letter stands not only for the other of *spiritus* – surely a resonance of Pauline theology (e.g. 2 Cor. 3.6) – but in its meaninglessness as an unreadable sign, as in the case of an unknown language, indicating both a hidden syntax and that which cannot be captured in speech (Lacan 1993). Here a correlation emerges between *pneuma* and *akatalēptos* – that which cannot be grasped or contained by the mind; the immeasurable, the infinite, the incomprehensible – as we find it used in Clement of Alexandria (Clem. *Strom.* 8.9; cf. Bucuk 2009) and in other Greek writers, and specifically in relation to the Holy Spirit in the seventh-century Byzantine *Chronicon Paschale* (PG 92: 772A).

The spiritual is understood here to indicate that which is somehow beyond language, outside the reach of culture. In its most fundamental sense, *pneuma* stands for that which resists symbolisation. This allows us some understanding of the difficulties inherent in securing a precise definition of spirituality. For paradoxically, the very word itself stands for what is *per se* unable to be assimilated because it is beyond description or comprehension. In the end spirituality signifies this out-of-reach. And yet, nevertheless, this realm of the real remains a sphere which language announces (Tugendhat 2003).

In this philological context, from the outset we cannot but be aware that the roots of the word psychosis lie in the Greek term *psuchē*. In *Phaedo* we see just what elastic a meaning this word can have (Kirk, Raven and Schofield 1984).[6] It is usually translated as soul (*anima* in Latin) and is distinguished from the body (*soma*)[7] – later we find Epiphanius referring to *psuchikōs* as the opposite of *sōmatikōs*[8] – or when described in a pejorative sense, from the flesh (*sarx*). Translating *psuchē* as soul also distinguishes it from *nous* (*mens*, 'intellect').[9] Aristotle defines *psuchē* as that thing, in virtue of which every living thing is alive (Arist. *De An.* 414a. 12). With the Stoics this becomes a subtle form of the spirit (*pneuma*). On this view, spirituality could very generally be defined as a concern for that which is most fundamental in a person and which includes, in some sense, that very self-concern. The proximity of these two terms, spirit and psyche, can be seen even in current usage. While in English we may seek peace of mind, the French hope to find *paix d'esprit* (peace of spirit).

In Xenophon we find *psuchē* contrasted with the law in a passage where Cyrus' mother tells the boy that his father was a free Persian who was accustomed to following the law and not his soul (Xen. *Cyrop.* 1, 3, 18). To follow one's soul is here to turn away from the law (*nomos*), a turning away which in psychosis is at its most radical and amounts to a fundamental non inscription (*Niederschrift* – literally, 'non-scriptural' – is the German word that Freud uses throughout his work) (Lacan 1993). This further lexical cleavage between *psuchē* and *nomos* mirrors that between *pneuma* and *gramma* which we have already noted. In the Septuagint, *psuchē* is used to translate the Hebrew *nephesh* (vital breath, life or being), which is distinct from *ruah*; something that St Paul mirrors by contrasting *psuchē* with *pneuma*.[10] In Genesis, when Yahweh breathed into man the breath of life, he became a living *nephesh* or being. *Nephesh* described the seat of the emotions and in the earlier biblical documents refers to the physical appetites. But later it comes to refer almost exclusively to desire, something that can never be satisfied (Staples 1928; cf. Lacan 1993).

Nearly all scholars agree that, by the time Augustine came to read Plotinus, he was already familiar with Cicero's treatise on the soul. Here Cicero argues that to locate the divine we must look within. In fact, both Cicero and Plotinus understand the Socratic dictum 'know thyself' to mean know your own soul; 'Hence Cicero is bold enough to say, like Plotinus, that the soul is a god' (Cary 2000: 83).

From *psuchē* to psychosis

Although our word psychosis has its foundation in *psuchē*, the words used for madness in classical Greek do not stem from this root. In antiquity, the words used to describe insanity are *mania* or *melancholia* (from *melas* meaning black, and *cholos*, bile). The former, *mania* (translated into Latin as *insania*, literally unwell) – from which we get our words mania and manic – indicates what we might call ordinary or temporary madness (Graver 2007), something that can beset anyone, perhaps in response to grief or other emotions. *Melancholia* (*furor* in Latin), on the other hand, more often refers to a deranged state in which a person's capacity for impressions (*phantasiai*) is disrupted, leading to a complete darkening of the mind. The person in this state required custodial care. As early as the Hippocratic texts we find certain forms of behaviour being treated as symptoms of exceptional mental conditions. These include hallucinations (*phantastikon*; cf. Sextus Adv. Math. VIII.56). For example, Orestes is chased by furies that no one else sees. It is only in the middle of the nineteenth century that the term psychosis was introduced, first in German by von Feuchtersleben, who defined it with the composite word *Seelenkrankheit* (mental illness). Two years later the word psyche appeared in English.[11] Given that *Seelen*, in its primary sense, means souls, Feuchtersleben's is, for our purposes, a rather circular definition.

The notion of reason (*logos*) had been invented by the Greeks (Jaeger 1973–86) and Greek culture has long been viewed as the triumph of rationalism. This led to a simplistic view of the positivism and secularism of Greek medicine (van der Eijk 2005), a view which has now largely had its day in scholarly circles but which continues to be repeated in popular accounts of the history of madness.[12] From the Presocratic period on Greek philosophers examined the concept and moved from the idea that it was the criteria for assessing everything, in the direction of an hypostatisation of reason and then towards a rejection of its adequacy, particularly in terms of its epistemological usefulness in the quest to uncover ontological truth (Diels 1906/1907). Thus, by the end of antiquity the Neoplatonist Damascius was to declare, over and above reason, the importance of the un-thought, unspoken (Ruelle 1966). Here we see reason rejected 'as a way of grasping the truly transcendent' (Mortley 1986: 242). This is not to say that rationality has no place in the analysis of religious experience or belief but that there is something in religious experience, even in its most primitive forms, that escapes rationalisation. This is most vividly expressed in the literature of mysticism. The trend, as we might call it, in Greek thought, away from an hypostatisation of reason in relation to the epistemology of being towards an appreciation of what Rudolf Otto called the numinous (Otto 1924), can be seen to be emerging in like the *Phaedrus*. According to Caelius Aurelianus (Cae. Aur. *Morb. Chron.* 1.5, A98) this idea originated with Empedocles (Guthrie 1965). Socrates argues that our greatest blessings come to us by way of four forms of madness – prophetic, ritual, poetic and erotic – all of which he describes as having a divine origin. These four kinds of sacred or supernatural madness are distinguished from an ordinary or natural kind of madness. The causes of natural madness, as opposed to supernatural madness, he identifies largely in physiological terms, for example, the effects of heavy drinking or the result of epilepsy (Rohde 1925).[13] This distinction between natural and sacred madness that we find in the *Phaedrus* is already, in Plato's time, rather an advanced view. It is a view which, in the light of the fact that the earlier belief which prevailed from Homer's time – that all forms of mental disturbance have a supernatural origin – can be understood as a limiting of the divine aspect of madness (Dodds 1951). That is to say, whereas many forms of madness can be understood by reason because they are caused through natural or physiological conditions that we can uncover through investigation, it was thought that there were other kinds of madness which were beyond the grasp of reason. However, the dividing line between common insanity and prophetic madness was in fact 'hard to draw' (Dodds 1951: 68). For us it is hard to know for sure whether any of the mental states which Plato identifies as madness correspond exactly to what we would today identify as a psychosis. But it is likely that they did, at least to some extent because he describes them as bringing changes in the person's normal social behaviour. There is, for example, an extant account of Menecrates who thought he was Zeus (Weinreich 1933).[14]

Mysticism, poetry and nothingness

The mystical cuts across the various traditions of belief and religious practice (Solignac and López-Gay 1980) and brings us to what is, perhaps, the heart of our subject matter. For in mystical language we encounter a spirituality,[15] which seems to come closest to insanity, as both the madman and the mystic confront the other of rationality (Höfer 2009). But the non-rational is not the same as the irrational. It refers to the limits of the symbolic, where divinity functions as a signifier that introduces '*always less* satisfaction and *always more* un-known in the subject's position' (de Certeau 2006: 44), while the irrational, we might say, is more like a structural failure within rationality itself (Davidson 1982).

Mysticism, as the cult of the secret, has its prehistory in a closing of the eyes (*muein*) (Liddell and Scott 1863). Here, the otherwise hidden meaning (*to mustagōgēma*) was revealed to those who passed through the secret rites of initiation (*mystagōgia*) (Lampe 1961). In this it seems to have embodied a desire both to create and destroy its own landscape. This amounts to a wish for loss within religious languages.[16]

> Mysticism operates as a process whereby the objects of meaning vanish, beginning with God himself; it is as though the function of

mysticism were to bring a religious *episteme* to a close and erase itself at the same time, to produce the night of the subject.

(de Certeau 2006: 37)

Bakan (1958) has shown just how deeply Jewish mystical thought, particularly in its later phase from the sixteenth century on, impacted on Freud.[17] He points out that psychoanalysis attempts to discern the nature of 'secret things' (Bakan 1958: 311).

> we are concerned with a secret, with something hidden . . . In the case of the criminal it is a secret which he knows and hides from you, but in the case of the hysteric it is a secret hidden from him, a secret he himself does not know. The task of the therapeutist is, however, the same as the task of the judge; he must discover the hidden psychic material.
>
> (Bakan 1958: 311)

When Lacan reviewed Freud's reading of the Schreber case, he saw a clear difference between Daniel Schreber's religious experiences and those of the mystics, particularly the sixteenth-century Spanish Carmelite John of the Cross. Lacan's interest in mysticism had probably begun while he was still at the Lycée. At that time his philosophy master, Jean Baruzi, was writing a doctoral thesis on the saint, which was eventually published in 1924 (Baruzi 1931).[18] Lacan would return to John of the Cross a number of times over the years.[19] The difference between the two, he thought, was to be found in the language they used, which somehow indicated, in the case of Schreber, his psychosis and, in that of John of the Cross, the authenticity of his mystical experience (Lacan 1993). Although a year or two earlier Lacan had said that, while everyone had read the *Dark Night of the Soul*, nobody had really understood it (Lacan 1988), he now argued that this difference in language would be apparent to everyone. He thought that the fundamental dissimilarity between the words of the two lay at the intersection between poetry and madness, for, while John of the Cross wrote in a poetic way, Schreber did not.[20] The point that Lacan was making was that the poet is someone who tunes into and responds to the linguistic environment, that is, to the discourse of other language users in which he or she participates. In this sense, poetic meaning is never a hermetic sealed off form of language, even when it stretches everyday usage. In other words, poetry is still language in the strict sense of the word, and therefore, however ambiguous or obscure it may be, a poem is not gibberish or nonsense, but rather part of a conversation and thus intelligible. The poetry of John of the Cross places great emphasis on distinguishing the desire for objective knowledge from what he calls unknowing or nothingness (*nada*). The latter is a kind of knowledge, but one that registers itself without an idea – an experience that resists analogue because it is beyond concepts and therefore cannot be spoken (Peers 1933–5). He describes mystic experience in these terms, as the experience of a knowledge which is hidden under a cloud of unknowing. In this dark cloud the divine is experienced directly but as unknown (de Sainte-Marie-Madeleine 1953). This knowledge-in-obscurity is not opposed to the precise or clear knowledge of things, as we find it in the empirical sciences – John does not conceive rational knowledge as a misunderstanding, but he does consider it an inferior kind of knowledge. Lacan concluded that in his poetry John of the Cross was able to open up another dimension of experience to the reader, of which she or he was previously unaware, whereas Schreber's psychotic language closed down shared understanding because it is wholly singular (de Certeau 1987).

This form of mystical or immediate knowledge takes on ecstatic characteristics which have overtly sexual connotations (Collin 1999).[21] In so doing, it is inscribed within a tradition of eroticism that goes back at least as far as Plato in paganism and to Origen and Gregory of Nyssa in Christianity. As Dodds puts it, 'it is not easy historically to draw a sharp line between Christian *agape*-mysticism and Platonist *eros*-mysticism' (Dodds 1965: 89 n. 2; cf. Armstrong 1961 and Rist 1966). It is no coincidence that erotic writing appears at the same time as does a flowering of mystical literature. This sexual dimension also adds to the proximity between the two discourses (Verdiglione 1977).

Lack, representation and transcendence

Mystical language also has an historical function in relation to a lack, or what de Certeau calls a 'labor of absences' (de Certeau 2006: 37) – absences which spring from both Jewish and Christian traditions where there is a defection and critique of religious orthodoxy that is closely connected to economic hardship (Ozment 1973). That these traditions are not always as far apart as we might imagine is illustrated by the fact that Teresa of Avila's grandfather was a Jewish convert, forced to abjure (Brenan 1973). Converted Jews in sixteenth-century Spain remained close to a repressed and internalised Jewish tradition – 'the tradition of the *gespaltete Seelen* [literally, 'split souls', meaning forced converts], divided, whose cleaved lives created a hidden 'interiority' and were 'prominent in the ranks of the *alumbrados* (illuminati)' (de Certeau 2006: 84; cf. van Praag 1948).[22]

Hegel had defined subjectivity as the presence of reflection and had endeavoured to give an account of self-consciousness and situate it, not abstractly but as something deeply embedded in the lived experience of the subject's relations to objects in the world. According to this schema, the subject is so impregnated by desire for the other and so dependent on the other, for a sense of self, that relations with the other are invariably conflicted. In fact, Hegel defines self-consciousness simply as desire itself (*Begierde überhaupt*).[23] As he saw it, the self depends on the object of desire to fill its lack and it was the notion of lack that was to become one of Hegel's major contributions to Lacan's thought (Williams 1992).[24] It represents a development of Husserl in that it underscores the way in which intersubjectivity is constructed. It is a lack of being (*manque de l'être*), Lacan suggests, that lies at the heart of the analytic experience (Lacan 2006). In part, this may be because psychoanalysis brings the practitioner face to face with difficulty in terms of the resistance of the patient. Here, both the difficulty experienced by the practitioner, and the gesture of resistance itself, can be described as ascetical, that is, as a kind of withholding (Harpham 1987). Hence Lacan refers to the 'the ascesis of psychoanalysis' (Lacan 1988: 126). Thus self-consciousness and desire are closely linked to an existential reticence and indicate an inability for human beings to be satisfied.

But, as well as being based on Hegel, Lacan derives his concept of lack, almost certainly, from Heidegger's analysis of lack and deficiency (*Mangel*, *Mangelhaftigkeit*) (Heidegger 1990). For Heidegger, absence of being is the experience a person has of the void or nothingness at the centre of her or his own consciousness. It is an absence of a foundation to the self that springs from the fact that, while consciousness can perceive objects, it is unable to perceive itself except as if it were an object external to itself. Heidegger describes this in terms of an inherent conflict between the necessity of saying the truth of being and the incapability of saying being which results from what he calls the silent call of being and being's occurrence as withdrawal (Taminiaux 1989). The distinction that Heidegger is making here between being (*Sein*) as it has traditionally been understood in the history of Western philosophy to indicate the hidden, enduring, metaphysical ground of existence and a dimension of the meaning of life which has not previously been articulated. *Seyn* (being)[25] suggests an elusive element in what is currently happening (Scott 2001). This is not a description of worlds-behind-the-scene but of a beyond that fundamentally marks the limit of the contained and thus signals that which cannot be unravelled. Thus lack-of-being refers to the other and to the limits of knowledge. But not just the limits of our present understanding; rather the essential structure of non-presence (Levinas 1961).

> It is not as knowledge of the world, of some world-behind-the-world, or as a *Weltanschauung* that we have tried to articulate the transcendence ... A transcendence that cannot be reduced to an experience of transcendence, for it is a seizure prior to all *positing* of a subject and to every perceived or assimilated content. Transcendence or awakening that is the very life of the human, already troubled by the Infinite.
>
> (Levinas 2006: 77)

In *Die Traumdeutung*, Freud had insisted that interpretation had its limits (Žižek 1989). Not everything in a dream can be understood or unravelled,

16

because some aspects of the unconscious always remain obscure and hidden. 'There is at least one spot in every dream at which it is unplumbable – a navel, as it were, that is its point of contact with the unknown' (Freud SE 1900: 111).[26] This is not as a result of the inadequate nature of the act of interpretation, but because something essential always 'falls outside the field of representation' (Shepherdson 2003: 119).

> There is often a passage in even the most thoroughly interpreted dream which has to be left obscure; this is because we become aware during the work of interpretation that at that point there is a tangle of dream-thoughts which cannot be unravelled and which moreover adds nothing to our knowledge of the dream. This is the dream's navel, the spot where it reaches down into the unknown.
>
> (Freud SE 1900: 525)

Lacan's critique of rationalism revolved around a consideration of the implications of the notion of representation (*Vorstellung*) and particularly of its limits (cf. Bernet 2002). The Cartesian notion of representation, which was a move away from Aristotle, demanded that a new mind–body distinction be drawn between consciousness and what is not consciousness (Rorty 2009). In his second proof for the existence of God, Descartes shows the need for something other than consciousness to sustain thought. This un-thought – something that is outside and beyond consciousness – could be described as the unconscious source from which consciousness arises (Boothby 2001).

> while it may be correct to say the unconscious can be followed through various symbolic manifestations (the lapsus, the dream, free association, negation), there is also an aspect of the unconscious which belongs to the order of the real, understood as a dimension irreducible to representation.
>
> (Shepherdson 2003: 120)

According to Laurent (1995), for Lacan the limits of representation point to an inherent dissonance between thinking and being. Signifiers, conscious and unconscious, never entirely capture the being of the subject, not because of the imaginary nature of the ego, formed as it is at the mirror stage and not because of the complex network of representations that characterise the symbolic nature of language, but because of a fundament lack in the real. This mirrors Wittgenstein's contention in the *Tractatus* that there is a whole realm of human life made up of the things that belong to the limit of the world – things, that is, that cannot be put into propositions. In other words, language cannot be the whole story and in this sense mysticism signifies the realm of the unsayable. However, Tugendhat in *Egozentrizität und Mystik* (2003) reminds us that the inexpressible is more than simply that which is not yet said, because when we think about the inexpressible we are already engaged in language. He thus describes mysticism as a retreat from oneself, from an egocentric view of the world in which there is no room for gratitude or thanksgiving for that upon which our existence depends. In this sense the mystical could be described in terms of a displacement of the self. 'One can perhaps say – to adopt the terminology of his [Wittgenstein's] later works – that he has given us an instance of one particular language-game, from which already the feeling of something "mystical" emerges' (D'hert 1978: 32). Thus language – and this includes the language of empiricism – always points beyond itself in the sense that 'aspects of things which are most important for us are hidden' (Wittgenstein 1999: 129).

Conclusion: Self-consciousness, mysticism and psychosis

Tugendhat (1986) points out that in Freud's *New Introductory Lectures on Psycho-Analysis* we find the astonishing sentence: 'We do not need to discuss what is meant by "conscious," since it is clear beyond all doubt' (Tugendhat 1986: 5). Here Freud seems naively unaware of the difficulties concerning consciousness and specifically self-consciousness, which have been central to philosophy since Descartes (Freud SE 1933). Namely, questions about the structure of self-consciousness and the relation of oneself to oneself. Key to this discourse has been the idea that consciousness is concerned with our relationship to objects and that a reflexive relation to oneself can give one access to oneself, as an object.

The philosophical assumptions which lie beneath psychoanalysis in its encounter with belief (and with religious belief more specifically) are frequently overlooked because of the conflict, within psychoanalytic self-understanding, which has led it largely to eschew all but the empirical in the uncovering of truth.

> On the basis of his limited knowledge of philosophy and, in particu-
> lar, his very narrow concept of consciousness, Freud maintained that
> philosophy as philosophy of consciousness would necessarily lack an
> appropriate understanding of the Unconscious and he expected
> nothing more from it than a reduction of the Unconscious to con-
> sciousness, that is to say, a sterile denial of the existence of the
> Unconscious . . . It is therefore quite understandable that Freud and
> his pupils and successors gave little attention to philosophical
> considerations concerning the Unconscious.
>
> (Bernet 2002: 328)

Thus psychoanalytic discourse has, in general, tended to dismiss the significance of religious belief and experience, and deem it purely pathological. This is because it has failed to take account of the fact that all forms of spirituality refer essentially to a way of treating language and are therefore social. However, when rescued by hermeneutic philosophy, psychoanalysis is well placed to take a lead in understanding the place of religious phenomenology precisely because of the attention it gives to language and to the limits of language. Thus Lacan's attempt at a transcendental-philosophical grounding of psychoanalysis gives us a far better foundation for understanding spirituality and its relationship to madness.

Spirituality is a term which, given its biblical resonance, already situates our thought within the confines of the Judeo-Christian tradition; that is to say, within the parameters of that convergence of Near Eastern and Hellenistic thought that forms the background to European culture. As a result, Christianising assumptions not infrequently lie behind our readings of spirituality. Even in the changed sense in which Plato describes the care of the soul (*psuchē*), it is difficult not to hear Christian overtones. Such a view also often distorts our understanding of what we might call, for want of a better term, non religious forms of spirituality – that is, spiritualities detached from institutions and traditions of belief and practice. While there is clearly continuity as well as discontinuity between the two approaches, religious forms of spirituality tend to become preoccupied in identifying the beyond with an 'afterlife', 'the other world' and so on.

Religious beliefs do not exist outside of language or within a special language. Rather, they make use of (a common, shared) language, albeit in a specific way. In other words, what makes or does not make sense within religious discourse is, therefore, 'determined by what constitutes sense or nonsense in other contexts' (Hudson 1969: 40). This applies to mystical language, which on a surface reading may appear to be very close to psychotic language. But, while psychotic language signifies the limits of symbolisation, the language of mysticism has coherence for a particular community, for it is shared meaning that gives it its significance. John of the Cross emphasised this point by dismissing the idea that (private) visions and inner voices were the essence of mystical experience. A religious psychosis, on the other hand, signifies not the limits of symbolisation but a rejection of symbolisation.

Notes

1 Although invisible, prior to Anaximenes *pneuma* in the sense of breath was certainly thought to exist. Anaximenes probably held that all things were surrounded by '*pneuma kai aēn*' (wind or breath and air) and that it was the originative substance (cf. Diels 1906 I, p. 18: 30–40). He compares the cosmic air with life giving breath, so as to understand the world as a mirror image of man, *pneuma* being seen as the life principle in the world as wind or air and in man as breath-soul – '*oion ē psuchē, phēsin, ē ēmatera aēr ousa suykratei ēmas, kai hlon ton kosmon pneuma kai aēr periechei*' (Diels 1906 I, p. 21: 17–19). But the idea that the soul holds the body together has no other parallel in any source prior to Aristotle (Kirk et al. 1984).

2 Cf. Guthrie (1962: 130).

3 Cf. also ibid.

4 For the critical edition of Augustine's *De Trinitate*, see E. Hendrikx, M. Mellet and Th. Ca-Mellet (ed. and trans.) (1955) *La Trinité* I–VII. Bibliothèque Augustinienne 15. Les oeuvres de saint Augustin. Paris: Institut d'Études Augustiniennes; and P. Agaesse and J. Moingt (ed. and trans.) (1955) *La Trinité* VIII–XV. Bibliothèque Augustinienne 16. Les oeuvres de saint Augustin. Paris: Institut d'Études Augustiniennes.

5 According to Lacan, there is a moment in the very early stages of infantile development in which the later emergence of a psychosis is determined.

6 For the text of *Phaedo*, see H.N. Fowler (ed. and trans.) (1914) *Plato Euthyphro, Apology, Crito, Phaedo, Phaedrus* Loeb Classical Library 36, Cambridge, MA and London: Harvard University Press: 193–404.

7 Cf. Matt. 10.28, which reads: *to sōma tēn de psychēn.*

8 *P.G.* 41.741A cited in Lampe (1961: 1554).

9 Following German scholars, who translate *nous* and *noētos* in Plotinus with *Geist* and *geistig*, Hadot consistently renders these terms in French not with *Intelligence* and *intelligible* but with *Esprit* and *spirituel*. He comments that by employing these terms '*afin exprimer du mieux possible le caractère mystique et intuitif de l'Intelligence plotinienne*' P. Hadot, *Plotin ou la simplicité du regard*. Paris: Études Augustiniennes, 1973; cf. also A.-J. Festugière (1954) *Personal Religion among the Greeks*, Berkeley: University of California Press.

10 Freud was aware of this ambiguity and grappled with it in his discussion of the equivalent German *Geist* (spirit) and *Seele* (soul), terms he uses almost interchangeably (SE XXIII, cf. Strachey's note on p. 114). Cf. S. Freud (1938) An Outline of Psycho-Analysis, *The Standard Edition of the Complete Psychological Works of Sigmund Freud*, vol. XXIII, 144–207 trans. J. Strachey. London: Hogarth Press/ Institute of Psycho-Analysis.

11 The first example of this use seems to be in the English translation of E.F. von Feuchtersleben (1845) *Lehrbuch der ärztlichen Seelenkunde*, Vienna: C. Gerold, which was published in London by the Sydenham Society in 1847 under the title *Principles of Medical Psychology*. The translation was made by H.E. Lloyd. This use of psychosis mirrors that of the word schizophrenia. See the paper by G.E. Berrios et al., Schizophrenia: A Conceptual History, *International Journal of Psychology and Psychological Therapy* 3(2): 111–40, where the authors situate the usage of the term schizophrenia within the broader historiographical context; also see the note by Laplanche and Pontalis in their dictionary: J. Laplanche and J.-B. Pontalis (1980) *The Language of Psycho-Analysis*. London: Hogarth Press/Institute of Psycho-Analysis: 370 and 372 note α.

12 Popular histories of madness and the treatment of those afflicted by a mental disorder invariably repeat the view that, while in pagan and Jewish antiquity demonic possession was considered the cause of insanity and ill treatment meted out to sufferers by priests, in the classical era in Greece reason prevailed over superstition and with it a kind of prelude to the Enlightenment approach to the causality of mental disorders was developed. Later, with the fall of Rome and the emergence of Christianity, superstition again prevailed cf. R.H. Major (1957) How Hippocrates made his diagnoses, *International Record of Medicine* 170: 479–85; R.E. Siegel (1964). Clinical observation in Hippocrates: An essay on the evolution of the diagnostic art, *Mount Sinai Journal of Medicine* 31: 285–303; and M. Jandolo (1967) Manifestazioni stomatiche dell psicosi in Ippocrate, *Revista di storia della medicina* 11: 45–8. This simplistic view, now largely eschewed by classical scholars, in which ideas in early modern science are conflated with ancient

enquiries into the natural world, not only fails in its account of reason in Greek thought and its lack of understanding of the role of demonology in the classical and late antique periods, but also in its inadequate understanding of the historical development of Judeo-Christian literature and the historiography of religious phenomenology. In so doing, they merely exchange one discourse for another. For more reliable guidance in the study of these distinct but interrelated areas, see B. Van Groningen (1958) Le traité hippocratique, *La Composition littéraire archaïque greque: procédés et realisations*, Amsterdam: N.V. Noord-Hollandsche Uitgevers Maatsschappij, pp. 247–55; G. Bratescu (1975) Eléments archaïques dans la médicine hippocratique, *La Collection hyppocratique et son rôle dans l'histoire de la médicine: Colloque de Strasbourg, 23–27 octobre 1972*, ed. L. Bourgey and J. Jouanna, pp. 41–9, Leiden: E.J. Brill; M. de Certeau (1986) *Histoire et psychanalyse entre science et fiction*, Paris: Gallimard; J. Jouanna (1988) La maladie sauvage dans la *Collection hippocratique* et la tragédie grecque, *Métis* 3: 343–60; G.E.R. Lloyd (1990) *Demystifying Mentalities*, Cambridge: Cambridge University Press; M.C. Nussbaum (1994) *The Therapy of Desire. Theory and Practice in Hellenistic Ethics*, Princeton, NJ: Princeton University Press; and F. Hoessly (2001) *Katharsis. Reinigung als Heilverfahen. Studien zum Ritual der archaischen und klassischen Zeit sowie zum Corpus Hippocraticum*. Göttingen: Vandenhoeck and Ruprecht.

13 Dodds points out that, despite the fact that Plato did not believe in the supernatural character of epilepsy, in general in antiquity *epilēpsis* was the sacred disease par excellence because it suggested the intervention of a daemon. This notion of supernatural intervention is retained in our use of the expression 'an attack' of a particular disease, or indeed our use of the words seizure or stroke (Dodds 1951).

14 Weinreich (1993: 105) suggests that the popular etymology connected Zeus with *zēn* and *dia*. We find an echo here of the Homeric clausula *theous aien eontas* in asserting the immortality of Zeus in Callimachus' *Hymn to Zeus* cf. N. Hopkinson (1984) Callimachus' Hymn to Zeus, *Classical Quarterly*, New Series 34(1): 139–48.

15 On the relationship between the terms mystical and spirituality, and the shift from the adjectival to substantive use, see G. Müller (1971) Ueber den Begriff der Mystik. *Neue Zeitschrift für Systematische Theologie und Religionsphilosophie* 13: 88–98.

16 De Certeau suggests that the convergence between psychoanalysis and mysticism can be seen in a return of Christian notions in Lacanian discourse, which is homologous to the link between *absprechen* (contestation) and *angehören* (belonging) – 'a zebrine patterning and labor of absences' – that ties Freud's writings to the Jewish tradition. He says that the 'wish for loss' is analogous to the death drive in Freud but directed towards the syntax which the mystics used as a tool to create linguistic journeys that simultaneously destroy the landscape and the way. This is the sense in which representations vanish, beginning with the concept of god, producing the mystic *noche oscura* (dark night) and *nada* (nothingness). Through this process they function to bring about a closure to an imaginary religious *epistēmē* which erases itself 'in much the same way that the analytic trajectory diminishes the signifying chain'; de Certeau (2006: 36–7).

17 Rice considers Bakan's view unpersuasive because he mistakenly equates the mystical in Judaism exclusively with the study of the kabbalah; see E. Rice (1990) *Freud and Moses. The Long Journey Home,* New York: State University of New York Press, esp. 119 and 224 n.9.

18 Jean Baruzi (1881–1953) was an historian and a philosopher and followed the famous modernist theologian Alfred Loisy as Chair of the history of religions at

the Collège de France from 1933–4. His works on John of the Cross, which included a substantive entry in 1948 in the *Histoire générale des religions* (Paris: Aristide Quillet), were highly regarded and informed much of the lengthy study on the mystic in the *Dictionnaire de Spiritualité,* Paris: Beauchesne (1953), LIII: 408–47. Baruzi, in common with Max Milner and Georges Morel, placed great emphasis on the poetry of John of the Cross; see M. Milner, *Poésie et vie mystique chez saint Jean de la Croix* Paris: Editions du Seuil, 1951 (to which Baruzi contributed the preface), and G. Morel, *Le sens de l'existence selons saint Jean de la Croix,* Paris: Aubier, 1960–1. For an English translation of the poems, see R. Campbell (1972) *The Poems of St John of the Cross. The Spanish text with a translation*, London: Harvill Press. See also Mark Agius' excellent translation of a study by Pius Sammut – P. Sammut (1992) *God is a Feast. A New Look at John of the Cross*, Rochester: New Life Publishing.

19 As Freud had considered his relationship to Judaism in *Totem and Taboo* (1912–13) and *Moses and Monotheism* (1937–9), Lacan in his *Ethique de la psychoanalyse* (1959–60) considered his relationship to Christianity. While Freud's Judaism has been discussed in detail, Lacan's Catholicism has been less closely examined. However, one cannot but notice that time and again he writes in relation to the New Testament, to theological texts, particularly Augustine, to Pascal, Meister Eckhart, Teresa of Avila, etc. For this reason, Michel de Certeau describes Lacan's discourse in its history, narratives and theoretical loci as Christian (de Certeau 2006). It is a view that Roudinesco echoes in describing mysticism and the Trinity as two of the great myths on which Lacan based his reading of Freud (Roudinesco 1993). On Freud's Judaism, see especially Y.H. Yerushalmi (1991) *Freud's Moses. Judaism Terminable and Interminable,* New Haven and London: Yale University Press; M. Ostow (1982) *Judaism and Psychoanalysis* New York: Ktav Publishing House; and D. Merkur (1994) Freud and Hasidism, *The Psychoanalytic Study of Society,* vol. 19, ed. L. Bryce Boyer, Ruth M. Boyer and Howard F. Stein, London: The Analytic Press.

20 We might compare this to the relationship between the poetry of Hölderlin, so beloved of Heidegger, and his psychosis which Laplanche analysed, following Lacan's notions of the paternal signifier and of foreclosure. Cf. J. Laplanche (2007) *Hölderlin and the Question of the Father*, trans. L. Carson, Victoria: ELS Editions. The best English edition of the poems is *Friedrich Hölderlin. Poems and Fragments*, trans. M. Hamburger, London: Anvil Press Poetry. See also R. Peacock (1938) *Hölderlin*, London: Methuen and Co. See also T. Kepes (1997) Psychoanalysis and God: A comparative analysis of Jacques Lacan and John of the Cross, *Journal of Faith and Science Exchange* 45–7.

21 In Seminar XX, Lacan points out the orgasmic posture that Bernini has Teresa of Avila adopt in his famous statue of the saint in the church of Santa Maria della Vittoria in Rome. See J. Lacan (1998) *On Feminine Sexuality. The Limits of Love and Knowledge 1972–1973. Encore, The Seminar of Jacques Lacan,* Book XX, ed. J.-A. Miller, trans. B. Fink, New York: Norton. Of course, Lacan was not the first to notice the erotic in regard to Teresa's mystical ecstasy. Indeed, D.-M. Bournville, the most vehemently anti-Catholic of Charcot's colleagues at the Salpêtrière, had diagnosed her with hysteria. See A. Hustvedt (2011) *Medical Muses. Hysteria in Nineteenth-Century Paris*, London: Bloomsbury.

22 *Alumbrados* (the enlightened) was a term used loosely to describe practitioners of a mystical form of Christianity in Spain during the fifteenth and sixteenth centuries. Some were only mildly heterodox, but others held views that were clearly heretical. Consequently they were vigorously suppressed and became one of the early victims of the Inquisition.

23 While the Standard Edition of Freud's works translate *Wunsch* as 'wish', Freud's French translators use *désir* rather than *voeu*. In Lacan's lexicon the notion of desire comes closer to Hegel's *Begierde* – the relationship between consciousness and the self – than to Freud's *Wunsch*. On Lacan's appropriation of Hegel's *Begierde* as distinct from *Wunsch* or *Lust*, see E. Roudinesco (1986) *Histoire de la psychoanalyse en France 2. 1925–1985*, Paris: Fayard.

24 Lacan had become interested in Hegel after attending Kojève's 1933–4 lectures, which Lévi-Strauss also attended (Birksted-Breen and Flanders 2010). As well as in his definition of desire as the desire of the Other, Lacan is probably more or less dependent of Kojève's Hegel for his conception of a decentred subjectivity defined in relation to the Other and his notion of the subject's alienation (Barzilai 1999).

25 *Seyn* is an earlier spelling of the word *Sein* (being). Some authors have attempted to mirror this by translating *Seyn* as 'beying'. Heidegger's works are full of examples of this kind of experimentation with language. Lacan's attraction to Heidegger was probably due in part to the obscure style which resulted from this experimentation and it may well have contributed to the syntactic obscurity which characterises much of his writing. Cf. D. Vallega-Neu (2001) "Beying-Historical Thinking", Heidegger's Contributions to Philosophy. In *Companion to Heidegger's Contributions to Philosophy*, ed. C.E. Scott, S.M. Schoenbohm, D. Vallega-Neu and A. Vallega, pp. 49–65. Bloomington and Indianapolis: Indiana University Press.

26 Levinas mirrors this when he speaks of the transcendent as the other of language. Paradoxically the transcendent, understood in this sense, is both limited and delimited by the other. That is to say, because transcendence is spoken in language it is necessarily intersubjective, yet at the same time it remains an ungraspable non-said and forms part of a network of inaccessible connections in meaning. Transcendence is thus described by Levinas as an aspect of language that is unheard because it is fundamentally inaudible (Levinas 1961). To put it another way, the absolute other that is alluded to in this concept of transcendence is that which cannot be contained in thought.

Abbreviations

Works by ancient authors are cited as follows:

Arist. *De An.*	Aristotle. *De Anima* , trans. W.S. Hett (1957). Loeb Classical Library 288. Cambridge and London: Harvard University Press.
Cae. Aur. *Morb. Chron.*	Caelius Aurelianus, *De Morbis Acutis et Chronicis*, ed. and trans. I.E. Drabkin (1950). Chicago: University of Chicago Press.
Cic. *De Nat. De.*	M. Tullii Ciceronis. *De Natura Deorum*, vol. 1, intro. and commentary J.H. Swainson (1880). Cambridge: Cambridge University Press.
Cic. *Pro Archia*	Cicero. *Pro Archia Poeta*, trans. N.H. Watts (1935). *Cicero. The Speeches:* 7–41. London: William Heinemann.
Clem. *Strom.*	Clement of Alexandria. *Stromata* books 7–8, ed. O. Stählin and L. Früchtel (1960). Clemens Alexandrinus II *Die griechischen christlichen Schriftsteller der ersten drei Jahrhunderte* 17. Berlin: Akademie-Verlag.

Eus. *Hist. Eccl.*	Eusebius. *Ecclesiastical History*, ed. G. Bardy (1960). *Eusèbe de Césarée. Histoire Ecclesiastique* IV. Sources chrétiennes 71. Paris: Editions du Cerf.
Sextus *Adv. Math.*	Sextus Empiricus, *Adversus Mathematicos VIII*, trans. R. Bett (2005). Cambridge: Cambridge University Press.
Theoph. *De Sen.*	Theophrastus. *De Sensu.* Diels, H. (1906/1907). *Die Fragmente der Vorsokratiker.* Diogenes A 19. vol. I(42): 331–28. Berlin: Weidmannsche Buchhandlung.
Xen. *Cyrop.*	Xenophon. *Cyropaedia,* 2 vols, trans. W. Miller (1914). Loeb Classical Library 51 and 52. Cambridge and London: Harvard University Press.
P.G.	*Patrologia Graeca*, ed. J.P. Migne (1857–66). Paris.

References

Armstrong, A.H. (1961). Platonic Eros and Christian Agape. *Downside Review* 79: 105.

Bakan, D. (1958). *Sigmund Freud and the Jewish Mystical Tradition*. Princeton: D. Van Nostrand Company Inc.

Baruzi, J. (1931). *Saint Jean de la Croix et le problème de l'expérience mystique*. Paris: Librairie Félix Alcan.

Barzilai, S. (1999). *Lacan and the Matter of Origins*. Stanford: Stanford University Press.

Bernet, R. (2002). Unconscious consciousness in Husserl and Freud. *Phenomenology and the Cognitive Sciences* I: 327–51.

Birksted-Breen, D. and Flanders, S. (2010). General Introduction. In *Reading French Psychoanalysis*, ed. D. Birksted-Breen, S. Flanders and A. Gibeault, pp. 1–51. London and New York: Routledge.

Boothby, R. (2001). *Freud as Philosopher. Metapsychology After Lacan*. New York and London: Routledge.

Brenan, G. (1973). *Saint John of the Cross*. Cambridge: Cambridge University Press.

Bucuk, B.G. (2009). *Angelomorphic Pneumatology. Clement of Alexandria and Other Early Christian Witnesses*. Supplements to Vigiliae Christianae 95. Leiden: Brill.

Burton, P. (2007). *Language in the* Confessions *of Augustine*. Oxford: Oxford University Press.

Cary, P. (2000). *Augustine's Invention of the Inner Self*. Oxford: Oxford University Press.

Collin, F. (1999). La Liberté inhumaine: ou le mariage mystique de Jacques Lacan et Simone de Beauvoir. *Les Temps Modernes* 54: 605.

Crouzel, H. (1960). *Origène et la connaissance mystique*. Paris: Desclée de Brouwer.

Davidson, D. (1980). *Essays on Actions and Events*. Oxford: Oxford University Press.

Davidson, D. (1982). Paradoxes of irrationality. In *Philosophical Essays on Freud*, ed. R. Wollheim and J. Hopkins, pp. 289–305. Cambridge: Cambridge University Press.

de Certeau, M. (1977). Le Corps folié: folie et mystique aux XVIᵉ et XVIIᵉ siècles. *La Folie dans la psychoanalyse*, ed. A. Verdiglione, pp. 189–203. Paris: Payot.

de Certeau, M. (1987). *La Faiblesse de croire*. Paris: Editions du Seuil.

de Certeau, M. (2006). *Heterologies. Discourse on the Other*, trans. B. Massumi. Minneapolis and London: University of Minnesota Press.

de Sainte-Marie-Madeleine, G. (1953). Nature de la contemplation – description psychologique. *Dictionnaire de Spiritualité* vol. 2(2): 2058–67. Paris: Beauchesne.

Deleuze, G. and Guattari, F. (1983). *Anti-Oedipus. Capitalism and Schizophrenia.* Minneapolis: University of Minnesota Press.

D'hert, I. (1978). *Wittgenstein's Relevance for Theology.* Bern: Peter Lang.

Diels, H. (1906/1907). *Die Fragmente der Vorsokratiker,* 2 vols. Berlin: Weidmannsche Buchhandlung.

Dodds, E.R. (1951). *The Greeks and the Irrational.* Berkeley, Los Angeles and London: University of California Press.

Dodds, E.R. (1965). *Pagan and Christian in an Age of Anxiety.* Cambridge: Cambridge University Press.

Fascher, E. (1927). *PROPHĒTĒS: Eine sprach- und religionsgeschichliche Untersuchung.* Geissen: Alfred Töpelmann.

Freud, S. (1900). *The Interpretation of Dreams.* In *The Standard Edition of the Complete Psychological Works of Sigmund Freud,* vol. 4, ed. and trans. J. Strachey. London: Hogarth Press/Institute of Psycho-Analysis.

Freud, S. (1933). *New Introductory Lectures on Psychoanalysis.* In *The Standard Edition of the Complete Psychological Works of Sigmund Freud,* vol. 22, ed. and trans. J. Strachey. London: Hogarth Press/Institute of Psycho-Analysis.

Graver, M.R. (2007). *Stoicism and Emotion.* Chicago and London: University of Chicago Press.

Guthrie, W.K.C. (1962). *A History of Greek Philosophy,* vol. 1, *The Earlier Presocratics and Pythagoreans.* Cambridge: Cambridge University Press.

Guthrie, W.K.C. (1965). *A History of Greek Philosophy,* vol. 2, *The Presocratic Tradition from Parmenides to Democritus.* Cambridge: Cambridge University Press.

Harpham, G. (1987). *The Ascetic Imperative in Culture and Criticism.* Chicago and London: University of Chicago Press.

Heidegger, M. (1990). *Being and Time,* trans. J. Macquarrie and E. Robinson. Oxford: Basil Blackwell.

Höfer, B. (2009). *Psychosomatic Disorders in Seventeenth-Century French Literature.* Farnham: Ashgate.

Hudson, W.D. (1969). Some remarks on Wittgenstein's account of religious belief. *Talk of God. Royal Institute of Philosophy Lectures,* ed. G.N.A. Vesey, vol. 2, pp. 36–51. London: Macmillan.

Jaeger, W. (1973–86) *Paideia: The Ideals of Greek Culture,* 3 vols. New York and Oxford: Oxford University Press.

Kirk, G.S., Raven, J.E. and Schofield, M. (1984). *The Presocratic Philosophers. A Critical History with a Selection of Texts.* Cambridge: Cambridge University Press.

Lacan, J. (1988). *The Seminar of Jacques Lacan, Book I. Freud's Papers on Technique 1953–1954,* ed. J.-A. Millar, trans. J. Forrester. Cambridge: Cambridge University Press.

Lacan, J. (1993). *The Psychoses. The Seminar of Jacques Lacan,* ed. J.-A. Miller, trans. R. Grigg. London: Routledge.

Lacan, J. (2006). *Écrits,* trans. B. Fink. New York and London: W.W. Norton and Company.

Lampe, G.W.H. (ed.) (1961). *A Patristic Greek Lexicon.* Oxford: Clarendon Press.

Laurent, E. (1995). Alienation and separation. In *Reading Seminar XI. Lacan's Four Fundamental Concepts of Psychoanalysis,* ed. R. Feldson, B. Fink and M. Jaanus, pp. 19–38. Albany: State University of New York Press.

Levinas, E. (1961). *Totalité et Infini: essai sur l'extériorité*. Paris: Livres de Poche.

Liddell, H.G. and Scott, R. (1863). *A Greek–English Lexicon*. Oxford: Clarendon Press.

Mortley, R. (1986). *From Word to Silence*, vol. 2, *The Way of Negation, Christian and Greek*. Bonn: Hanstein.

Otto, R. (1924). *The Idea of The Holy*, trans. J.W. Harvey. London: Humphrey Milford, Oxford University Press.

Ozment, E. (1973). *Mysticism and Dissent. Religious Ideology and Social Protest in the 16th Century*. New Haven: Yale University Press.

Rist, J.M. (1966). A note on eros and Agape in pseudo-Dionysius. *Vigiliae Christianae* 20: 235–43.

Rohde, E. (1925). *Psyche: The Cult of Souls and the Belief in Immortality among the Greeks*, trans. W.B. Hillis. London: Routledge and Kegan Paul.

Roudinesco, E. (1993). *Jacques Lacan. Esquisse d'une vie, histoire d'un système de pensée*. Paris: Fayard.

Ruelle, C.A. (ed.) (1966). Damascius. Dubitationes et solutiones de Primis principiis. *Platonis Parmenidem*. Amsterdam: Hakkert.

Shepherdson, C. (2003). Lacan and philosophy. *The Cambridge Companion to Lacan*, ed. J.-M. Rabaté, pp. 116–52. Cambridge: Cambridge University Press.

Solignac, A. and López-Gay, J. (1980). Mystique. *Dictionnaire de Spiritualité*, vol. 10, *1889–1902*. Paris: Beauchesne.

Staples, W.E. (1928). The 'soul' in the Old Testament. *American Journal of Semitic Languages and Literature* 44(3): 145–76.

Taminiaux, J. (1989). *Lectures de l'ontologie fondamentale. Essais sur Heidegger*. Grenoble: Jerome Millon.

Tugendhat, E. (2003). *Egozentrizität und Mystik*. München: C.H. Beck.

van der Eijk, P. (2005). *Medicine and Philosophy in Classical Antiquity*. Cambridge: Cambridge University Press.

van Praag, J.A. (1948). *Gespleten zielen*. Groningen: J.B. Wolters.

Weinreich, O. (1933). *Menekrates Zeus und Salmoneus. Religionsgeschichtliche studien zur Psychopathologie des gottmenschentums in Antike und Neuzeit*. Stuttgart: W. Kohlhammer.

Williams, R. (1992). *Recognition. Fichte and Hegel on the Other*. Albany: State University of New York Press.

Wittgenstein, L. (1999). *Philosophical Investigations*, trans. G.E.M. Anscombe. Oxford: Blackwell.

Žižek, S. (1989). *The Sublime Object of Ideology*. London: Verso.

2

FREUD, MADNESS AND THE DELUSION OF RELIGIOUS BELIEF

Josè Mannu

Introduction: foundations

In this chapter I shall seek to demonstrate how the religious thought of Judaism is the matrix within which Freud develops his theoretical arguments about religion. I shall therefore have little to say about the historical truthfulness of his arguments, although I shall touch on this, but rather I shall seek to demonstrate how Freud's critique of religion is based on a mode of thought that stems precisely from the Judeo-Christian tradition. This hypothesis is not widely shared. Peter Gay (1998), for example, traces the cultural foundations of psychoanalysis to the philosophical tradition of the enlightenment and of scientific positivism. I shall go through the works in which Freud explicitly examines religion: 'Obsessive Actions and Religious Practices' (1907); *Totem and Taboo* (1913); *The Future of an Illusion* (1927) and *Moses and Monotheism* (1939). Religion does appear in other works, such as the case of Little Hans, in *Leonardo da Vinci and a Memory of his Childhood* (1910); *Civilization and its Discontents* (1930); the letters; *The Interpretation of Dreams* (1900); 'On Narcissism: An Introduction' (1914b); 'The Moses of Michelangelo' (1914a) and *Group Psychology and the Analysis of the Ego* (1921). But the places where references to religion appear are not as important as the question of how religion is defined by Freud in his construction of the psychoanalytical method. Spencer Brown, in his classic book *Laws of Form* (Spencer-Brown 1979) argued that to indicate something it is necessary to first draw a distinction (Spencer-Brown 1979); and Martin Buber (1951) wrote an article, which has also become a classic, on the need to distance oneself from the other in order to construct a relationship. I shall therefore take as my point of departure the distinction that Freud traces between his scientific thought and religious thought, and the animistic thought on which it is based: 'The human race, if we are to follow the authorities, have in the course of ages developed three such systems of thought – three great pictures of the universe: animistic (or mythological), religious and scientific'

(Freud SE 1913: 77). For Freud these three systems are not separate, although they do employ different logical systems and languages, which are incommensurable. This incommensurability is due to the different explanations of phenomena. Whereas animism is totalising in that it 'gives a truly complete explanation of the nature of the universe' and 'contains the foundations on which religions are later built' (Freud SE 1913: 77), scientific thought is characterised by its incompleteness: 'Our god λογος is perhaps not a very almighty one, and he may only be able to fulfil a small part of what his predecessors have promised. If we have to acknowledge this we shall accept it with resignation' (Freud SE 1927: 54). However, Freud's view did not take into consideration the fact that the *logos* of religion coincided for a long time with the logos of science, and that the separation occurred in a precise context. This is usually identified as the dispute between Galileo and Robert Bellarmine. In the dispute the nub of the question was whether the telescope used to observe objects on earth was of any value in also observing heavenly bodies existing in the Aristotelian fifth essence, i.e. the ether – this fifth element (or essence) not being part of the earth, as distinct from the other four: earth, water, air, fire. Cardinal Bellarmine, who represented the establishment, made (as we now know) a fundamental error, but ever since then religion has abandoned knowledge of the universe and left it to science. That is to say, the separation between religious and scientific thought did not centre on the study of humanity, the psyche or the soul, but concerned the study of the universe.

To return to Freud, the three systems of thought follow irreconcilable paths of logic, but from an evolutionary point of view they are connected, in the sense that they are the result of a process evolving from animistic to religious thought (during the infancy of humanity) to scientific thought, which is the expression of the maturity of humankind but which is characterised by only partial and limited vision. For Freud it is therefore possible to establish a parallel between the thought of humanity and the thought of the individual:

> No one can have failed to observe, in the first place, that I have taken as
> the basis of my whole position the existence of a collective mind, in
> which mental processes occur *just as they do* in the mind of an individual.
> (Freud SE 1913: 157; my emphasis)

Later, Freud will point out that the development of a person occurs through recognition of his or her own limits, and the abandoning of infantile (primary) narcissism. However, this stage of primary narcissism will not be abandoned altogether by the person in the course of his or her psychic development, but only modified through subsequent superimpositions. To explain this concept, Freud will use, as a metaphor for this evolution, the history of the city of Rome:

> Now let us, by a flight of imagination, suppose that Rome is not a
> human habitation but a psychical entity with a similarly long and

copious past – an entity, that is to say, in which nothing that has once come into existence will have passed away and all the earlier phases of development continue to exist alongside the latest one . . . it is rather the rule than the exception for the past to be preserved in mental life.

(Freud SE 1927: 70–2)

Freud will return to this parallel between the history of humanity and its myths on the one hand, and the psychic life of the individual on the other, over the whole span of his works. Already in *The Interpretation of Dreams* (1900) he treats the Oedipus complex as a story that explains the drama of the first years of an infant's life, from which there arise a moral consciousness and taboos that penalise desire, while at the same time providing social stability. In other words, the myth of Oedipus is the expression of an emotional problem of the individual infant, translated into the mythical story that is a product of animistic thought.

Basic hypotheses and method of interpretation

We therefore have three (two plus one) premises that can be considered as general hypotheses for Freudian theory and that characterise Freud's theoretical writings. The first is that the functioning of the human mind is universal, i.e. that the mechanisms underlying human thought are common to all, so that the recourse to myths (which are an expression of the infancy of the human race) can serve as an explanation and interpretation of the stages through which any person passes in the course of their evolution; the second (a consequence of the first) is that the development of humanity can be compared to and explained by the development of the individual and vice versa; and the third, of Lamarckian origin – and which is more open to criticism – holds that mutations of the species are exclusively due to environmental factors and linked to the needs of survival which, becoming fixed in the genetic code, are transmitted through heredity.

It came to appear all the more fantastic because it required a theoretical underpinning that modern biology discredited decisively. When Freud wrote *Totem and Taboo*, some responsible students of man were still ready to believe that acquired traits can be genetically handed on through the generations. The science of genetics was still in his infancy around 1913, and could accommodate the most varied conjectures about the nature of inheritance. Darwin himself, after all, though caustic in his references to Lamarck, had been something of a Lamarckian in hypothesizing that acquired characteristics may be inherited.

(Gay 1998: 347)

A consequence of this is that human civilisation evolves towards a gradual improvement, and civilisation can be used as a metaphor for the development of the individual and vice versa. According to Foucault Freud's system of interpretation breaks with the interpretative systems of the sixteenth and seventeenth centuries (Foucault 1994) and introduces a hermeneutics that is, in fact, biblical. Freud himself will say, in *An Autobiographical Study* (SE 1925):

> My deep engrossment in the Bible story (almost as soon as I had learnt the art of reading) had, as I recognized much later, an enduring effect upon the direction of my interest.
>
> (Freud SE 1925: 8)

That the reading of scripture was important in Freud's life is shown by the dedication his father wrote in a bible that he gave him on his thirty-fifth birthday. This bible was, in fact, the same one Freud had read as a child and that his father had had rebound for the occasion. The Freud family was a Jewish family, and his father Jakob never abandoned Jewish tradition, even if he lived his religion in a very liberal fashion. Here is the dedication that Jakob wrote in the bible he gave to his son Sigmund:

> Son who is dear to me, Shelomoh. In the *seventh in the days* of the years of your life the Spirit of the Lord began to move you and spoke within you: Go, read my Book that I have written and there will burst open for you the wellsprings of understanding, knowledge, and wisdom. Behold, it is the Book of Books, from which sages have *excavated* and *lawmakers* learned knowledge and judgement. A vision of the Almighty did you see; you heard and strove to do, and you soared on the wings of the Spirit.
>
> Since then the book has been *stored* like the fragments of the tablets in an *ark with me*. For the day on which your years were filled to five and thirty I have put upon it *a cover of new skin* and have called it: 'Spring up, O well, sing ye unto it!' And I have presented it to you as *a memorial and as a reminder* of love from your father, who loves you with everlasting love.
>
> Jakob son of R. Shelomoh Freid [sic]
> In the capital city Vienna 29 Nisan [5]651 6 May [1]891 [71]
> (Derrida 1996: 23)[1]

The culture born of reading the biblical text is a hermeneutic culture based on reflection and interpretation. It is a culture that poses the eschatological problem of the end of life and hence of man's death. But that is not all. In Hebrew *dābār* corresponds to λόγος understood as word and action: the word of God is also action. These two elements – hermeneutics as a search that goes beyond the letter of the text, and the importance of the word as action – are at the basis of the construction of Jewish culture and may therefore have a part in Freudian thought.

While some have maintained that Freud received no religious education (Mannoni 1970: 157), I find this partly incorrect (cf. Bakan 2004; Ostow 2007). Mannoni does quote the letter that Freud wrote to the editor of the Jewish Press Centre in Zurich:

> I can say that I stand as far apart from the Jewish religion as from all other religions: that is to say, they are of great significance to me as a subject of scientific interest, but I have no part in them emotionally.
> (Gresser 1994: 181–2)

The partial incorrectness probably stems from the fact that Mannoni lays his stress on religion as belief, whereas the Jewish religion and the reading of the bible in particular are important to Freud as a means of acquiring a method of thinking based on interpretation, and this method is intrinsic to the Jewish cultures founded on the reading and interpretation of the bible as it has evolved over the course of centuries (cf. Schneider and Berke 2010). From the method of reading based on textual interpretation there emerges the possibility of applying a perspective that is alternative to the traditional one:

> Social justice means that we deny ourselves many things so that others may have to do without them as well . . . And the same germ is to be found in the pretty anecdote of the judgement of Solomon. If one woman's child is dead, the other shall not have a live one either. The bereaved woman is recognized by this wish.
> (Freud 1921: 121)

In other words Freud – and hence the psychoanalysis – uses a method of interpretation that shifts its attention to the emotions that are less visible: the interest lies not in observing the love of the mother who gives her son up in order to see him live (any human love would do as much), but rather in understanding why the other women would accept to see the baby cut in half. This, which Ricoeur (1967) has defined as a hermeneutics of suspicion makes it possible to analyse the grief of the other mother (the one who has lost her own baby) and the envy felt towards the mother who still has her child, an envy that becomes an appeal for justice – the dividing up of the baby. This suggests that the sense of social justice, an expression of civilisation, is not innate but emerges from a loss and/or renunciation and from envy, itself the product of a narcissistic wound, felt towards someone who has not yet suffered this loss and/or renunciation. It is important to consider this example as an expression of Freud's originality in a reading of the event, which is, in this case, a biblical event. In other words, Freud reinterprets the judgement of Solomon using the hermeneutic method, but the viewpoint is absolutely new, a product of his particular genius: 'the Kabbalistic forms of interpretation were now to be used in the appreciation of any human being' (Bakan 2004: 246).

An ingenious reading makes a known event suddenly become new. There is a saying that 'if a person is pointing at something, it's silly to look at the person's finger', but Freud teaches us that, on the contrary, it is as important to look at the finger of the person doing the pointing, and that this can generate new ideas. On this point, Derrida writes:

> Who wants to substitute him- or herself for Freud's phantom? How can one not want to, as well? The moment has perhaps come to risk, in a few telegrams, a thesis on the subject of Freud's theses. The thesis would say in the first place this: all the Freudian theses are cleft, divided, contradictory, as are the concepts, beginning with that of the archive. Thus it is for every concept: always dislocating itself because it is never one with itself. It is the same with the thesis which posits and arranges the concepts, the history of the concepts, their formation as much as their archivization.
>
> (Derrida 1996: 84)

Religion and psychopathology

For Freud, religion must become an object of knowledge since it is an expression of humanity. As a consequence of this hypothesis, Freud introduces the concept that religious tradition in general and the historical religious tradition of the Jewish people in particular – that is to say, the monotheistic religious tradition – is the product of a primitive desire. This point is not clarified however, so that Yerushalmi can say:

> The true challenge for psychoanalysis is not to plunge the entire history of tradition into a hypothetical group consciousness, but to help to clarify, in a nonreductive way, what unconscious needs are being satisfied at any given time by living within a given religious tradition.
>
> (Yerushalmi 1991: 89)

Freud's interest is, however, directed at illness, so he also remains a clinician in his sociological analyses. His relationship with religion arises as he tackles the problem of ritual, and the relationship between religion and obsessive-compulsive neuroses. Religion is, he considers, in its ritualistic forms basically obsessive by nature. Freud therefore treats religious thought for the first time in an article entitled 'Obsessive Actions and Religious Practices' (Freud SE 1907), which appeared for the first time in the *Zeitung Religions-psychologie* in 1907. Freud treats religion here not for its doctrinal content, which he would do in later writings, but as a set of shared rituals. He identifies the point of intersection between obsessive rituals and religious practices in the concept of ceremonial.

> It is easy to see where the resemblances lie between neurotic ceremonials and the sacred acts of religious ritual: in the qualms of conscience brought on by their neglect, in their complete isolation from all other actions (shown in the prohibition against interruption) and in the conscientiousness with which they are carried out in every detail.
>
> (Freud SE 1907: 119)

Freud is obviously aware that the differences may appear obvious. While the minutiae of religious ceremonial are full of significance and have a symbolic meaning, those of neurotics seem foolish and senseless. But it is precisely here that Freud's genius comes through. The psychoanalytic technique of investigation, which he introduces, completely changes the picture. This shows the true meaning of the foolish and senseless rituals.

> It is only thanks to the efforts of psycho-analytic treatment that he becomes conscious of the meaning of his obsessive action and, with it, of the motives that are impelling him to it . . . the obsessive action serves to express unconscious motives and ideas.
>
> (Freud SE 1907: 122)

In particular, the compulsive actions are the result from an unconscious sense of guilt. This concept will be dealt with in greater depth in *The Ego and the Id* (Freud SE 1923a), but it is no accident that it appears for the first time here, precisely when Freud is dealing with the subject of religion and obsessive ceremonials. The concept of guilt and expiation is at the very basis of religious rituals and an analysis of them shows that they arise from the repression of an instinctual impulse (another concept introduced for the first time here) which gives rise to prohibitions: 'Against the temptation the protective measures seem soon to become inadequate; then the prohibitions come into play, with the purpose of keeping at a distance the situation that gives rise to temptation' (Freud SE 1907: 124). 'The formation of a religion, too, seems to be based on the suppression, the renunciation, of certain instinctual impulses' (Freud SE 1907: 125). Freud thus makes a link between obsessive neurosis and religious practice in rituals, in the meticulous ceremonials that 'push aside the under-lying thoughts' (Freud SE 1907: 126).

From a methodological point of view, the lumping together of religion and obsessive neurosis on the basis of ritual behaviour is certainly arbitrary, in the sense that if a universe of meaning contains ritual practices that are repeated in ceremonies, this does not demonstrate that the body of meaning contained in religious thought is an expression of psychical illness. For Freud, ritual becomes morbid when it is carried out as a sacred act, with a special scrupulousness and anxiety that follows its neglect or if it is performed badly, and he therefore seizes on one aspect, which cannot, however, represent the whole. Freud's conclusion is that 'one might venture to regard obsessional neurosis as a pathological counterpart of the formation of a religion, and to describe that neurosis as an individual religiosity and religion as a universal obsessional neurosis' (Freud SE 1907: 126–7), but adding that 'the chief difference would lie in the nature of those instincts, which in the neurosis are exclusively sexual in origin, while in religion they spring from egoistic sources' (Freud SE 1907: 127); that is to say, those instincts that we might suppose are related to the ego. We might be able to glimpse here a foreshadowing of the concept of ego drives.

The problem that was immediately raised by Oscar Pfister,[2] a protestant pastor who was a psychoanalyst and friend of Freud, is that, 'while it is difficult to argue against the presence of this obsessive impulse in the first stages of religion, we need to ask whether it is part of its intrinsic nature' (Pfister 2009: 113). Freud will seek to reply to this objection in his subsequent book, *Totem and Taboo* (SE 1913).

Totem and taboo

This book is made up of four studies first published in the journal *Imago* directed by Freud in the years 1912–13. It represents 'a first attempt on my part at applying the point of view and the findings of psycho-analysis to some unsolved problems of social psychology' (Freud SE 1913: xiii). What is being attempted is, as already stated above, finding an analogy between the individual psyche and the primitive history of humanity. Totemism is a primitive form of religion that is the basis of the identity of a people and is founded on two prohibitions.

> The most ancient and important taboo prohibitions are the two basic laws of totemism: not to kill the totem animal and to avoid sexual intercourse with members of the totem clan of the opposite sex [i.e. the imposition of exogamy].
>
> (Freud SE 1913: 31–2)

Since, according to Freud, prohibitions are born of desire – 'a thing that is forbidden with the greatest emphasis must be a thing that is desired' (Freud SE 1913: 69) – the killing of the totem-animal that impersonates the figure of the father, and the desire of the woman that belongs to one's own totem (i.e. of the mother), are primeval desires of man. In reality, Freud is aware of a contradiction in totemism, which is founded on the cohesion of the group yet prohibits precisely the thing that would knit the group even more closely together – sexual relations between men and women of the same totem; but it is precisely this prohibition that introduces the taboo that is at the root of moral consciousness. Freud is fully aware of the whole range of problems – 'Everything connected with totemism seems to be puzzling' (Freud SE 1913: 108), and this includes prohibitions: 'the fact that exogamous sexual restrictions were imposed intentionally throws no light on the motive which led to their imposition. What is the ultimate source of the horror of incest which must be recognized as the root of exogamy?' (Freud SE 1913: 122). At this point Freud finds the solution: the killing of the father and the totem meal.

> One day the brothers who had been driven out came together, killed and devoured their father and so made an end of the patriarchal horde. United, they had the courage to do and succeeded in doing what would have been impossible for them individually.
>
> (Freud SE 1913: 141)

This is the source of what Freud defines as deferred obedience, an example of which is also to be found in the case of Little Hans: 'What had up to then been prevented by his actual existence was thenceforward prohibited by the sons themselves, in accordance with the psychological procedure so familiar to us in psycho-analysis the name of "deferred obedience"' (Freud SE 1913: 143). The concept of deferred obedience is important in the development of Freud's thought, not only with regard to religion but also in general for the development of psycho-analytical theory. It is not only limited to the children's sense of guilt at having killed their father, so that through deferred obedience they together carry out his teachings or else fail in their endeavours precisely in order to demonstrate that they cannot do without the lost father; but deferred obedience also relates to the pattern of analytical work itself, the results of which sometimes manifest themselves only a considerable time after the end of the analysis.

Christianity as well as Judaism belongs to this matrix of ideas, even though in a more sophisticated manner: 'In the Christian doctrine, therefore, men were acknowledging in the most undisguised manner the guilty primeval deed, since they found the fullest atonement for it in the sacrifice of this one son' (Freud SE 1913: 154). Given his great intellectual honesty, Freud adds in a note that:

> derivations which I have proposed in these pages do not in the least overlook the complexity of the phenomena under review. All that they claim is to have added a new factor to the sources, known or still unknown, of religion, morality and society – a factor based on a consideration of the implications of psycho-analysis.
>
> (Freud SE 1913: 157 n.2)

In *Totem and Taboo*, religion is for the first time treated explicitly, although the elimination of the father remains only one hypothesis of interpretation, which is therefore susceptible to further modifications, as Yerushalmi maintains and who observes that Freud's emphasis is strange.

> Why it is that throughout his work, he have concentrated so exclusively on patricide, why only the Oedipus complex and not a 'Cain complex,' has remained an enigma to me . . . Whereas you took Oedipus as your paradigm for our malaise, Augustine found his in Cain, and in The City of God he universalized him by making him the founder of the earthly city . . . Though it lacks your sophisticated notion of the return of the repressed, Augustine's view of the first fratricide as an archetype seems to me not that far removed in spirit from your own view of the repetition of the murder of the primeval father.
>
> (Yerushalmi 1991: 92, 93)

Again in *Totem and Taboo* no consideration is given to the problem of a matured religion, but only to a primordial animistic religiosity. Freud would tackle head on his relation with his own religion only in one of his last books, *Moses and Monotheism*.

In 1922 Freud wrote another essay, in which he took up again the idea of the primeval father, this time identified with a demonic figure, in 'A Seventeenth-Century Demonological Neurosis' (1923b). In this essay, although one of Freud's minor studies, Freud nevertheless emphasises the ambivalence surrounding the central idea: 'It does indeed sound strange that the Devil should be chosen as a substitute for a loved father. But this is only so at first sight for we know a good many things which lessen our surprise' (Freud SE 1923b: 85). In the son were present

> two sets of emotional impulses that were opposed to each other: it contained not only impulses of an affectionate and submissive nature, but also hostile and defiant ones. It is our view that the same ambivalence governs the relations of mankind to its Deity.
>
> (Freud SE 1923b: 85)

The father thus becomes an archetype of both God and the devil.

One year earlier Freud had written *Group Psychology and the Analysis of the Ego* (1921), which, together with 'On Narcissism: An Introduction' (1914b), 'Papers on Metapsychology' (1915), *Beyond the Pleasure Principle* (1920) and *The Ego and the Id* (1923a), forms part of those theoretical writings in which he develops his conception of the workings of the psyche. In *Group Psychology and the Analysis of the Ego* (1921) religion is dealt with only in passing, but the work does introduce some important concepts, such as that of groups with a leader and the concept of identification, as well as picking up again other concepts such as that of the ego ideal. The Catholic Church is presented as a stable artificial group organised around a commander-in-chief, Christ, 'who loves all the individuals in the group with an equal love. Everything depends upon this illusion' (Freud SE 1921: 94). The second concept is that of identification, 'known to psycho-analysis as the earliest expression of an emotional tie with another person' (Freud SE 1921: 105), which is presented in all its ambivalence with regard to the chosen object: 'the object that we long for and prize is assimilated by eating and is in that way annihilated as such' (Freud 1921: 105). Identification is a more primordial form of bond and it often happens that from the object-choice a person regresses to identification: in other words, the object-choice is the father one would like to have, while identification is the father one would like to be. Another concept, again picked up from 'On Narcissism: An introduction' (Freud, 1914b: 466), is that of the ego ideal: 'The heir to the original narcissism in which the childish ego enjoyed self-sufficiency' (Freud 1921: 110); it gradually gathers up from the influences of the environment the demands which that environment makes upon the ego and which the ego cannot always rise to; so that 'a man, when he cannot be satisfied with his ego itself, may nevertheless be able to find satisfaction in the ego ideal which has been differentiated out of the ego' (Freud 1921: 110).

The future of an illusion

Freud launched his first real critique of religion in 1927, with *The Future of an Illusion*. He wrote to his friend Oskar Pfister,

> In the next few weeks, a pamphlet of mine will be appearing which has a great deal to do with you. I had been wanting to write it for a long time, and postponed it out of regard for you, but the impulse became too strong. The subject-matter – as you will easily guess – is my completely negative attitude to religion, in any form or however attenuated, and, though there can be nothing new to you in this, I feared, and still fear, that such a public profession of my attitude will be painful to you. When you have read it you must let me know what measure of toleration and understanding you are able to preserve for the hopeless pagan.
>
> (Meng and Freud 1963: 110)

In the book itself, the critique of religion comes within a general critique of the culture of which religion is a part. Freud begins by referring back to the primordial taboos: 'with the prohibitions that established them, civilization – who knows how many thousands of years ago? – began to detach man from his primordial animal condition' (Freud SE 1927: 10). The prohibitions relate to the instinctual wishes regarding incest, cannibalism and the lust for killing.

These prohibitions, which then go to make up the superego, are the foundation of civilisation. The problem then is: what does civilisation give back to people in return? Here Freud cites important compensations, such as a 'different kind of satisfaction is afforded by art to the participants in a cultural unit, though as a rule it remains inaccessible to the masses, who are engaged in exhausting work and have not enjoyed any personal education' (Freud SE 1927: 13). But the most important compensation for civilisation's prohibitions is religion: 'The defence against childish helplessness is what lends its characteristic features to the adult's reaction to the helplessness which *he* has to acknowledge – a reaction which is precisely the formation of religion' (Freud SE 1927: 24).

Freud thought that the evidential arguments that religion is not an illusion are extremely weak, based as they are exclusively on the faith of believers. Religion represents a method whereby nature is humanised and therefore made friendly, so it performs an important role in calming human anxiety in the face of a hostile nature, in particular of death (which inevitably human beings have to face and of which they are well aware), and of the difficulties of living together in society. The problem therefore becomes: why is religion so firmly rooted and why does it exert such a great influence over humanity? The answer is that it serves to provide reassurance, as Freud had already written in *Leonardo da Vinci and a Memory of his Childhood*:

> Biologically speaking, religiousness is to be traced to the small human child's long-drawn-out helplessness and need of help; . . . The protection against neurotic illness, which religion vouchsafes to those who believe in it, is easily explained: it removes their parental complex, on which the sense of guilt in individuals as well as in the whole race depends, and disposes of it, while the unbeliever has to grapple with the problem on his own.
>
> (Freud SE 1910: 123)

Having defined religion as man's need for consolation and protection when faced with the prohibitions of civilisation and man's impotence before nature, Freud goes on to criticise religion as non-scientific. *Credo quia absurdum* (I believe because it is absurd) – a saying ascribed to Tertullian [160–220 CE], one of the early church fathers, sums up for Freud an attempt to remove religious belief from the jurisdiction of reason, which he identifies with the scientific method.[3] The same holds good for the 'as if' philosophy outlined by Hans Vaihinger (Vaihinger 1967).[4]

> They are called 'fictions', but for a variety of practical reasons we have to believe 'as if' we believed in these fictions. This is the case with religious doctrines because of their incomparable importance to the maintenance of human society.
>
> (Freud SE 1927: 28–9)

The Future of an Illusion attracted a great deal of criticism, but two responses in particular are of importance – one from Oskar Pfister and the other from the writer, musicologist, playwright and essayist and winner of the 1915 Nobel Prize for Literature, Romain Rolland. Rolland, who corresponded with Freud, raised the question of the difference between spiritual impulse – an expression of a profound human need – and religion, understood as a social practice in which the spiritual impulse has been lost as a result of ecclesiastical institutionalisation. Rolland, although in agreement with Freud's analysis of religion, argues for a religious feeling which he terms an oceanic feeling, a sensation of unity with the world.

Freud took two years to reply to Rolland and did so with a subsequent work, *Civilisation and its Discontents*, in which he expands the concept of narcissism. Freud's introduction places his investigation squarely within the context of scientific research.

> I cannot discover this 'oceanic' feeling in myself. It is not easy to deal scientifically with feelings. One can attempt to describe their physiological signs . . . If I have understood my friend rightly . . . it is a feeling of an indissoluble bond, of being one with the external world as a whole.
>
> (Freud SE 1930: 65)

Freud had already dealt with the concept of narcissism in his 1914 essay, which represented a turning point in the construction of his theory, introducing the distinction between ego-related and object-related drives. In *Civilisation and its Discontents* he deepens his conception of the ego, defining it in direct connection and continuation with the id, which is a kind of facade of the ego, and operates clear and sharp lines of demarcation with respect to the outside world, except in some circumstances. One of these is the state of being in love; the other is pathological. But Freud goes further in his reflection, underlining that 'the adult's ego-feeling cannot have been the same from the beginning' (Freud SE 1930: 66). The infant learns that the withdrawal of his mother's breast brings a sensation of pain and displeasure: 'In this way there is for the first time set over against the ego an "object", in the form of something which exists "outside" and which is only forced to appear by a special action' (Freud SE 1930: 67). This recognition of the existence of an outside world brings with it the inevitable pain for which religion provides a consolation, precisely with this oceanic feeling. Here, Freud is aware of a change to his theory:

> alterations in it became essential, as our enquiries advanced from the repressed to the repressing forces, from the object-instincts to the ego. The decisive step forwards was the introduction of the concept of narcissism – that is to say, the discovery that the ego itself is cathected with libido . . . This narcissistic libido turns towards objects, and

thus becomes object-libido; and it can change back into narcissistic libido once more.

(Freud SE 1930: 118)

The oceanic feeling is therefore the continuance of primary narcissism. It represents, that is, the experience of oneness with the mother; and the feeling of the infinite is nothing but nostalgia for the pre-oedipal condition, when there is still no perception of the object as something other than oneself. The fact that it is an infantile experience obviously does not mean that it is immature but rather that it is deeply rooted in human beings. The theory of narcissism represents a turning point in psychoanalytical theory and is also central for the psychoanalytical interpretation of religion. The ego, as a differentiated structure, must come to terms with the reality principle embodied, for example, in the parents' prohibitions. Faced with these frustrations, the reaction is to interiorise them, forming the super-ego – that is an inner impulse that, precisely because it has been interiorised, turns the failure to satisfy a drive into an act of narcissistic pride, because the demands of the super-ego have been satisfied. The satisfaction of the drive is suspended and replaced by the narcissistic pleasure of having satisfied one's own super-ego.

Pfister's response to Freud's *The Future of an Illusion* was to write a book entitled *Die Illusion einer Zukunft* (The Illusion of a Future). Pfister's grounds for his criticism are different from those of Rolland, because he sees the chief issue as a problem of knowledge. Taking as his point of departure Freud's statement that religions are a product of desire, Pfister asks, 'but can the whole of religious thought be explained in this way? And is such an exchange between desire and reality something that is exclusive to religion?' (Pfister 2009: 119). Pfister introduces a fundamental distinction between the various religions, analysing the Christian religion and developing an argument aimed at refuting Freud's hypotheses without trying to refute his theses about religion in general.

> it is often said that according to the Christian conception, everything that is denied the believer during earthly life will be granted him in the beyond. That is false: the renunciation of sexual activity is compensated in the Islamic paradise, certainly not in the Christian one.
>
> (Pfister 2009: 122)

In the second stage of his argument, Pfister challenges the opposition between scientific thought and religious thought in the sense that they follow paths of development which are different from one another. Ricoeur makes the same point.

> Freud is completely uninterested in the development of religious sentiment. He has no interest in the theology of an Amos or an Osee, of an Isaiah or an Ezechiel, nor in the theology of Deuteronomy . . .

40

> The idea of the 'return of the repressed' enabled him to dispense with a hermeneutics that would take the circuitous path of an exegesis of the texts and rushed him into taking the shortcut of a psychology of the believer, patterned from the outset on the neurotic model.
>
> (Ricoeur 1970: 246)

In fact, except in his last work on Moses, Freud never uses biblical quotations, basing himself exclusively on his analytical experience with people affected by neurotic disorders, while Pfister's criticism is founded on a religious perspective. This distinction is, to my way of thinking, central. Freud's failure to address the issue from the perspective of theology was to be a thread running through the criticisms of and objections to Freudian thought by a number of different authors such as Hans Küng. Küng asked, 'is he [Freud] really sure that behind the religious beliefs and actions of these primitives there is really nothing and that everything can be reduced to an error?' (Küng 1979: 333).

> Freud and his followers have tried to explain religion as the universal obsessional neurosis of humanity ... Arieti traces the psychological development of religion through the ages and convincingly shows that Freudian reductionism is mistaken in the assertion that religion has failed to evolve and develop parallel to other advances in civilization.
>
> (Bemporad 1974: 1001–2)

This critique, which argues that different levels of knowledge – mystical, religious and, naturally, scientific – are possible, although important, is not entirely correct. It is, however, a critique that finds its origin in the observations made by Pfister.

> I do not believe in science as a replacement for religion ... let us not forget that the most daring and grandiose developments in ethics can only be produced in the form of religion. For the great developments in ethics we have to thank not the scientists but the founders of the religions.
>
> (Pfister 2009: 151)

Two forms of knowledge with an objective that for Pfister is one and the same: 'the truth shall make you free' (Pfister 2009: 158).

Moses and monotheism

To his son Ernst, Freud wrote (on 17 January 1938):

> I have had posted to you an essay on Moses, one of my few recent works which may arouse general interest. I am afraid this interest

41

may exceed justified proportions and be blown up into something sensational. But I may be mistaken. It is my first appearance as a historian; late enough!

(Freud 1990: 368)

The final work is a text made up of three essays. The first two appeared in *Imago* (1937), while the complete book with the third essay included was published in 1938. The third essay is disproportionately long compared with the other two and is full of repetitions and recapitulations, a sign of Freud's dissatisfaction with what he was writing. In a letter to Andreas-Salomé, he confessed, with regard to the figure of Moses, 'he has pursued me through my whole life' (letter to Andreas-Salomé, 6 January 1935; Freud and Andreas-Salomé 1983).

Freud attributes the origin of monotheism to the culture of the Egypt of the Pharaohs. Such an analysis had already been made by Abraham in a study written in 1912, to which, curiously, Freud never referred. *Moses and Monotheism* is a very complex work, introduced by an hypothesis about the origins of Moses. Following the lead of Abraham and other authors, Freud formulates the hypothesis that Moses was Egyptian and that the name itself is of Egyptian origin and means 'child'. If Moses was Egyptian, how, Freud asks, did he construct a rigidly monotheistic religion such as Judaism, starting from a culture, such as Egypt's, which contained an innumerable series of divinities? The answer he proposes is: 'if Moses was an Egyptian and if he communicated his own religion to the Jews, it must have been Akhenaten's, the Aten religion' (Freud SE 1939: 24). In Freud's view circumcision was of Egyptian origin. Moses therefore was an Egyptian, and he became the leader of the Jewish people following Akhenaten's ruin. Freud considers Moses to be the father of his people and referring back to his much earlier book, *Totem and Taboo*, he writes of the tradition that Moses was murdered by his people, although there exists little basis for this conjecture. Among historians, only the German theologian Ernest Sellin, in 1922, espoused this theory based on an interpretation of a passage by the prophet Hosea (second half of the 8th century BCE) and passages in other Old Testament prophets. Most other historians disputed the truth of this hypothesis – as did Sellin, later on – but Freud maintained it to be true from a psychological point of view. Moses can be the father of the Jewish nation precisely because he is not one of its sons (Esposito 2004).

In the third essay, Freud repeats the thesis expressed in *Totem and Taboo*, according to which religious phenomena are comprehensible only when related to the neurotic symptoms of an individual. The pattern of individual neurosis, translated into the history of the Jewish people, leads Freud to argue that Moses is the father who is murdered, in order then for his people to revive the religion that he had taken from that of the god Aten and given to the Jews, after it had lain dormant for a period. Moses is a key figure for Freud and represents what he calls the 'great man'.

Moses and the 'great man'

It may be interesting to dwell on the characteristics of the great man in Freud. He introduces here the concept of overdetermination, which means that each event never presents itself as self-sufficient but is always the effect of several convergent causes and is itself the cause of other events. The characteristics that contribute to a person being a great man are not to be sought in his capacities but in how he affects others. This he does in two ways: 'by his personality and by the idea which he puts forward' (Freud SE 1939: 109). But this is not sufficient; another element is needed. 'We know that in the mass of mankind there is a powerful need for an authority who can be admired, before whom one bows down' (Freud SE 1939: 109). Here Freud again returns to the figure of the father. It is the nostalgia for the father of childhood that drives everyone to search constantly for this figure and, once found, invest him with all the paternal characteristics: 'The decisiveness of thought, the strength of will, the energy of action . . . the autonomy and independence of the great man' (Freud SE 1939: 109–10).

The God of Moses had, for Freud, the characteristics of Moses himself (wrathful temper and relentlessness). Moses therefore reflected for his people the figure of the father, but he too had been a child and son. 'The great religious idea for which the man Moses stood was, on our view, not his own property: he had taken it over from King Akhenaten' (Freud SE 1939: 110). The great idea therefore never has a single mind as its origin. The Pharaoh who introduced it in his turn adapted the new religion of the god Aten to Egyptian culture, centred on the figure of the Pharaoh, as sole lord and master of his people. Moses, once he had become father of a people, like the primordial father in *Totem and Taboo*, was murdered. At this point the religion of Moses might have ended, as happened in Egypt, but here another event characteristic of the great man occurred. The successors of Moses, the prophets, kept alive his religion and made possible his rebirth over a long distance of time. The rebirth however, after the Babylonian exile, was a rebirth that represented the fusion of the popular god Yahweh with the God of Moses. The prophets and the culture of the Babylonian period are part and parcel of the great man syndrome.

Thus the culture of a people (Egyptian), the father (the Pharaoh), the idea accepted by the son (Moses), his character, the desire of the masses to have a father, his murder, his latent presence, the prophets (sons) who keep the idea alive, the rebirth of the idea from a fusion with other ideas born during the period of latency – all this forms part of the concept of the great man. But why was the great idea lost in Egypt, and why, in the Jewish people, did it remain latent and was then reborn? Here Freud has a very ingenious intuition. The God of Moses could not be represented in an image and he considers this fact decisive: 'it meant that a sensory perception was given second place to what may be called an abstract idea – a triumph of intellectuality over sensuality or, strictly speaking, an instinctual renunciation, with all its necessary psychological consequences' (Freud SE 1939: 113).

This conversion from sensuality to spirituality was for Freud the reason why the Jewish people remained faithful to their religion. The de-materialised God, which cannot be represented in visible form, became the grandiose God who becomes part of the identity of the person. In fact, Freud's thinking at this point is enriched by a concept that had been introduced when he was dealing with the subject of narcissism: that of the ego and the super-ego. When the parent has been internalised and the prohibitions are owned by the super-ego, obedience to the super-ego is for the ego a source of pride and hence of pleasure.

Freud was clearly not interested in an exegesis of the biblical texts, or in an analysis of the development of religious thought, but stopped at the psychology of the believer, using the pattern of neurosis as the key to interpretation. This is certainly a great limitation to his thinking from the religious point of view, but he was simply not interested in tackling these other problems. However, Freud does press on with his analysis in order to understand the phenomenon of faith, the famous *credo quia absurdum* – 'The persuasive force of religions is linked to the return of the repressed' (letter to L. Andreas-Salomé 6 January 1935, in Freud and Salomé 1983: 201) – which supports the historical truth.

The return of the repressed and the religion of the son

'It has long since become common knowledge that the experiences of a person's first five years exercise a determining effect on his life, which nothing later can withstand' (Freud 1939: 125). These first experiences are identified with the instinctual impulses from which the ego defends itself through repression. The impulse nevertheless remains and subsequently finds a replacement satisfaction that is identified with the symptom: 'All the phenomena of the formation of symptoms may justly be described as the "return of the repressed"' (Freud SE 1939: 127). This concept, according to Yerushalmi (1991), is central to the book, and is 'the problem of tradition, not merely its origins, but above all its dynamics', and this has to do with the inter-generational transmission of the trauma (Bernstein 1998). The rebirth of Yahweh, in an irresistible manner after a period of latency lasting some centuries, represents a recovery of tradition, which Freud explains in its dynamic aspects, in terms of neurosis.

> Early trauma – defence – latency – outbreak of neurotic illness – partial return of the repressed. Such is the formula which we have laid down for the development of a neurosis. The reader is now invited to take the step of supposing that something occurred in the

life of the human species similar to what occurs in the life of individuals.

(Freud SE 1939: 80)

But this further step contains a new element. The return of the repressed does not just produce anxiety but is also, as Yerushalmi has pointed out, 'the rediscovery of the purest teachings of Moses, which had been forgotten' (Yerushalmi 1991: 116). The attempt to explain monotheism makes Freud travel along an arduous road. Monotheism cannot be the result of a spontaneous historical evolution, since it is not found in the great civilisations of Greece and Rome. The solution of the collective unconscious is not acceptable: 'I do not think we gain anything by introducing the concept of a "collective" unconscious' (Freud SE 1939: 132). The search for a solution leads him to take up again the idea of the primitive horde from *Totem and Taboo*. The admiration and fear of the father, his murder and reinstatement, represent historical truth since they are an expression of psychological truth. Monotheism was successful because it recalls that the relation to the father and the religion of Moses took root, because it responds to a psychological need in humankind. Continuing along this track, Freud also explains the obvious evolution of the religion as it goes beyond Judaism through the agency of Saul of Tarsus, a Jew who as a Roman citizen took the name of Paul. Christianity frees mankind from the guilt of killing the father by immolating the son.

It is worth noticing how the new religion dealt with the ancient ambivalence in the relation to the father. Its main content was, it is true, reconciliation with the father, atonement for the crime committed against him; but the other side of the emotional relation showed itself in the fact that the son, who had taken the atonement on himself, became a god himself beside the father and, actually, in place of the father . . . Christianity became a religion of the son.

(Freud SE 1939: 136)

Over and above the criticisms that these interpretations might provoke, it should be remembered that what is important for Freud, and underlies his thought, is clinical practice: his interest for the person who is suffering. This means that the viewpoint is not philosophical but clinical even when interpreting religion, since religion is a product of human thought. This means that precisely since it is an expression of mankind, it too contains pathological elements, defences against suffering and desire. The effort that a reading of Freud invites us to make is to think clearly, recognising both the health and the pathology residing in religious experience. Within the experience of human-kind, the relation with an internal representation of the paternal image of God in some form (whether one believes in God or not) is universal, and can explain the approach of human beings to reality in every age and epoch.

Some reflections

I think that I should premise these concluding reflections with an important consideration. The merit of thinkers should not be judged on the basis of the solutions they bring to problems, but rather on the manner in which they present their arguments. From this point of view, Freud is a shining example of clarity even as he revises his conclusions or admits his uncertainties. As we have seen, Freud's relation to religion is fraught with problems. However, three key points for reflection clearly emerge.

First, it is necessary to distinguish between a critique of religion in toto and Freud's identification of problematic elements in religious practice, focusing on duty and a sense of guilt. Second, it is necessary to distinguish between religion and a concept of God on the one hand, and between a relationship with God as an inner object and identification with a community of believers on the other. Third, there is the problematic distinction between the individual and the group.

On the first point, I think that Freud's critique does identify an important issue that is a source of unease within religious tradition ('religion' remains too vague a term), and this is the view that desire is the enemy of a religion founded on duty. We should nevertheless remember that the Freudian perspective is that of a clinician and therefore one that emphasises with most clarity the dangers lurking in religious practice: 'the exclusion of desire from the ethical sphere has disastrous consequences: the objective of happiness is excluded from the field of moral consideration' (Ricoeur 1977: 467). To consider religious morality as an obligation and also as desire, the one not in conflict one with the other, has consequences that Freud emphasises in his definition of God as object of inner representation, and therefore present in every person independently of religious faith or practice, but also independently of a person's actually known father.

But there is a further aspect to consider, and that is the model of knowledge that Freud employs. For Freud, religion represents a more evolved stage of animism, even if it incorporates numerous animistic features. Even within religious thought itself, there are developments, for instance, when Freud underlines the importance of the absence of images (quite different from iconoclasm) in Judaism, which takes it to a higher level of spirituality. Yet, for Freud, religion remains an infantile mode of knowledge, belonging to the childhood of humanity and destined to be replaced by that adult mode which is scientific knowledge. In reality, the relation between scientific reasoning and religion has never been that separate.

In the bible, the word *dābār*, the Hebrew equivalent of the Greek *logos*, means 'word' and 'action'. The word of God created order. Light is the measure and number of the hours and of all time, in which is expressed the divine intention to bring together and give order to the things that had been dispensed (Zellini 2010). After order comes numeration, the power of counting:

in the book of *Numbers*, Yahweh delegated to Moses the census of the entire community (Zellini 2010). Calculating distinguishes what is calculable from what is not, what can be determined and ordered from what cannot.

We have seen how the first separation between religious thought and scientific thought took place on non-problematic grounds far removed from the human person, i.e. the study of the universe. The scientific study of man would come much later and would develop in the context of important social changes such as the French Revolution. It would be carried forward on the basis of studies of madness and its medical treatment. Initially this would take definite shape through Freudian psychoanalysis, and Freud would inevitably have to come to terms with religious thought. In reality, the division between religious thought and scientific thought, as proposed by Freud (a product of the positivism of the time), does not stand up to the changing times and has always raised new issues inviting further reflection. Knowledge posited by religion, in other words, is a form of knowledge on a par with scientific knowledge, evolving in a different but equally important channel.

Freud analysed the relation between animism and monotheistic religion in *Totem and Taboo*. Monotheistic religion is, in a certain way, the product of a social structure: the God of the Jews originates from the Egyptian god Aten, the expression of a society powerfully centred on the figure of Pharaoh. The God of the Jews would then take the likeness and characteristics of the personality of Moses. The development from the totem-animal to God who is pure un-representable spirit is enormous, but it is the expression of the progress of civilisation. In reality, the relation with religion remains very problematic from a cultural, not clinical, point of view. From a clinical point of view Freud singles out those elements of religion (rituals, beliefs, oceanic feeling itself) that are an expression of clinical malaise, reaching the conclusion that religion may represent in and of itself a psychopathological condition. On the basis of this affirmation, which emerges in numerous of his writings, such as 'Notes upon a Case of Obsessional Neurosis' (the case of the ratman; Freud SE 1909), *Leonardo da Vinci and a Memory of his Childhood* (1910), as well as in 'Obsessive Actions and Religious Practices' (1907), Freud considered individual neurosis as a metaphor for the development of humanity.

The great intuition of Freud was surely to demonstrate the psychological elements contained in religious thought. We are less inclined to share his vision of a kind of hierarchy of knowledge, with scientific thought as an expression of adult thought while religious thought is only childish; nevertheless, this will lead him to develop a series of important theoretical concepts such as that of narcissism, or to stress the importance of the concepts of the ego, super-ego, and ego ideal. He would not countenance his pupil Jung's concept of a collective unconscious because of the hostility he felt towards him. However, religious thought would accompany him for the whole of his life.

To consider God as an inner object is the basis of the construction of a person's identity, whether that person believes or refuses it. As Rosenzweig (1985) observes, the self is born precisely from this inner confrontation, with a warning about feelings of distress that one aspect of religion can sometimes bring with it. But one *aspect* – not the idea of God. This is the difference. The concept of God is an individualising concept only in terms of identification; the rituals and the emotions that these rituals arouse may lead to pathologies; and the identification with the Son of God urged by the Church can be a regressive process. This distinction is central and was captured by Freud in all its implications. If we do not take account of this distinction, we run the risk of considering religious or pseudo-religious groups as healthy for the individual practitioner, while they are only apparently so on the basis of the urge for a primitive bond such as that of group identification, with the spread of anxiety and its resolution in ritual ceremonial.

Referring to a religious system founded in 1866 called Christian Science, according to which every illness of the spirit and of the body can be conquered through full comprehension of the word of Jesus, Freud observes that, although he considers it a regrettable aberration, it should not be forbidden: 'Are the authorities so certain of the right path to salvation that they venture to prevent each man from trying to be saved after his own fashion' (Freud SE 1926: 236).

Notes

1 The dedication is a mélange of quotations from the bible, identified by Ostow in a study of 1989. Cf. M. Ostow (1989) 'Sigmund and Jakob Freud and the Philippson Bible – (With an analysis of the birthday inscription)', *International Review of Psycho-Analysis* 16: 483–92.
2 Oskar Pfister (1873–1956) was a Swiss Lutheran minister and psychoanalyst and belonged to a psychoanalytical circle in Zurich that was centred around Bleuler and Jung. In 1919, he formed the Swiss Society for Psychoanalysis. Between the years 1909 and 1939 he corresponded with Freud. He thought theology and psychoanalysis compatible and is remembered particularly for his work involving the application of psychoanalysis to education.
3 *Credo quia absurdum* is, of course, a misquotation. Tertullian's actual words are *credibile est, quia ineptum est* (*De carne Christi* 5.4).
4 Vaihinger's philosophy of 'as if' influenced Adler's theory. Adler believed that life is inherently meaningless and applied the concept of fiction to individuals

References

Bakan, D. (2004). *Sigmund Freud and the Jewish Mystical Tradition*. New York: Dover.
Bemporad, J. (1974). Psychiatry and Religion *American Handbook of Psychiatry*, vol 1. New York: Basic Books.
Bernstein, R.J. (1998). *Freud and the Legacy of Moses*. Cambridge: Cambridge University Press.
Buber, M. (1951). Distance and Relation. *Hibbert Journal* 49: 105–13.
Derrida, J. (1996). *Archive Fever. A Freudian Impression*, trans. E. Prenowitz. Chicago and London: University of Chicago Press.

Esposito, R. (2004). *Bios.* Turin: Einaudi.

Foucault, M. (1994). Nietzsche, Freud, Marx. *Aut-aut* 262/3: 99–111.

Freud, S. (1900). *The Interpretation of Dreams.* In *The Standard Edition of the Complete Psychological Works of Sigmund Freud*, vol. 4, ed. and trans. J. Strachey. London: Hogarth Press/Institute of Psycho-Analysis.

Freud, S. (1907). Obsessive actions and religious practices. In *The Standard Edition of the Complete Psychological Works of Sigmund Freud,* vol. 9, ed. and trans. J. Strachey. London: Hogarth Press/Institute of Psycho-Analysis.

Freud, S. (1909). Notes upon a case of obsessional neurosis. In *The Standard Edition of the Complete Psychological Works of Sigmund Freud*, vol. 10, ed. and trans. J. Strachey. London: Hogarth Press/Institute of Psycho-Analysis.

Freud, S. (1910). *Leonardo da Vinci and a memory of his childhood.* In *The Standard Edition of the Complete Psychological Works of Sigmund Freud,* vol. 11, ed. and trans. J. Strachey. London: Hogarth Press/Institute of Psycho-Analysis.

Freud, S. (1913). *Totem and Taboo.* In *The Standard Edition of the Complete Psychological Works of Sigmund Freud*, vol. 13, ed. and trans. J. Strachey. London: Hogarth Press/Institute of Psycho-Analysis.

Freud, S. (1914a). The Moses of Michelangelo. In *The Standard Edition of the Complete Psychological Works of Sigmund Freud,* vol. 13, ed. and trans. J. Strachey. London: Hogarth Press/Institute of Psycho-Analysis.

Freud, S. (1914b). On narcissism: An introduction. In *The Standard Edition of the Complete Psychological Works of Sigmund Freud*, vol. 14, ed. and trans. J. Strachey. London: Hogarth Press/Institute of Psycho-Analysis.

Freud, S. (1915). Papers on metapsychology. In *The Standard Edition of the Complete Psychological Works of Sigmund Freud*, vol. 14, ed. and trans. J. Strachey. London: Hogarth Press/Institute of Psycho-Analysis.

Freud, S. (1920). *Beyond the Pleasure Principle.* In *The Standard Edition of the Complete Psychological Works of Sigmund Freud* , vol. 18, ed. and trans. J. Strachey. London: Hogarth Press/Institute of Psycho-Analysis.

Freud, S. (1921). *Group Psychology and the Analysis of the Ego.* In *The Standard Edition of the Complete Psychological Works of Sigmund Freud*, vol. 18, ed. and trans. J. Strachey. London: Hogarth Press/Institute of Psycho-Analysis.

Freud, S. (1923a). The ego and the id. In *The Standard Edition of the Complete Psychological Works of Sigmund Freud*, vol. 19, ed. and trans. J. Strachey. London: Hogarth Press/Institute of Psycho-Analysis.

Freud, S (1923b). A seventeenth-century demonological neurosis. In *The Standard Edition of the Complete Psychological Works of Sigmund Freud,* vol. 19, ed. and trans. J. Strachey. London: Hogarth Press/Institute of Psycho-Analysis.

Freud, S. (1925). An autobiographical study. In *The Standard Edition of the Complete Psychological Works of Sigmund Freud,* vol. 22, ed. and trans. J. Strachey. London: Hogarth Press/Institute of Psycho-Analysis.

Freud, S. (1926). *The Question of Lay-Analysis.* In *The Standard Edition of the Complete Psychological Works of Sigmund Freud*, vol. 20, ed. and trans. J. Strachey. London: Hogarth Press/Institute of Psycho-Analysis.

Freud, S. (1927). *The Future of an Illusion.* In *The Standard Edition of the Complete Psychological Works of Sigmund Freud,* vol. 21, ed. and trans. J. Strachey. London: Hogarth Press/Institute of Psycho-Analysis.

Freud, S. (1930). *Civilization and its discontents.* In *The Standard Edition of the Complete Psychological Works of Sigmund Freud,* vol. 21, ed. and trans. J. Strachey. London: Hogarth Press/Institute of Psycho-Analysis.

Freud, S. (1939). *Moses and Monotheism.* In *The Standard Edition of the Complete Psychological Works of Sigmund Freud,* vol. 23, ed. and trans. J. Strachey. London: Hogarth Press/Institute of Psycho-Analysis.

Freud, S. (1990). *Epistolari. Lettere alla fidanzata e ad altri corrispondenti. 1873–1939.* Turin: Boringhieri.

Freud, S. and L. Andreas-Salomé (1983). *Eros e conoscenza (lettere 1912–1936).* Boringhieri. Turin: Boringhieri.

Gay, P. (1998). *Freud: A Life for our Time.* London: Norton.

Gresser, M. (1994). *Dual Allegiance: Freud as a Modern Jew.* New York: State University of New York Press.

Küng, H. (1979). *Dio esiste?* Milan: Mondadori.

Mannoni, O. (1970). *Freud.* Bari: Laterza.

Meng, H. and Freud, E.L. (eds) (1963). *Psychoanalysis and Faith. The Letters of Sigmund Freud and Oskar Pfister,* trans. E. Mosbacher. New York: Basic Books.

Ostow, M. (2007). *Mind and Brain: A Psychoanalytic Examination of Spirituality and Religion.* New York: Columbia University Press.

Pfister, O. (2009). *L'illusione di un avvenire,* trans. S. Candreva, S. Daniele, E. Panaitescu and C. Spinoglio. Turin: Boringhieri.

Ricoeur, P. (1967). *Della interpretazione,* trans. Daria Filippi. Milan: Il Saggiatore.

Ricoeur, P. (1977). *Il conflitto delle interpretazioni,* trans. R. Balzarotti, F. Botturi and G. Colombo. Milano: Jaca Books.

Rosenzweig, F. (1985). *La stella della redenzione,* trans. Gianfranco Bonola. Casale Monferrato: Editore Marietti.

Schneider, S. and Berke, J. (2010). Freud's meeting with Rabbi Alexandre Safran. *Psychoanalysis and History* 12: 15–28.

Spencer-Brown, G. (1979). *Laws of Form.* New York: Elsevier-Dutton.

Vaihinger, H. (1967). *La fiosofia del come se.* Rome: Astrolabio.

Yerushalmi, Y.H. (1991). *Freud's Moses: Judaism Terminable and Interminable.* New Haven and London: Yale University Press.

Zellini, I.P. (2010). *Numero e logos.* Milan: Adelphi.

3

JUNG'S DIVINE MADNESS

Christopher MacKenna

Introduction

Belief in divine madness – the idea that we can be out of our rational minds but inspired in life enhancing and creative ways – can be traced back at least to the ancient Greeks (Dodds 1951). Jung's own account of his crisis and the way he responded to it has recently been published in the *Red Book* (Jung 2009); making this an opportune moment to reassess our understanding of Jung and to enquire what light his achievement can throw on our understanding of spirituality in relation to psychotic states of mind.

Divine madness

Jung experienced a series of visions that caused him to fear for his sanity. In retrospect, though, he came to believe both that they were prophetic and that the insights gained through the sixteen years of introspection that followed could have wider therapeutic value for many other people. Such beliefs raise questions about the relationship between individual psychology – perhaps psychopathology – paranormal experience, and psychotherapeutic practice. Towards the end of his life Jung wrote that all his thoughts circled round God like the planets round the sun and were as 'irresistibly attracted' by God (Jung 1976: 236). This was no late conversion on his part. In the first chapters of *Memories, Dreams, Reflections* (Jung 1963), he described the haunting religious dreams and fantasies that elevated and disturbed his lonely early years. Now that the *Red Book* has been published, we can also see the quite remarkable extent to which Jung – at a critical moment in his adult life, when he appeared to be sliding into a psychotic illness – apparently turned his back on external forms of help and appealed directly to the Spirit of the Depths[1] to come to his aid.

Jung's disturbance

Jung first spoke publicly about the disturbance that gave rise to the contents of the *Red Book* in a seminar for advanced students of his ideas, held in 1925.

On 20 April that year, he recalled a dream he had had in 1912, while he was working on the Miller fantasies, in which he had dreamed of Freud in the guise of an Austrian customs official; but Jung's companion (he suggests it was his shadow) said, 'Did you notice him? He has been dead for thirty years, but he can't die properly.'[2] The scene then changed and Jung found himself in a medieval southern town on the slopes of mountains. The sun was blazing at full noon – the hour, he said, spirits are abroad in southern countries – when he saw a crusader dressed in a coat of mail with the Maltese cross in red on his back and front. '"Did you notice him?" Jung's shadow asked, "He has been dead since the twelfth century, but he is not yet properly dead"' (Jung 1990: 38f.). Jung says this dream bothered him for a long time. He claimed that when he dreamed it he was still unaware of the conflict his book on the Miller fantasies would precipitate with Freud. At the same time he felt there was an antagonism between the figure of Freud and the crusader, yet there was also a similarity between them. Both were dead but they could not die properly. Jung says the dream left him feeling 'oppressed and bewildered' and that Freud was similarly affected, and could not interpret it (Jung 1990: 39f.). In retrospect, it is not difficult to imagine that the dream's judgment on Freud – that he had died thirty years ago – might express Jung's growing impatience with the older man; but what of the crusader? Jung himself was physically tall and of a crusading temperament, as is shown by his combative defence of psychoanalytic ideas in medical circles.[3] Although, theoretically, he was still Freud's heir apparent, tension was growing between them. At the same time, although Jung says that he was no longer living in the Christian myth (Jung 1963: 166), the *Red Book* reveals how deeply he was imbued with it; and his later decision to create the *Red Book* (Jung 2009) almost in the form of a medieval manuscript with elaborate calligraphy and illuminated capitals demonstrates his affinity with this era.

Jung's crusader is a complex figure. At one level I think he represents Jung's conscious understanding of the Christian Church, which, although still locked in the thought world of the Middle Ages, had not been able to die. On the other hand, I think the crusader also depicts an insignificantly recognised religious part of Jung himself. Writing about this dream towards the end of his life, he recalled that the stories of the quest for the Holy Grail had been of the greatest importance to him since the age of 15. In the deepest sense the Grail quest was Jung's quest,[4] which had scarcely anything to do with Freud's. Like the Grail knights, Jung was desperate to find something still unknown that might confer meaning upon the banality of life.

> To me it was a profound disappointment that all the efforts of the probing mind had apparently succeeded in finding nothing more in the depths of the psyche than the all too familiar and 'all-too-human' limitations.
>
> (Jung 1963: 161)

We can hear the note of desperation in Jung's voice. The great tragedy of Jung's teenage years had been to witness his father's loss of Christian faith and premature death (Jung 1963). Now, as he approached midlife, Jung seemed to be caught in the same blind alley. Psychoanalysis had discovered nothing, in the depths of the psyche, beyond all-too-human limitations. Although Jung always eschewed the role of preacher, the contents of the *Red Book* suggest that, through his experiences of divine madness in his encounters with the 'spirit of the depths', he felt he had been able to glimpse the nature of ultimate reality and that his vision somehow provided a resolution to the deepest needs of the unquiet spirits of the dead – doubtless his father among them – which had beset him. In this sense the *Red Book* is a messianic text and the reader must decide – as with Schreber's *Memoirs of my Mental Illness* (Schreber 2000) – if its contents are inspired. In neither case, though, can an objective test be applied. If we are to follow Jung and Schreber we will have to engage with them from the depths of our own beings – and then see whether they have addressed the deepest questions of our souls.

Jung had a second bewildering dream at Christmas time in 1912, in which a white dove transformed into a little girl with golden hair. When she was gone, the dove reappeared and slowly said, 'I am allowed to transform into a human form only in the first hours of the night, while the male dove is busy with the twelve dead' (Jung 1990: 40). The dream disturbed him, and puzzled Freud. Until this time, Jung had shared Freud's understanding of the repressed unconscious, but now he began to entertain the idea that 'the unconscious did not consist of inert material only, but that there was something living down there' (Jung 1990: 40).[5] During 1913, confused by his dreams and troubled by increasing symptoms of disturbance, Jung attempted to re-analyse his infantile memories, but found no relief. In a further attempt at self-cure he sought to recover the emotional tone of his childhood by playing at building 'houses of stone, all sorts of fantastic castles, churches, and towns'. But, although he enjoyed this 'like a fool' (Jung 1990: 41), his disturbance persisted until

> Towards autumn [1913] I felt that the pressure that had seemed to be in me was not there anymore but in the air. The air actually seemed to be darker than before. It was just as if it were no longer a psychological situation in which I was involved, but a real one, and that sense became more and more weighty.
>
> (Jung 1990: 41)

In October 1913, while in this disturbing state of mind, Jung was on a train when he fell into a fantasy in which he was looking down on a map of Europe. As he watched, the northern part of Europe sank down and was inundated by the sea. When the water reached Switzerland, the mountains rose to protect it. As he watched the wreckage of Europe and dead bodies tossing in the water, which turned to blood, Jung's dispassionate observation gave way to a sense of catastrophe that gripped him with 'tremendous power' (Jung 1990: 41). He tried to repress the fantasy, but it came again, holding him bound for two hours. Three or four weeks later it was repeated, with the blood more prominent (Jung 1990: 42). Identifying himself with Switzerland, Jung feared the visions showed that he was 'an over-compensated psychosis',[6] yet he lacked confirmatory symptoms (Jung 1990: 43f). The outbreak of the First World War in August 1914 reassured Jung, because it proved, to his satisfaction, that his visions of Europe being submerged in water, ice and fire were genuinely prophetic; that the spirit of the depths, which had furnished his vision, was also driving world affairs. Sometime after he had received this reassurance, he began to inscribe the contents of the dreams and fantasies that followed his Europe visions into the *Red Book*.

The *Red Book*

To open the pages of the *Red Book* is to be transported into another world. Jung tells us that he transcribed the dreams and active imaginations that followed the flood vision from his original notebooks into a large, leather-bound volume, known by its colour as the *Red Book*, because he knew that his experiences contained something precious and could think of nothing better than to write and paint them in a valuable book, reliving the original experiences as best he could. As the recently published reproduction of the *Red Book* shows, it is a work of art. The text is executed in elaborate calligraphy, with illuminated capitals, reminiscent of medieval manuscripts. Jung also illustrated the text with pictures and designs, some relating directly to the text, others of which have simply to be pondered. The book looks and feels arcane, as if it comes from another time and place. Jung would say that it does: it has the strange rather compelling foreignness, which both attracts and repels, that he would associate with the spirit of the depths.

Some passages, like the opening section, are composed in a high-flown scriptural style. These passages are interspersed with lively dramatic interludes – Jung's active imaginations – in which he encounters a cast of characters who emerged spontaneously from his inner world, with whom he engages in animated activity, discussion and debate. When he argues with them he is very much his conscious self. At other times, they challenge, confound and instruct him. Along the way, through this apparently unsystematic journey, Jung was initiated into the paradoxical workings of his unconscious mind. Readers used to therapeutic conversations, in which the patient's personal life is to the fore, are likely to find themselves puzzled by the contents of this book. At first sight it has nothing to do with Jung's daily life. Where are his wife, his children, his professional colleagues, his patients – the world he inhabited? Strangely missing. Instead the book is taken up with the conflict and collision between two opposed points of view that he refers to as the spirit of this time and the spirit of the depths.

The spirit of this time is concerned with practical questions of use, value, justification and meaning; but the spirit of the depths, whose activity Jung detected in his flood visions and in the outbreak of the First World War, is more powerful than the spirit of any age. According to Jung, during his introverted journey:

> The spirit of the depths took my understanding and all my knowledge and placed them at the service of the inexplicable and the paradoxical. He robbed me of speech and writing for everything that was not in his service, namely the melting together of sense and nonsense, which produces the supreme meaning.
>
> (Jung 2009: 229)

As these two spirits collided within him, Jung struggled to discover if he was speaking 'the greatness and intoxication and ugliness of madness', or deeper truth, as the spirit of the depths avowed (Jung 2009: 230). Jung's divine madness begins here, because to be in harmony with the spirit of the depths, as Jung believed all truly inspired religious people are, is to appear mad according to the spirit of this time. In an amusing but disturbing section, Jung imagines himself admitted to a psychiatric hospital where the professor of psychiatry rapidly diagnoses religious paranoia on the grounds that he is manically aroused, hearing voices, hallucinating and using neologisms. To cap it all, the prognosis is bad, because Jung appears to lack insight; he is not behaving according to the dictates of rational common sense (Jung 2009: 295f.). In another place, he writes,

> if you enter into the world of the soul, you are like a madman, and a doctor would consider you to be sick. What I say here can be seen as sickness, but no one can see it as sickness more than I do.
>
> (Jung 2009: 238)

Composition

The engine that drives the *Red Book* and provides its underlying drama is the almost daily record of dreams and active imaginations, which sometimes read like visions, which Jung dates between 14 November 1913 (within a month of his first flood vision) and 11 February 1914. There are then some entries for April and May 1914, after which the spirit of the depths appears to have been silent until June 1915, when Jung saw an osprey rising from the water with a fish and his soul said, 'That is a sign that what is below is born upward' (Jung 2009: 336f.). Thereafter, there are dated entries for September and December 1915; then January and February 1916, which include the *VII Sermones ad*

Mortuos (Jung 1925). There are a few further entries, dated April, May and June 1916, and one from July 1917, but it seems that the essential material on which the *Red Book* is based was predominantly delivered in late 1913 and early 1914, with further, more occasional amplificatory material emerging during the next three years. As the notes to the published edition indicate, Jung's original material underwent substantial development and some modification as he transcribed it into the *Red Book*. At the end of the text Jung tells us that he worked on it for sixteen years, until his study of the Chinese alchemical text, *The Secret of the Golden Flower*, later reprinted in Jung's *Alchemical Studies* (Jung 1967), began to supersede it.[7] He finally stopped in 1930, when his alchemical researches convinced him that the contents of the *Red Book* were not some private madness, but his own initiation into experiences familiar to the alchemists before him:

> To the superficial observer, it will appear like madness. It would also have developed into one, had I not been able to absorb the over-whelming power of the original experiences. With the help of alchemy I could finally arrange them into a whole.
>
> (Jung 2009: 360)

The *Red Book* is too massive to be summarised in an essay, but it is important to introduce the reader to its contents and flavour. The quality of Jung's divine madness must be experienced, not abstracted, if we are to make any assessment of its worth. For reasons of space, I will concentrate on the first section – *Liber Primus* – which gives a sense of the underlying nature of Jung's disturbance. I will then sketch some of Jung's more significant discoveries about the dynamics of the unconscious world, relating to my theme. Sadly – because my focus is divine madness – there will not be room to consider the original version of the *Seven Sermons to the Dead* (Jung 2009), which suggest Jung's most developed understanding of the emergence of conscious processes from the unfathomable depth of the unconscious world. This revisioned metapsychology finally allows Jung's dead to rest.

Liber Primus

The first part of the *Red Book* is prefaced by four messianic texts from the bible,[8] suggesting the revelatory nature of its contents and its healing potential. Yet, although his thoughts are often scriptural in form, Jung insists he is not giving general teaching, but merely describing his own path (Jung 2009). He tells us that in October 1913, when the first flood vision came, he was in his fortieth year and at a stage in life when he had achieved all his desires, 'honor, power, wealth, knowledge, and every human happiness' (Jung 2009: 231). From a psychotherapeutic point of view it may be significant that Jung is wrong about his age – he was actually in his thirty-eighth year.[9]

Equally, it is difficult to reconcile his claim to total contentment with what we know of his life at this time. The Fourth Private Psychoanalytic Meeting had taken place on 7 and 8 September 1913, in an atmosphere described by Ernest Jones as 'disagreeable', and by Freud as 'fatiguing and unedifying' (Freud and Jung 1974: 550). At this meeting, when Jung stood for re-election as president, 22 out of 52 participants abstained from voting so that Jung's election would not be unanimous. The following month – the month of the first flood vision – only one letter passed between Jung and Freud. On 27 October 1913, Jung wrote:

> Dear Professor Freud,
> It has come to my ears through Dr Maeder that you doubt my *bona fides*. I would have expected you to communicate with me directly on so weighty a matter. Since this is the gravest reproach that can be levelled at anybody, you have made further collaboration impossible. I therefore lay down the editorship of the *Jahrbuch* with which you entrusted me. I have also notified Bleuler and Deuticke of my decision. Very truly yours, DR. C. G. JUNG.
> (Freud and Jung 1974: 550)[10]

The rupture with Freud had been coming for several years, but its gravity to Jung, in personal and professional terms, can hardly be overstated. Years later, Jung would write that although he had always had some doubts and hesitations about aspects of Freud's theories, Freud was the first man of real importance he had ever met. In Jung's experience up to that time, no one else could compare with him (Jung 1963). Loss of Freud's friendship, under whatever circumstances, would have been a grievous blow to Jung. Far from being full of contentment, as Jung asserts, we know both from the seminar on analytical psychology (Jung 1990) that he gave in 1925, and from *Memories, Dreams, Reflections* (Jung 1963), that he was becoming increasingly isolated. The floods that threatened Europe were also threatening him. If, in the eyes of the spirit of this age, he had achieved 'honor, power, wealth, knowledge, and every human happiness', inwardly – in terms of the spirit of the depths – he was still a pauper.

Jung evidently found the process of introversion – his introspective search for the spirit of the depths – difficult. His rational and intellectual defences were very strong. He needed to be in control of his life and thoughts. Until now he had regarded the soul as an object of intellectual enquiry. It was only when the spirit of the depths forced him to address his soul as 'a living and self-existing being' that he became aware that he had lost his soul (Jung 2009: 232).[11] In desperation, during the nights of November 1913, Jung began to cry out to his soul as if she was an independent person. Despite his psychoanalytic training, he still had to learn that dreams, which he revealingly calls 'the dregs of my thought', were actually the speech of his soul; that dreams determine us without our understanding their action.[12] In this quest, scholarliness alone was not enough; 'there is a knowledge of the heart that gives deeper insight' (Jung 2009: 233). The thought that his soul possessed a life of her own, a life not controlled by his conscious mind, seems to have terrified Jung. Must he learn to do without rational meaning? But this would be nonsense and madness. Is there a supreme meaning? But he must not think, only learn to trust – to love his soul. Fearfully, he begins to sense that, in the world of the depths, meaning gives way to meaninglessness and eternal disorder, from which nothing can deliver us since this is the other half of the world. But – and this saving thought develops through the *Red Book* – he will discover that there is a pattern even here, because order and meaning grow out of disorder and meaninglessness. In fact, there is something dead about order and meaning alone, because what has become is no longer becoming.

For six nights Jung failed to elicit any reaction from his soul, while he swayed between fear, defiance and nausea, and was 'wholly prey to my passion'; then, on the seventh night, he received the command to 'look into your depths, pray to your depths, waken the dead' (Jung 2009: 234). In the light of what is to come this was a terrifying command, but it was also central to Jung's task because, as we will discover, Jung was haunted by the dead, and:

> not just [Jung's] dead, that is, all the images of the shapes you took in the past, which your ongoing life has left behind, but also the thronging dead of human history, the ghostly procession of the past, which is an ocean compared to the drops of your own life span. I see behind you, behind the mirror of your eyes, the crush of dangerous shadows, the dead, who look greedily through the empty sockets of your eyes, who moan and hope to gather up through you all the loose ends of the ages, that sigh in them. Your cluelessness does not prove anything. Put your ear to that wall and you will hear the rustling of their procession.
>
> (Jung 2009: 296)

But this is to anticipate. After twenty-five nights of fruitless introspection, Jung was torn between scorn for the spiritual task he was attempting and the conviction that he was really writing a book. Yet it seems that he reached a point where he finally desired to become 'an empty vessel for his soul' (Jung 2009: 237). The following night, he says, accompanied by an excited chorus of voices, he allowed himself to fall great depths into the world of his soul. In a dark cave, full of shrieking voices, he glimpsed a luminous red stone covering an opening in the rock where '*something wanted to be uttered*' (Jung 2009: 237; my emphasis). At this point in the narrative, hearing and speech become confused because, although Jung places his ear to the opening, he sees the bloody head of a man on the dark stream. 'Someone wounded, someone slain floats there' (Jung 2009: 237). Shuddering, he wondered what it meant.

A plausible interpretation might wonder about a connection with the slain or wounded Jung. Was he finally becoming aware of his distress at being ostracised by the psychoanalytic community? If there is any truth in this interpretation, Jung characteristically rejects it, just as he dissented from Freud's reductive interpretation of Schreber's paranoia.[13] He claims that the imagery was so archetypal it needed no personal associations (Jung 2009: 238, n.85). Instead, as the vision continued, he noted a large black scarab floating past and then a red sun in the depths of the water with many tiny serpents striving towards it. Night fell, and a stream of thick red blood sprang up, surging for a long time before it ebbed. Jung was terrified. What had he seen? If Jung was harbouring any murderous rage about his coming break with Freud and the psychoanalytic world, he somehow absorbs it into larger thoughts about life and death. He interprets the black beetle as the death that is necessary for renewal, and seeks for life within, rather than without. Again, rather than nursing illusions about his own innocence, he says boldly, 'I myself am a murderer and murdered sacrificer and sacrificed. The upwelling blood streams out of me' (Jung 2009: 239).

From one point of view, this attitude seems grandiose. By embracing the symmetric logic of the spirit of the depths, according to which he can be both the murdered and the murderer, Jung is occluding others from his field of view. This could be interpreted as a strategy for maintaining an illusion of responsibility for events that were largely beyond his personal control. On the other hand, given that the vision belongs to December 1913, when Europe was spiralling towards war, we might think that Jung was refusing the war-mongering madness which projected evil into a foreign foe. Instead, says Jung, we should sacrifice the hero in ourselves, for we only murder our brothers because we do not know our brother is ourselves. 'Frightful things must happen until men grow ripe' (Jung 2009: 239). The timing of Jung's visions, and his interpretation of them, give pause for thought. In August 1914, when Europe was possessed by collective paranoia, Jung – who had reason to feel aggrieved – refused to impute his suffering to other people, but tried rather to use its energy to explore his own blood guilt.[14] In part, this may explain one of the most poignant features of the *Red Book*, which is the deep sense of isolation that pervades it. Although Jung talks with many people, they all belong to his inner world. By opting for the spirit of the depths Jung had chosen a solitary path, but his choice may not be unconnected with the fact that he appears deeply suspicious of love; of anything that might inhibit him. Much later in the *Red Book* he reveals that to love would be to hoist the fate of another onto his shoulders. He wants love, but that

> really would be too much and would bind me like an iron ring that would stifle me . . . Love, I believe wants to be with others. But my love wants to be with me. I dread it.[15]
>
> (Jung 2009: 324)

Why did Jung fear love? Towards the end of his life he recalled a time, when he was 3, when his mother was hospitalised for several months, apparently for problems associated with difficulty in his parents' marriage. He tells us that he was 'deeply troubled' by her absence and that, thereafter, he always felt mistrust when he heard the word 'love' (Jung 1963: 22). Difficult as this separation must have been, his mother's return created its own terrors. By the time Jung was 7 or 8, he was sleeping in his father's room – his parents slept apart. At night, strange and mysterious presences emanated from her room. He experienced them as luminous visions. It was as if 'the nocturnal atmosphere had begun to thicken' (Jung 1963: 31) – reminiscent of Jung's experience in October 1913, when 'the air actually seemed to be darker than before' (Jung 1990: 41). Small objects became large. Once, a tiny ball gradually approached until it grew into a 'monstrous and suffocating object' (Jung 1963: 31). Again, we can note the echo between this 'suffocating object' and Jung's fear that love will stifle him (Jung 2009). If there is a psychotic core to the *Red Book*, I believe it lies in Jung's childhood nightmare of being unable to separate from the mother, whose psyche threatened to engulf him. As we will see, this primal terror appears also to be reflected in the *Red Book*'s constant preoccupation with the God, 'who makes us sick'; the God from whom we must heal ourselves, 'since he is also our heaviest wound' (Jung 2009: 338). Finding a relationship with God, which avoided the inflationary risks of identification, yet allowed the unknowable mystery to incarnate and transform itself in him, was Jung's ultimate achievement. I think that this was the Holy Grail he sought all his life. But in late 1913, Jung was still at the beginning of his journey. Faced with the vision of the murdered man, Jung says that if we slay it in ourselves, instead of seeking to kill the heroic spirit in our brother, the sun of the depths will begin to rise in us. In other words, unconscious contents will begin to be activated by the energy no longer needed consciously to sustain a heroic image of ourselves. This is far from being a glorious or inflationary experience. As unconscious contents were animated within him, Jung's darkness came to life. He experienced this as the crush of total evil, as the conflicts of life that lay buried in the matter of his body – a significant recognition of the way repressed experiences can be somatised – began to stir. The serpents in his vision are now found to be 'dreadful evil thoughts and feelings'. But, in stark contrast to the spirit of this age, which glorifies achievement, the spirit of the depths maintains that 'The one who learns to live with his incapacity has learned a great deal' (Jung 2009: 240). Jung may have been determined to locate the villain in himself, but the battle was far from won. In his fantasy, an assassin appeared from the depths and levelled his murder weapon at the 'prince'. Jung felt transformed into a 'rapacious beast'. His heart glowered in rage against the 'high and beloved, against my prince and hero'. Might this be Freud? Or, perhaps, Jung's father or God or Jung himself?

I felt betrayed by my king. Why did I feel this way? He was not as I had wished him to be. He was other than I expected. He should be the king in my sense, not in his sense. He should be what I called ideal . . . It was civil war in me. I myself was the murderer and the murdered. The deadly arrow was stuck in my heart, and I did not know what it meant.

(Jung 2009: 241)

Jung's rage and the rebirth of God

Jung's murderous thoughts spread like poison through his body. Disturbingly, he says that 'the murder of one' (Jung 2009: 241) – does he mean the Archduke Ferdinand? Or was this a psychotic fantasy, which caused Jung to blame himself for the First World War? – 'was the poisonous arrow that flew into the hearts of men and kindled the fiercest war'. Yet, Gods must die. 'Everything that becomes too old becomes evil, the same is true of your highest . . . If a God ceases being the way of life, he must fall secretly' (Jung 2009: 241). During the following night, in a 'frightful dream' (Jung 2009: 241, n.112), Jung found himself enacting these murderous fantasies when he assisted in the assassination of Siegfried, the archetypal hero prince (Jung 2009: 241).[16] In the *Red Book* Jung describes Siegfried as 'my power, my boldness, my pride', who seems to have personified Jung's rather grandiose defences (Jung 2009: 242). Later in his life, in *Memories, Dreams, Reflections* (Jung 1963), Jung associates Siegfried with the Germanic desire to achieve, heroically to impose their will, to have their own way; and admits that this is what he had wanted to do.

These associations are probably correct. But there may have been a more painful, personal and poignant motif underlying Jung's sacrifice of Siegfried. The great underlying theme of Wagner's opera *Der Ring des Nibelungen*, which revolves around the birth, life, and death of Siegfried – is the renunciation of love in the quest for the Ring.[17] As is now widely accepted, between the years 1908 and 1911 Jung had a passionate relationship with his former patient, Sabina Spielrein (McCormick, 2001).[18] During their romance, Spielrein dreamed of mothering their love child, a boy who would be called Siegfried. Following the termination of her relationship with Jung, Spielrein – who had qualified as a medical doctor – married and gave birth to her first child, a daughter, in September 1913. On the 29th of that month – almost exactly a month before Jung's letter to Freud, quoted above – Freud, who was familiar with the details of Jung's affair with Spielrein, wrote to congratulate her, incidentally expressing his own feelings about 'Siegfried':

Dear Frau Doktor,
Well, now, my heartiest congratulations! It is far better that the child should be a 'she'. Now we can think again about the blond Siegfried and perhaps smash that idol before his time comes.

For the rest, the small She will speak for herself. May she fare well, if wishes still have a vestige of omnipotence!
Yours, Freud.

(Carotenuto 1984: 121)

Jung was also aware of the birth, 'I congratulate you most warmly on the happy event!' he wrote, probably at the end of December 1913 (Jung 2001: 186). It is difficult to believe that such deeply personal associations to 'Siegfried' are unrelated to Jung's assassination of him in the *Red Book*, although, even here, Jung seems more overtly to associate him with grandiosity and power.

As always happens with Jung, though, the personal aspect of his conflict is transmuted into archetypal imagery: the assassination of Siegfried, which Freud interpreted in personal terms, becomes the prelude to profound reflections on the birth, life and death of our images of God. At one level, Jung longs for stasis. Ambitiously, he would like to have succeeded as Siegfried. Siegfried's death leaves him defenceless, as his proud self-image crumbles into the bitter and conflicted conflicts of his internal world. Yet, through his self-analysis, pictured in the *Red Book*, Jung is coming to believe that this is the necessary fate of every self-image, of every image of God that has become static and rigid – beyond its sell-by date. The bitterest truth for mortal men, Jung contends, is that 'our Gods want to be overcome, since they require renewal' (Jung 2009: 242). An ageing God image becomes nonsense, and the greatest truth becomes the greatest lie. So meaning must become absurdity to enable fresh meaning to arise. In the mythological language beloved by Jung, the 'blond savage of the German forests' had to betray 'the hammer-brandishing thunder to the pale Near-Eastern God' (Jung 2009: 242). Christianity succeeded the old Germanic images of God; but Christian images of God are equally vulnerable. They too must die.

It is very important that we try to read these statements in a psychological way. Throughout his life Jung was adamant that our images of God are a *complexio oppositorum*: a complex of opposites (Henderson 2010). They are not simple. As a child, growing up in his father's parsonage, Jung had been taught that God is simply love. But love is complex – as Jung well knew. His mother had taught him a prayer, which was meant to comfort him at night. To the young Jung, though, it seemed to picture Jesus as a bird who took children. Jung associated this with the activity of Satan and of the undertakers' men, whom he saw at work in his father's churchyard. As a result he began to distrust Lord Jesus (Jung 1963: 24), a distrust that grew with his earliest dream – at the age of 3 or 4 – when he encountered 'Lord Jesus' as an underground phallus and heard his mother calling, 'Yes, just look at him. That is the man-eater!' He awoke 'sweating' and 'scared to death' (Jung 1963: 25). These early terrors were compounded, a few years later, when the sight of the local cathedral, its new roof glittering in the sun, precipitated a fantasy of God dropping a great turd from under his throne, which shattered the building's roof and walls (Jung 1963). For the rest of his life – whatever the church might teach – Jung knew that God was as dangerous as God was loving.

In the *Red Book* three things seem to move in parallel. First, there is Jung's quest to liberate himself from his two-dimensional identification with Siegfried. He needs to own his own shadow, even if this means killing his heroic self-image. Second, there is the terrible object lesson of what failure to do this can lead to, provided by the crowds that cheered when the First World War broke out. They could identify with Siegfried because they had projected their murderousness into their enemies. Third, at the deepest archetypal level, there are the images of God, which sanction and drive both personal and national self-images. Much later in his life, Jung would write:

> As the highest value and supreme dominant in the psychic hierarchy, the God-image is immediately related to, or identical with, the self, and everything that happens to the God image has an effect on the latter. Any uncertainty about the God-image causes a profound uneasiness in the self, for which reason the question is generally ignored because of its painfulness. But that does not mean that the question remains unasked in the unconscious.
>
> (Jung 1968: 109)

When war broke out, the British and the Germans each claimed the Christian God as their ally; as God is righteous, so their causes were righteous too, they maintained. But, beginning with the *Red Book* and throughout his life, Jung would contend for a darker truth. Mythologically speaking, he believed that the church's picture of a sinless Christ was only achieved by splitting off Jesus' shadow and locating it in Satan, whom Jung interprets as Christ's alter ego. In Jung's reading of the Easter story, when Christ descends into hell after his crucifixion, he does so in order to unite with antichrist. In due course, Jung believed, their union would lead to the birth of a new God image, which would transcend them both. In Jung's opinion, 'Gods are unavoidable. The more you flee from the God, the more surely you fall into his hand' (Jung 2009: 242).

As the *Red Book* unfolds, though, a terrible option emerges: either we go into the depths and confront the forces that drive world events within ourselves, as Jung is attempting to do, or the depths change themselves into death and get enacted on the world stage. In contrast to the euphoric sense of universal brotherhood that Jung experienced, as he travelled through northern Europe at the beginning of the First World War, the spirit of the depths called him into icy solitude.[19] Why? Because, Jung contends, new life comes not from following the crowd, but only from becoming centred in ourselves – where the life of God within us can begin. Jung believed that the assassination of Siegfried, his conscious hero, would lead to the birth of a new God image in his soul. The psychotic potential of this notion is evident when Jung says that it seemed to him, for a time, that his soul was God. In due course, though, he resisted this identification, helped, perhaps, by his ambivalence, because he says that he pursued his soul to kill the image of the divine child within it, 'for I am also the worst enemy of my God' (Jung 2009: 244). At the same time he also claims that his enmity was decided on in God, since God's ambiguity means that he is also mockery and hate and anger. These are awesome and paradoxical thoughts. What becomes of human agency, if we believe that everything happens from beyond us? That God lives us, rather than us living our own lives? Jung was haunted by these questions for decades, until they finally erupted in *Answer to Job*, where he sought to express the 'shattering emotion which the unvarnished spectacle of divine savagery and ruthlessness produces in us' (Jung 1969b: 366). In my opinion, Jung's whole *oeuvre* was driven by his need to discover how he could both be lived by God, but also, somehow, take responsibility for his own actions. In intensely paradoxical language, Jung says that, far from imitating heroes, the new God needs no imitators or pupils, for 'He forces men through himself. The God is his own follower in man. He imitates himself' (Jung 2009: 245). If we are outside ourselves, living a communal life, our self suffers 'privation' (Jung 2009: 245). But if God moves into the self, 'he snatches us from what is outside us and we arrive at singleness in ourselves' (Jung 2009: 245). Paradoxically, Jung claims it is only when we are solitary that God leads us to the God of others and through that to the true neighbor, to the neighbor of the self in others (Jung 2009: 245). By owning our own incapacity, we are freed from the need to be heroes and no longer have to compel others to be heroes in our place.

Elijah, Salome and Jung's deification

During the night when Jung was preoccupied with these profound specula-tions, he had his first conversation with three figures who appeared spontane-ously from his internal world: an old man, Elijah; his blind daughter Salome; and a serpent. Elijah personified the power of forethinking, while Salome rep-resented pleasure. Their association, given their biblical backgrounds, scan-dalised Jung. But he had to learn that, in the depths of the unconscious, the opposites are joined. Here the serpent has a vital role to play in bringing them to consciousness because it writhes from right to left and left to right between them; being an adversary, but also a bridge. A crystal, which had appeared in an earlier fantasy, is now found to represent the thought that arises in the tension between these opposing forces.[20] In another image, Jung likens this emerging third to the divine son, the supreme meaning, the symbol, the passing over into a new creation. In an important clarification, given the danger of psychotic identification with God, Jung states that he does not become the supreme meaning or the symbol, but the symbol becomes in him such that it has its substance, while he retains his own (Jung 2009: 250). Although not the divine son, he has effectively become a mother to God (Jung 2009: 250).

Through this visionary encounter, Jung's understanding of psychic reality is enlarged. At one point Elijah chides Jung for imagining that his thoughts are part of him: 'your thoughts are just as much outside yourself as trees and animals are outside your body' (Jung, 2009: 249).[21] In another place, Jung tries to distance himself by declaring that Salome and Elijah are symbols, but Elijah rejects this: 'We are just as real as your fellow men' (Jung 2009: 246). Somehow this rebuke brings Jung to the point where he can acknowledge his yearning – its exact nature is not revealed – which requires unusual honesty, because usually we do not wish to know, fearing that the object of our yearning will be impossible or too distressing. Yet, yearning is the way of life. If we deny our yearning we will be tempted to follow the way of the hero, which means seeking to live our life through others' achievements. Instead, Jung learns that the greatest psychological and spiritual imperative is to live oneself; to be one's own task. This is not a call to narcissistic indulgence but to protracted suffering, since we must become our own creator, beginning not with our best and highest qualities but with the worst and deepest. The culmination of the first part of the *Red Book* is reached when Jung sees further visions in the crystal: Christ is in his final torment on the cross, the black serpent coiled at its foot. The serpent winds itself around Jung's feet, and then around his whole body, his arms held wide. Salome appears, saying, 'Mary was the mother of Christ.' Jung demurs, but she continues, 'You are Christ.' As he is entwined, Jung finds his face transformed into the Mithraic *Deus Leontocephalus* (Jung 2009: 252 n.211).[22] Blind Salome kneels at Jung's feet, her hair twined around them, his blood streaming down, till she exclaims that she can see. Commenting on this fantasy in 1925, Jung interpreted Salome as a representation of his feeling function, which, being his inferior function, was surrounded by an aura of evil. In other words, he was afraid of his ability to feel. Because his feeling function was poorly developed – in contrast to his thinking function – feeling and thinking, Salome and Elijah, needed to be harmonised in Jung, for 'whoever distances himself from love, feels himself powerful' (Jung 2009: 253).[23] Commenting on these vivid archetypal images of divinisation and healing, he said:

> One is assailed by the fear that this perhaps is madness. This is how madness begins, this is madness. You cannot get conscious of these unconscious facts without being gripped by them. If you can overcome your fear of the unconscious and can let yourself go down, then these facts take on a life of their own. You can be gripped by these ideas so much that you really go mad, or nearly so.
>
> (Jung 1990: 97)

Despite his reservations, Jung later asserted the supreme importance of such an experience of deification – experienced in the ancient world by the devotees of Mithras – because it gave 'immortal value to the individual' (Jung 1990: 97). Perhaps it was here, in this internal experience of deification, which gripped Jung with all the certainty of divine madness, that he finally found the antidote to his despair. Perhaps this was the 'something still unknown which might confer meaning upon the banality of life' (Jung 1963: 161), which he had failed to find in his father's religion or with Freud.

In a more symbolic interpretation of this union of opposites, Jung likened the lion to the young, hot, dry July sun – the culminating light of summer – and the serpent to humidity, darkness, earth, the winter (Jung 1990: 98). Through this union, effected by Jung's willingness to make himself his own enemy and symbolically enacted in his identification with the Mithraic *Deus Leontocephalus*, we learn that Jung's blind pleasure is converted into sighted love. According to Jung, if we try to evade the spirit of the depths it will force us into the mysteries of Christ. This was evidenced, for him, in the Great War, when Christians who wanted heroes and ran after redeemers piled up a mountain of Calvary all over Europe. But the result, according to Jung's implacable vision of the spirit of the depths, is that:

> If you succeed in making a terrible evil out of this war and throw innumerable victims into this abyss, this is good, since it makes each of you ready for sacrifice himself. For as I, you draw close to the accomplishment of Christ's mystery.
>
> (Jung 2009: 254)

We have choice. Either we can practise voluntary self-sacrifice and contain conflict within ourselves, as Jung sought to do, thus becoming a Christ. Or, by externalising conflict into the terrible forces of war we will be propelled into sacrifice despite ourselves. The first part of the *Red Book* ends on a note of promise: one day the opposites would be harmonised in Jung: 'The mystery showed me in images what I should afterwards live. I did not possess any of those boons that the mystery showed me, for I still had to earn all of them' (Jung 2009: 254).

Liber Secundus

The first part of the *Red Book* is marked by a huge sense of internal desperation and conflict. It tells us something about Jung's initial disturbance and his need to overcome his Siegfried complex before he could move fluently in the depth of his unconscious. With the opening of the second part – *Liber Secundus* – we find ourselves in a slightly different world. Here Jung records a vivid sequence of encounters with figures who seem to have emerged spontaneously from his internal world, as he turned his consciousness within. From these meetings, Jung learns about the dynamics of the unconscious. With the Red One, Jung discovers how opposites can experience mutual transformation. A process he would come to know as the 'Transcendent Function' (Jung 2009: 259). Through his encounter with a scholar's daughter, being held captive by her father's love, he discovers that the contra-sexual principal – the anima in men and the animus in women – must be allowed free rein, because 'humankind is masculine and feminine, not just male and female' (Jung 2009: 263). The most difficult thing is 'to be beyond the gendered and yet remain within the (limit of) the human' (Jung 2009: 261). Meeting a hermit in the desert, Jung learns about the importance and the limitations of religious language and concepts. In a deeply poignant encounter with the God of nature – Jung calls him Izdubar – Jung discovers more about the ways in which our conscious images of God are always subject to change. They live and die, but we, like Mary, by our conscious attitude towards the emergent symbols in our internal worlds, can assist in the rebirth of God. Jung finds this process deeply painful. Science may have destroyed our capacity for belief but, characteristically, he still yearns for a God against whom he can rail, 'That way I would at least have a God whom I could insult, but it is not worth blaspheming against an egg that one carries in one's pocket' (Jung 2009: 285). At the same time, in a passage which reveals his ambivalence towards God and, perhaps, echoes his feelings towards his reliable but powerless father, he asks:

> did I not sing the incantations for his incubation? Did I not do this out of love for him? I do not want to tear the love for the Great One from my heart. I want to love my God, the defenceless and hopeless one. I want to care for him, like a child.
>
> (Jung 2009: 286)

Significantly, Jung learns that if we project all our goodness into God we may feel overwhelmed by emptiness and evil. On this deflated note, Jung's thoughts are drawn to envy. Years before Melanie Klein, he reflects on the devil's envy – which must be his own envy – in relation to God: 'Because the emptiness lacks the fullness it craves fullness.' The devil 'sees the most beautiful and wants to devour it in order to spoil it' (Jung 2009: 289).

Divine madness

These intense preoccupations profoundly disturb Jung, who finds himself commanded to eat a piece of liver cut from the corpse of a murdered child. It is a form of communion, but Jung wants to be reasonable. The divine now appears to him as irrational craziness; an absurd disturbance of his meaningful human activity; an unbecoming sickness which has stolen into the regular course of his life. Unfortunately, as Jung is discovering, 'You can ... leave Christianity but it does not leave you' (Jung 2009: 292). In this frame of mind, while Jung is reading *The Imitation of Christ,* a host of dead spirits come rushing in on their way to Jerusalem to pray at the Holy Sepulchre.[24] They have no peace, even in death. It is at this point that Jung is carted off to the madhouse, as mentioned above.[25] Jung seems to be torn between two points of view. In Jesus' kingdom other laws are valid than the guidelines of Jung's wisdom. Here the 'mercy of God,' which Jung could never rely on, is the highest principle of action (Jung 2009: 295). At the same time Jung is in a state of confusion. Everything appears accidental, everything apparently misleads. With this thought:

> to your shivering horror it becomes clear to you that you have fallen into the boundless, the abyss, the inanity of eternal chaos. It rushes toward you as if carried by the roaring winds of a storm, the hurtling waves of the sea . . . Chaos is not single, but an unending multiplicity. It is not formless, otherwise it would be single, but it is filled with figures that have a confusing and overwhelming effect due to their fullness.
>
> These figures are the dead.
>
> (Jung 2009: 295)

Although Jung does not make the connection he seems to be describing, in more personal terms, his fantasy of Europe being flooded. He is falling into a void:

> Madness is a special form of the spirit and clings to all teachings and philosophies, but even more to daily life, since life itself is full of craziness and at bottom utterly illogical. Man strives toward reason only so that he can make rules for himself. Life itself has no rules. That is its mystery and its unknown law. What you call knowledge is an attempt to impose something comprehensible on life.
>
> (Jung 2009: 298)

In a terrifying sentence, Jung records: 'This is the night in which all the dams broke, where what was previously solid moved, where the stones turned into serpents, and everything living froze' (Jung 2009: 299).

In face of this apparently total loss of meaning, the *Red Book* asserts that we build the road by going on; that our life is the truth that we seek. We create the truth by living it. While there may be no distinctions in primal chaos, we grow if we stand still in the greatest doubt and therefore steadfastness in great doubt is a veritable flower of life.

The onward journey

To the end, Jung was preoccupied with God. In a passage which seems to encapsulate the meaning of Jung's internal struggle to achieve a working distance from God, he wrote:

> in the first instance the God's power resides entirely in the self, since the self is completely in the God, because we were not with the self. We must draw the self to our side. Therefore we must wrestle with the God for the self. Since the God is an unfathomable powerful movement that sweeps away the self into the boundless, into dissolution.
>
> Hence when the God appears to us we are at first powerless, captivated, divided, sick, poisoned with the strongest poison, but drunk with the highest health.
>
> We must strive to free the self from the God, so that we can live.
>
> (Jung 2009: 338f)

These sentences suggest a desperate developmental struggle to achieve separation and individuation from a primal other. Freud would doubtless have interpreted Jung's dilemma in terms of his oedipal struggle with his father, whereas Jung was aware that his fundamental problem lay in relation to his mother.[26] As I read the *Red Book*, Jung's constant resort to archetypal, rather than personal, language was, at least in part, driven by his need to relate his personal experience to universal themes. Had he kept it on the personal level it might either have overwhelmed him or led to the banality of reductive interpretation he so greatly feared. In words that might serve as Jung's *credo*, he wrote:

> I daily weigh up my whole life and I continue to regard the fiery brilliance of the God as a higher and fuller life than the ashes of rationality. The ashes are suicide to me. I could perhaps put out the fire but I cannot deny to myself the experience of the God. Nor can I cut myself off from this experience. I also do not want to, since I want to live. My life wants itself whole
>
> . . . the God I experienced is more than love; he is also hate, he is more than beauty, he is also the abomination, he is more than wisdom, he is also meaninglessness, he is more than power, he is also powerlessness, he is more than omnipresence, he is also my creature.
>
> (Jung 2009: 339)

The *Red Book* is not so much an evasion of personal analysis as Jung's mighty attempt to free himself from being enslaved to God and to establish himself on sounder foundations than he was able to achieve in childhood. In this sense the *Red Book* is indeed an engagement with the madness of his inner world. Looked at this way, Jung's whole psychological enterprise is about the self-redemption of the self. Not exorcising or denying God, but seeking to establish the self at a safe distance from God, who may also be the mother whose terrifyingly dual nature is described in *Memories, Dreams, Reflections* (Jung 1963), and given greater psychological objectivity in chapter 7 of *Psychology of the Unconscious*, aptly titled 'The Dual Mother Rôle' (Jung 1991: 294–368).

Discussion

What might Dr Jung, the psychiatrist, have made of the *Red Book* had it been the work of a patient? By happy chance we have two papers, both addressing psychotic processes, read by Jung to medical audiences in Aberdeen and London in July 1914. Although he does not refer to his then ongoing self-analysis, these contemporary papers provide the theoretical rationale that must have informed his approach to his own internal world. *On the Importance of the Unconscious in Psychopathology* (Jung 1960) begins by suggesting that the function of the unconscious is to compensate for the one sidedness of our conscious attitudes and opinions.[27] This process can be seen at work in the parapraxes highlighted by Freud and in dreams. In more severe forms of mental disturbance, though, the sufferer refuses 'to recognise the compensating influence which comes from the unconscious' (Jung 1960: 207), with the result that when unconscious material finally erupts into consciousness it comes clothed in the language of the unconscious.

> Such material includes all those forgotten infantile fantasies which have ever entered into the minds of men, and of which only legends and myths remain . . . [such] material is frequently found in dementia praecox.
>
> (Jung 1960: 209)

Perhaps this is a sober reference to the dead who stalk Jung through the pages of the *Red Book*, and an acknowledgment that the archetypal nature of the material that erupted during Jung's confrontation with the unconscious was due to the fact that for too long he refused to recognise the compensating influence which comes from the unconscious.

In *On Psychological Understanding* (Jung 1960), Jung comments on Freud's study of Schreber's *Memoirs of my Nervous Illness* (Schreber 2000).[28] While conceding that Freud had been able to suggest a plausible oedipal interpretation of Schreber's delusions, Jung felt he had failed adequately to engage with Schreber's enormous symbolic creativity (Jung 1960). A reductive approach to Goethe's *Faust* would yield similar results, but the point of reading *Faust* is not to learn how 'Goethe deals with these human banalities', but 'how he redeems his soul from bondage to them' (Jung 1960: 180).[29] In place of Freud's 'retrospective understanding', Jung was seeking a 'prospective understanding', through the application of what he called his 'constructive method' (Jung 1960: 181). Applied to *Faust*, this would demonstrate how Faust redeems himself as an individual. In this way, we will have '*understood ourselves* with the help of *Faust*' (Jung 1960: 181; my emphasis). In the *Red Book* Jung is clearly attempting to redeem himself by means of his creative and symbolic capacity. In his opinion, subjective creation is a means of redemption, and he quotes Nietzsche as his authority for saying that 'Creation – that is the great redemption from suffering; that is the ease of living' (Jung 1960: 186).

Interestingly, by inviting us to discover the meaning of *Faust* through evaluating our subjective reactions to it, Jung is anticipating psychoanalytic ideas about the positive value of the counter transference by several decades. He is also indicating his belief that 'subjective creation' – as in the *Red Book* – might offer a path towards redemption. As he sees it, the psyche is the point of intersection between two points of view. On the one hand, it contains the remnants and traces of previous human development, pointing towards universal principles of human psychology. On the other hand, it can outline what is to come, in so far as the psyche creates its own future. Applied to psychiatric work, the crucial question is what goal is the patient trying to reach through the creation of what may appear to be a psychotic system? Two things stand out: the patient is aiming at something, and he devotes all his willpower to the completion of his system (Jung 1960: 186). Instead of offering reductive interpretations, Jung's concern was to understand the patient's fantasy system in terms of its typical components, as he had done with the Miller fantasies. What we know in the present state of our knowledge, says Jung, is that pathological and mythological formations are unconscious creations and that myths furnish useful material for comparative study of delusional systems (Jung 1960). Then, in a most significant passage, he writes:

> Closer study of Schreber's or any similar case will show that these patients are consumed by a desire to create a new world system, or what we call a Weltanschauung, often of the most bizarre kind. Their aim is obviously to create a system that will enable them to assimilate unknown psychic phenomena and so adapt themselves to their own world.
>
> (Jung 1960: 188)

When we consider the contents of the *Red Book* we can see that Jung was himself in search of a new *Weltanschauung*; one that would honour the mythological outpourings of the unconscious, but in a scientifically acceptable way. The dilemma of modern men and women, Jung felt, was that, although our psyche is invincibly mythological/religious, we can no longer fall back uncritically on the great religious traditions of the past. Instead, we have to find new ways of relating to the myth-making potential of the unconscious, or risk living a dangerously unbalanced life of hyper-consciousness, which invites a compensatory incursion by unconscious forces. As the twentieth century wore on, Jung saw the vast collective madnesses enacted by the communist and fascist states as evidence of the correctness of this view. Jung was not sanguine about psychosis; he knew how destructive mental illness can be. But he also believed that a patient's intense preoccupation with his apparently bizarre system of thought could be seen as the first stage in the normal creative process in an introverted personality. Introverts, like Jung, look for the solution to the world's problems within themselves. Through introspection they can assimilate precious unconscious contents; but they have then to bring the fruit of their introspection into relation with outer reality. Creative breakthroughs in scientific thought have occasionally been heralded by dreams, but the dilemma of the psychiatric patient is that he:

> remains stuck in this [introverted] stage and substitutes his subjective formulation for the real world – which is precisely why he remains ill. He cannot free himself from his subjectivism and therefore does not establish any connection with objective thinking and with human society.
>
> (Jung 1960: 189)

Listening to these words in July 1914, the members of the Psycho-Medical Society of London could have had no idea that Dr Jung, so poised, professional and eloquent by day, was, by night, immersed in the most extraordinary conversations with the inhabitants of his inner world. As we know, it was not until 1930 that Jung felt able to abandon work on his *Red Book*. He did this when his researches into alchemy finally provided, to his satisfaction, external confirmation that his inner formulations were not simply the messianic or artistic creations of a mad professor, but that he had accurately intuited the archetypal structures of the unconscious mind. He quotes Feuerbach: 'understanding is real and effective only when it is in accord with that of other reasonable beings. Then it becomes objective and connects with life' (Jung 1960: 189). For Jung, the alchemists were the other reasonable beings who provided the connection between his labours in the *Red Book* and the external world.

Jung's divine madness

Virginia Woolf once wrote, 'Madness is terrific I can assure you, and not to be sniffed at; and in its lava I still find most of the things I write about' (Dunn 2000: 251). Carl Jung and Daniel Paul Schreber both recorded their experiences of divine madness, but only Schreber insisted on publishing his work – believing it to be literally true. Jung was more circumspect, being

72

more aware of the symbolic and psychological factors at work in his creation. Because of this, he was able to develop valuable insights into the archetypal dimension of the psyche. Depth psychology as a whole, though, continues to suffer from the rift between Jung and Freud. As Donald Winnicott wrote:

> Freud's flight to sanity could be something we psychoanalysts are trying to recover from, just as Jungians are trying to recover from Jung's 'divided self,' and from the way he . . . dealt with it.
>
> (Winnicott 1989: 483)

It is one of history's more poignant ironies that the one person who might have been able to bridge the gulf between Jung and Freud, at a theoretical, if not at a personal level – the person who made original contributions to both Jung's and Freud's theoretical understandings, but has only recently been recognised as the brilliantly original mind she undoubtedly was – was Sabina Spielrein (Cifali 2001).

In Winnicott's (1989) mature judgment, Jung was a case of childhood schizophrenia who managed to heal himself. This was an astonishing achievement. But, even those like Judge Schreber, whose madness remains unhealed, can also be inspired. In his book *My Own Private Germany, Daniel Paul Schreber's Secret History of Modernity,* Eric Santner (1996) summarises the work of scholars who have charted profound connections between Schreber's writings and the social and political fantasies undergirding Naziism. And Santner argues that, although Schreber was blind to the political significance of his ideas, he was right to believe in their importance, because they represented a form of insight into the profound malfunctions that underlay the politico theological structure of the Nazi state.

If Schreber achieved this, then his madness was indeed divine. Sadly, just as utterances of the Delphic Oracle and the priestesses of Dodona were difficult to understand, so the tragedy of Schreber's *Memoirs* is that no one was able to comprehend the warning they contained. Jung's achievement, on the other hand – and this was his life's work – was to transmute the divine madness of the *Red Book* into coherent psychological and psychotherapeutic perspectives which continue to offer profound insight into the common wellsprings of psychosis, creativity and spiritual experience.

Notes

1 Jung (2009: 8f.).

2 In Jung's terminology the shadow represents those aspects of the self that have not yet been brought into the light of consciousness or are actively occluded by that light.

3 An example of Jung's crusading attitude in defence of psychoanalysis, in a letter to Freud: 'I was amazed by your news. The adventure with "Schottländer" is marvellous; of course the slimy bastard was lying. I hope you roasted, flayed, and

impaled the fellow with such genial ferocity that he got a lasting taste for once of the effectiveness of psycho-analysis. I subscribe to your final judgment with all my heart. Such is the nature of these beasts. Since I could read the filth in him from his face I would have gone for his throat. I hope to God you told him all the truths so plainly that even his hen's brain could absorb them. Now we shall see what his next coup will be. Had I been in your shoes I would have softened up his guttersnipe complex with a sound Swiss thrashing' (Freud and Jung 1974: 325).

4 The recovery of the Holy Grail, traditionally understood to have been the chalice used by Christ at the Last Supper, was the goal of the Grail knights' quest of medieval legend. In Jung's more developed psychological thinking the Holy Grail stands for the (unachievable) goal of individuation: the complete realisation of all the conscious and unconscious aspects of our being.

5 Jung was well aware that repressed contents can behave in extremely dynamic ways. What he is beginning to suspect here, though, is that there might be a genuinely transpersonal presence in his psyche. In this dream, the white bird appears to be the harbinger of Jung's soul (Jung 2009: 264).

6 Jung's fear was that his immensely strong intellectual defences might be masking an underlying psychosis, which could erupt and overwhelm him.

7 Alchemists are popularly thought of as primitive chemists, who tried to turn base matter into gold. Studying their texts, though, Jung realised that their chemistry, in which the elements are personified, was actually a wonderfully rich, pre-psychological, description of unconscious processes projected into matter. In Jung's view, though, and as the more enlightened alchemists themselves realised, the true purpose of their experiments was not the creation of precious metal but personal transformation. Discovering their works convinced Jung that his was not an isolated venture, but part of a centuries-long tradition of understanding and research.

8 Isaiah 53: 1-4; Isaiah 9: 6; John 1: 14 and Isaiah 35: 1–8.

9 He was born on 26 July 1875.

10 Jung resigned as President of the International Psychoanalytic Association on 20 April 1914 and from his post as Privatdocent in the medical faculty of Zürich University on 30 April of the same year (Freud and Jung 1974: 358 and n.2). The *Jahrbuch*, to which Jung refers in this letter, was the *Jahrbuch für psychoanalytische und psychopathologische Forschungen*: the official journal of the psychoanalytic movement between 1909 and 1914.

11 On Jung's use of the word 'soul': Jung tells us that while recording these fantasies he heard a woman's voice (in his mind) saying, 'It is art.' He took such exception to this that, when the comment came again, he said, 'No, it is not art! On the contrary, it is nature.' Intrigued by the fact that a woman should interfere with him from within, he decided that she must be the soul, in a primitive sense. From these early experiences he derived the idea that the soul or anima, the counter-sexual principle in men, plays an archetypal role in male psychology; just as the animus plays a corresponding role in the psychology of women (Jung 1963: 178f.).

12 Jung once defined dreams as 'a spontaneous self-portrayal, in symbolic form, of the actual situation in the unconscious' (Jung 1969a: 263). In his opinion, dreams tend to compensate for the one-sidedness of our conscious perceptions and can be interpreted both from a causal and a purposive point of view. From the latter perspective, dreams may be said to determine us because they can point to an altered psychological situation, which has yet to impinge on our conscious understanding (Jung 1969a: 246). According to Jung, Freud's approach to dreams

was partial, because he restricted himself to a causal, reductive point of view (Samuels, Shorter and Plaut 1986).

13 Richard Noll insightfully comments about this tendency in Jung: 'By reframing his experience as a way of suffering for the good of humanity rather than just over, "the debris of my former relationships," indeed by seeing the universal in the particular, Jung healed himself' (Noll 1994: 207).

14 If there is an historical parallel, I am reminded of Teresa of Avila and her Carmelite sisters. In the sixteenth century, while her compatriots the *conquistadores* were seeking to subjugate the populations of Central and South America in their lust for gold, Teresa and her companions chose to face the dangers of their interior castles, seeking an inner spiritual treasure rather than an earthly one. But, poor as they were and few in number, Teresa's sisters at least had each other for support. Jung's *Red Book* appears to chart a very solitary journey.

15 Even in 1928, when he was completing the *Red Book*, Jung could write: 'By temperament I despise the "personal", any kind of "togetherness", but it is so strong a force, this whole crushing unspiritual weight of the earth, that I fear it. It can rouse my body to revolt against the spirit, so that before reaching the zenith of my flight I fall lamed to earth' (Jung 1973: 49).

16 Siegfried or Sigurd, was the legendary dragon-slaying hero of the *Nibelungenlied*.

17 That is for gold: the alchemical quest!

18 The primary documents are reprinted in Carotenuto (1984) and in the *Journal of Analytical Psychology* 46(1). I am grateful to Mrs Hester Solomon for drawing my attention to the themes of Wagner's opera and Jung's relationship with Sabina Spielrein.

19 Cf. Jung (2009: 231, 245 and 244, n.137).

20 At the end of *Liber Primus*, Jung writes, 'The symbol of the crystal signifies the unalterable law of events that comes of itself. In this seed you grasp what is to come' (Jung 2009: 254). See also Jung (2009: 239).

21 These thoughts that are outside ourselves are reminiscent of Bion's 'wild thoughts', such as dream-thoughts, or intrauterine thoughts, where there is no possibility of being able to trace immediately any kind of ownership or even any sort of way of being aware of the genealogy of that particular thought (Bion 1997: 27).

22 This lion-headed god encircled by a snake was a Mithraic deity, called Aion, or the eternal being (Jung 1990: 98). He is pictured in the frontispiece of Jung's book *Aion* (Jung 1968). Mrs Hester Solomon comments, 'Jung was born on 26th July so, astrologically, it makes him a Leo, or lion and indeed he was "lion headed", physically and psychologically. Aion is an apt self-image' (private communication).

23 As described above, the conflict between love and power was evident in Jung's turmoil over the sacrifice of Siegfried.

24 *The Imitation of Christ* was an extremely popular work of Christian devotion, usually attributed to Thomas à Kempis (1380–1471).

25 Cf. Jung (2009: 295).

26 'The conjecture that I have succumbed to a personal complex does indeed spring to mind when one knows that I am a clergyman's son. However, I had a good relationship with my father, so no "father complex" of the ordinary sort. True, I didn't like theology because it set my father problems which *he* couldn't solve and which *I* felt unjustified. On the other hand, I grant you my personal mother complex' (Jung 1976: 65).

27 First read to the Neurology and Psychological Medicine Section of the British Medical Association, at the British Medical Association's Annual Meeting held in Aberdeen, in July 1914.

28 A lecture delivered to the Psycho-Medical Society, London, in July 1914.

29 Again, we might note Jung's determination to escape the 'banality of life' (Jung 1963: 161).

References

Bion, W. (1997). *Taming Wild Thoughts*. London: Karnac Books.

Carotenuto, A. (1984). *A Secret Symmetry, Sabina Spielrein between Jung and Freud*. London: Routledge and Kegan Paul.

Cifali, M. (2001). Sabina Spielrein, a woman psychoanalyst: another picture. *Journal of Analytical Psychology* 46(1): 129–138.

Dodds, E.R. (1951). *The Greeks and the Irrational*. Berkeley and Los Angeles: University of California Press.

Dunn, J. (2000). *Virginia Woolf and Vanessa Bell: A Very Close Conspiracy*. London: Virago Press.

Freud, S. and Jung, C. (1974). *The Freud/Jung Letters: The Correspondence between Sigmund Freud and C.G. Jung*, ed. W. McGuire, trans. R. Manheim and R.F.C. Hull. London: Hogarth Press/Routledge and Kegan Paul.

Henderson, D. (2010). The coincidence of opposites, C.G. Jung's reception of Nicholas of Cusa. *Studies in Spirituality* 20: 101–13.

Jung, C.G. (1925). *VII Sermones ad Mortuos*. London: John M. Watkins.

Jung, C. (1960). *The Psychogenesis of Mental Disease. Collected Works*, vol. 3, ed. H. Read, M. Fordham, G. Adler and W. McGuire. London: Routledge and Kegan Paul.

Jung, C.G. (1963). *Memories, Dreams, Reflections: Recorded and Edited by Aniela Jaffé*, trans. R. Winston and C. Winston. London: Collins/Routledge and Kegan Paul.

Jung, C.G. (1967). *Alchemical Studies. Collected Works*, vol. 13, ed. H. Read, M. Fordham, G. Adler and W. McGuire. London: Routledge and Kegan Paul.

Jung, C.G. (1968). *Aion, Researches into the Phenomenology of the Self. C.G. Jung Collected Works*, vol. 9(ii), ed. H. Read, M. Fordham, G. Adler and W. McGuire. London: Routledge and Kegan Paul.

Jung, C.G. (1969a). *The Structure and Dynamics of the Psyche Collected Works*, vol. 8, ed. H. Read, M. Fordham, G. Adler and W. McGuire. London: Routledge and Kegan Paul.

Jung, C.G. (1969b). *Psychology and Religion: West and East. Collected Works*, vol. 11, ed. H. Read, M. Fordham, G. Adler and W. McGuire. London: Routledge and Kegan Paul.

Jung, C.G. (1973). *Letters, Volume 1: 1906–1950*, ed. G. Adler and A. Jaffé, trans. R.F.C. Hull. London: Routledge and Kegan Paul.

Jung, C.G. (1976). *Letters, Volume 2: 1951–1961*, ed. G. Adler and A. Jaffé, trans. R.F.C. Hull. London: Routledge and Kegan Paul.

Jung, C. (1990). *Analytical Psychology: Notes of the Seminar Given in 1925*, ed. W. McGuire. London: Routledge and Kegan Paul.

Jung, C.G. (1991). *Psychology of the Unconscious: A Study of the Transformations and Symbolisms of the Libido: A Contribution to the History of the Evolution of Thought*, trans. B.M. Hinkle. London: Routledge.

Jung, C.G. (2001). The Letters of C.G. Jung to Sabina Spielrein. *Journal of Analytical Psychology* 46: 173–199.

Jung, C.G. (2009). *The Red Book, Liber Novus*, ed. S. Shamdasani. New York and London: Norton and Company.

McCormick, K. (2001). Biographical note. *Journal of Analytical Psychology* 46: 13–14.

Nietzsche, F. (1974). *The Gay Science with a Prelude in Rhymes and an Appendix of Songs*, trans. W. Kaufmann. New York: Random House.

Noll, R. (1994). *The Jung Cult, Origins of a Charismatic Movement*. New Jersey: Princeton University Press.

Samuels, A., Shorter, B. and Plaut, F. (1986). *A Critical Dictionary of Jungian Analysis*. London: Routledge and Kegan Paul.

Santner, E.L. (1996). *My Own Private Germany, Daniel Paul Schreber's Secret History of Modernity*. Princeton: Princeton University Press.

Schreber, D.P. (2000). *Memoirs of my Nervous Illness*. New York: New York Review of Books.

Winnicott, D.W. (1989). *Psycho-Analytic Explorations*, ed. C. Winnicott, R. Shepherd and M. Davis. London: Karnac Books.

Part 2

ANTHROPOLOGY, HISTORY AND HAGIOGRAPHY

The Stoics, for instance, declared explicitly that philosophy, for them, was an 'exercise'. In their view, philosophy did not consist in teaching an abstract theory – much less in the exegesis of texts – but rather in the art of living . . . it is a progress which causes us to *be* more fully, and makes us better. It is a conversion which turns our entire lives upside down, changing the life of the person who goes through it.

(Hadot 2008: 82–3)

INTRODUCTION TO PART 2

Conversion and the fragmented body

John Gale

In antiquity we find two quite different descriptions of conversion: one dramatic, the other ascetic. The first is known in Greek as *metanoia*, which becomes largely a Christian term, the second as *epistrophē*. In its original sense, *metanoia* means a change of mind or even an afterthought (Liddell and Scott 1863); later it refers to the related notion of repentance or penitence; and later still to prostration as an act of penance (Lampe 1961). In its primary sense it is characterised by a momentary realisation, a sudden and dramatic event. Horace tells us how he was converted by a sudden thunderclap in a clear sky. Dramatic conversions of this kind were often marked by visions (Nock 1933) – Valentinus saw the logos under the form of a newly born baby – auditory hallucinations and a new treatment of language which included unusual figures of speech, turning words round (de Certeau 2006) and the rapid formation of sentences (Underhill 1911). Examples proliferate in biblical and in secular literature throughout the centuries culminating in the period from the twelfth to the seventeenth centuries. Teresa of Avila's works abound with references to visions and most notably to three distinct types of *hablas* (voices) – translated in English rather quaintly as 'locutions'. When a person's fears assume hallucinatory qualities, they may be described as religious in the original sense of the Latin *religio*, which indicates an uneasy fear of the supernatural. *Religio* is connected to the verb *religare*, *religo*, an emotional misgiving that somehow binds or restrains a person. Hence, *religio* comes to mean a pious scruple about doing something.[1] This, as Freud was vividly aware, brings religion structurally near to an obsessional neurosis.

Metanoia amounts to a violent break for the subject – we might even say breakdown. Following dramatic experiences like this, the newly reborn feel they have been converted, once and for all. The work has been done and the slate wiped clean. It is as if everything previously known to the convert ceases to exist. Freud described the work of delusional formation (*Wahnbildungsarbeit*) functioning in much the same way. This sudden and complete conversion often corresponds to a change of identity in which a crisis in a person's life, a psychic catastrophe, is somehow resolved. Thus conversion (*metanoia*) may be an attempt to rebuild meaning and restore equilibrium by blocking off archaic, inner conflicts that surfaced in the crisis (Salonen 1989). Here we see both dramatic conversion and psychotic delusion working to hold the subject's world together in an attempt at recovery and reconstruction. Like the delusions of someone experiencing psychosis, the beliefs of the 'born again' may well be important attempts to make the unbearable bearable. Augustine, insightful as ever, knew that no such dramatic experience could so easily free him from his past identity. 'When you hear a man confessing' he wrote, 'you know that he is not yet free' (Brown 2000: 171).

Epistrophē (from the verb *epistrephein* – to turn around, pay attention to) describes a very different experience. It has its roots in the *Timaeus* and becomes something of a technical term in Neo-Platonism. Despite its pagan origin, it is used extensively in the patristic era to indicate a religious conversion. It is more or less equivalent to the expression *conversatio morum* as we find it in late Latin[2] and indicates a change of activity which results in a gradual reorientation in the relationship a person has with himself. When Epictetus speaks, for example, of *epistrophē eis heauton* (conversion to oneself), it implies a shift to a more ascetic lifestyle that has as its goal the cultivation of systematic introspection in order to gain access to aspects of oneself previously out of sight (Foucault 1984). In this sense conversion (*epistrophē*) amounts to a form of self-care, the adoption of a lifestyle that privileges a particular kind of knowledge, akin to what Lacan refers to as *savoir* and which he distinguishes from an imaginary understanding or flawed recognition. The continuing nature of this form of conversion is emphasised in Latin where *conversatio* is linked to *processus* (advance, progress), in which the kind of knowledge that is gained is a form of psychological insight. This is not something acquired through study but from recollection or turning to one's memory (*memoria*). The change of direction in life that is marked by *epistrophē* may make it appear somehow mundane because, rather than being enunciated in a new doctrine, it is manifested in seemingly insignificant yet concrete changes in the subject's life such as diet, timetable and form of dress. That is to say, it is characterised by a behavioural change rather than a cognitive one. These changes in life style are not the conversion itself but merely the beginning of a process (*askēsis tēs psuchēs*) in which the subject changes his focus of attention onto himself and every aspect of his way of life (Foucault 2001; cf. Lacan 1999).[3] This new focus is directed towards an inner shift from an inauthentic life, darkened by unconsciousness, to authenticity (Dodds 1965). If we are to believe Pierre Hadot (1953) this draws a person face to face with their unconscious and in this sense a religious conversion may already come close to an analysis (Marcus 2003) because it involves working through or working over of psychic material (*memoria*) through a protracted period of time. It is this turning inward, *eis to eisō* (into the inside), to use Plotinus' idiom,[4] that becomes with Augustine the experience of conversion in the West (Bochet 2003) and paves the way for the development of the intellectual climate in which psychoanalysis emerges.

We encounter *epistrophē* vividly in the tantric tradition of asceticism. Here, we find a way of life that dramatically challenges our conceptions of sanity and madness. Leaving society, the *sannyasi* dons the *kavi* (habit), goes barefoot, sits on the floor and renounces the symbolic. Even in the context of Hinduism his behaviour seems bizarre, if not meaningless. It would be easy to read this as an instance of the enactment of unconscious fantasies and parallels can be seen in the case studies of psychotic patients (Jackson 2001). But what marks the life of the saddhu is repetition or recollection and the passing of time. Not in a pathological sense but in the way in which recollection was used in classical antiquity to denote a lifetime of re-evaluation of what has passed and of that which is present. It is a way of coming to terms with oneself, through an understanding of what has formed us. The changes that take place are real enough but the lifestyle remains constant. The *Gita* also falls within the discourse of *epistrophē*. That is to say, the transformation that is described in the text is an ascetic conversion, hence its emphasis on action – what to do – in which Arjuna grapples with his desire in the quest for self-understanding.

Imagos of fragmentation

Hagiography favoured stories of exorcism because they emphasised the power of the saint. And, for an exorcism you need a demonic possession. The exorcism functioned like a psychodrama – often drawn out with periods of relapse – in which the 'unhinged' worked through his or her inner psychological torment with the saint (Horden 1993: 180). In other words, the encounter was critical. But there were instances in classical antiquity, as well as in medieval Islam (Dols 1987) and in the early Byzantine world, of chronic mental disturbance that 'no psychodrama could alleviate' (Horden 1993: 180).[5] The distinction between the possessed and the insane was clear enough in Byzantium. Chrysostom was able to distinguish between endogenous depression (*athumia*) and demonic possession, and Augustine between possession and *phreneticus*, the medical term for insanity (Horden 1993: 186). Gregory the Great, writing in the 590s CE, speaks of the cure of a *freneticus* (madman) who was a patient in a house for the sick.

When we think of the mystics, we tend to think of characters from the sixteenth century, but mystical literature does not begin there (de Certeau 1982). In fact, its origins go back at least to Palladius' account, written in 420 CE, of a nun who was *salē* (Butler 1904) 'for thus they style the mentally afflicted' (Lowther Clarke 1918: 119). *Sale* is an obscure term but one that may come from the Syriac *sakla*, which had been used to translate the Greek word *mōros* (fools or dull of mind) in a passage from 1 Cor. 4.10.[6] It refers to a person in a state of agitation, trouble, tumult (Špidlík 1964);[7] an imbecile, someone half-witted or mad (Lampe 1961) but who, nevertheless, was thought to be the recipient of supernatural revelations. From the fourth century in Egypt, to the fifth and sixth centuries in Syria and Mesopotamia, right up to nineteenth-century Russia, a host of mad ascetics appear (Špiklík 1964).[8] It is perhaps partly in this tradition of spiritual insanity that the vita of Francis of Assisi is best read. His conversion, at the age of 25, was marked by a series of visions, physical illness and depression. Undressing in the crowded square in Assisi, he cultivated an unkempt appearance and announced that his father was no longer his father. The details of Francis' conversion bear considerable resemblance to that of the Wolf-Man, one of Freud's famous patients, who also went through a religious conversion and dramatically broke off his relationship with his father. The Wolf-Man was about the same age when he came to Freud as Francis was at the time of his conversion. In both cases physical illness seems to have triggered some kind of breakdown, which in the case of the Wolf-Man, Freud understood as a blow to narcissism (Yarom 1992). His symptoms included masochism and compulsively performed religious rituals. Freud found the key to understanding the Wolf-Man's disorder through a dream which revealed a deep-seated fear of his father and of castration.

However, it would be simplistic to imagine that the distinction between *metanoia* and *epistrophē* was, in practice, so clear cut. In the account of Francis' life written by Thomas of Celano, we see hagiography functioning at different levels. As well as remembering a man's life, it also idealises it in its use of repetition, in its resistances and in its adherence to a scriptural typology. In doing so a new mythology is articulated in which the historical takes on a vertical dimension. In this sense the narrative can be described as the origin of the life of the saint. It is a structural foundation in which 'language *is* conversion' (Harpham 1987: 104). Despite her repetitive references to experiences of *arrobamiento* (rapture), *arrebatamiento* (transport), *amortecimento* (swooning), *elevamiento* and *levantamiento* (elevation) and *embebecimiento* (absorbtion), following her second conversion in 1555, which took place as she read Augustine's *Confessions*, Teresa of Avila lived, as did Francis of Assisi, a largely mundane life albeit one dramatically changed. While sharing many of the features and phenomena of psychosis – notably an unshakable certainty, hallucinations, voices and idiosyncratic figures of speech – the perceptions and beliefs of Teresa and Francis were inscribed socially. That is to say, they were part of a shared discourse and as such they were contained within the confines of a defined syntax which regulated what de Certeau (1987) describes as the collective imaginary.

For Francis, the crisis of conversion is the reverse image of another major event in his life – the stigmata – a symptom for which there was no organic cause. Here conversion becomes a mechanism of symptom formation. In fact Freud introduces the term conversion (*Konversion*) in the *Studies on Hysteria* in the case history of Frau Emmy von N. The question being framed concerns the symptom articulated in relation to an imaginary anatomy and not only the historical development of symptomatology (Foucault 1961). Here, psychic, inner conflict – including repressed ideas, and its attempted resolution – is transposed onto the medium of the body (Laplanche and Pontalis 1985). This poses a fundamental question concerning the subject's sexual position (Yarom 1992).

Freud, having studied under Jean-Martin Charcot, developed psychoanalysis around his work with hysterical patients like Dora, a 16-year-old girl whom he treated for just two months towards the end of 1900.[9] Dora's symptoms included aphonia, depression and thoughts of suicide (Didi-Huberman 2012). At the Salpêtrière, Freud saw many more extreme cases of hysteria. Indeed, just two years before he arrived in 1885, Louise Lateau, a famous Belgium stigmatic, had died there.[10] She had been examined by one of Charcot's colleagues, Désiré-Magloire Bourneville, at the time the stigmata appeared (Bourneville 1875). Hustvedt (2011) argues that by not dismissing Lateau as a fraud, as other doctors had done, Bourneville shifted the conceptual framework for understanding her symptoms.

As with Freud, Lacan's theory of hysteria revolves around the inner conflict of sexuality. Both regarded hysteria as one of the two main forms of neurosis – the other being obsession. In the neuroses the question which haunts the subject is the question of death. What is the meaning of my existence given the inescapable fact that my life is going to end? In obsessional neurosis the subject works frenetically to justify his or her existence by somehow making life seem worthwhile. This also explains the central place of guilt and fear of future catastrophe, frequently found in obsessive-compulsive disorder. Freud had described how one of his obsessional patients, whom he called the Rat Man, performed compulsive rituals in order to protect his father from punishment. These rituals suggested to Freud that there was probably a link to be found between obsessional neurosis and religious practice. In the neuroses, symptoms function as an alternative language in which those things that have been the subject of repression are somehow expressed or spoken physically. Lacan argued that what differentiates the two forms of neurosis is the fundamental question they pose for the subject. Commenting on the two dreams which form the core of the 'fragment of a case' which was Dora (Gay 2006: 246) and on Dora's identification with Herr K, Lacan concluded that hysteria concerns the question of sexual identity. Lacan links this to his notion of the *corps morcelé*, the fragmented body which is the other side of the mirror image. In the mirror, the infant sees itself as whole and this contrasts with his own, uncoordinated body (Dolto 1961). The anxiety caused by this dichotomy generates the construction of an image of the body's totality, in the form of the synthesis of the ego (Shentoub 1963) – which is fundamentally an alter ego – and thus essentially alienated (Lacan 1981). Yet the ego remains haunted by the primitive terror of 'imagos of the fragmented body' – images of castration, mutilation, dismemberment, evisceration and of the body bursting open – which appear in hallucinations, dreams and associations (Lacan 2006: 85). This fragmented body 'appears in the form of disconnected limbs . . . that define the hysteric's fantasmatic anatomy which is manifested in schizoid and spasmodic symptoms' (Lacan 2006: 78). This is to speak of the body as distinct from the organism, as a compound of identifications and the first signifier. That is, not in relation to the physiological structure of the nervous system but to the way the body is broken up in fantasy. In order for the body, in this sense, to acquire meaning for the subject, 'it must first have had significance for the mother' (Prado de Oliveira 2001: 132).

The fragmentation of which Lacan speaks and which has its counterpart in Kleinian theory is the fragmentation of the self, as well as of others, and is a characteristic unconscious mechanism found in psychosis (Lacan 1981; cf. Pankow 1956). Schreber recounted hallucinations in which he lived for years without a stomach, intestines, lungs or bladder, and with shattered ribs and a torn oesophagus. From this, Deleuze argues, the psychotic body is, par excellence, a body devoid of organs (Deleuze and Guattari 1980) or, perhaps more exactly, a body lacking the sense of unification that derives from the ego.

Notes

1 In Greek *eusebeia* (reverence towards the gods), *hosiotēs* (disposition to observe divine laws) and *eulabaia* (the character and conduct of discretion, caution, reverence and piety) are the words most frequently used to describe religion.

2 The word *conversatio* is from the root *converti, convertere* (to turn). In monastic literature from the fourth through to the sixth centuries it meant following an ascetic observance, rule of life or, as we would say, lifestyle.

3 In Gregory of Nyssa we find the Christian way of life described in exactly the same terms as the earlier pagan philosophic life (*ho kata philosophian* or *philosophos bios*). Cf. W. Jaeger (1954), *Two Rediscovered Works of Ancient Christian Literature: Gregory of Nyssa and Macarius*, Leiden: E.J. Brill, p. 82, and *Early Christianity and Greek Paideia* Cambridge, MA: Belknap Press of Harvard University Press, p. 90 and p. 141 n. 9.

4 Enneads 1: 6.8. This is from a passage of Plotinus' treatise *On Beauty*, which Augustine interweaves with the parable of the prodigal son in the Confessions 1: 28 and 8: 19. See Cary (2000: 159 n.25).

5 Although in ancient Rome there were examples of hospitals for slaves and for soldiers, it was in late antiquity that a revolution occurred in the medical scene with the proliferation of hospitals. This brought those with a psychosis within the scope of medical care (Van Minnen 1995). According to Grey (2005), these establishments, frequently run by monasteries (Crislip 2005) and based initially on the monastic infirmary (Horden 2005), looked after and treated those 'who might now be diagnosed as insane, epileptic or mentally ill' or with conditions we would label 'psychosis or schizophrenia' (Grey 2005: 43, 47). However, it was recognised that most conditions, mental as well as physical, could have a number of sources including the environment and that 'by no means all serious mental disorders' including psychosis would have been interpreted as demonic in character (Horden 1993: 186). Cf. P. Van Minnen (1995), Medical care in late antiquity, *Clio medica* 27: 153–69; A.T. Crislip (2005), *From Monastery to Hospital:*

Christian Monasticism and the Transformation of Health Care in Late Antiquity. Michigan: University of Michigan Press; P. Horden (2005), The earliest hospitals in Byzantium, Western Europe, and Islam, *Journal of Interdisciplinary History* 35(3): 361–89; C. Grey (2005), Demoniacs, dissent, and disempowerment in the Late Roman West: Some case studies from the hagiographical literature, *Journal of Early Christian Studies* 13(1): 39–69.

6 Špidlík's (1964) derivation of *salos* from the Syriac was repeated by Bartelink in 1974 but Guillaumont remained unconvinced. Cf. G.J.M. Bartelink (1985; orig. 1974), *Palladio. La Storia Lausiaca*, Milan: Arnoldo Mondadori Editore, p. 363 n. 32 and A. Guillaumont (1996; orig. 1984), La folie simulée, une forme d'anachorèse, *Études sur la Spiritualité de l'Orient Chrétien*, Bégrolles-en-Mauges: Abbaye de Bellefontaine, pp. 125–30.

7 Draguet, in his translation of the Syriac Lausiac History, has 'elle se faisait folle' and 'elle est agitée' – cf. R. Draguet (1978), *Les Formes syriaques de la matière de l'Histoire Lausiaque,* Louvain: Corpus Scriptorum Christianorum Orientalium, vol. 2, pp. 164, 166.

8 There are a vast number of primary sources which describe this phenomenon as well as contemporary studies, the most up-to-date literature review and summary being J.-C. Larchet's (1992), *Thérapeutique des maladies mentales. L'expérience de l'Orient chrétien des premiers siècles.* Paris: Les Éditions du Cerf.

9 Bakan (1958) had thought, perhaps rather fancifully – but nevertheless delightfully – that Freud might have intended by Dora to indicate the word Torah (the Pentateuch). That is to say, he may have wished to imply that an analysis is like biblical exegesis. The Hebrew word torah has the same connotations as the Egyptian *sbâye(t),* Coptic *sbô* and shares with the Latin *doctrina* (from *doceo* to teach) and *disciplina* (from *disco,* to learn) the dual sense of a system of teachings and correction, even punishment. On the etymology of *tôrah* and the denominative origin of *hôrâ* (to teach), see W.F. Albright (1927), The names Israel and Judah with an excursus on the etymology of TôDâh and Tôrâh, *Journal of Biblical Literature,* 151–85. See also B. Paperon (1999), Exégèse juive de la Bible et notions modernes d'inconcient, *Pardès* 27: 99–127.

10 Foucault points out that although, unlike many hospitals run by religious orders the Salpêtrière was a lay organisation, nevertheless it was conceived on a quasi-monastic model. Cf. M. Foucault (1963), *Naissance de la clinique*, Paris: Presses Universitaires de France.

Bibliography

Bochet, I. (2003). *Augustin dans la pensée de Paul Ricoeur.* Paris: Editions faculties jésuites de Paris.

Bourneville, D.-M. (1875). *Science et Miracle: Louise Lateau ou la Stigmatisée Belge.* Paris: Delahaye.

Brown, P. (2000). *Augustine of Hippo. A Biography.* London: Faber and Faber.

Butler, C. (ed. and trans) (1904). *The Lausiac History of Palladius. The Greek Text Edited with Introduction and Notes,* vol. 2. Cambridge: Cambridge University Press.

Cary, P. (2000). *Augustine's Invention of the Inner Self.* Oxford: Oxford University Press.

de Certeau, M. (1982). *La Fable mystique XVᵉ–XVIIᵉ siècle.* Paris: Gallimard.

de Certeau, M. (1987). *La Faiblesse de croire.* Paris: Éditions du Seuil.

de Certeau, M. (2006). *Heterologies. Discourse on the Other*, trans. B. Massumi. Minneapolis and London: University of Minnesota Press.

Deleuze, G. and Guattari, F. (1980). *Mille Plateaux: capitalisme et schizophrénie II*. Paris: Minuit.

Didi-Huberman, G. (2012). *Invention de l'hystérie*. Geneva: Editions Macula.

Dodds, E.R. (1965). *Pagan and Christian in an Age of Anxiety*. Cambridge: Cambridge University Press.

Dols, M.W. (1987). The origins of the Islamic hospital: Myth and reality. *Bulletin of the History of Medicine* 61: 367–90.

Dolto, F. (1961). Personnologie et image du corps. *La Psychanalyse* 6: 59–92.

Foucault, M. (1961). *Histoire de la folie à l'âge classique – folie et déraison*. Paris: Plon.

Foucault, M. (1984). *Le Souci de soi*. Paris: Editions Gallimard.

Foucault, M. (2001). *L'Herméneutique du sujet: Cours au Collège de France 1981–1982*. Édition établie sous la direction de François Ewald et Alessandro Fontana. Hautes Études. Paris: Gallimard et Seuil.

Gay, P. (2006). *Freud. A Life for Our Time*. London: Max.

Hadot, P. (1953). Epistrophē et metanoia dans l'histoire de la philosophie. *Actes du XIeme congrès international de philosophie XII*. Louvain: Editions E. Nauwelaerts.

Hadot, P. (2008). *Philosophy as a Way of Life. Spiritual Exercises from Socrates to Foucault*, trans. M. Chase. Oxford: Blackwell.

Harpham, G.G. (1987). *The Ascetic Imperative in Culture and Criticism*. Chicago and London: University of Chicago Press.

Horden, P. (1993). Responses to possession and insanity in the earlier Byzantine world. *Society for the Social History of Medicine* 6(2): 177–94.

Hustvedt, A. (2011). *Medical Muses. Hysteria in Nineteenth-Century Paris*. London: Bloomsbury.

Jackson, M. (2001). Psychoanalysis and the treatment of psychosis *A Language for Psychosis. Psychoanalysis of psychotic states*, ed. P. Williams (pp. 37–53). London and Philadelphia: Whurr Publishers.

Lacan, J. (1981). *Le Séminaire de Jacques Lacan,* Livre III, *Les Psychoses. 1955–1956*. Paris: Editions du Seuil.

Lacan, J. (1999). *The Ethics of Psychoanalysis 1959–1960. The Seminar of Jacques Lacan Book VII*, ed. J.-A. Miller, trans. D. Porter. London: Routledge.

Lacan, J. (2006). *Écrits. The First Complete Edition in English*, trans. B. Fink with H. Fink and R. Grigg. New York, London: W.W. Norton.

Lampe, G.W.H. (1961). *A Patristic Greek Lexicon*. Oxford: Clarendon Press.

Laplanche, J. and Pontalis, J.-B. (1980). *The Language of Psycho-Analysis*, trans. D. Nicholson-Smith. London: Hogarth Press/Institute of Psycho-Analysis.

Liddell, H.G. and Scott, R. (1863). *A Greek–English Lexicon*. Oxford: Clarendon Press.

Lowther Clarke, W.K. (trans.) (1918). *The Lausiac History of Palladius*. London: SPCK.

Marcus, P. (2003). *Ancient Religious Wisdom, Spirituality, and Psychoanalysis*. Westport: Praeger.

Nock, A.D. (1933). *Conversion. The Old and the New in Religion from Alexander the Great to Augustine of Hippo*. Oxford: Clarendon Press.

Pankow, G. (1956). *Structuration dynamique dans la schizophrénie. Contribution à une psychothérapie analytique de l'expérience psychiatrique du monde*. Bern: Hans Huber.

Prado de Oliveira, L.E. (2001). On autism, schizophrenia and paranoia in children: the case of little Jeremy, *A Language for Psychosis. Psychoanalysis of Psychotic States*, ed. P. Williams (pp. 126–48). London and Philadelphia: Whurr Publishers.

Salonen, S. (1989). The restitution of primary identification in psychoanalysis. *Scandinavian Psychoanalytic Review* 12: 102–15.

Shentoub, S.A. (1963). Remarques sur la conception du moi et ses references au concept de l'image corporelle. *Revue Française de Psychanalyse* 27: 271–300.

Špidlík, T. (1964). Fous pour le Christ. En Orient. *Dictionnaire de Spiritualité* 5: 752–61.

Underhill, E. (1911). *Mysticism. A Study in the Nature and Development of Man's Spiritual Consciousness*. London: Methuen and Co.

Yarom, N. (1992). *Body, Blood and Sexuality. A Psychoanalytic Study of St Francis' Stigmata and their Historical Context*. New York: Peter Lang.

4

DIVINE MADNESS

Tantric ascetics on the cremation ground in Tarapith, Birbhum District, West Bengal

Audrey Cantlie

In the *Phaedrus*, Socrates introduces the idea of divine madness. Of this he distinguishes four kinds: the madness of the oracle, the madness of possession, the madness of the poet and the madness of love. The madman (the prophet, the possessed, the poet, the lover) is endowed with a clarity of vision by which he passes through the door into truth so that, as Socrates puts it, 'the sane man is nowhere at all when he enters into rivalry with the madman'.

(Plato Phaedrus: 245, 8–9, in Jowett 1871: 579)

In the early 1980s I was initiated into Tantra by a guru in Calcutta, where I was making a study of Kalighat Temple, and I also worked for short periods in 1981 and 1985 among Tantric ascetics living on the cremation ground at Tarapith, a village in the Birbhum District of West Bengal. A Tantric ascetic is by definition expected to be mad and is often known as the 'Mad One' *(Khepā Bābā)* or the 'Naked One' (*Lengtā Bābā*).[1]

Tara's place

The little village of Tarapith (literally, 'Tara's Place'), with its famous temple to the goddess Tara and the adjacent cremation ground where she is said to walk at night, has become one of the most important pilgrimage centres in eastern India. People remember when it was a wild and desolate place in the jungle with tigers, bears, hyenas and jackals, but today the only remaining trees are in the cremation ground itself, which give it a nostalgic charm often commented on by visitors. Birbhum District is one of the poorest districts of West Bengal and, in the absence of local timber, most people cannot afford to buy wood for burning the dead. Although Hindus traditionally cremate their dead, in the cremation ground at Tarapith more corpses are buried than burnt.[2] After removing all clothes and garlands that might bind or attach them to their earthly existence, bodies are placed in shallow graves and the earth shovelled back on top to form a low mound. In the rainy season, the River Dwaraka floods the lower reaches of the cremation ground so that the mounds are flattened and, when the water recedes, no trace of the graves remains. As a result, when new graves come to be dug, they disturb the bones of the previous occupants, which are unceremoniously turfed out and left lying about. It is these bones that the sadhus collect in order to communicate with the spirits from whom they derive their baleful and sinister powers.

The factor of place is of great importance for the success of Tantric *sādhanā* (ritual practices). The sadhus who build their huts on the cremation ground are living above the remains of previous sadhus, whose powers filter up to them through the earth. But it would be too narrow to see this as the worship of relics. The sadhus who used to live there, the events that once happened there, continue to inhabit the soil, the trees, the atmosphere, the very ambience of a particular spot and give to it its defining qualities. The repetition (*japa*) of a given mantra may be successful in one place and unsuccessful in another. Only when its vibration coincides with the goddess in her auditory form does she appear to the adept in a vision of light, who becomes thereby a perfected being (*siddha puruṣa*).[3] Ordinarily a dead body is considered polluting. If one touches a man returning from the cremation ground, one takes a bath; if one touches a man who has touched a man returning from the cremation ground, one takes a bath; if one sees a man returning from the cremation ground, the orthodox may take a bath. But there are certain cremation grounds, of which Tarapith is one, that were made holy (*pabitra*) by the presence of the sadhus, so that visitors are required to remove their shoes before entry. In the world of Tantra, the polluting is pure, and the pure is polluted.

History and legend

Like other temples, the Temple to Tara has its myth of origin. Oral history tends to evolve over time, changing with changing circumstances, and what follows below are versions of stories that I collected while in the field. They are to be understood here, not as an account of the past, but of the past as viewed from the present — the living past, as it were.

Some 3,000 or 4,000 years ago, the sage Vasistha Muni was practising austerities in the name of the goddess Tara without success. He became angry and cursed the mantra. The goddess then advised him to go to Tibet, where he received a new mantra from Vishnu, who also instructed him in an esoteric form of worship in which there is no difference between pure and impure. He told him to go to a particular place in India, which he described, and to perform this worship there. The sage found the place described, which is now called Tarapith, where he placed under a cotton tree an image of the goddess he had brought with him from Tibet. In a short time he was successful. He left Tarapith and no one knows where he was buried.

Much later, about 400 years ago, a merchant called Jaya Dutta came to Tarapith with his wares by boat, accompanied by his only son. The son died, some say by snake bite, others say by cholera. The boatmen were cooking their food on the bank of a tank called Vasistha's Pond, when suddenly the fish they had cooked came alive and jumped into the water. They told the merchant, who at first did not believe them, but then he thought, 'If the fish can come to life, why not my son?' He immersed the body of his son in the water and the son came back to life, saying, 'Mother, Mother'. That night the merchant dreamt of a beautiful woman who said to him, 'I am Mother, Goddess Tara. My stone image is in the ground under the cotton tree. Find it and arrange for its worship.' The merchant dug up the ground as instructed, found the image and established it in a temple on the fourteenth day of Ashwin (September/ October).

Today, in the evening, visitors to the Temple are given *darśan* (viewing) of a metal image of Tara, 3–4 feet high, with four arms, a garland of skulls, a projecting tongue and long unbound hair. The image is then removed to a cot for the night, revealing inside it on the altar a slab of black stone, perhaps 24 inches across, 20 inches high and 4–6 inches deep, representing in shadowy relief Shiva sucking from the breast of Tara to relieve his throat from the pain of the poison which he drank at the churning of the ocean. This is described by the priest as the original image established by Vasistha Muni. Some people said it was the third eye of Sati.[4] The fusion of fierce (*ugra*) and protective qualities represented here by Tara's double image, is a characteristic of all forms of the *mysterium horrendum*. I will not elaborate here on the details of worship in the Temple. With the influx of pilgrims the priests have become rich and own most of the hostels and shops in the village. Their relation with the sadhus is ambivalent. They disapprove of their drunk and disorderly lives, but they bring wealth to Tarapith.

Tarapith owes its importance as a centre of pilgrimage to an ascetic called Vama Khepa or Vama Deb (1843–1911). There are three organisations now working in his name and two temples dedicated to him at Tarapith. Of the innumerable stories told about him, the most famous is the occasion when he was seen eating the food (*bhog*) for the Goddess before the offering and giving to her his food remains (highly polluting) saying, 'Mother, eat.' He was beaten senseless by the priests. That night the goddess appeared in a dream to the Rani of Nator who owned the Temple, a pitiable figure with her back bleeding and full of cuts. She said that she had taken on her own body the injuries of her son and was going to leave Tarapith: 'You have driven away my beloved son, I am not going to eat your *bhog*.' Next day, when they began to prepare the *bhog* at the Temple, the fire would not light. The Rani said, 'Let him do whatever he likes. Don't disturb him.' One day he was seen urinating on the image. The priests asked, 'Why are you doing this?' He replied, 'When a small child pisses on his mother's lap, no one asks him what he is doing. So why do you ask me?' He is said to have effected many miraculous cures and was credited with powers to control the weather. He was on very familiar terms with the goddess, often abusing and cursing her, a tradition not wholly lost today. One of the sadhus I met observed, 'I said to goddess Tara, "You sit high and mighty up there on your throne. But if I catch you by the leg, I will pull you down to the River Dwaraka".'

Vama Khepa is an example of an uneducated villager, innocent of formal ritual and Sanskrit mantras, whose simple faith (*bhakti*) touched the goddess. He attained enlightenment under the same tree where Vasistha Muni once sat. He said if a man performed 300,000 *japa* (repetitions) of the Tara mantra at Tarapith, the man would become *siddha* (perfected). My guru observed that he believed what Vama Khepa said.

The Tantric path

No single path (*mārg*) claims a monopoly of the truth, for, just as all rivers end in the sea, so it is said that all paths lead to enlightenment. But to the adherent his chosen path will be justified on the grounds that it is the most appropriate in this current age and that it is easier and quicker than other paths. Tantrics, however bizarre their practices, may maintain continuity with tradition by describing themselves as including the paths of ritual (*karma*), knowledge (*gyān*) and devotion (*bhakti*) and as containing the essence of the Veda. In this way the tradition evolves without losing contact with its roots. Similarly, the dubious credentials of many wandering mendicants today are neutralised by a distinction between true sadhus and false sadhus, the first associated with famous names from the past and the second used to describe contemporary examples. One often hears, 'There are no good sadhus nowadays.' Thus the ideal is preserved while its manifestations are rejected.

The purpose of Tantric *sādhanā* is to attain union with a goddess who is the object of worship. This takes the form of a momentary vision of the goddess, who appears to the adept in a blaze of light, a coincidence in time and place, as a result of which he becomes a perfected being (*siddha puruṣa*). In this union, worshipper and worshipped, subject and object, adept and goddess, become one and the same. An Italian sadhu put it this way: 'One day when you look in the mirror you will see the face of God.' Hence the man-gods worshipped throughout India and, occasionally, abroad.

Without placing it within the context of Indian thought, the answer to the question 'What am I (*āmi*)?' or, perhaps better, 'What is the I?' is likely to mislead, for its aim is not to establish identity but to delete or erase its possibility. By way of introduction I take up here briefly two notions, the status of the phenomenal world (*saṃsāra*) and the meaning of the term 'god' (*bhagavān, īsvar*), the two being intrinsically related.

The world (saṃsāra), a term that carries with it the flavour of limitation and confinement, is said to be māyā, which has the double meaning of illusion and created. From one point of view it could be said that nothing that is created really exists; it only seems to be. Sometimes it is spoken of as the play (līlā) of the gods, sometimes as the dream of Vishnu lying on the waters whence the creator god, Brahma, bodies forth the universe each day to re-absorb it the same night, a day and a night in the life of Brahma lasting 8,640,000,000 years in human time. Thus the process of creation and destruction is endlessly repeated in successive cosmic cycles, each cycle having four ages (yuga), of which the first, the Satya Yuga, is the most perfect, and the last, the Kali Yuga, in which we are now living, the most degenerate. In Tantric cosmology creation is understood as the union of Shiva/Shakti, passivity and activity, male and female, represented pictorially as the goddess standing on the dead body of Shiva (sada-Śiva). She mounts him, he opens his eyes, and from their union the universe is born, to be re-absorbed by the goddess at the end of the cosmic cycle. The creation and destruction of the universe is repeated symbolically as a spiritual practice (sādhanā) by many sadhus, the male worshipping the body of the female as the Mother, and she him as Shiva, before they engage in intercourse. It is perhaps consistent with the degenerate character of the present age that Shiva and Kali are considered to be mad deities in a mad world. There is a popular song on the cremation ground beginning 'Father is mad, Mother is mad'.[5] Beyond time and space, creation and destruction, being and non-being, is brahman (as it is called), which does not change as the world changes. It has no qualities (nirguṇa) and is ineffable. A sadhu explained it negatively thus: 'If you cut it, it won't cut; if you kill it, it won't die; if you burn it, it won't burn.' The aim of the sadhu is to realise his identity with brahman, that he himself is soul (ātman), and his soul is brahman, sometimes also called paramātman.

The status of the world in Tantra is equivocal. Although brahman does not exist in the world as the thing-in-itself which has no form, nevertheless the world as its manifestation participates in it, in the sense that Krishna as Arjuna's charioteer both is and is not Krishna. Tantra is said to be derived from tanu (the body), understood not as a seat of mortification but of enjoyment and, as such, an affirmation of life. It is on the body that the adept concentrates his religious practices, enjoying forbidden foods and forbidden pleasures. He does not proceed by rejecting the world and denying the flesh. As Makhan Baba explained, 'First the gross (stūla), then the subtle (sūkṣma). Unless you work on the gross body, the subtle will not come.' For the Tantric the world is not without substance. He views it as the body of the goddess and, being of that world, he looks to the goddess in himself to realise the knowledge that he is the goddess.

Because the phenomenal world is a manifestation of the one ineffable reality, the distinctions and differentiations we see in it are mistaken perceptions.

There is no difference between self and other, subject and object, inside and outside. 'What is there [macrocosm] is here [microcosm]. What is not here is nowhere.' If everything is of everything else, the sadhu by looking within himself can arrive at knowledge (*vidyā*). By seeing things differently, they become different and he becomes a quite different seer of them. In the Indian context, knowledge (*vidyā*) and ignorance (*avidyā*) largely replace the Christian emphasis on virtue and sin, and are to be understood not as states of cognition, but as states of being. It has been said that in India there are more gods than people. However that may be, the terms which we translate as 'god' (*bhagavān, īśvar*) do not carry the same implications as the Christian term 'God' or the Islamic term 'Allah'. They are included in the phenomenal world and will disappear at the end of this Kali Yuga to reappear in the next cosmic cycle.

When I went out in the morning on my first visit to Tarapith, I passed the Vama Deb Ashram, where there was a life-size image of the holy man in white marble. On my return at dusk, I noticed that a shawl had been placed round his shoulders against the chill night air. I did not suppose, any more than the keeper of the Ashram, that a marble statue could feel the cold. This simple act of piety reminded me of an observation of my guru: 'The goddess does not need our offerings – the food, the clothes, the jewels – for she is the whole world, she has everything. We give not for her sake, but for our own, to show our devotion.' In the Temple Tara leads a human life, she is woken at four each morning by the priest who claps his hands three times at the door, saying, 'Mother, I am coming in.' The image is then bathed, dressed, fed and worshipped. But, as my guru remarked, 'We like to see our deities with hands and feet. But who knows if god is a human being? He may be a cat, or a rat, who knows?' There is a saying: 'For the benefit of the *sādhak* (adept) the form of *brahman* is imagined.'

As all deities are seen as manifestations, as it were, of the one ineffable reality, the distinction between them may be blurred. It is common to hear that 'All the Mothers are one' or 'There is no difference between Krishna and Kali.' In the vicinity of Kalighat Temple, two temples represent this unity iconographically: in one near the cremation ground, the image is of Kali to the waist and Krishna below; while in the other the image is divided vertically, Kali on the right side and Krishna on the left. On the walls of Choto Baba's Ashram near Tarapith is written, 'As is *Śyāma* [Krishna, the dark-skinned], so is *Śyāmā* [Kali, the dark-skinned].' He worshipped both deities. This awareness of the contingent nature of divinity is illustrated below by conversations with two sadhus. The first is a sadhu from Bangladesh who had lived in Tarapith for ten years:

> Tantra derives from *tanu* (body). We have a body and because of it we have a name. Ten days after we were born our mother and father gave

us a name. If you call someone by his name, he will reply. But what is within this body has no name. Because of it we see, we talk, we move. What is within us having no name, that is I (*āmi*), soul (*ātman*), power (*śakti*). The more you feel the *ātman*, the more you get the power (*śakti*). By *sādhanā* (spiritual discipline) we realise, 'I am god (*param īśvar*)'.

The second is a recorded interview with another sadhu, Lahiri Baba, who had an Australian disciple, Margaret. For eleven months she lived in a hut on the cremation ground and meditated on the goddess Tara according to his instructions. Then one day he said to her:

'What is the Goddess? She is nothing. For whom are you saying this sound, "God"? Everything is God. Don't give any name to it. Don't think of any particular shape. Everything is one thing – One God. You are also God.' After I said this to Margaret, she sat in the crema-tion ground for three days, without eating, without drinking, without speaking. From great knowledge this condition occurs. Then she packed her bags and returned to Australia.

This anecdote can of course be interpreted in different ways. To the uninitiated reader I would point out that Lahiri's exposition of what we might perhaps call a version of 'immanence' is consistent with the method of preparing consecrated liquor (*kāran*) described on page 102.

The Tantric sadhu

What then is a Tantric sadhu? Ramakrishna Paramhamsa said that a *sannyāsī* has four qualities. He should be like a five-year-old child (innocent, without sin). He should be like a learned man (versed in the sacred texts). He should be like a *piśāca* (a ghoul delighting in foul smells and eating human flesh). He should be like a madman.[6] Tantric knowledge is described as 'knowledge from the mouth of the guru' (*guru mukhiyā vidyā*), and in every hut on the cremation ground there was a garlanded photograph of the occupant's guru testifying to his initiation and vouching, as it were, for his spiritual credentials. During initiation the guru imparts to the initiate certain secret mantras, which are secret only in the sense that they are to be kept secret and not revealed. Although widely available in written texts, a mantra has no efficacy unless imparted during initiation by the guru ('*Hriṃ, kriṃ* have no power unless given by guru.') The idea of the guru is omnipresent. 'Guru is Brahma, guru is Vishnu, guru is Maheshvar, guru is *param brahman*'; 'The guru is greater than god. If guru is annoyed, no god can help you. If guru is pleased, nobody can harm you'; 'Guru holds the key to the gate, without him I cannot get god, so naturally he is greater to me than god'. 'My guru may be a wicked man, he may be an ignorant man, but I am not to think of him like that. If you think of your guru as an ordinary man, you go straight to hell.' All these sayings and sentiments I have heard, but in practice the relationship is not without its tensions. The disciples may love the guru very much, but they feel he belongs to them and should do what they want. Sometimes it leads to quarrels.

My guru was of the Tirtha *sampradāya*, one of the ten sects established by Shankaracarya in the eighth century. This group is on the right-handed side and performs Kumari Puja (worship of a virgin as the goddess) instead of ritualised sexual intercourse.[7] After the first initiation (*dīkṣā*) he imparted further instruction through six higher stages.[8] Because knowledge comes only from the mouth of the guru, the guru's knowledge is confined to what he has been given by his own guru; he may 'know about' other practices but he does not 'know' them and cannot transmit them. Should a disciple wish to be versed in additional practices, he must take another guru. The first guru is called the *dīkṣā* (initiating) guru and subsequent gurus, whose number is not limited, are called *śīkṣā* (learning) gurus. Thus, those who define themselves as Tantric are not under the authority of a single 'church' and may vary in their practices.

In spite of the variations between different sects and different stages of initiation, the principle of 'all-the-sameness' remains the basis of almost all Tantric *sādhanā* (religious practice), whatever is repugnant to ordinary sensibilities and contrary to custom being embraced in Tantra, its success measured in certain contexts by the absence of feelings of revulsion and disgust. At the time of my visits, one sadhu was eating human flesh and another was eating excrement. Caste is not observed ('When we take the work of sadhu, we have no caste'). Under the *pañcamuṇḍī āsana* (seat on five heads) where the sadhu traditionally sits for his meditation are buried the skulls of five animals, one of them human, which have died violent deaths. The principle of all-the-sameness is formalised in the five forbidden Ms: *māṃsa* (meat), *matsya* (fish), *madya* (liquor), *mudrā* (parched grain), *maithuna* (sexual intercourse). These are not to be understood in a natural way. The sadhu eats but not to satisfy his appetite, drinks but not to get drunk, has intercourse but the seed must not fall. As one sadhu put it, 'Liquor is not liquor, fish is not fish, meat is not meat.' His purpose is the attainment of enlightenment, the realisation of the self as god.

The path of transgression bestows on its practitioners certain powers (*siddhi*), popularly understood as issuing from traffic with the spirits dwelling on the cremation ground. For example, *kāyā siddhi* makes the body invulnerable, *bāk siddhi* is the power that whatever one says in speech becomes so in fact. If a sadhu carrying a bottle of liquor says it is milk, it will be found to be milk. Lengta Baba had the gift of seeing at a distance, subtle sight (*sūkṣma dṛṣṭi*) as it is called, as distant from the gross sight (*sthūla dṛṣṭi*) of ordinary people. While in Calcutta he saw in his mind's eye the cremation ground at Tarapith. 'Two men are coming, looking for me. "He is not here," they are told, "he has gone away." They say they will return in three days.' Because of the powers attributed to them, thousands of pilgrims consult the sadhus every year to cure sickness, conceive a child, pass an examination, obtain a job and other problems and difficulties of householder life. It is enough for the sadhu to mutter, 'It will be, it will be [*habe habe*]', perhaps accompanied by a little packet of ash from the fire in his hut, for their wish to be fulfilled. But the notoriety of the Tantric, the fear of offending him, derives from more sinister practices. There was a sadhu at Tarapith who claimed to perform *uccātan* (persecution), *baśikaraṇ* (making obedient to one's will), *māran* (killing). I was fortunate enough to attend a performance held between midnight and three o'clock on the night of Amābasyā (when the earth is in menses). He used a small rag doll and an arrow to kill the 'enemy' of a Calcutta client. I do not know if the ritual was successful, but people often complain of wasting illnesses allegedly caused by Tantrics.

The 'suspended *status quo* of death'

On the cremation ground, the sadhu assumes his specific relationship with death. For the householder, death may be natural or unnatural, timely (*kāla*) or untimely (*akāla*). In the first case the body is cremated and the soul transformed by funerary rites into an incorporated ancestor (*pitṛ*). In the second (young children, death by accident, suicide, violence and certain diseases such as leprosy), no funerary rites are performed, so that the deceased remains a disembodied ghost. But for the sadhu there is a third category, which Piatigorsky calls 'that which has always been, as it were, already dead, which is within death, and not "before" or "after", being thereby supernatural' (Piatigorsky 1985: 232). Before leaving householder life, a sadhu should perform his own funerary rites (although this is not always done), becoming thereby dead to the world. Although now immunised, as it were, against death – for he has already died – he dwells in the 'suspended *status quo* of death' symbolised by the skull (Piatigorsky 1985: 233). Not all the sadhus traffic with bones, but they are everywhere to be seen on the cremation ground. It is said that Vama Khepa threw 10,000 skulls into a pit, and his hut, its walls embedded with skulls, is still in use today. While those who die naturally remain bound in the cycle of birth and death and will be reincarnated, sadhus look to a different fate: 'People like us, who recognise by our *sādhanā* that man is god [*manuṣa devatā*], we are not coming any more. We vanish into the body of Mother.' Their departure (or passing) is called *samādhi* (salvation), a term both for spiritual salvation and physical death, for in their case both are understood as the same.

Tantra in practice

Tantra manifests itself on the cremation ground both externally in appearances and rituals, and internally in meditative practices. According to the path that Vasistha Muni rather unwillingly undertook, there is no difference between purity and impurity, they are all-the-same. By openly flouting the distinctions of the world, the renouncer constitutes himself as an inversion or anti-model, adopting what the world rejects, practising what it prohibits, evidencing what it is not, and so in a way evoking the shadow of a presence made absent. His positive is the world's negative, which he demonstrates in his uncouth appearance, strange manners and polluting practices. In forsaking householder life, he also abandons its security (relative though that may be) for the uncertain and solitary life of a renouncer, for there is no group or association of sadhus on the cremation ground where he can find a place. As one sadhu put it, 'We came alone, we go alone, so we must live alone.' A visiting sadhu should address another living on the cremation ground with 'Om, I salute Narayana [an epithet of Vishnu].' Each sadhu is equivalent to every other sadhu; no one can claim rank or precedence over another. Each follows the separate path given him by his guru(s).

I met and made notes on thirty sadhus at Tarapith, twenty-one male and nine female. They included three Aghoris, distinguished by their black clothes.[9] The biographical material I could obtain was scanty – it is not considered appropriate for a renouncer to dwell on his former life – and I cannot of course vouch for the accuracy of local gossip. The motives for becoming a sadhu are sometimes divided into pull and push, attraction and repulsion. Without denying an almost universal openness to religious experience, my overwhelming impression is that at Tarapith push prevails. There is Nogen Baba, a Sikh who fled Delhi to escape the reprisals following Mrs Gandhi's assassination; Sushila Ma, who allegedly strangled her husband and was said to be wanted by the Calcutta police for drug trafficking and pimping; Mukul Baba, who lost his livelihood after a stroke; Bina Ma, deserted by her husband for a younger woman; Krishna Ma, who became mad and was guided by the goddess in a dream to Tarapith, where madness is the norm; the young student, who remarked with disarming frankness that 'Jobs are very hard to get nowadays'; Kalini, an Italian Bhairavi,[10] said of the reasons for becoming a sadhu, 'A murderer to escape jail, a thief to steal more easily, a beggar to beg more nicely.'

It would, however, be a mistake to view such sadhus as other than genuine. In accordance with the doctrine of karma, no distinction is made between what a man is or does and what happens to him. If someone sees the goddess, he is considered fit to do so; there are no unprepared visions. Whatever their motives or circumstances, they all find themselves living on the cremation ground as devotees of the goddess. And to this end they are all in one way or another committed. Over time what they do becomes what they are.

Tantrics are distinguished by their red or reddish clothes, and the men usually wear necklaces of silver with *rudrākṣa* (dried fruit) beads and silver rings and bangles. Hair is always left long, but a *juṭhā* (matted hair) is considered a gift from the goddess.

In the cold weather the sadhus lived reasonably well, but when the pilgrimage season came to an end, survival was difficult. Not many had grey hair and all were thin. Sadhus may repeat, 'If food comes, that is good. If food does not come, that is also good', a precarious existence described as 'living under Mother's feet', but each sadhu is in competition with every other sadhu for attracting alms. I have heard visitors, asking for the whereabouts of a popular sadhu called Lengta Baba, being told that he was dead (but they could of course be directed to another very good sadhu . . .). The rivalries on the cremation ground are not just about money; sadhus are also jealous of their prestige and reputation. Many stories circulate of prominent sadhus being poisoned or beaten to death (evidence of which occurred during my visits). As against this, there are sadhus who offer each other food when they have it to spare.

Conversation with the sadhus suggested a great variation of practice (*sādhanā*). An interesting difference is the understanding of *bhūt*, which may be internal/external, mental/physical, essence/appearance. In its external, material form, it is understood as referring to spirits called *bhūt*, which may be either (a) a disembodied ghost for whom no funerary rites have as yet been performed by which the chief mourner under the direction of the priest creates ritually the ten limbs of a new and subtle body for the deceased in the ten days after death so that he can go away to his 'own place', or (b) a category of (usually) malevolent spirits who, together with *piśācas* (flesh-eating demons), *yoginīs* and *dakinīs* (both companions of the Mother), live on cremation grounds. When I asked Bina Ma if she had seen a *bhūt*, she replied, 'How have I seen? When have I seen?' I took her to mean that only those spiritually advanced could actually see spirits. She did not traffic with bones, but, before she ate her one meal of the day, she sprinkled a handful of food on the ground for the *bhūts*. It was also not uncommon for sadhus to say, perhaps ironically, 'We are the *bhūts* of the cremation ground.' But the term '*bhūt*' is also used in an internal, quite different way to refer to the five elements of the physical or gross body: earth, air, fire, water, ether. There is a ritual called *bhūtaśuddhi* by which the adept in meditation purifies his body of these gross elements before proceeding to the worship of and identification with the deity. Of the four sadhus understanding *bhūt* in this more subjective way, the most emphatic was Lahiri Baba:

> The ordinary Tantrics know nothing about the inner meaning of Tantra. In giving food and liquor to the *bhūts,* they are making a mistake. There is no *bhūt*, there is no *piśāca*, only the five *bhūts* making up the body are real. By eating meat and fish, how can you get knowledge? These are outer things only, childish play. The image you

worship in the Temple is a thing of clay or stone; it is not real. It is useful only to you. I used to worship but now I take help only from within myself. The Mother is everything. She is me, she is the universe. You are also the universe. Your soul is god, you are god.

This tension between external ritual actions and internal meditative practices is characteristic of the many schools of Tantra and of Indian religion generally.

The overall impression left by the sadhus is that, however active they may once have been, many of them are now doing very little. They live on the cremation ground, that is their *sādhanā*; nothing that they do (*kriyā karma*) is as important to their self-definition as the cremation ground itself. Sadhus tend to travel and most have visited other cremation grounds before settling at Tarapith, where some have been for 10, 20, up to 55, years. They describe it as a place of peace (*śānti*), of happiness (*ānanda*), their contentment testifying to their success on the path, for a discontented sadhu is no sadhu. Perhaps this contributes to their view of the cremation ground. Many stories circulate of adjusting reality to what is expected of it, the changing arrangement of features on the ground being interpreted to accord with their history. The successive temples to Tara built on different sites are all built on the spot where Vasistha Muni obtained enlightenment; the seat on five skulls (*pañcamuṇḍī āsana*) used for his meditation by the sage, and by reputation the same seat as used by Vama Khepa, is identified with the one today on the cremation ground, although it is also said that no one knows where Vasistha Muni used to sit; the cotton tree accidentally burnt down by Vama Khepa when he set fire to his leg in a fit of insensibility can still be seen by the pilgrim, miraculously regrown. In short, Tarapith is a place of legend where things are as they should be.

What follows is a brief account of three episodes observed on the cremation ground, showing the life of a sadhu from day to day in his relations with the public.

Five young men were squeezed into the little hut of a sadhu, who told them to stare into the piercing black eyes of his guru's photograph and make a wish, which would be fulfilled. One youth muttered that he didn't believe it, and was immediately rebuked by another youth, alluding to the mysterious powers attributed to the sadhus: 'Be quiet. This is a matter of your life.' A middle-aged woman appeared in the doorway. Baba shouted at her that he didn't want money but was short of *dhūp* sticks. She left, returning a little later with a packet of sticks. Then she touched her forehead to the lintel of the door and went away.

A woman with a little girl of three, accompanied by her husband and brother, came to consult Kala Baba in his hut on the cremation ground. 'Look, Baba, my child is not feeling well. Bless her so that she does not give me any more trouble in her life.' Baba asked for money to buy *dhunā* (resin), which was brought and sprinkled on the fire. He instructed the woman to repeat a mantra while she offered the *dhunā*. After a time, Baba took some ash and applied it with his thumb to the child's forehead from the bridge of the nose to the hairline, saying, 'Jai Tara Ma, look after this child. Let her be free of this disease.' The woman bowed down at Baba's feet and gave him five rupees.

At 8.30 in the morning Lengta Baba was preparing some *gañja* (marijuana) to smoke. Five or six young men came to his hut and asked for some. He did not reply. They asked again. He said, 'This is not a shop. Go and buy some.' They came in and sat down. He passed round the pipe. Then one of them said, 'Can I have some liquor?' Lengta Baba rose to his feet, swore at him (the sadhus have a very rich vocabulary), smashed the bottle of liquor and threatened him with his tongs. They were frightened and ran off. He said people were always coming to take something but they never brought something to give.

The meditative practices (*dhyāna*) of the sadhus, given by the guru, I was not able to enquire into, for they are secret (*gupta*). However, there was one sadhu on the cremation ground, called Amar Baba, whose guru was the third guru of my guru and we were at the same stage of initiation. When this came to light, he invited me to a ritual meal. Two features of the evening particularly interested me. The first was that, as a woman, I ranked above him so that he offered me liquor and meat first, before I offered them to him, an order of precedence reflecting the relative positions in Tantra of Shiva and Shakti. The second was the mantra he used in preparing and purifying the liquor, which had the effect of changing it into *kāran* (consecrated liquor). It began as follows: 'I am *brahman*, this ghee is *brahman*, everything is *brahman*, I am sacrificing *brahman* to *brahman*. . .'

The sacralisation of food by mantras transforming the paraphernalia of articles used in cooking into different aspects of Brahman is not peculiar to Tantra. What Amar Baba described is reminiscent of very similar ritual practices among Vaisnavas which have the effect of joining the soul of the individual (*jīva ātman*) to the universal soul (*param ātman*). 'The cook,' a guru explained, 'is to consider the fire as one part of Brahman, the rice, water, the very pot, spoon and the cover, all are to be considered different aspects of Brahman. The cook himself is *param brahman* (the highest god).' The eater offers this food, Brahman to Brahman and eats as Brahman itself. Khare reports similar practices in other parts of India (1976).

In considering Indian meditative practices, it is well to remember their particular idea of 'knowledge' as a state of being. To know something is to be that which you know. As a sadhu put it, 'To know milk, you have to mix yourself up with the milk.' To know a god is to be that god. This position distinguishes 'knowing about' (information) from 'knowing' (identification). The goal of all paths to salvation is to know what you already are. Here *vidyā/avdiyā* (knowledge/ignorance) largely replace notions of virtue/sin in Christian tradition. The meditative practices of a Tantric saddhu are designed to identify his consciousness with the object of his meditation resulting in his realisation that he himself is the deity he worships. It is an ecstatic state, akin to madness.

At Tarapith there was only one sadhu, the 'mad Shankar' as his mother called him, who was widely recognised as having attained this state, and another, Lengta Baba, who was believed to be close to it.

'There are only two sadhus at Tarapith, Shankar Baba and Lengta Baba. The rest just put on red clothes' (observation of Gyan Babu). From what follows below, it is not difficult to understand why they acquired their reputation.

Shankar Baba

I first heard the name of Shankar Baba from an astrologer in Calcutta: 'At Tarapith there is a sadhu called Shankar Baba who is very good. Like a madman, but very good.'

On the day after I reached Tarapith, I ate at the Temple, where Gyan Babu organised a lunch for pilgrims, taking the opportunity of a captive audience to preach his daily sermon, which always began, 'There is no difference between Tara Ma and your own mother.' Afterwards we talked about Shankar Baba, whom he described as the 'only real sadhu in Tarapith'. The distinguishing mark of a *siddhapuruṣa* (perfected being), he told me, 'is that he has no attraction for money or clothes or women or health or anything, including food. If you give Shankar Baba a valuable cloth, he will take it. But after two or three hours, you will see someone else wearing it. Shankar Baba likes *muri* (puffed rice). If you give him 100 rupees, he will give it to the shopkeeper for two paisa of *muri*.[11] When enraged, he is notorious and throws rocks. But if hit by a rock, people take it as a blessing.'

Shankar Baba lived on the cremation ground at Tarapith from the age of 12, but so many people came to see the 'mad Shankar', as his mother called him, that he moved out to stay with the family of a married sister in neighbouring Bellia, a weaver village. But even then he had about a hundred visitors a day. When I first saw him he was seated naked on a cane mat on the verandah while his sister's son's wife was rubbing his body with oil. He had black hair, bald on top, and a long white beard. On the wall behind him were several pictures of Tara Ma decorated with garlands and with incense burning before them. Baba seemed to live in a world of his own detached from his surroundings, unaware of the throngs of visitors. Now and then he would exclaim, 'Tara, Tara', in a thin, high-pitched, birdlike voice. When he noticed the visitors in the courtyard – this happened every ten minutes or so – he ejected them forcibly, 'Go, go', often dragging women along the ground by their hair. Visitors always come bearing gifts – *bidi*, cigarettes, sweetmeats, cooked rice, and afterwards they would enquire if Baba had taken anything. If, for example, he half-smoked a cigarette, the remainder became *prasād* (remains of food eaten by a deity), charged with his essence, his being. Baba's sister's son's wife said he took tea and *muri* in the early morning and later rice with egg. He could not eat too much at a time, but whatever he wanted they had to provide. On my next visit I was shown on to the verandah to take *darśan* (viewing) of Baba in a room inside. He was sitting naked on a rug eating earth from a metal plate. As he threw balls of earth into his mouth, little pebbles fell down with a clatter on to the metal. He was restless, often coming out of the room to sit for a short time on a red cloth on the verandah. He urinated on the floor of the room.

When I went again to see Shankar Baba, a little tea stall had been set up outside the house to sell the *bidis*, cigarettes and sweets for again offering to Baba. He was in a furious temper, screaming, 'Give me a blanket.' When a blanket was brought, he threw it down swearing. Another was brought, also rejected. Someone said he had asked for some food, which was not brought him, and this upset him. He went inside uttering a string of obscenities, which I taped but have been unable to translate. His sister's son released an enormous mosquito net, which had the effect of calming him.

On my last visit Baba was inside sleeping. Three parties were waiting to see him. When Baba woke, he came out on to the verandah, saying, 'I will eat rice.' His brother's widow (whom he once described as a black snake) said, 'Wait, wait. I will prepare some.' Baba was angry at the delay but a woman visitor managed to touch his feet to cure a disease. Later in the day he resumed eating earth, and my most vivid memory of him is the sound of pebbles falling back with a clatter on to the metal plate below. Kalini, who was Lengta Baba's disciple and Bhairavi, said that two or three years earlier Shankar Baba used to visit the cremation ground. One day he passed Kalini and shouted to her that her guru would die and she would be left a widow. They were concerned, but nothing has happened yet. In spite of his reputation, there are those who consider Shankar Baba to be a case of clinical madness rather than religious madness or, in Socratic terminology, of ordinary madness, not divine madness.

Lengta Baba

I asked Lengta Baba how he became a sadhu. This is what he told me. He was playing with some boys at worshipping Kali and, after making a straw image of the goddess, was looking for a sacrifice (*bali*). Perhaps one of the cows that were eating the corn? Or perhaps a *kumarha* (pumpkin)? Then one of them said, 'I will be like this today,' assuming the position of the goat. He replied, 'All right, you will be the goat today and I will make the sacrifice.' He split a bamboo and with it cut off the head of the boy. Then he fainted and was in a coma for three days.

> Then, slowly I became a sadhu. I went to many places where no man was living, only water and jungle, tiger, bear, jackal. I lay on the ground and took *ganja*. I saw *bhūt, pret* [spirits]. Wandering here and there, I came to Tarapith. There was one man here. With my guru, slowly, slowly I came to stay. For one year I did work (ascetic practices), then I took initiation (*dīkṣā*) from him.

I was told that at Noon Bazaar, Ahmedpur, there is now a temple where Lengta's straw image of Kali is worshipped, because it is the only image to which a human sacrifice has been made in recent times. I visited Noon Bazaar and there is indeed a temple there with a straw image, but when I tried to verify his story I always met with, 'Lengta Baba is a very good boy. He would never do anything wrong.'

Baba was an impressive figure walking across the cremation ground in a narrow red loincloth, wearing a silver necklace, belt and bangle. His complexion was dark and he had several *jaṭās*. In spite of his resolute air, his eyes often seemed troubled. I was told that one of his disciples had been a German woman married to a Japanese who made a film about him. Lengta Baba said there were three kinds of knowledge of the dead: the knowledge of god, the knowledge of doctors and the knowledge of Tantric sadhus. He had a little hut on the cremation ground near the *chita* (cremation pyre) so that he could see when a suitable body was coming for his work (*sādhanā*). In his hut were four skulls and a *mahāpātra* (literally, 'great vessel', made from the top of a skull).

> This skull has one spirit moving around in this area. When I call him, he comes to this skull. It is necessary to know the name of the dead. I ask them who brought him. Three or four types of dead are coming useful for work: some are run over by train, some hang themselves, some take poison. Their skulls, their bones are needed. With these all work [*sādhanā*] can be done. I have to give them food. I take mango wood and use it for stirring. I cook rice, fish and meat with liquor. While I cook this I will be completely naked. I do it in the middle of the night. I give it naked to the heads. By eating, the *bhūt* [dead man's spirit] becomes obedient to me and will do my work. If you give food to a man, eating, eating, he becomes obedient. If you put liquor in a skull and cover it, after an hour you will see it has gone.

Lengta Baba has some rich disciples in Calcutta. The story goes that Gauranga Rai from Ultradanga had a wayside stall selling potatoes. After he was initiated by Lengta Baba his fortunes changed and he is now extremely rich. He persuaded Lengta Baba to initiate two of his friends living in the same street. They too prospered. The three families come to Tarapith every year at the festival of Shiva Ratri when Vama Deb was born and finance the feeding of about a thousand sadhus and beggars in Lengta Baba's name. After the festival, they take him back with them to Ultradanga in Calcutta, where they have built a temple to Kali, beautifully decorated with skulls. They remarked, 'Lengta Baba's god is Kali, but our god is Lengta Baba.'

Lengta Baba's popularity has attracted the hostility of other sadhus, as did his guru, Sadananda Baba. A witness to Sadananda's murder gave the following account of it.

Many people used to come to Sadananda. Some gave watch, some gave money, some gave cloth. The people hired to kill him asked him to perform a sacrifice on the pyre on the dark night of the moon. When it was finished, they asked for his watch. Baba said, 'What will you do with this watch? Take something which you can keep forever.' But they didn't listen to him. A quarrel started and he was killed. When the police came, they were bribed and the matter ended, though everyone knows the man responsible.

Sadananda Baba's *sādhanā* is described as *ugra* (fierce) and Lengta Baba has adopted the same mode. After he performed a sacrifice on the *dhuni* (sacrificial fire) in his hut for the well-being of a middle-aged man, the man rose and said he had completed what he came for and was going home. Lengta Baba became angry, hit him violently on the back several times and also kicked him with his feet. The man decided to stay. There followed an offering of liquor to the fire before it was distributed to everyone present. The man then asked in a mild voice if he could go. 'Go,' said Lengta Baba. The man stooped to touch his feet. Baba hit him four times on his back and spat on him. The man touched his feet and left.

Like every other sadhu, Lengta Baba had a sacrificial fire (*dhuni*) in his hut, which was lit from half-burnt logs from the funeral pyre and burns continuously. When his hut was broken into, he managed to rescue a smouldering log and it was only when he went on a visit to Italy with Kalini (where he particularly enjoyed performing rites among the Etruscan tombs) that he let his fire go out after twenty years. It is on this fire that he cooks his food and performs his sacrifices. In *yājñā*, unlike *pūjā*, the offering is destroyed. Agni, the fire god, destroys the material quality of the offering while carrying its essence to the gods. Fire is transformative, changing the offering from one mode of being to release another. As such, the *dhuni* represents for the sadhu the agent and embodiment of his transformation. Being already in a sense dead to the world, he can no longer die. One day I asked Lengta Baba about eating the flesh of corpses, a *sādhanā* he had learnt from his guru. For that, he said, he needed an untimely (*akāl*) death like a fatal accident or hanging. He pointed to a tape recorder that I had used to record the Bauls (a sect of itinerant musicians) who sang at the festival of Shiva Ratri on the cremation ground.

The Bauls have gone, but something still remains in the machine. It is this that we 'hear' when we eat the flesh. When the soul leaves the body, certain organs keep warm longer than the rest – the brain, the lungs, the liver. Before it grows cold, I must take the flesh. I prepare it with spices and liquor.

He went on to explain that, by eating the flesh, he entered into the state of mind of the dead man at the moment of his death, and by passing it through his body he took into himself and neutralised its inauspicious nature so that the relatives could live in peace.[12] Considerable attention in general is paid to the moment of death (whether at an auspicious or inauspicious time) and to the orifice from which the soul leaves the body, for these indicate the next incarnation of the deceased.

Lengta Baba's popularity has not been without cost. Some days he said he would not go to the cremation ground, because too many people wanted him to do something for them. When visitors came, he often pretended to be asleep. I heard a man ask him if his sister would find a husband, to which he replied that if he was worrying so much about his sister, what was the use of two men worrying about her. About the time of Shiva Ratri I saw ten to twelve important-looking men from Calcutta squeezed into his hut. One of them said to Baba, 'Oh Lengta, why don't you give something to Ajit Bose so that he can prosper in his business, he is not getting very good customers these days? Otherwise how will he manage with his family?' Baba said, 'Yes, yes. Let come the time. Let's see the situation. Then I will give.' The man persisted, 'Do something for us. Last time you gave me one flower, I remember, without asking. But this time what happened to you? What's wrong with you? We have to ask.' Lengta Baba said he needed some money for liquor, which was supplied. He stood up and broke off one by one the flowers and baal leaves from a garland on an image of the goddess and distributed them singly. Then he took some ash from the sacrificial fire, called the man and asked him to sit before him. With his right thumb he drew a line of ash from between his eyebrows to the top of his forehead, and put some ash in his mouth, saying, 'Eat.' Someone said, 'Oh, Baba, why don't you give me something?' 'I don't have any more.' 'There is one flower.' 'All right, share it amongst you.' So some people got a piece of flower. Baba then sat down, saying, 'It will be. It will be.' So, one might say, the guru was distributed among his disciples, to the last petal of the last flower.

Unlike many sadhus, Lengta Baba, a devotee of Kali since his childhood, found in the cremation ground his natural habitat. He said of his life, 'Others say my life is bad. No house, no food, nothing. But I say it is good. I say all is good.'

Then something happened. He had been living for some time with an Italian girl from Naples who had taken the name of Kalini (little Kali). She came to India in search of spiritual enlightenment ten years previously, and had found her way to Tarapith, where she took initiation from Lengta Baba and afterwards went to live with him. They became very close. 'What I have got from Lengta Baba,' she said, 'cannot be put into words.' He was both her guru and her Bhairava (sexual partner). She became pregnant and gave birth to a boy, whom they called Digambar (dressed in the wind).

For a Tantric sadhu to take a female partner for the purpose of sex is a recognised *sādhanā* (religious practice).[13] But to beget a child is a spiritual catastrophe. In Hinduism the *ātman* (soul), a particle of the divine soul, is believed to pass in the semen so that ejaculation weakens a man and results in a loss of essence. In the case of a Tantric, he loses all his powers. A sadhu said of Lengta Baba, 'I have seen that he has made great efforts in his life. From his mouth fire would come, gold would come. But now it won't be.' All the same, when I saw him playing with his little son, I could not find it in my heart to regret it. The little boy grew up very wild on the cremation ground; his language was full of the obscenities used by the sadhus and he began to throw heavy objects at people. He lasted only one day at school and was sent home. It was decided that Kalini should take him to Italy and leave him with her mother. Lengta Baba became moody. He often said to Kalini that he would die soon. Perhaps in Sadananda's death he anticipated the manner of his going. I do not know: 'If I die, you [Kalini] won't be able to stay here. If I stay here, I will stay. If I go, I will go. But you look after Digambar. Take him to your country. On the cremation ground people are disturbing me. They are doing devilry. You cannot stand it, you cannot, you will die.'

He showed us his palm: 'All sides are jungle. The lines are bad, they peter out, no way through. This is trident [Shiva]. There is a house. Look, four houses. These are the body of Baba. Men will kill me. It says here they will destroy me. As long as Mahakal [Shiva] is here, the planets cannot do anything. I have no fear. But someone is trying to do evil work on me.' So saying, he strode off across the cremation ground, muttering that 'too much talking is not good'.

Postscript: the truth in madness

In the last chapter of his remarkable book *Madness and Civilization*, Foucault takes the view that madness is not simply an absence such as unreason; it has a positive content of its own. In other words, madness is a form of knowledge and it is in that knowledge that the truth of madness can be found (Foucault 2001).

It would not only be out of time (anachronistic), but also out of place to apply the categories of Western thought to Indian material of the mid-1980s. All the same, there are two notions that might be helpful even in an alien context. The first is the Kleinian notion that so-called normal/neurotic people also have a psychotic part to them (Bion 1987: 162) – ergo, being ourselves psychotic, we can understand psychosis. The second is the advantage of bin-ocular vision for an understanding of the object, when it is seen from two points of view simultaneously, a development noted by the psychoanalyst Bion (López-Corvo 2006: 12–13). The case of Shankar Baba raises the ques-tion of the difference between ordinary madness and religious madness. Of these it can be said that they are both different and the same. There is some linguistic distinction, '*pāgla*' being more often used for the first and '*khepā*' for the second, but the behaviour expected of a madman is much the same in both cases. The stereotypic features of the madman are listed by Bhattacharyya as follows: (1) he has no home; (2) he eats anything; (3) he does not bathe; (4) he is naked; (5) he does whatever he likes; (6) he speaks gibberish (Bhattacharyya 1986). Later she comments that the stereotypic view of the madman might equally well describe the *sannyāsī*, one who has renounced the world. Behaviour classed in the world as mad, because it is not the norm, is adopted in Tantra as normal precisely for that reason. For it is the world (*saṃsāra*) and the ways of the world that the renouncer renounces, changing his name and personality to re-align himself as another being in another place.

But his is not the vacuous path of negation. In place of the structures of the world, he substitutes an anti-structure in which, like Alice's looking glass, white is black and black is white; not antinomian in the sense of an opposition to oppositions, but in the sense of itself being an opposition. The sadhu arranges his life against the world as a savage commentary on an illusion. And he reconstructs himself by focusing on the materiality of the physical body, although this is not the body as we know it. The fluidity of body/mind, material/mental in Indian thought is such that they are continuous, inseparable, the one an aspect of the other. A man eating heating foods raises the temperature of the blood and inflames the passions.[14] A man eating food cooked by a thief becomes a thief. Softness and mutability are associated in particular with women, which enables them on marriage to be ritually detached from their natal family and to acquire the bodily substance of their husband's family. It also makes them more susceptible or open to states of madness, trance and divine possession. It is against this background that the sadhu performs his *sādhanā*, secure in the expectation that practices focusing on his body have a moral dimension and that what he does can transform what he is.

The denial of the world is a recurrent theme among the sadhus, usually on the grounds that material possessions do not last.[15] They are fond of the saying, 'You entered the world naked, you will leave it naked.' The Vaishnava ascetic also withdraws from the world, but his method is to multiply its restrictions in order to protect himself against invasion by the pollution surrounding him. I remember when I was a little girl in Assam, the head of a Vaishnava monastic institution called on my father as Deputy Commissioner. A new carpet was ordered from Calcutta and was laid on the stairs so that no foot trod on it before his. The Tantric denial takes a different form characterised by irony, mockery, derision. By reflecting the world in reverse, his madness calls the world to account, exposing its hollowness and challenging it to justify itself before its other. Where is the truth to be found? In the wretched life of men, the prison of the world, or in the savage freedom of the renouncer?

At this point I would like to introduce an external viewpoint, as it were. In talking to the sadhus, I did not form the impression that they are mad.[16] To me they seemed different in their behaviour more than in their being, but, unlike the ordinary madman, different by choice. The critical distinction between the two is self-awareness. The sadhus are aware both of the life that they have left and of the life that, for whatever motives, they have now decided to adopt. Their focus is binocular. By their spiritual disciplines (*sādhanā*) they will doubtless induce states of altered consciousness unfamiliar to me, but theirs is not madness as we know it.

This opinion stands at the limit of my knowledge as an outsider (or, at best, an inside-outsider). And also, I would suggest, it goes beyond my authority to speak on that which I am not, on what I can know about but cannot know. What qualifies us to pronounce on that to which we are strangers? The order of things has many voices and does not answer to a simple 'yes' or 'no'. The diverse threads (*guṇa*) that make up the fabric of the world are multicoloured, but the fabric itself, containing all colours, is itself colourless (*nirguṇa*). This the Tantric knows. The defining quality of divine madness is that the sadhu knows himself as mad and knows the nature of that madness. It is a knowledge that he has of himself.

Acknowledgements

I acknowledge with gratitude the help of my guru and of the many sadhus kind enough to spend time with an inquisitive stranger. Golok Mukherjee was a great help with the language and his amiable character an invaluable asset in the field. I am indebted to Jeanne Openshaw and John Gale for their helpful comments on an earlier draft of this paper and to Hanna-Ruth Thompson for correcting some diacritics. Its residual errors and defects are entirely my responsibility. I also acknowledge the untiring patience of Nina Balogh and Michelle Lawson in transcribing an almost illegible manuscript.

Notes

1 The material that follows is taken from my unpublished field notes. Unless otherwise stated all quotations in inverted commas are observations made by the sadhus at Tarapith during conversation or, in a few cases, recorded on a tape recorder and transcribed. The names of some sadhus have been changed to protect their identity.

2 In Bengal, in addition to deaths that are untimely (*akāl*), caste Vaishnavas, low castes, children and sadhus are usually buried, the last in a sitting position.

3 *Siddha* literally means 'boiled', but is used metaphorically in the sense of 'perfected'. A *siddhi* is a magical power.

4 At the time of my visit, the general opinion in Tarapith was that it was a *siddha pīṭh* (propitious for enlightenment), not a *pīṭhasthān* (where one of the limbs of Sati fell to earth). I visited all the *pīṭhasthāns* in West Bengal and gained the impression that there was a tendency for neglected sites to be forgotten over time, and more popular pilgrimage sites to lay claim to this distinction. If Kinsley's information is representative, this now seems to have taken place in respect of Tarapith (Kinsley 1998: 109).

5 The madness of Kali is a prominent theme in *Rama Prasada's Devotional Songs*: 'Thou art mad; Thy husband is mad; Thou livest in company with the mad' (Sinha 1966: 95).

6 Ramakrishna (1974) was fond of homely parables for the exposition of his teaching. There are numerous collections of stories he is said to have told or were attributed to him.

7 Tantric sects are classed as 'right-handed' or 'left-handed' according to their degree of departure from convention, the right hand being associated with purity and the left hand with pollution.

8 The stages of initiation by my guru were *dīkṣā, śaktabhiṣeka, pūrṇabhiṣeka, krama dīkṣā, samrājya, mahāsamrājya, Brahman.*

9 The Aghoris are an ascetic sect of ferocious reputation said to have originated in the second half of the eighteenth century. They are described by Parry in *Indian Religion* (1981), eds R. Burghardt and A. Cantlie, London: St Martin' pp. 51–78, which is commented on by Piatigorsky on pp. 231–7 of the same book.

10 Bhairavi is the feminine of Bhairava, a ferocious form of Shiva, and all the women sadhus on the cremation ground are called Bhairavi Ma. More specifically, Bhairavi is used to indicate the female partner of an adept with whom he performs a highly ritualised form of sexual intercourse re-enacting the union of Shiva and Shakti in the creation of the universe. My guru remarked, 'We have no way of thinking of creation except in terms of procreation.' A distinguishing feature of Hindu thought is its high degree of self-awareness.

11 There were 64 old paise to the rupee.

12 Cf. the idea of the sin-eater (Puckle 2008: 46–7).

13 I have not discussed here erotic practices in Tantra, so prominent in its image in the West, because they were not found in the crowded conditions of the cremation ground.

14 All foods are classed as 'heating' or 'cooling' according to their effect on the temperature of the blood.

15 I am reminded of what Sadanana said when robbers asked for his watch: 'What will you do with this watch? Take something that will last forever?'

16 From this impression I exclude Shankar Baba, who was much of the time in a mental state or trance (*bhāva*), unaware of his surroundings, such that madness seemed fused with religiosity.

References

Bhattacharyya, D. (1986). *Pāgalāmi: Ethnopsychiatric Knowledge in Bengal*. New York: Maxwell School of Citizenship and Public Affairs, Syracuse University.

Bion, W.R. (1987). *Second Thoughts*. London: Karnac Books.

Foucault, M. (2001). *Madness and Civilization*, trans. R. Howard. London: Routledge.

Jowett, B. (1871). *The Dialogues of Plato*, vol. 1, pp. 541–615, section 245. Oxford: Clarendon Press.

Khare, R.S. (1976). *Culture in Reality*. Sinta: Indian Institute of Advanced Study.

Kinsley, D. (1998). *Tantric Visions of the Divine Feminine*. Delhi: Motilal Banarsidass Publishers.

López-Corvo, R.E. (2006). *Wild Thoughts Searching for a Thinker*. London: Karnac Books.

Parry, P.J. (1985). The Aghori ascetics of Benares. In *Indian Religion, Collected Papers on South Asia*, ed. R. Burghart and A. Cantlie, vol. 7, pp. 51–78. London: Curzon Press.

Piatigorsky, A. (1985). Some phenomenological observations on the study of Indian religion. In *Indian Religion, Collected Papers on South Asia*, ed. R. Burghart and A. Cantlie, vol. 7, pp. 208–58. London: Curzon Press.

Puckle, B.S. (2008). *Funeral Customs*. Charleston, SC: Forgotten Books.

Ramakrishna, Sri (1974). *Tales and Parables of Sri Ramakrishna,* 5th ed. Madras, India: Sri Ramakrishna Math.

Sinha, J. (1966). *Rama Prasada's Devotional Songs*. Calcutta: Sinha Publishing House PVT Ltd.

5

MODELS OF WISDOM AND SANCTITY

The conversion of St Francis of Assisi

Michael Robson

Conventions and codes of conduct are devised by many societies for their members. Families educate their young and produce a programme of praiseworthy acts to be imitated and they identify their opposites to be avoided; an emphasis is placed upon the promotion of the common good and honour of the unit in a particular society. Hagiography champions the wholesome values that parents and teachers ought to communicate to children from an early age (Menestò and Brufani 1995a). Children are trained to follow the precepts of their parents and to benefit from the experience of older relations. One of the earliest lessons taught to children is that their behaviour should not besmirch the good name and reputation of their family. The family is the microcosm of the wider society that seeks to foster its distinctive set of values that are deemed to be life-enhancing and to encapsulate the accumulated wisdom of the ages. The link between social *mores* and right reason bubbles beneath the surface of innumerable groups, which regulate their members' behaviour. Eccentric and deviant deeds invite firm judgement and one person's individualism or selfishness is said to jeopardise the fortunes of a family or broader community. Wayward behaviour is not only portrayed as inappropriate; it is depicted in terms of folly, madness or even suicide. Perpetrators of such deeds are deemed to have lost their senses and to be acting out of character. In many cases penalties are imposed and ostracism ensues.

A similar set of conventions was invoked by groups of the religious. The religion of the Old Testament arose within a community context in which God was revealed as the protector and leader of his people. The descendants of Abraham were schooled to give priority to the Divine Law over social conventions and to listen attentively to the prophets who articulated the Word of God. Fidelity to religious observances was identified with a spirit of wisdom that finds expression in the text: *the fear of the Lord is the beginning of wisdom* (Proverbs 9: 10). This sagacity was the sure guide of the pilgrim people, moulding and informing their lives. Inexplicable conduct raised questions of probity and sanity. Some of those celebrating the festival of Pentecost in Jerusalem asked whether the apostles' preaching was the result of inebriation (Acts 2: 13). The pre-eminence of the Word of God passed into the nascent Christian tradition that challenged men and women to embrace *metanoia* and to live a new life shaped by the Gospel. Candidates for baptism underwent a protracted period of scrutiny and testing to gauge their suitability for the sacrament of initiation. Converts were routinely admonished to seek the wisdom revealed in the person of Jesus Christ and they were exhorted to be countercultural. Christian morality differed markedly from the *mores* of contemporary society and this bifurcation was articulated in a classical text, the *De civitate Dei,* of St Augustine of Hippo. The cessation of the epoch of persecution of the Church generated a more congenial society in which the majority were baptised, but it did not remove the friction between the Gospel and the rules of secular society. This was one of the *stimuli* for the emergence of the monastic world (Knowles 1966; Lawrence 1994) that in turn sired a series of reform movements between the eleventh and thirteenth centuries (Lawrence 1994).

The citizens of Assisi in Umbria were fiercely proud of their Christian origins and heritage. They celebrated the heroism of San Rufino, the bishop who had established Christianity in the city, sealing his ministry with his blood in 238. Devotion to the saint received a boost in the eleventh century with the recovery of the martyr's *passio* (Brunacci 1948) and the proliferation of miracles, some of which were associated with the new cathedral of San Rufino. A sermon by the eminent reformer, Cardinal Peter Damian (†1072), celebrated the heroism of the martyred bishop who was the protector of Assisi and its champion against the neighbouring city of Perugia (Lucchesi 1983). The rebuilding of the cathedral was continued into the thirteenth century (Langeli 2007) and the martyr's relics were recovered in 1212. The bones of San Vittorino, the second martyred bishop of the city, were interred in the Romanesque church of San Pietro inside the city walls during the thirteenth century (Manca 1995). Despite devotion to local saints, Assisi experienced some of the tensions between local government and the Gospel in a turbulent period. Although leper hospitals were a feature of cities in Western Europe (Borthwick Prob. Reg.1, fol.83rv), the urban officials of Assisi met the threat of leprosy by framing legislation that effectively discouraged them from entering the city (Brown 1982; Fortini 1926; Riley 1974).

Although Francis of Assisi had been nurtured on the accounts of the valiant heroism of these intrepid martyred bishops of Assisi (Fortini 1940), he imbibed his initial values from the prevailing attitudes of his neighbours. This was manifest in his treatment of lepers, whom he dreaded. The lazar houses filled him with deep revulsion and nausea and he habitually shunned the company of lepers (Menestò and Brufani 1995a), as he declares so openly in his *Testament*. His disposition towards lepers exemplified the tension between the principles of the Gospel and the conventions of society. His early life, conversion, the civil war and its wake, the emergence of a new life shaped by the Gospel and early responses to his fraternity form the basis of this study.

Francis' early life

The son of Pica and Pietro, Francis was born into the prosperous Bernardone family in 1181 or 1182. His father was a highly successful merchant who imported cloth from the markets of France. Francis' education was provided by the canons of San Rufino at the school adjacent to the church of San Giorgio, where he preached his first sermon and where he found temporary burial before the construction of the basilica (Menestò and Brufani 1995a). Despite his self-deprecatory words (Paolazzi 2009), which were on occasion echoed by others (Menestò and Brufani 1995e), he was an outstandingly resourceful teacher and was a young man with a highly developed sense of drama and symbolism; his love of music remained with him for life. His formal education fitted him for his career in the world of commerce; it also served him in later years as a deacon. Dr Rosalind Brooke regards Francis as an exceptionally gifted communicator who taught by parables, example, exaggeration, paradox and dramatisation. The *Chansons de Geste* and the Arthurian cycle were chosen as vehicles to convey the kernel of the Gospel (Brooke 1970).

Francis' name was derived from his father's love of France (Menestò and Brufani 1995d). From his earliest years Francis developed a strong love for that country, whose fairs he had probably attended with his father. He spoke French in moments of special joy following his act of renunciation before the bishop (Menestò and Brufani 1995a), and spiritual intoxication or prophecy, when he predicted that the dilapidated church of San Damiano outside Assisi would become the home of women renowned for their zealous service of God in voluntary poverty (Menestò and Brufani 1995b). His love of France was nurtured by its music, literature and fidelity to the Catholic tradition, especially its devotion to the Eucharist, whose theology was being clarified towards the end of the twelfth century. His attempts to minister in France were thwarted by the advice of Cardinal Hugolino, the influential bishop of Ostia, friend and protector of the fledgling fraternity, who prevailed him to return to Umbria and protect the interests of his nascent community (Menestò and Brufani 1995b, 1995e).

As an adolescent Francis followed his father's profession (*artem patris id est negociationem exercuit*) (Menestò and Brufani 1995d) and enjoyed the trappings of an affluent lifestyle. The cloth trade provides part of the context of his early life and conversion. Piles of cloth for sale were in the Bernardone household (Menestò and Brufani 1995a). Cloths of different colours were sold by Pietro at Umbrian markets, including Foligno (Menestò and Brufani 1995d). Pietro's wealth enabled Francis to dress in the finest of garments from the family's shop (*apotheca*) in Assisi (Menestò and Brufani 1995c). Francis had the money to finance his gastronomic tastes and his extensive wardrobe. His new vocation would eschew fine clothes and prompt him to dress in penitential sackcloth (Menestò and Brufani 1995e). His earlier life as a merchant was exploited by his biographers, who styled him as the divine merchant.

From his youth Francis was of frail and weak constitution (Menestò and Brufani 1995e). The *legenda trium sociorum* relates that he was given over to revelry and song with his friends. He roamed the streets of the walled city of Assisi day and night and was so lavish in his spending that his earnings were squandered in feasting and other pursuits. Such conduct earned him a timely rebuke from Pietro and Pica Bernardone, who reflected that he was behaving as though he were the son of a great prince rather than a merchant. Nonetheless, parental love cast a veil over their son's profligacy. Neighbours, too, commented on his extravagant conduct. Francis spent more money on expensive clothes than his income warranted. His vanity made him crave the limelight. He was elected as king of the revels, holding his badge of office (*portans in manu in baculum quasi dominus*) (Menestò and Brufani 1995d).

He had an innate compassion for the needy members of society, who would be allocated a major part in series of events leading to his conversion. Thomas of Celano, too, describes Francis as the ringleader of the frivolous set in Assisi who invited him to dinner parties, where the suggestive and vulgar prevailed. He goes on to speak in sour terms about the reasons for Francis' popularity, maintaining that his companions selected him as their leader because they had already tasted his munificence and knew that he would foot the bill for them. His neighbours were not disappointed, because he prepared a sumptuous meal for them, serving them elegant food (Menestò and Brufani 1995b).

The civil war and its aftermath

The turn of the thirteenth century was a time of reappraisal and social realignment in many cities and towns in Italy against the landscape of the protracted tussle between the papacy and the emperor. The cities of Umbria were not exempt from such tensions and internecine struggles, as Franciscan literature attests. Although Assisi was placed under the control of its Germanic overlord, there was an uprising in the last years of the twelfth century, when the *Rocca maggiore*, the symbol of subjection and oppression in the duchy of Spoleto, was sacked by the men of Assisi; the youthful Francis may have been among them in toppling a symbol of alien rule. Within a few years the tensions between the local nobility and the newly assertive mercantile classes, the *maggiori* and *minori* of Assisi, flared up again, reached a state of crisis and divided the city, leading to a civil war in which the nobility found support from the neighbouring city of Perugia.

As a member of the mercantile class, Francis was drawn into this conflict. In November 1202 he was a combatant at the battle of Collestrada, land close to Ponte San Giovanni, a village situated between Assisi and Perugia. From the hill Francis could see his own city. Thomas of Celano refers to a great massacre (*non modica strages ex belli conflictu*) and the battle in which the young Francis was captured and led to Perugia, where he was incarcerated by the perennial foe of the people of Assisi. While many of his fellow prisoners were depicted as being miserable on account of their imprisonment, Francis bore his captivity, a symbol of original sin, with better humour than his fellow citizens (Menestò and Brufani 1995b). Some of the biographers exaggerate his cheerfulness and spirit of detachment in this period. Francis remained in prison for the better part of two years before he was released. One hypothesis is that he was ransomed by his wealthy father and allowed to return home to resume his career as a lucrative merchant.

The period in jail gave Francis the time to review his conduct, to reflect upon its priorities and to plan his future. His biographers are united in their report that it was a markedly changed young man who returned to his native city and to the family's home close to the city's ancient *piazza del comune*. A sense of disorientation remained with him and this was accompanied by physical infirmity. Apart from these perfectly natural explanations, it is probable that Francis carried some deep psychological scars from his experience of violence. He had seen the fierce divisions and the indiscriminate destruction of property; he probably witnessed the brutal deaths of some of his neighbours and friends in skirmishes and exchanges on the field of battle. Such experiences undoubtedly scarred Francis for some time, if not for the rest of his life. His biographers were well acquainted with internecine strife and wars in the cities of Umbria, Tuscany and the Marches of Ancona. Their reticence on the subject of Francis' emotional equilibrium should not be cited as evidence that his psyche had emerged unscathed from warfare and detention; the horrendous deeds that he had seen with his own eyes were unforgettable. Were his hands stained with the blood of his neighbours and fellow citizens? Is this why he subsequently behaved so generously towards former foes, like the impoverished knight whom he clothed? He was aged 22 or 23 at the time of his return to Assisi. Warfare played a crucial part in the life of Francis, who responded by pioneering the greeting of peace to all whom he encountered. The near future would see him as an agent of peace and reconciliation in the troubled communes of Italy. He was also active in this role in Assisi.

The period of convalescence provided Francis with space to re-examine his life, to walk in the fields outside Assisi and to spend time in reflection with some prayer. The moment of crisis brought him face to face with the purpose of life, its frailty and its uncertainty. He began to search for a new and more satisfying form of life. Restlessness and some unpredictability now stamped his behaviour. Meditation began to claim more of his time and energies as he pondered the next stage in his life. The change in his conduct seems to have occurred step-by-step, with an evolving understanding. His sense of alienation from previous pleasures, however, coexisted with his ambition to become a celebrated knight. When his physical strength had returned, he enlisted with a local knight who was enrolling in the army of Walter de Brienne, who was opposing the armies of the German emperor in southern Italy. His former ostentation returned when he set out for Apulia in search of knighthood and renown; he had gone no further than Spoleto, where he had a decisive dream about conditions of service. This was interpreted as a divine directive to abandon his aspirations for knighthood and to return to Assisi with his military ambitions turned to rubble (Menestò and Brufani 1995a, 1995b). One explanation for the remarkable change in his life was that he was in love (Menestò and Brufani 1995b), a theme that was later spiritualised in terms of Lady Poverty.

Francis' act of renunciation

The chronology of Francis' conversion and act of renunciation is unclear with three interlocking events, beginning with the unexpected encounter with a leper. While the information on Francis' life has been supplied largely by biographers, who were prone to exaggerate their case and to contrast his earlier behaviour with the life of grace (Moorman 1979), the most authentic account of his conversion comes from his own pen, the *Testament*, a document dictated in the late summer of 1226, a short time before his death on the evening of 3 October. The pivotal moment was the decisive meeting with a leper outside the city. Hitherto lepers had been viewed with fear and loathing, which the penitent Francis attributed to original sin and actual sin. This was a providential moment of grace in which he overcame his customary aversion from the suffering members of society. A radical change was occurring and what had previously been a source of bitterness and a cause of distortion was transformed into a new vision and sweetness. The impact of this encounter was so powerful that Francis immediately mounted his horse and withdrew from Assisi; thereafter he devoted himself to the care of the lepers (Paolazzi 2009), perhaps at the *lazaretto* in the valley between Rivo Torto and the Portiuncula, close to the small chapel of Santa Maria Maddalena. His language – *exivi de seculo* – reflects the traditional vocabulary of the religious life with its sharp criticism of secular society and its values. The act of conversion was the antithesis of urban life with its pursuit of security and its welter of man-made regulations.

This seemingly chance encounter exposed two flaws in the values that obtained in Assisi. First, it demonstrated the weaknesses of the conventions that prevailed in the city, which had framed legislation to protect its inhabitants from the scourge of leprosy; the citizens were inclined to shun lepers, whose ulcerated wounds terrified them (Menestò and Brufani 1995e). Obedience to human conventions was shown to be limited because the principles of urban government were not immutable. Moreover, the norms of a society were not unfailingly sensitive to the spirit of the Gospel. Francis responded by withdrawing from the city and devoting himself to the care of

117

the lepers; Franciscan hagiography contains several references to lepers and their hospitals where the early friars ministered. Thereafter the key moments in the revelation of his new vocation were located outside the city. Second, the meeting with the leper called into question the temptation to gloss uncomfortable passages from the Gospel. Such a practice was now shown to be running the risk of diluting the teaching of the Son of God. Francis reacted to the second of these by adopting a literal interpretation of the sacred texts, which would be his sure guide for the future.

This event occurred about the time that Francis received another divine communication in the church of San Damiano, whose ruinous state is captured by the artists from the school of Giotto in the upper basilica of San Francesco in Assisi. On one occasion the figure from the crucifix admonished the praying Francis to repair his house. Thomas of Celano concedes that these startling words had a deranging effect (*stupet non modicum*) upon Francis. This biographer delighted in a new and unheard-of miracle, which stimulated Francis' devotion to the cross, thereafter one of the focal points of his piety and the heart of his preaching. The message from the Crucified Christ was taken literally by Francis, who immediately set about the restoration of the old church, giving the priest money to purchase a lamp to burn before the image of the cross (Menestò and Brufani 1995b). Francis' new plans startled the priest, Peter, who had heard of his reputation for excesses. His resolution was, however, manifest by the collection of stones for the repair of the church; sometimes he purchased stones for the restoration (Menestò and Brufani 1995b).

Francis' novel demeanour set him on a collision course with his increasingly bewildered and perplexed father. In the streets of Assisi he begged oil for the lamps in San Damiano. Despite his earlier inhibition, he confessed his fears and begged in French for oil and received it. His former delicacy gave way to physical labour in which he impressed the resident priest who fed him. The former spendthrift started to beg for food from door to door (*ostiatim*) (Menestò and Brufani 1995a). The profound change in his life prompted many to laugh at him and insult him, deriding him as mad (*pro insano*) (Menestò and Brufani 1995c). Former friends covered him with insults, calling him a fool and a madman (*insanumque ac dementem*) and threw stones and mud at him. His life had so altered that they deemed him to have been out of his mind (*dementiae imputabant*). Hearing this commotion, Pietro Bernardone hurried out to find his son, whom he intended to castigate (Menestò and Brufani 1995d). He regarded his son's new ideas as utter folly (*insania*) and hurled abuse at him (Menestò and Brufani 1995b). His son's seemingly bizarre conduct was at odds with the values that he and his wife had communicated to him.

When Pietro Bernardone concluded that he was unable to move his intransigent son, he had recourse to the commune of the city; he denounced his son and demanded restitution for the money squandered at the fair in Foligno. This summons was rejected by Francis, who now presented himself as the servant of God; he claimed an exemption from the jurisdiction of the local commune and his plea was accepted. Pietro then took his complaint to the episcopal authority, Guido I, bishop of Assisi (D'Accunto 1995, 1996, 2002, 2008), who cited Francis to respond to the charges. This time Francis readily agreed to the hearing. Guido firmly reminded Francis that, if he wished to serve God, he must begin by restoring his father's property (Menestò and Brufani 1995d). The dramatic act, whereby Francis returned even the clothes in which he stood, was both a renunciation of his former lifestyle and a quasi-baptismal moment in which he reaffirmed his faith in God his Father; it was a confessional event which imparted a new direction to his life. This flamboyant gesture signalled Francis' intentions of embarking upon a new life within a religious framework which would be revealed to him at a later date (Menestò and Brufani 1995e). For the time being he was content to have freed himself from the shackles of parental expectations and the social conventions of his native city. In the interim he lived as an oblate or hermit and returned to his work of restoring ruined churches in the vicinity of Assisi, especially Santa Maria degli Angeli, the Portiuncula, San Pietro and Santa Maria Maggiore, the old cathedral (Frugoni 2000).

Francis was now resolved to peer beyond human regulations and expectations and to anchor his life in the teaching of the Bible. One expression of this was his openness to the words of the New Testament. At different times he had the book of the Gospels opened at random to proffer guidance on the principles by which he wished to live. Thus, for example, after hearing the proclamation of the Gospel at Mass in Santa Maria degli Angeli, he suddenly glimpsed his new vocation as one called to perpetuate the preaching of the apostles and, swapping his hermit's dress, he clothed himself as an apostle in sackcloth. Thomas of Celano relates that Francis obeyed the Gospel to the letter (Menestò and Brufani 1995a), a trait that would become a feature of the conversion. Thenceforth the mutable decisions of human institutions were to be subordinate to the primacy of the sacred Scriptures.

Francis and the model of the apostolic Church

After the momentous reading from the Gospel during Mass at Santa Maria degil Angeli, Francis remained outside Assisi, living first at Rivo Torto and then at the Portiuncula, which became the friars' spiritual home. While earlier generations of ascetical figures left their homes and sought admission to a monastery, Francis was touched by a new spirit that saw sanctity in terms of engagement with secular society (Lawrence 1994). It is undeniably true that he had turned his back upon his earlier lifestyle. No effort was made to set out for distant mission fields, until he made three attempts to reach the Holy Land. His new vocation, however, called him to be an urban evangelist and to preach the Gospel in his native city. The cities and towns of Umbria were to be the first theatre of his ministry. His apostolate took him back to Assisi, a city that he had left two or three years earlier.

It was a very different Francis who climbed the paths from the valley to the hillside city of Assisi, where his message echoed the preaching of the apostolic Church, calling his former neighbours to repentance for the forgiveness of sins. The extravagant youth with a fine wardrobe was now dressed simply as a poor evangelist aflame with a sacred and urgent message. His powerful words and altered demeanour struck the people of Assisi, who saw him as a man whose life had acquired a new orientation, vitality and power. He spoke vigorously, attractively and imaginatively about the Gospel and his message was conveyed by word, example and drama. Among those who monitored the change in Francis was Bernard of Quintavalle, a wealthy man, who invited him to his home on the street which now bears his celebrated name, close to the small church of San Gregorio in Assisi. He was impressed not only by the fervour of Francis' words, but also by his asceticism and devotion. He concluded that Francis was a man of God and his decision to seek his spiritual advice gave birth to the new fraternity.

Instead of formulating a penitential and pastoral strategy the two men proceeded to the church of San Nicolò close to the *piazza del comune*, where they prayed after Mass and had the book of the Gospels opened thrice at random. The texts on which their eyes fell became the kernel of the incipient fraternity. The first text was 'if you wish to be perfect, go, and sell what you own and give the money to the poor' (Matthew 19: 21). The second was 'take nothing for the journey' (Luke 9: 3) and the third, 'if anyone wants to be a follower of mine, let him renounce himself and take up his cross and follow me' (Matthew 16: 24 and Luke 9: 23) (Voorvelt and van Leeuwen 1989). This advice was scrupulously followed by Bernard (Menestò and Brufani 1995b), who divested himself of his possessions, selling them and giving the money to the poor; thereby he fulfilled the advice proffered to the rich young man in the Gospel (Menestò and Brufani 1995a). The tension between the principles of the New Testament and those of the marketplace manifested themselves in the opportunism of Sylvester, an elderly priest and canon of San Rufino, who grumbled at the price which he had earlier received from Francis for some stones; the latter responded by giving the priest some of the coins disbursed by Bernard. This avaricious complaint subsequently shamed the priest, who began to do penance a few days later and then joined the fraternity, where he died in an edifying manner (Menestò and Brufani 1995c). News of Bernard's dramatic renunciation of his possessions on the Piazza di San Giorgio attracted comment and reached the ears of Giles, another native of Assisi, who wished to follow Francis' spiritual counsel and join Bernard and Peter as his disciples (Brooke 1970). The colourful conversion of Bernard was thus instrumental in triggering the vocations of Sylvester and Giles. Rumour of the friars' penitential lives brought others to the fraternity (Menestò and Brufani 1995e). The friars were accustomed to explain that they were voluntarily poor by the grace of God and in fulfilment of His counsel. They had renounced their possessions for the love of God and had given them to the poor (Menestò and Brufani 1995c).

A novel vocation

Innocent III expressed amazement that Francis wished to form a community without the customary material possessions. Nonetheless, he recognised that God was speaking through Francis, whose simplicity of life was enlivened by a profound spiritual wisdom (cf. 1 Corinthians 2: 4) (Menestò and Brufani 1995c). Francis' first recruits were natives of Assisi and it was the natural setting for their ministry of calling people to penance and peace in the wake of the recent civil war. While urban centres provided the friars with their natural habitat, the latter were no longer at home there and formed a community that was based on the precepts of the Gospel. They had all turned their backs on the values of the commercial world that flourished in such centres. The friars' detachment was demonstrated by their retreat from the city at the end of their labours. The heartbeat of the founder and his fraternity was in rural hovels, wayside chapels and hermitages outside Assisi. Francis' perception of the apostolic life drew upon the new ideas adopted by a series of ascetical and penitential figures and groups in the twelfth century (Brooke 1975). He freely embraced the concept that religious life entailed pastoral engagement with society rather than flight from it, despite his talk of *leaving the world* after his interaction with the leper. Nonetheless, Francis was touched by the simplicity and starkness of the Cistercian ideal and he freely borrowed from the monastic lexicon for the organisation of communal life and its penitential norms. He fostered good relations with Benedictine communities in the vicinity of Assisi.

Francis' conversion featured encounters with the impoverished members of society, such as the beggar who sought alms in the Bernardone shop in Assisi, the poor knight and the paupers of Assisi and Rome to whom he gave his clothing, presaging his new identity. These episodes acquired a more spiritual dimension through the series of readings from the book of the Gospels; the sacred texts were instrumental in mapping out his new vocation. Francis quickly passed from a focus on the *vita apostolica* to reflection on the *imitatio Christi*. He believed that the Son of God had become poor in this world to enrich humanity. His period of reflection and meditation helped him to enter more fully into the mode of redemption whereby creature and Creator were reconciled through Jesus Christ. The self-emptying of the Incarnation became the model for Francis' own life of poverty and his wish to renounce himself, as he states in the opening chapter of the Rule.

The friars' vocation was to live according to the manner of their divine mentor. Their voluntary poverty was a salient feature. They lived in penury and poor clothing, a mark of their retreat from the city and its excesses; evangelical poverty was their emblem. In this they differed markedly from contemporary religious, such as the Benedictine monks and the Augustinian canons who were individually poor while enjoying membership of an institution which might be rich in corporate terms through its estates and rents. By the end of the twelfth century this model of religious life was already ceding some of its perennial appeal. Although Francis seems to have displayed some interest in the monastic world in his dealings with San Verecundo in Gubbio (Menestò and Brufani 1995a), he was later adamant that he was not called to be a monk or hermit (Menestò and Brufani 1995a) or to observe the Rules of Saints Benedict or Augustine. His vocation was to become a new fool in the world (*novellus pazzus in mundo*) (Menestò and Brufani 1995e). His *Testament* affirms that he was divinely inspired and that no one showed him what to do; the Lord told him what He wanted (Paolazzi 2009). He and his disciples worked with their hands for their living and they accepted payment in kind (Menestò and Brufani 1995e); money was to be shunned at all costs. When their supply of food ran out, the friars had recourse to questing for alms, something of a novelty for members of religious communities. While Francis had been able to do this individually, the small group of friars encountered some hostility in doing the same. The people of Assisi complained that these new religious, who had recently renounced their possessions, were becoming especially burdensome. Bishop Guido I was drawn into this controversy and raised the matter with Francis, pressurising him to accept some property to supply the community's need for food. Francis retorted in a perceptive and magisterial manner that, if he had possessions, he would need alms to protect them because they were a source of discord and some litigation (Menestò and Brufani 1995c, 1995d); his response was based on the evidence of his own eyes and the innumerable divisions which he had observed in families and even religious institutions, which were prone to legal disputes regarding property and money (Knowles 1948).

The first friars were well known to the people and clergy of Assisi and its environs, where they bore witness to the Gospel by exhortation and example. Their first confrères in France, Germany and Hungary took no trouble to prepare themselves for their new ministry and neglected to study the languages and customs of these people; accordingly, they suffered the consequences when they were taken for heretics (Boehmer 1908; Menestò and Brufani 1995c). Francis dispatched the fledgling community into neighbouring provinces where the friars were not immediately recognised as men of God. *The Anonymous of Perugia*, completed in 1240–41, recounts the impression created by the first friars who called men to fear and love God and to live in penance. While some marvelled at the friars' message, other took them for fools and drunkards. They differed from all others in their dress and lifestyle, appeared like wild men (*silvestres*) and abuse was sometimes meted out to them. Some willingly listened to their words of peace and their exhortations to penitence on the piazza or in the streets, while others jeered them. Many relentlessly questioned them, with some asking them whence they came and the religious order to which they belonged. The friars styled themselves as penitents of Assisi (Menestò and Brufani 1995c, 1995d).

Some people regarded the friars as impostors or fools (*deceptores vel fatui*), denying them hospitality. The friars suffered many insults and were reduced to finding lodging in the porticos of churches or houses. Two friars were looking for a place to stay in Florence and found a house with a portico containing a bread oven. When they sought lodging, the woman denied it, but she reluctantly permitted them to spend the cold night near the oven. On his return her husband upbraided her for allowing two rogues (*ribaldi*) to lodge there. She justified herself by saying that they would be unable to steal anything from the portico. During the night the two friars arose and attended Matins in the nearest church. The following morning the lady attended Mass and observed the friars in devout and humble prayer. She concluded that such men were not evildoers, as her husband judged them. As these thoughts passed through her mind, a man named Guido went around the church distributing alms to the poor; he attempted to press a coin upon each of the friars. One of them, Bernard, explained that he and his companion were voluntarily poor by the grace of God and in fulfilment of His counsel. The woman regretted her hardness of heart and recognised the friars as true Christians who had renounced their possessions for the love of God and had given them to the poor. She invited the friars to return to her house (Menestò and Brufani 1995c).

Despite such an inauspicious start, the hagiographical tradition narrates the triumph of *il poverello d'Assisi*, who serves as a prophetical figure, promoting reconciliation and fostering peace; leading ecclesiastical figures benefited from his insights and profound teaching. The band of twelve friars who travelled to the papal court in search of the blessing of Innocent III in 1209 had become a vast army by the time of Francis' death seventeen years later. The friars had already established themselves throughout the various provinces of Italy, France, Germany, Spain, Portugal, England, Ireland and Scotland by the 1230s. The bishop of Terni attended one of Francis' sermons and regarded him as a divine messenger for the rejuvenation of the Church (Menestò and Brufani 1995e). Francis moved in exalted circles and enjoyed access to the dying Innocent III at Perugia in July 1216. His close friendship with Cardinal Hugolino, the future Gregory IX, enabled the fraternity to become a major religious order, whose Rule of life was approved by Honorius III on 29 November 1223. Nobles sought his spiritual advice and became his early benefactors. Orlando, count of Chiusi, donated the mountain of La Verna for the friars' use and it was there that Francis received the stigmata, the five wounds that had marked the body of the Crucified Christ. Towards the end of his life Francis was feted by members of the papal court (Menestò and Brufani 1995e) and was treated as a saint (Menestò and Brufani 1995e). One of the ironies is that Francis, who had travelled to the fairs and markets of France, was honoured by the king and queen of that country, who venerated the pillow used by the dying saint (Menestò and Brufani 1995a). He was canonised by Gregory IX in the Piazza di San Giorgio on 16 July 1228 in the presence of a vast concourse of prelates, religious, princes and civic officials, including one monarch (Menestò and Brufani 1995a). The next day the pope laid the foundation stone for the new basilica to be built in honour of *il poverello* (Menestò and Brufani 1995d).

Opposition to the Franciscan vocation

Francis' new vocation caused a well-ventilated division in his family. Following his act of renunciation in the episcopal court, his younger brother, Angelo, followed his father's example and poured scorn upon him (Menestò and Brufani 1995b). Francis' reputation, enhanced by his stirring sermons in Assisi's newly rebuilt cathedral of San Rufino, attracted the attention and admiration of Clare di Favarone di Offreduccio and her sister, Agnes. Both sisters encountered fierce opposition to their decision to become the disciples of *il poverello*. Clandestine meetings between Francis and Clare were arranged, with Philip of Atri and Bona di Guelfuccio of Assisi in attendance, to consider her future and a way of her sharing the ideals of evangelical poverty. The outcome was Clare's profession at Santa Maria degli Angeli and her temporary refuge at San Paolo, the Benedictine monastery, at nearby Bastia (Menestò and Brufani 1995f). Clare's relations attempted to drag her from this monastic church. There was a further violent response from her uncle and a dozen men sixteen days later, when Agnes joined her older sister at San Angelo di Panzo, another Benedictine community outside Assisi, where Clare had been given temporary asylum (Menestò and Brufani 1995g). Had Clare and Agnes joined one of the established Benedictine monasteries in Umbria, the opposition would have been less virulent. The fact that these daughters of one of the most noble families in Assisi (Fortini 1982) were exchanging the security of the comfortable lifestyle of their home on the Piazza di San Rufino for the instability and uncertainties associated with the impecunious Francis and his followers fuelled the anger of their family.

The obstacles placed in the paths of the pillars of the Franciscan cosmos were to be repeated on numerous occasions in the first century of the movement's history. There were signs of the order's growing respectability in the canonisation of three saints – Francis of Assisi, Anthony of Padua and Elizabeth of Hungary – by Gregory IX as early as 1235; some twenty years later, Clare of Assisi would also be enrolled in the catalogue of saints. The order had already established itself in virtually every diocese of the Western Church by the 1240s and the friars were becoming a feature of the landscape of the Church; they were also increasingly prominent at the new universities, where their masters of theology were highly influential and some friars were being raised to the episcopate. Before the end of the century a friar, Nicholas IV, would be installed on the throne of St Peter. Despite such marks of success in secular terms, some families continued to oppose their sons becoming friars. For example, Richard Gobium, the benefactor who had accommodated the friars in Northampton, drew a line at his son, John, taking the habit. When John defiantly chose to persevere in his new vocation, the friars were ordered to vacate the premises close to the church of St Edmund outside the new wall of the town (Little 1951). Vigorous and sometimes violent attempts to thwart such aspirants became a topos of the order's hagiographical tradition, its chronicles and *exempla* literature, as the following example demonstrates.

An unnamed friar of Dublin narrated the fate of those who laid siege to the friary there in 1258, when David de Burgh, brother of Walter, the future earl of Ulster, was received into the order. When Walter heard about the clothing of his brother, he immediately went to the friary in Dublin with his knights, men at arms and retainers and broke down the partition in the middle of the church, inflicting dreadful violence on the convent. David was violently snatched from the convent and deprived of his religious habit. The source of this *exemplum* continued to talk about society as an arena bristling with challenges to Christian morality and talked of the novice going back to the world (*ad seculum reduxerunt*). The anecdote exemplifies the fate of those who oppress the Church and indirectly the Franciscan order, especially one Thomas Court, who beat repeatedly on the inner doors of the church and inflicted as much violence as he could. He was described as acting like a drunkard before dying in the presence of numerous witnesses (Fitzmaurice and Little 1920; Little 1908).

Pellegrin Reppellin, a child, was cured from a paralysis that had afflicted him from birth, through the intercession of St Douceline (*c.* 1215–74). As soon as the boy was healed, the saint prevailed upon his mother to make a promise to give her son to the Cordeliers. Pellegrin described how, when he was about to become a friar, his brother – *fraire seglar* – objected strongly and wanted him to become a monk instead at the monastery of St Victor. Fearful of his brother, Pellegrin reluctantly yielded. Suddenly he felt a terrible pain in one of his ears that had earlier been healed through the intercession of the saint. The pain increased with each step towards the monastery. When he was about to be clothed in the monastic habit, his ear, neck and throat became so swollen that he could barely speak and he was obliged to return home; this happened on two occasions. His speech failed him until he remembered the vow that he had made to the saint. He promised her that, if she cured him, he would fulfil his promise to become a friar. This resolution was no sooner formed than the swelling in his neck and ear went down, his throat was clear and his speech returned. The friars were reluctant to accept him, but, reassured by the miracle, they clothed him as a friar. Received into the order at the appropriate age, he became a great preacher, confessor and precentor of the friary. He recounted the blessings that he had received from St Douceline, whose shrine was in the church of the Cordeliers at Marseilles (Albanès 1879; Garay and Jeay 2001).

The vocation of Robert de Ware, a member of the custody of London, illustrates another allegation brought against the friars. He was the eldest son of a merchant of franklin of Hertford. At the University of Oxford he fell under the influence of the friars, who were increasingly accused of enticing young scholars to join their ranks; this became another topos of anti-mendicant literature, finding its champion in Richard FitzRalph, archbishop of Armagh (1346–60). Robert entered the order between 1265 and 1268, to the great dismay of his family. His father and mother, brother, relatives and friends were dispatched to induce him to withdraw from the order. In vain his father tried to obtain a formal release from the order for his son in the court of the papal legate, Ottobuono de' Fieschi, cardinal deacon of San Adriano. Paternal anger followed this rebuff and he refused to set eyes on his son again. One day Robert and another friar reappeared at the gates of the family home in Ware. His father sent the servants to tell his son that he would not be admitted; he swore to kill his son if he dared to enter the house. About the Octave of the Blessed Virgin, his father fell ill and was confined to his bed. One night he dreamed that he was once again riding his horse from Hertford to Ware. As he climbed a certain knoll, he met three beautiful ladies, one of whom asked whether he was on good terms with his son, Robert. On hearing the negative reply, the lady instructed him not to proceed until he had rectified the situation. On waking, he confided his dream and promise to a member of the household and it was agreed that it was the Blessed Virgin who had spoken to him. He had Robert fetched from London, a journey of some 22 miles (35 km), and a reconciliation ensued (Owst 1925; Röhrkasten 1997).

One of the fullest accounts of parental opposition is narrated in the chronicle of Salimbene de Adam. His father, Guido de Adam, a crusader in the time of Baldwin, count of Flanders, had four sons, of whom the chronicler, Salimbene, was the third. Salimbene was admitted to the order at the age of 15 on 4 February 1238 and was clothed by Elias of Cortona, minister general at Parma. This was to the dismay of his father, who was inconsolable and continually lamented the loss of his son and heir. He complained to the emperor, Frederick II, who was visiting Parma, that the friars had stolen his son. The emperor wrote to Elias, asking for Salimbene to be restored to his father. Guido travelled to Assisi to hand a copy of the emperor's letter to Elias. When he was passing through Fano, the friars hid Salimbene and his brother, also a friar and named Guido de Adam, at the house of Lord Martin, a master of law. After reading the letter, Elias wrote to the friars to state that, if Salimbene wished to leave the order, he was free to do so without delay. Conversely, if he wanted to stay, he was to be allowed to do so. Accompanied by a large group of knights, Guido proceeded to the convent at Fano to speak with his son in the presence of a crowd of friars and others in the chapter house. The scene was a classic confrontation between paternal pressure and the choice of new recruit to the friars. Guido produced Elias' letter in the presence of the custos (regional superior of the order) and urged his son to return home with him, using uncomplimentary language about the friars. When Salimbene declared that his new vocation was a matter of his salvation, his father accused the friars of brainwashing his son.

A private meeting achieved nothing and eventually Guido prostrated himself on the ground and cursed his son. The convent of Fano, outside the city walls and only a few streets from the sea, was vulnerable to manoeuvres by Guido, who had arranged for pirates from Ancona to kidnap his son if he ever took a walk along the beach. Moreover, Guido had offered a reward for his son's capture. For this reason Salimbene was transferred to the friary at Iesi, where he spent the whole of Lent. Even after his move to Pisa, his father continued to lay traps to detach him from the order and was never reconciled with him (Scalia 1998/99). Guido spent the rest of his life in trying to remove his son and unsuccessfully enlisted the intervention of Innocent IV (Scalia 1998/99). Many of the emotions felt and expressed by Guido serve as a medieval precursor for those parents who are aghast to find their sons and daughters attracted by religious groups or sects that they accuse of brainwashing and destabilising.

Conclusion

The conversion of St Francis of Assisi illustrates the conflicting cultures or civilizations, one secular and the other religious. The tension between them is noted by Professor Diarmaid MacCulloch, who asserts that 'religious belief can be very close to madness. It has brought human beings to acts of criminal folly as well as the highest achievements of goodness, creativity and generosity' (MacCulloch 2009). Francis spurned the laws and conventions of medieval Assisi and gave himself to the fulfilment of the Gospel, to which everything else was subservient. The circumstances of his conversion and his new vocation expose the clash between two views of the world and their respective values. His conduct caused consternation on the part of his family and former friends, whom the hagiographical tradition pilloried for their inability to comprehend the radical change in his character; the language of madness appears regularly in the responses to the dramatic change in Francis' life. The friction between the Gospel and expediency is demonstrated in the response of the people of Assisi to the friars renouncing their possessions and then seeking alms in the city.

Aspects of the friars' apostolate caused criticism and consternation even within Christian circles. For example, when a friar, James, was accustomed to take a leper to the church of Santa Maria degli Angeli, people attending the chapel were horrified and feared contagion. Francis' biographers present his treatment of a leper as a moment of self-mastery in which he shared the latter's bowl (Menestò and Brufani 1995e). His victory over his own prejudices and weaknesses was a moment of grace; the saint was reaffirming the priority of the Gospel. Another perspective is that is this was no more than irresponsible conduct. The protocol of hospitality and the table clashed with the demands of sanctity in Francis' decision to quest for alms as a guest of Cardinal Hugolino. Although the cardinal had reserved a seat of honour for him,

Francis insisted on begging in the streets and, having arrived late, he then distributed what he had collected among the startled knights and chaplains (Menestò and Brufani 1995e). Thus, even the most senior cardinal in the Church was either insulted or honoured, depending on the vantage point. Francis is depicted as a prophetical figure, who reaffirmed the principles of Christianity, regardless of the norms of secular society. The hagiographical tradition of *il poverello* shows a mutual unease and suspicion and hostility between the conventions of society and the call of the Gospel. Within a short time the friars stood accused of brainwashing their recruits and turning them against their families and the principles of their early education. Such accusations were also levelled against those who converted to Catholicism in late nineteenth- and early twentieth-century Britain, often resulting in disinheritance and ostracism. What the penitent and saintly Francis cherished and revered was sometimes abhorrent or insane from a worldly perspective.

Abbreviation

Borthwick Prob. Reg.   Borthwick Institute Archives *Probate Registers*. University of York, will dated 14 May 1395, Reg. 1, fol. 83rv.

References

Albanès, J.H. (ed.) (1879). *La Vie de Sainte Douceline fondatrice des béguines de Marseille.* Marseille: Etienne Camoin.

Boehmer, H. (ed.) (1908). *Chronica Fratris Jordani (Collection d'études et de documents sur l'histoire religieuse et littéraire du moyen âge*, vol. 6). Paris: Librairie Fischbacher.

Brooke, R.B. (ed.) (1970). Vita Beati Fratris Egidii. In *The Writings of Leo, Rufino and Angelo Companions of St. Francis*, pp. 305–349. Oxford: Clarendon Press.

Brooke, R.B. (1975). *The Coming of the Friars*. London: Allen and Unwin.

Brown, R. (1982). *The Roots of St Francis: A Popular History of the Church in Assisi and Umbria Before St Francis as Related to His Life and Spirituality*. Chicago: Franciscan Press.

Brunacci, A. (1948). Leggende e culto di S. Rufino in Assisi. *Bollettino della deputazione di Storia Patria per l'Umbria* 45: 5–91.

D'Acunto, N. (1995). Vescovi e canonici ad Assisi nella prima metà del sec. XIII. In *Assisi al tempo di Federico II,* serie VI, ed. F. Santucci, vol. 23, pp. 49–132. Assisi: Accademia Properziana del Subasio.

D'Acunto, N. (1996). Il vescovo Guido oppure i vescovi Guido? Cronotassi episcopale asssiana e fonti francescani. *Mélanges de l' École Française de Rome* 108(2): 479–524.

D'Acunto, N. (2002). Assisi nel Medio Evo. Studi di storia ecclesiastica e civile. *Quaderni dell'Accademia Properziana del Subasio* 8: 103–55.

D'Acunto, N. (2008). Il vescovo di Assisi Guido I presso la curia Romana. *Francesco a Roma dal signor Papa: Atti del VI Convegno storico di Greccio*, ed. A. Cacciotti and M. Melli, pp. 41–60. Milan: Edizioni Biblioteca Francescana.

Fitzmaurice, E.B. and Little, A.G. (ed.) (1920). *Materials for the History of the Franciscan Province of Ireland AD 1230–1450*. Manchester: Manchester University Press.

Fortini, A. (1926). *Nova Vita di San Francesco*, 4 vols. Milan: Alpes.

Fortini, A. (1940). *Assisi nel Medioevo Roma*. Rome: Edizioni Roma.

Fortini, G. (1982). The noble family of St Clare of Assisi. *Franciscan Studies* 42: 48–67.

Frugoni, C. (2000). La prima attestatione pubblica di Francesco d'Assisi. *Archivum Franciscanum Historicum* 93: 503–10.

Garay, K. and Jeay, M. (2001). *The Life of Saint Douceline, a Beguine of Provence*. Woodbridge: Boydell and Brewer.

Knowles, D. (1948). *The Religious Orders in England*. Cambridge: Cambridge University Press.

Knowles, D. (1966). *From Pachomius to Ignatius: A Study in the Constitutional History of the Religious Orders*. Oxford: Clarendon Press.

Langeli, A.B. (2007). II Patto di Assisi: Ritorno sulla *Carta Pacis* di 1210. *Franciscan Studies* 65: 1–7.

Lawrence, C.H. (1994). *The Friars: The Impact of the Early Mendicant Movement on Western Society*. London: Longman.

Little, A.G. (ed.) (1908). *Liber exemplorum ad usum predicantium, saeculo XIII compositus a quodam fratre minore Anglico de provincia Hiberniae*. Aberdeen: British Society of Franciscan Studies.

Little, A.G. (ed.) (1951). *Fratris Thomae vulgo dicti de Eccleston Tractatus de adventu Fratrum Minorum in Angliam*. Manchester: Manchester University Press.

Lucchesi, J. (ed.) (1983). *Sancti Petri Damiani sermons. Corpus Christianorum, continuatio mediaevalis* 57: 217–22. Turnhout: Brepols.

MacCulloch, D. (2009). *A History of Christianity: The First Three Thousand Years*. London: Allen Lane.

Manca, B. (1995). *San Vittorino vescovo e martire di Assisi nella legenda e nel culto*. Assisi: Libreria Fonteviva.

Menestò, E. and Brufani, S. (eds) (1995a). Thomae de Celano vita prima Sancti Francisci. *Fontes Francescani* 273–424. Assisi: Porziuncola.

Menestò, E. and Brufani, S. (eds) (1995b). Thomae de Celano vita secunda Sancti Francisci. *Fontes Francescnai* 441–639. Assisi: Porziuncola.

Menestò, E. and Brufani, S. (eds) (1995c). Anonymi Perusini de inceptione vel fundamento ordinis. *Fontes Franciscani* 1311–51. Assisi: Porziuncola.

Menestò, E. and Brufani, S. (eds) (1995d). Legenda trium sociorum. *Fontes Francescani* 1373–1445. Assisi: Porziuncola.

Menestò, E. and Brufani, S. (eds) (1995e). Compilatio Assisiensis. *Fontes Francescani* 1471–1690. Assisi: Porziuncola.

Menestò, E. and Brufani, S. (eds) (1995f). Testamentum sanctae Clarae virginis. *Fontes Francescani* 2311–19. Assisi: Porziuncola.

Menestò, E. and Brufani, S. (eds) (1995g). Legenda Sanctae Clarae Assisiensis. *Fontes Francescani* 2415–50. Assisi: Porziuncola.

Moorman, J.R. (ed.) (1979). *Saint Francis of Assisi*. London: SPCK.

Owst, G.R. (1925). Some Franciscan memorials at Gray's Inn. *Dublin Review* 176: 276–84.

Paolazzi, C. (ed.) (2009). *Francesco d'Assisi Scritti. Spicilegium Bonaventurianum* 36. Grottaferrata: Editiones Collegii S. Bonaventura ad Claras Aquas.

Riley, P.V. (1974). Francis' Assisi: Its political and social history, 1175–1225. *Franciscan Studies* 34: 393–424.

Röhrkasten, J. (1997). Mendicants in the metropolis: The Londoners and the development of the London friaries. In *Thirteenth Century England VI*, ed. M. Prestwich, R.H. Britnell and R. Frame, pp. 61–75. Woodbridge: Boydell and Brewer.

Scalia, G. (ed.) (1998/99). *Salimbene de Adam, Cronica a.1168–1287. Corpus Christianorum continuatio mediaevalis*, vols 125, 125a. Turnhout: Brepols.

Società internazionale di studi francescani (1978). *Assisi al tempo di san Francesco: Atti del V convegno internazionale, Assisi, 13–16 Ottobre 1977*. Assisi: La Società.

Voorvelt, G.C.P. and van Leeuwen, B.P. (1989). L'Evangéliaire de Baltimore. Etude critique su le missel que saint François aurait consulte. *Collectanea Franciscana* 59: 261–321.

6

SPIRITUAL CONVERSION IN
THE BHAGAVAD GITA
A psychoanalytic study

Satish Reddy

> But thou canst not see Me
> With this same eye of thine own:
> I give thee a supernatural eye:
> Behold My mystic power as God!
> (*Bhagavad Gita* 11: 8)[1]

God revealing his divine-cosmic self to a human is a theme in many religions. Arguably, the most dramatic example of such spiritual epiphany occurs in the most profound and influential sacred text of Hinduism, *The Bhagavad Gita* (*Gita*). The *Gita* is a poetic dialogue between the God Krishna and his human pupil and devotee, the warrior Arjuna, set in the context of an apocalyptic fratricidal war between the rival cousins, the Pandavas and the Kauravas. Arjuna is the Pandava epic hero and the disguised Krishna is his chariot driver. Unaware of Krishna's divinity, Arjuna considers Krishna a fellow warrior and intimate friend. As war is about to begin, Arjuna loses his resolve to fight and becomes despondent and depressed. Paralysed by sadness and guilt, he tells Krishna that he cannot fight and asks him to help him resolve his spiritual crisis. Krishna's counsel to Arjuna comprises the content of the *Gita*. In its eighteen concise and dense chapters, Krishna conveys to Arjuna the essential teachings of Hinduism and the path to salvation – a magisterial resolution to Arjuna's existential crisis.

In chapter 11 of the *Gita*, 'Manifestation of the Cosmic Form', Arjuna asks Krishna to see his divine form. In this pivotal and transformative chapter, Krishna gives Arjuna divine vision so that he may see the cosmic-universal form of God. Upon seeing Krishna's divine form, Arjuna is spiritually and existentially transformed – he is spiritually converted. And yet Arjuna's vision of the divine is not beatific – it is horrific. His emotional reaction to Krishna's divinity combines awe, dread, fear, amazement and humility. Arjuna trembles and bows before Krishna, as he is made to understand the true nature of God. He comprehends emotionally what he had previously been able to understand only intellectually what Krishna has been trying to teach him all along.

This chapter is a psychoanalytic study of the process of spiritual conversion in the *Gita*. By spiritual conversion, I follow William James's *Varieties of Religious Experience* (James 1902).

> To be converted, to be regenerated, to receive grace, to experience religion, to gain an assurance, are so many phrases which denote the process, gradual or sudden, by which a self hitherto divided, and consciously wrong, inferior and unhappy, becomes unified and consciously right, superior and happy, in consequence of its firmer hold upon religious realities. This is at least what conversion signifies in general terms, whether or not we believe that a direct divine operation is needed to bring such a moral change about.
>
> (James 1902: 171)

My interest is in the affective reactions of the mundane self when confronted with the ineffable and holy Other, and the subsequent transformations and transmutations that the self undergoes as a consequence. In other words, how does a human being react to the perception of God revealing himself? In exploring the psychodynamics of the process, I suggest in particular that the precondition of guilt, the affective reaction of awe and the sensory modality of vision are central to the process of spiritual conversion. I approach the topic as a psychoanalyst, recognising at the onset that psychoanalytic paradigms of understanding mysticism and spirituality are often reductive and relegate mysticism and spirituality to the defensive functions of the ego, as opposed to looking at the matter as ego-edifying and possibly ego-transcendent (Meissner 1984; O'Neil and Akhtar 2009; Parsons 1999).

The setting of the *Gita*

Part of the *Mahabharata* (1899), the *Gita* is the jewel in the crown of this great Sanskrit Hindu epic, as it is considered the teaching of God himself. *The Mahabharata* is the longest recorded epic in the world, a text of about 75,000 verses. It is the story of a great eschatological war between the five Pandava brothers and their cousins, the 100 Kauravas, who are fighting for dominion over a kingdom. This long, complex and fascinating text consists of eighteen major books (*parvans*), each subdivided into chapters. The chapter entitled 'The Book of the Bhagavad Gita' is located in the sixth major book, *Bhismaparvan*, named after Bhishma, great-grandfather and patriarch to both warring parties. This book chronicles the killing of Bhishma by Arjuna. The central plot of the *Mahabharata* revolves around Bhishma's voluntary renunciation of his father's throne and his vow of lifelong celibacy so that his father may marry a low-caste woman. Bhishma's submissive oedipal action results in progressive problems to the royal succession, ultimately culminating in the war between the Pandavas and the Kauravas. In the epic, most of the protagonists on both sides die, including Arjuna and Krishna. The war marks the transition between two *Yugas*, or world ages, in Hindu cosmogony.[2] The conflict between the Pandavas and the Kauravas occurs at the end of the *Dvaparayuga*, or Dvarupa age, and formally begins our current *Kaliyuga,* or Kali age, which according to Hindu calculations began on 18 February 3102 BCE.

The logic and structure of the Gita

The *Gita* is a relatively short treatise: 700 stanzas divided into eighteen chapters. It is narrated as a poetic dialogue between the bard Samjaya and his patron, the blind king Dhrtarastra, father of the Kauravas. Samjaya has been given the gift of telepathy by Vyasa, author of the *Mahabharata* and is relating the details of the war to the blind king.[3] The first verse of the *Gita* begins with Dhrtarastra asking:

> In the Field of Right, the Kuru-field,
> Assembled ready to fight,
> My men and the sons of Pandu as well,
> What did they do, Samjaya?
> *(Gita* 1: 1)

The field is literally the battlefield where war is waged, but metaphorically and more importantly, it is the intrapsychic battlefield of a conflicted self. The conflict on a simplistic level is one between good and evil. On a more meta-physical level, it is a conflict between the conditioned, conflicted, ephemeral and divided self (*ahamkara*), in contrast to the unconditioned spiritual self. Unconditioned self in Hinduism refers to the self that is everlasting, unchanged by worldly experience and exists, and persists before and after the mortal body. Heinrich Zimmer eloquently summarises the self in Hindu thought.

> *Ahamkara*, the ego function, causes us to believe that we feel like acting, that we are suffering, etc.; whereas actually our real being, the *Purusha*, is devoid of such modifications. *Ahamkara* is the centre and prime motivating force of 'delusion'. *Ahamkara* is the misconception, conceit, supposition, or belief that refers all objects and acts of consciousness to an 'I' (*aham*). *Ahamkara* – the making (*kara*) of the utterance 'I' (*aham*) – accomplishes all psychic processes, producing the misleading notion 'I am hearing; I am seeing; I am rich and mighty; I am enjoying; I am about to suffer.' It is thus the primal cause of the critical 'wrong conception' that dogs all phenomenal

experience; the idea, namely, that the life-monad (*Purusha*) is implicated in, nay is identical with, the processes of living matter (*Prakti*). One is continually appropriating to oneself, as a result of the *Ahamkara*, everything that comes to pass in the realms of the physique and psyche, superimposing perpetually the false notion (and apparent experience) of a subject (an 'I') of all the deeds and sorrows.

(Zimmer 1989: 319)

In chapter 13 of the *Gita*, Krishna tells Arjuna:

This body, son of Kunti,
Is called the field.
Who knows this, he is called
Field knower by those who know him.

Know that I am the field knower,
In all fields, son of Bharata.
Knowledge of the field and the Field-knower,
This I hold to be true Knowledge.

(*Gita* 13: 1–2; my emphasis)

Chapter 1 of the *Gita* begins with a detailed description of both warring parties and the development of Arjuna's psychological and existential crisis. Arjuna asks for Krishna's counsel at the beginning of chapter 2, marking the point where Krishna formally takes on the role as Arjuna's teacher and *guru*.[4] Chapters 2 and 3 are a synopsis of Krishna's entire teaching, as he instructs Arjuna on the three paths to realising God: the intellect (*jnanayoga*), actions (*karma yoga*) and emotions (*bhakti yoga*). The sequence is important, as Krishna appeals to all three levels unsuccessfully to the sceptical Arjuna before he reveals his cosmic, mystical self. In chapter 4, Krishna explicitly tells Arjuna of his divinity:

For me have passed many
Births, and for thee, Arjuna;
These, I know all;
Thou knowest not, scorcher of the foe.

Tho unborn, tho My self is eternal,
Tho Lord of beings,
Resorting to My own material nature
I come into being by My own mysterious power.

(*Gita* 2: 5–6)

But Arjuna does not believe in or understand Krishna's divinity. If he accepted what Krishna was trying to teach him, the *Gita* would have ended with chapter 3 and the epiphany of chapter 11 would be unnecessary. Instead, he remains sceptical, asking many questions.

> In typical traditional pictures of the *Gita* scene, Arjuna is shown with palms joined in reverence, looking at Krishna in an attitude of devotion and faith. But this is not what is described in the *Gita* itself, in which Arjuna shows from the very beginning that he does not really recognize Krishna as a teacher or as a god.
>
> (Legget 1995: 38)

As a man of action, Arjuna is unmoved by rational arguments. The discourse in chapters 2–9 is heavily intellectual, and shows little insight on Arjuna's part. In chapter 10, 'The Yoga of Manifestations', Arjuna asks Krishna:

> In full detail, Thine own mystic power
> And supernal-manifestation, Janardana
> Expound further; *for satiety*
> *Comes not as I listen to Thy nectar!*
> (*Gita* 10: 18; my emphasis)

Krishna indulges Arjuna and tells him of his various worldly and divine manifestations. Though more gratified (primarily through the sensory modality of aural speech), Arjuna's doubts remain and Krishna is very well aware of this. Chapter 10 closes with Krishna asking:

> *After all, this extensive*
> *Instruction – what boots it thee, Arjuna?*
> *I support this entire*
> *World with a single faction of Myself, and remain so.*
> (*Gita* 10: 42; my emphasis)

What is needed for Arjuna's conversion is an actual experience of Krishna's divinity, not arguments and words. This happens in chapter 11 as a special act of grace from God Krishna himself. In chapter 11, Arjuna is transformed and spiritually converted. His conditioned and ephemeral self are negated and annihilated through a cosmic vision of Krishna's infinite, ineffable and incomprehensible being. After this epiphany, Arjuna enters a different and higher level of consciousness. His perspective of himself and his existential conflict undergoes a radical spiritual transformation. He emotionally and spiritually understands what his *guru* has been trying to teach him all along in the *Gita*. Chapters 12–18 continue the teaching, with the emphasis now on *bhakti*, the uniquely Hindu form of emotional love and devotion to god. Arjuna listens attentively. His questions and doubts, characteristic of chapters 2–10, are gone. From chapter 12 onwards, Krishna is addressing a different audience – the everyday man, who without the intervention of divine grace, but through love and devotion, can approach the perimeters of the divinity that Arjuna, through God's grace directly experienced. The *Gita* ends in chapter 18 with Arjuna saying:

> Destroyed the confusion; attention to the Truth is won,
> By Thy grace, on my part, O Changeless One;
> I stand firm, with doubts dispersed;
> I shall do Thy word.
>
> (*Gita* 18: 73)

Who is Krishna?

In the *Mahabharata,* Krishna oscillates between the human and divine, similar to Christ in the New Testament. In the *Mahabharata*, Krishna is Arjuna's cousin and close friend.

> Of the Pandavas, Arjuna was the same age as Krishna. He always bowed to Dharma (his eldest brother) and Bhishma as his elders, and was, in turn, shown respect by the twins (his youngest brothers), but he always embraced Krishna as his equal. These two picnicked together, drank together, and were intimate friends.
>
> (Karve 1991: 163)

Krishna is also a warrior and an epic hero himself. His identity in the epic can be confusing, perhaps intentionally so by the authors. Krishna is human to most, recognised as divine by a few, and actually revealed as God himself to one. He stays impartial in the war, though his sympathies and affinity are with the Pandavas, particularly Arjuna. In the *Mahabharata*, Krishna offers his army to one side and his presence as a non-combatant in the war to the other side. Arjuna chooses Krishna's presence, while Duryodhana (the Kaurava king) opts for Krishna's army. Duryodhana is quite pleased with the arrangement that he has Krishna's formidable army – a better deal in his eyes than Arjuna having only Krishna's presence. Duryodhana thinks of Krishna only as a mortal – yet another warrior king with a powerful army vying after his own self-interest. Arjuna, on the other hand, is delighted to have his close friend and soulmate Krishna as his advisor in the role as his chariot driver. Did Arjuna have an unconscious inkling that Krishna was more than he appeared?

> Who then is Krishna who persuades Arjuna to accept the warriors fate? He is a *Vrisni* prince, for the nonce acting as Arjuna's charioteer, a seemingly subordinate role to which he has agreed in order to be a non-combatant in the thick of battle. Loyal to both warring parties, he has conceded his troops to Duryodhana (the King of the Kauravas)

and his presence to Arjuna . . .This role assumed by Krishna, because of the conventional camaraderie between warrior and driver, provides the intimacy which makes his exhortations possible and appropriate. Traditionally, the *suta* (chariot driver), on the chariot of the warrior, is witness to the warrior's triumphs and occasional lapses; in danger, he protects him. The triumphs of the warrior, he celebrates in song, hence *suta* also means bard. The lapses he condemns in private.

(van Buitenen 1981: 4–5)

Krishna is importantly an *avatar* of God – in Hinduism, a descent of God into man or God coming down to earth to re-establish morality and order. An *avatar* is a voluntary and deliberate act or incarnation of God, as opposed to humans, who are involuntarily reincarnated until they attain spiritual release or *moksha*. In Hinduism, Vishnu, the supreme Godhead, has ten avatars, and Krishna is the eighth *avatar* (Buddha is the ninth, and the tenth is yet to come at the end of our current age, *Kaliyuga*).[5] In chapter 4 of the *Gita*, Krishna tells Arjuna:

> For whenever of the right,
> A languishing appears, son of Bharata,
> A rising up of unright,
> Then I send Myself forth.
>
> For the protection of the good,
> And for destruction of evil-doers,
> To make a firm footing for the right,
> *I come into being in age after age.*
> (*Gita* 4: 7–8; my emphasis)

Krishna's human form is a munificent act of condescension for the benefit of mankind:

> This is the beginning of the famous system of avatars or incarnations of god, which became so characteristic of later Visnuism and a prime source of its strength. No Christian community needs to be told how such a doctrine of a loving God who is born upon earth to save the world can conquer the hearts of men.

(Edgerton 1944: 155)

Arjuna's crisis: the sick and divided self

Arjuna's crisis or his dark night of the soul is vividly described in chapter 1 of the *Gita*. As war is about to begin, Arjuna asks Krishna to place his chariot between the two armies so that he may survey them.[6] Krishna does so. Arjuna

137

sees in both armies his family, friends and teachers. He becomes sad, despondent and depressed. He tells Krishna:

> My limbs sink down,
> And my mouth becomes parched,
> And there is trembling in my body,
> And my hair stands on end.
>
> The bow, Gandiva, falls from my hand,
> And my skin, too, is burning,
> And I cannot stand still,
> And my mind seems to wander.
> I see portents
> That are adverse, Keseva;
> And I foresee no welfare,
> Having slain my kinsfolk in battle.
>
> I wish no victory, Krsna,
> Nor Kingdom nor joys;
> Of what use to us were kingdom, Govinda,
> Of what use enjoyments or life?
>
> (*Gita* 1: 29–32)

Note the dejection, guilt, anhedonia and hopelessness in Arjuna's words; he is illustrating the classical emotional and psychosomatic symptoms of melancholic depression. Arjuna drops his *Gandiva* (celestial) bow and sits dejected and helpless in his chariot, saying that he will not fight. Recalling James's description of 'the extreme of melancholy' Arjuna's self is paralysed by inaction for it 'is completely bankrupt and without resource, and no works it can accomplish will avail' (James 1902: 216).

It is important to note that in a text as short and succinct as the *Gita*, a whole chapter is devoted to describing Arjuna's despondency. From a psychoanalytic view, Arjuna's inhibition to fight and his depression are precipitated by Oedipal guilt – specifically the killing of Bhishma, the paternal figure par excellence and Drona, Arjuna's teacher and *guru* (another oedipal object). Bhishma, the supreme commander of the Kaurava army, is loved and revered by Arjuna. Arjuna grows up in the same house as Bhishma and a special affection develops mutually between them. It is no coincidence that the *Gita* is located in the 'Book of Bhishma' in the *Mahabharata*; it reflects and emphasises the oedipal dynamics of patricide and guilt. Arjuna has profound ambivalence in fighting and killing Bhishma and Krishna is well aware of this.

> How, Krishna, shall I fight in battle, with the venerable and aged preceptor of the Kurus, the grandsire of accomplished understanding and intelligence? Krishna, while playing in the days of childhood,

I used to soil the garments of the high souled and illustrious one by climbing on his lap with my body smeared with dust. Krishna, in my childhood, climbing on the lap of the high souled father of Pandu (our father), I used to say 'father'. 'I am not your father, but your father's father, Arjuna', were the words he used to say in reply to me. Oh how he used to treat me thus; how could he be now slain by me.

(*Mahabharata* 6.108: 90–3)

A closer look at the first chapter shows us that Arjuna not only questioned the morality of war and killing, but also Krishna's morality when the latter repeatedly prompts him to fight and kill Bhishma.[7] As van Buitenen notes:

Arjuna's dilemma is a real one and, despite Krishna's sarcasm, an honorable one. In effect, on the level of *dharma* (duty), Arjuna will be proved to have been right; but in the *Gita* Krishna offers him the choice of another level of values, which will absolve him from guilt.

(van Buitenen 1981: 3)

Arjuna's depression is an important and necessary precondition for his spiritual conversion. His battlefield paralysis, his neurasthenia, goes far beyond the moral questioning of war; it reflects a deeper spiritual and existential crisis. As a warrior, Arjuna had fought and killed many times before – without becoming overwhelmed by remorse or guilt. This was his 'profession' – his *Dharma* or duty in life as defined by the Hindu caste system, a role at which he excelled and, indeed, was considered incomparable. It is implausible that moral doubts alone paralysed Arjuna before the war. It was guilt over slaying parental surrogates and his teachers (*gurus*) that led to him questioning his self and his moral duty. James posits that such a guilty sense of sin is a prerequisite for conversion.

To begin with, there are two things in the mind of the candidate for conversion: first, the present incompleteness or wrongness, the 'sin' which he is eager to escape from; and, second, the positive ideal which he longs to compass. Now with most of us the sense of our present wrongness is a far more distinct piece of our consciousness than is the imagination of any positive ideal we can aim at. In a majority of cases, indeed, the 'sin' almost exclusively engrosses the attention, so that conversion is a process of struggling away from sin rather than of striving towards righteousness.

(James 1902: 187)

As James notes, a necessary precondition for spiritual conversion is a self that is plagued by guilt about what it has done or what it is going to do rather than a narcissistic self that is looking to abstractly prefect itself. It is the negative and painful emotions that motivate men to seek spirituality and other worldly reassurance; the comfortable are poor candidates for spiritual conversion. Arjuna's problem was that he did not know how to act – specifically, should he fight and kill? It was an existential problem; one of morality, not will. Specifically, it is the extremity of Arjuna's guilty and emotional consciousness that makes him a suitable candidate for his dramatic spiritual conversion. Arjuna asks Krishna:

> How shall I in battle against Bhishma,
> And Drona, O Slayer of Madhu,
> Fight with arrows,
> Who are both worthy of reverence, Slayer of Enemies
>
> For not slaying my revered elders of great dignity
> Twere better to eat alms – food, even, in this world;
> *But having slain my elders who seek their ends, right in this world*
> *I should eat food smeared with blood.*
>
> (Gita 2: 4–5; my emphasis)

'I should eat food smeared with blood'! It is eating his elders and gurus – overt oedipal destructive references. Note the psychic dimension of orality – eating tainted with blood – guilt. Eating is to take in and to identify – an elementary process in psychoanalysis of the mechanism of internalisation of the object – good or bad. The act of eating carries the dual connotation of taking in – digesting and incorporating (an identification), as well as chewing and destroying – a negation of the identification. Cannibalism reflects this ambivalence as an action that fuses love and aggression. The point is that Arjuna is overwhelmed by ambivalence and guilt: to kill his elders and teachers is to defile and negate the nourishing sustenance he gained from them. It is to kill a part of his 'self' – his empirical ego defined by its internalisations and identifications with parental and authoritative figures. Conflicted and compromised, his cognition and judgment impaired, and his will to act paralysed, Arjuna formally asks for Krishna's help:

> My very being afflicted with the taint of weak compassion,
> I ask Thee, my mind bewildered as to the right:
> Which were better, that tell me definitely;
> *I am Thy pupil, teach me that have come to Thee for instruction.*
>
> (Gita 2: 7; my emphasis)

Krishna obliges in chapter 11. By revealing his divinity, he changes Arjuna's perspective of himself in a manner more compelling, overarching and profound than Arjuna's sense of guilt.

Viswarupadarsham: the manifestation of God's cosmic form

Chapter 11 is entitled *Viswarupadarsanam*. *Darsana* is a Sanskrit word meaning 'vision and sight', derived from the Sanskrit root *drs,* which means 'to see', and hence 'comprehend'. *Darsana* in Hindu religious practice refers to viewing god, in whatever form, but carries the very profound connotation that it is not only seeing a form of god, but also actually being in his presence. *Viswa* means 'cosmos', and *rupa* means 'form'. Hence, *Viswarupadarsanam* = 'manifestation of the cosmic form'.

James describes the four qualities of mystical experience: ineffability, noesis, transiency and passivity (James 1902). Ineffability refers to something that defies expression and cannot be put into words, a state of feeling as opposed to intellect. 'Noesis' is a term for the knowledge gained through the mystical experience.

> They are states of insight into depths of truth unplumbed by the discursive intellect. They are illuminations, revelations, full of significance and importance, all inarticulate though they remain; and as a rule they carry with them a curious sense of authority for after-time.
>
> (James 1902: 329)

Transiency means not only short-lived but also something beyond time – atemporality. Passivity is something beyond voluntary control, an experience that is not actively sought out by the self but passively received. It is not through one's will that a mystical experience occurs, but through the grace and will of a higher power or superior being. Chapter 11 begins with Arjuna asking directly and somewhat brazenly to see Krishna's supreme form.

> Thus it is, as Thou declarest
> Thyself, O Supreme Lord.
> *I desire to see Thy form*
> *As God, O Supreme Spirit.*
>   (*Gita* 11: 3; my emphasis)

The following verse has Arjuna toning down the directness of his request. Referring back to James's notion of passivity, a vision of the divine is not something one demands but rather one receives through the grace of God. With more humility and perhaps a preconscious intuition of who Krishna really is, Arjuna qualifies his request by adding in the next verse, 'If Thou thinkest that it can be seen by me, O Lord' (*Gita* 11: 4). Krishna responds:

> *But thou canst not see Me*
> *With this same eye of thine own;*

I give thee a supernatural eye:
Behold My mystic power as God.
(*Gita* 11: 80; my emphasis)

What follows is a secondary description by Samjaya to the blind king Dhrtarastra of what Arjuna saw. What indeed Arjuna directly saw exceeds human comprehension. It is beyond words and description. It is in the realm of psychoanalytic primary process.[8] It is important that Arjuna's experience of God is narrated in the second person. It would have been impossible for Arjuna to put his own experience into words – his vision was ineffable noetic, and transient. Indeed the only description of Krishna's divinity has come to us secondarily through Samjaya – himself given a gift of telepathic vision by the author of the *Mahabharata*. Samjaya says:

Of a thousand suns in the sky
If suddenly should burst forth
The light, it would be like
Unto the light of that exalted one.
(*Gita* 11: 9–12)

Arjuna's response to Krishna's theophany

Otto Rudolf, in his extraordinary work *The Idea of the Holy* (Otto 1923), coins the term *'mysterium tremendum'* to describe the complex of emotions that characterise the human response to experiencing God. He notes three elements that constitute the feeling: awe, overpoweringness, and energy or urgency, strikingly similar to Arjuna's reaction to Krishna's theophany.

Hearing these words of Keseva,
Making a reverent gesture, trembling, the Diademed Arjuna
Made obeisance and spoke yet again to Krsna,
Stammering, greatly affrighted, bowing down.
(*Gita* 11: 35; my emphasis)

With utter humility, fear and self-abnegation, his hair standing upright, Arjuna asks:

Tell me who art Thou, of Awful form?
Homage be to Thee: Best of Gods, be merciful!
I desire to understand Thee, the primal one;
For I do not comprehend what Thou has set out to do.
(*Gita* 11: 31)

Krishna answers:

> I am time, Death, cause of destruction of the worlds, matured
> And set out to gather in the worlds here.
> Even without thee, thy action, all shall cease to exist,
> The warriors that are drawn up in the opposing ranks.
>
> Therefore arise thou, win glory,
> Conquer thine enemies and enjoy prospered kingship;
> *By Me, Myself they have already been slain long ago;*
> *Be thou the mere instrument, left-handed archer!*
>
> (*Gita* 11: 32–3; my emphasis)

Arjuna is overwhelmed by awe and fear. His ego boundaries are distorted and obliterated by the horrific vision of Krishna's divinity. He remembers how he treated Krishna as his friend, soulmate and his equal, and how he doubted him when earlier in the *Gita* he told him of his divine nature as god. Overwhelmed, shamed, frightened and humbled in the presence of God, Arjuna asks Krishna to return to his original human form:

> Having seen what was never seen before, I am thrilled,
> And at the same time my heart is shaken with fear;
> Show me, O God, that same form of Thine as before!
> Be merciful, Lord of the Gods, Abode of the World!
>
> Wearing the diadem, carrying the club, with disc in hand,
> Just as before I desire to see thee;
> In that same four-armed shape
> Present Thyself, O Thousand-armed one, of Universal form!
>
> (*Gita* 11: 41–6)

Arjuna's emotional response to directly experiencing God has parallels in the Judeo-Christian tradition – from Moses and the prophets Isaiah, Ezekiel and Jeremiah in the Old Testament to the vision of St Paul in the New Testament.[9] Indeed, Moses, like Arjuna, wishes to see God in his true form. God tells Moses that no one can see him and live, but offers Moses an alternative way of experiencing his divinity without actually seeing him. Quoting from Exodus:

> Then Moses said, 'Now show me your glory.' And the Lord said, 'I will cause all my goodness to pass in front of you, and I will proclaim my name, the Lord, in your presence. I will have mercy on whom I will have mercy, and I will have compassion on whom I will have compassion?' But, he said, 'you cannot see my face, for no one may see me and live.' Then the Lord said, 'There is a place near me where you

may stand on when my glory passes by. I will put you in a cleft in the rock and cover you with my hand until I have passed by. Then I will remove my hand and you will see my back; but my face must not be seen.'

(Exodus 33: 18–23)

Arjuna's response to the vision of Krishna's divinity is primarily frightening – not beautiful or ecstatic. Note the terms Samjaya uses to describe Arjuna's response: 'amazement', 'reverence', 'fright', 'thrill', 'fear' and 'trembling'. Perhaps the most compelling and encompassing description of the complex of emotions experienced by Arjuna is awe, essentially verbatim defined in the Oxford English Dictionary (1971) as: 'Immediate and active fear, terror and dread. From its use in reference to the Divine Being this passes into: Dread mingled with veneration, reverential or respectful fear; the attitude of a mind subdued to profound reverence in the presence of supreme authority, moral greatness or sublimity, or mysterious sacredness.' Accordingly, Keltner and Hait note 'Awe figures prominently in religious discussions of the relationship between humans and their gods. One of the earliest and most powerful examples is found in the dramatic climax of the *Bhagavadgita*' (Keltner and Hait 2003: 298).

In psychoanalytic literature, Phyllis Greenacre wrote that awe derives from the phallic stage of psychosexual development, specifically, awe of the father's phallus. She notes: 'One of the most interesting parts of the awe reaction is with its association with inspiration, with creativity and with *religious feelings*' (Greenacre 1956: 30; my emphasis). Mortimer Ostow elaborates on the role of awe in religio-mystical experience. Distinguishing fearful awe from pleasant awe, Ostow proposes, like Greenacre, that the feeling of awe experienced by adults has its origins in the infant's preverbal sensory experience of his parents, and writes, more persuasively than Greenacre, that 'the sense of awe derives from the newborn's non-declarative memory of his impressions of his adult, giant parents' (Ostow 2001: 231). Ostow correctly emphasises the visual perception of disproportionate scales of size as central to the feeling of awe. Dwarkanath Rao, in his paper 'God Playing Psychoanalyst: Lessons from the *Bhagavad Gita*', arrives at the same point, stating: 'One wonders if the cosmic vision of Krishna can be understood as the terrifying, omnipotent, omniscient parent of vulnerable childhood' (Rao 2001: 183). Keltner and Hait discuss the cognitive dimensions of the development of awe as relating to importance of size and scale from within the Piagetian framework of accommodation.

Accommodation refers to the Piagetian process of adjusting mental structures that cannot assimilate a new experience. The concept of accommodation brings together many insights about awe, such as that it involves confusion (St Paul) and obscurity (Burke), and that is heightened in times of crisis, when extant traditions and knowledge structures do not suffice (Weber). We propose that prototypical awe involves a challenge to or negation of mental structures when they fail to make sense of an experience of something vast. Such experiences can be disorienting and even frightening, as in the cases of Arjuna and St Paul, since they make the self feel small, powerless, and confused.

(Keltner and Hait 2003: 304)

The cognitive understanding of awe reinforces the importance psycho-analysts place on the interpersonal and emotional dimensions of awe: both describe the early developmental experiences of a child trying to com-prehend and assimilate an experience that is beyond their cognitive and maturational ability. Sudhir Kakar, in his insightful book *The Analyst and the Mystic* (1991) suggests that awe is an emotion that distances rather than unites.

> Vaishnava mysticism, being a mysticism of love, does not consider awe as a legitimate bhava (feeling or mood) in relation to the Divine. Thus there are no feelings of reverence, of the uncanny, or of mystery. Nor are there the degrees of fear associated with awe where, in extremity, terror and dread can reign. Awe is perhaps the central *bhava* of what Erich Fromm called authoritarian religion. Vaishnava devotionalism, on the other hand, would consider awe as an obstacle in the mystical endeavour. It distances and separates rather than binds and joins.

(Kakar 1991: 17)

Vaishnava refers to Vishnu, the Supreme godhead in Hindu mythology. As noted before, Krishna is an *avatar* of Vishnu. While important, Kakar's observation does not reflect nor relate to the unique, dramatic and exceptional interaction between Arjuna and Krishna that leads to Arjuna's conversion. What Kakar says bears significantly on what is taught in the *Gita before* and *after* the terrifying theophany of Krishna in chapter 11. The mysticism of love (*bhakti yoga*) is indeed the central message of the *Gita,* but it does not explain Arjuna's conversion. The approach to realising god through the sentiments of love and affection is meant for the everyday man seeking spiritual closeness to the divine. But love, affection, devotion (*bhakti*) and intellectual arguments (*jnana*) are not sufficient for the dramatic conversion of the doubtful and sceptical Arjuna, who ultimately requires an overpoweringly horrific and kaleidoscopic vision of Krishna's true being as the omnipotent and omniscient deity. It is precisely the exaggerated magnitude of Arjuna's paralysis and the extremity of his guilt, in the metaphorical setting of the battlefield of a cataclysmic war that slices time into different epochs that occasions Krishna's divine grace and intervention. This serves as a temporal metaphor for the

145

overwhelming, all-encompassing change the ego confronts in circumstances of spiritual conversion. Krishna reassures:

> By Me showing grace towards thee, Arjuna this
> Supreme form has been manifested by My own mysterious power;
> This form made up of splendour, universal, infinite, primal,
> Of Mine, *which has never been seen before any other than thee.*
>
> Have no perturbation, nor any state of bewilderment,
> Seeing this so awful form of Mine;
> Dispel thy fear; let thy heart be of good cheer: again do thou
> Behold the same former form of Mine: here!
>
> (Gita 11: 41–9; my emphasis)

'Never before seen by anyone other than thee' positions Krishna's revelation to Arjuna as an event that is unique and unparalleled, in the past, present and the future. It allows Arjuna the possibility of identifying with the divine. This is, perhaps, a bridge across the distance imposed by awe, that when crossed permits the mysticism of love. It is a paradigm of what Krishna has to say to Arjuna after the cosmic revelation – a message meant not so much for Arjuna but, more importantly, to the Arjunas of the mundane world – you and I. Krishna says:

> *This form that is right hard to see,*
> *Which thou hast seen of Mine,*
> *Of this form even the gods*
> *Constantly long for the sight.*
>
> *Not by the Vedas nor by austerity,*
> *Nor by gifts or acts of worship,*
> *Can I be seen in such a guise,*
> *As thou has seen Me.*
>
> *Doing my work, intent on Me,*
> *Devoted to Me, free from attachment,*
> *Free from enmity to all beings,*
> *Who is so, goes to Me, son of Pandu.*
> (*Gita* 11: 51–5; my emphasis)

The visual realm – seeing is believing

Most of the discourse in the *Gita* occurs within the aural realms of spoken speech. Krishna talks, and Arjuna listens and questions. Chapter 11 is the notable exception, wherein vision and sight figure predominantly. Indeed, Krishna gives Arjuna divine vision to view his cosmic self: 'I give thee a supernatural eye' (*Gita* 11: 8). The role of vision and sight are critical to Arjuna's spiritual conversion, as it is through the eyes that the specially selected Arjuna introjects and identifies with Krishna's divinity. It is through seeing that Arjuna understands what Krishna tells him in chapter 10: 'Of the Sons of Pandu, I am Arjuna' (Gita 10: 37).

In 'A Disturbance of Memory on the Acropolis', Freud writes:

> Now it would be easy to argue that this strange thought that occurred to me on the Acropolis only serves to emphasize that seeing something with one's own eyes is after all quite a different thing from hearing or reading about it. But it would remain a very strange way of clothing an uninteresting commonplace. Or would it be possible to maintain that it was true that when I was a schoolboy I had *thought* I was convinced of the historical reality of the city of Athens and its history, but that the occurrence of this idea on the Acropolis had precisely *shown* that in my unconscious I had not believed in it, and that I was now only acquiring a conviction that 'reached down to the unconscious'.
>
> (Freud 1936: 241; my emphasis)

Otherwise stated, Freud had read about or was taught about the grandeur of the Acropolis as a child (intellectual knowledge). But he neither believed nor appreciated its emotional profundity until he actually *saw* it as an adult. His seeing the Acropolis – in its visual and actual physical vastness – ocular perception emphasised and facilitating and reinforcing affectively – leads to an alternation of his consciousness. Unlike the child taught about the Acropolis, the adult Freud understood what was an intellectual precept as an emotional truth. Going back to Arjuna, we see a parallel process. Intellectual discourse by Krishna is not emotionally compelling. But an actual vision of the Cosmic Krishna jolts the schoolboy mentality of Arjuna's mundane consciousness into a profoundly higher emotional state: Arjuna's consciousness is altered and reconfigured by a vision of the divine-terrifying Krishna. Intellectual abstractions transform into affective reality via the sensory modality of vision.

In psychoanalytic theory, seeing is intimately associated with internalisations and identifications; with devouring and incorporation, literally, 'eating with one's eyes'. Going back to chapter 11 of the *Gita*, Arjuna, having seen Krishna cosmic form, says:

As moths into a burning flame
Do enter unto their destruction with utmost impetuosity,
Just so unto their destruction enter the worlds
Into Thy mouths also, with utmost Impetuosity.

Devouring them Thou lickest up voraciously on all sides
All the worlds with Thy flaming Jaws;
Filling with radiance the whole universe
Thy terrible splendours burn, O Vishnu
(*Gita* 11: 29–31; my emphasis)

Note the explicit visual imagery of devouring, which on the surface level carries the connotation of destruction. But from a psychoanalytic viewpoint, it is also a mechanism of identification with the all-powerful other. The equation would be: looking = devouring = oral incorporation = introjections = identification. Karl Abraham spoke of oral incorporation as a primary mechanism of identification with the object (Abraham 1924). Oral incorporation is extended to a perhaps more powerful and enduring modality of introjection and identification-vision. In Otto Fenichel's description:

> Whenever conformity to the demands of another person involves *looking up* to him we have, on the one hand, a proof of the existence of ocular introjections . . . There are hundreds of different instances of this sort. For example, he who stumbles looks at the image of God and stands firm again. Or, we derive moral strength by looking at the picture of someone whom we desire to copy – the very word 'copy' implies looking . . . it is not merely a question of reinforcing one's moral courage by acquiring visual evidence that other people are moral and that they behave in such and such a way. Rather it is a question of *the magical property of a look*: through the look itself the characteristics of that which is looked at are acquired by the person who looks.
>
> (Fenichel 1937: 29)

Witness the magical properties of looking that Fenichel stresses: by looking, one is mysteriously, even miraculously taking in the other. For Arjuna, looking at Krishna's cosmic self amounted to identification with God. Arjuna's mundane consciousness is converted to a higher spiritual consciousness through the act of looking – no ordinary looking, and no ordinary identification. It is looking at God himself and identifying with him. Such identification may appear presumptuous and narcissistic, but is in keeping with the Hindu philosophical paradigms that the spiritual unconditioned timeless self is present, though hidden and obfuscated, in all of us by the bodily conditioned, mundane self.

The role of vision – of ocular introjection as a precursor to identification in Arjuna's conversion – is highly relevant to the Hindu practice of worship. The climax in the Hindu ritual of worship is to view the Deity – a *darshan*. The notion of seeing, a *darshan,* has an important and profound place in Hindu ritual worship. It underlies the basis for the more gradual approach for the everyday man to approach God and spiritual understanding. A *darshan* is not a unique or singular event, as was Krishna's theophany, but the norm of everyday practice of Hinduism. After the priest makes oblations to the God, the devotees place their hands in reverence as they view the deity in the inner sanctorum. The viewing of the deity, the *darshan*, can be and is emotionally translated in Hindu worship as being in presence of God. The stone or bronze deity in a typical temple takes on a magical significance of being, for a brief moment, in the presence of God – not a mental or physical representation, but a concrete and actual presence. However, the emotion is, and must be, short-lived. The requirement of the transience of the *darshan* goes back to James's notion of the mystical as being transient. Just as Arjuna's vision of the divine was short – he in fact begged for it to end – so too is the *darshan*. For the feeling of being present in, with and within God – a power far greater than oneself – both nullifies and edifies the ego, negating the mundane self and edifying the transcendent self. Being, however transiently, in the presence of God, seeing, experiencing and taking him in, makes one more receptive to similar states and motivates one to a more permanent, internalised relationship with the deity.

In the novel *Anil's Ghost*, Michael Ondaatje, a noted Sri Lankan author, writes about artisans painting images of the divine Buddha. It was considered heresy to paint the eyes directly, as this would mean looking into the deities' eyes as they were created: an act of reverence but also of fear, trepidation and retribution through the human encountering the divine, with all its oedipal connotations. Thus, when artisans created painted deities, they could only paint the eyes by looking at their work through a mirror:

> Without the eyes there is not just blindness, there is nothing. There is no existence. The artificer brings to life sight and truth and presence . . . He climbs a ladder in front of the statue. The man with him climbs too. This has taken place for centuries, you realize, there are records of this since the ninth century. The painter dips a brush into the paint and turns back to the statue, so it looks as if it is to be enfolded in the great arms. The other man, facing him, holds up the mirror, and the artificer puts the brush over his shoulder and paints in the eyes without looking directly at the face. He uses just the reflection to guide him – so only the mirror receives the direct image of the glance being created. No human eye can meet the Buddha's during the process of creation . . . he never looks at the eyes directly. He can only see the gaze in the mirror.
>
> (Ondaatje 2000: 99)

Conclusion

As described in *Bhagavad Gita*, Arjuna's dramatic vision of God and his subsequent spiritual conversion was a unique and unparalleled event. I propose that Arjuna's dire psychological crisis of guilt and emotional pain was a necessary precondition for his conversion. The sensory modality of vision – actually gazing upon God – is crucial to the process of Arjuna's spiritual conversion, as well as to his subsequent internalisation and identification with Krishna as the supreme deity. The overwhelming awe and wonder Arjuna experiences as he witnesses the revelation of Krishna's cosmic self figure critically in the change and alteration in his consciousness and eventually, his spiritual conversion. The shocking, overwhelming, ego-distorting scale of the divine vision are necessary ingredients in jolting Arjuna's mortal consciousness to a higher spiritual level, providing an ideal greater in magnitude, intensity and reality to his guilt. The spiritual conversion that is effected by seeing God as a frightening and incomprehensible entity has its psychological antecedent in the infant's perception of his parents as at once grand, fearful, unfathomable and incomprehensible, and yet loving, caring and benign. The worship of an all-powerful, divine yet parental figure, dissolves and absolves the child in us of our inevitable patricidal guilt, as embodied by Arjuna, *avatar* for us all.

Notes

1 All references to the *Gita* are from Franklin Edgerton's 1944 translation, *The Bhagavad Gita*, Cambridge, MA: Harvard University Press.

2 Heinrich Zimmer summarises the concept of *Yugas* in Hinduism: 'According to the mythologies of Hinduism, each world cycle is subdivided into four *Yugas* or world ages. These are comparable to the four ages of the Greco-Roman tradition, and like the latter decline in moral excellence as the round proceeds. The classical ages took their names from the metals – gold, silver, brass and iron – the Hindu from the four throws of the Hindu dice game – *Krita, Treta, Dvapara*, and *Kali*. In both cases the appellations suggest the relative virtues of the periods, as they succeed each other in a slow, irreversible procession' (Zimmer 1974: 13).

3 The blind king has the overt meaning of a monarch who is unaware of what is going on in his own kingdom – blind to what is right and wrong. It also has an oedipal connotation of emasculation, as it is the king's son, Duryodhana, who is in charge and is making the decisions – i.e. to go to war. Moreover, blindness emphasises the sensory realm of vision as a critical modality that operates on multiple interlacing levels in the text as both a literary device and a psychological construct. Indeed, Samjaya was given the gift of visual telepathy by the author of the *Mahabharata*, the sage Vyasa, parallel to Arjuna being given the divine eye by Krishna to Arjuna so that Arjuna may see his real form.

4 The *guru* is a critically important concept in Hinduism. Literally meaning 'teacher', the *guru* is the spiritual guide. Sleeping with the *guru*'s wife is considered one of the most heinous sins in Hindu law, equating the role of the *guru* with the father. The *guru* represents the teacher who guides his *sishya* (pupil) to the divine. He is considered sacred and inviolate. The guru represents the conduit between the paternal and the divine.

5 The concept is similar to the biblical Book of Revelation, where the battle between the Christ and the Antichrist (i.e. good vs evil) is played out with its eschatological consequences.

6 Note the multiple connotations of the middle. It reflects the middle as a neutral yet ambivalent space. Psychoanalytically, middle may refer to Anna Freud's notion of the analyst being equidistant between the ego, id and the super-ego. Middle may also connote Winnicott's notion of transitional space – somewhere between reality and fantasy.

7 Indeed, Krishna not only prompts Arjuna to kill Bhishma many times but is also instrumental in having the Pandavas kill all the generals of the Kaurava

army (Bhishma, Drona and Karna) by morally questionable tactics. See Matilal (1991).

8 'The processes of the system *Ucs.* are timeless; i.e. they are not ordered temporally, are not altered by the passage of time; they have no reference to time at all. Reference to time is bound up, once again, with the work of the system *Cs.* The *Ucs.* Processes pay just as little regard to *reality.* They are subject to the pleasure principle; their fate depends only on how strong they are and on whether they fulfil the demands of the pleasure–unpleasure regulation. To sum up: *exemption from mutual contradiction, primary process, timelessness* and *replacement of external by psychical reality* – these are the characteristics which we may expect to find in the processes belonging to the system *Ucs*' (Freud 1915: 187).

9 See Arlow (1951).

References

Abraham, K. (1924). The influence of oral eroticism on character formation. *Selected Papers of Karl Abraham*, pp. 393–406. New York: Brunner/Mazel.

Arlow, J.A. (1951). The consecration of the prophet. *Psychoanalytic Quarterly* 23: 374–97.

Dutt, M.N. (trans.) (1899). *The Mahabharata*. Delhi: Parimal Publishers.

Edgerton, F. (ed.) (1944). *The Bhagavad Gita*. Cambridge, MA: Harvard University Press.

Fenichel, O. (1937). The scopophilic instinct and identification. *International Journal of Psychoanalysis* 18: 6–34.

Freud. S. (1915). The unconscious. In *The Standard Edition of the Complete Psychological Works of Sigmund Freud,* ed. and trans. J. Strachey, vol. 14, pp. 166–204. London: Hogarth Press/Institute of Psycho-Analysis.

Freud, S. (1936). A disturbance of memory on the Acropolis. In *The Standard Edition of the Complete Psychological Works of Sigmund Freud*, ed. and trans. J. Strachey, vol. 22, pp. 237–48. London: Hogarth Press/Institute of Psycho-Analysis.

Greenacre, P. (1956). Experiences of awe in childhood. *The Psychoanalytic Study of the Child* (11): 9–30.

James, W. (1902). *The Varieties of Religious Experience*. New York: Barnes and Noble Classics. Reprinted 2004.

Kakar, S. (1991). *The Analyst and the Mystic*. Chicago: University of Chicago Press.

Karve, I. (1991). *Yuganta: The End of an Epoch*. Hyberdad: Disha Publishers.

Keltner, D. and Hait, J. (2003). Approaching awe, a moral, spiritual, and aesthetic emotion. *Cognition and Emotion* 17(2): 297–314.

Legget, T. (1995). *The Bhagavad Gita Yogas*. London: Kegan Paul.

Matilal, B.K. (1991). Krsna: In defence of a devious divinity. In *Essays on the Mahabharata*, ed. S. Sharma. New Delhi: Motilal Banarsidass Publishers.

Meissner, W.W. (1984). *Psychoanalysis and Religious Experience*. New Haven: Yale University Press.

Ondaatje, M. (2000). *Anil's Ghost*. New York: Vintage Books.

O'Neil, M.K. and Akhtar, S. (2009). *On Freud's 'The Future of an Illusion'*. London: Karnac Books.

Ostow, M. (2001). Three archaic contributions to the religious instinct: Awe, mysticism, and apocalypse. *Does God Help? Developmental and Clinical Aspects of Religious Belief*, ed. S. Akhtar and H. Parens, pp. 197–233. Northvale, NJ: Jason Aronson.

Otto, R. (1923). *The Idea of the Holy*, trans. J.W. Harvey. Oxford: Oxford University Press.

Parsons, W.B (1999). *The Enigma of the Oceanic Feeling: Revisioning the Psychoanalytic Theory of Mysticism*. Oxford: Oxford University Press.

Rao, D. (2001). God playing psychoanalyst: Lessons from the *Bhagavad Gita*. In *Does God Help? Developmental and Clinical Aspects of Religious Belief*, ed. S. Akhtar and H. Parens, pp. 177–95. Northvale, NJ: Jason Aronson.

van Buitenen, J.A.B. (1981). *The Bhagavad Gita in the Mahabharata*. Chicago: University of Chicago Press.

Zimmer, H. (1974). *Myths and Symbols in Indian Art and Civilization*. Princeton: Princeton University Press.

Zimmer, H. (1989). *The Philosophies of India*. Princeton: Princeton University Press.

7

DID AUGUSTINE FORESHADOW PSYCHOANALYSIS?

John Gale

As early as 1908, the year of the first international meeting of psychoanalysts at Salzberg and just eight years after the publication of Freud's *Die Traumdeutung*, an English editor of Augustine's *Confessions* noted that Book X amounted to a true and psychological analysis of the phenomena of the conscious and unconscious aspects of the mind (Gibb and Montgommery 1908).[1] This sentiment was repeated in 1922 by the Benedictine scholar Cuthbert Butler (Butler 1951). The inclusion of a section on Augustine by Dom Butler in his *Western Mysticism* had been an afterthought but he was later to consider it the most valuable portion of his book.

Augustine of Hippo (CE 354–430) was born in Tagaste in North Africa of a pagan father and Christian mother, Monica, and received a Christian education. He studied rhetoric at the University of Carthage in order to become a lawyer but decided to devote himself to literary pursuits. He abandoned the Christianity of his infancy and took a mistress with whom he lived for fifteen years. In 373, while reading Cicero's lost *Hortensius*[2] he became interested in philosophy and became a *Ciceronianus* 'in a wider and deeper sense than before' (Hagendahl 1967: vol. 2, 488) and a Manichaean. He moved to Rome and then to Milan, where he taught rhetoric and came under the influence of Ambrose. In Milan he became a Neo-Platonist and soon afterwards a Christian. Augustine would be acclaimed by later generations as one of the most gifted Latin writers of his day and his influence on Western thought has been immense (Cross 1963).

While some serious objections have been raised to the view that the *Confessions* amounts to a psychoanalytic study, notably by Schmaltz (1952) and Meserve (1965), who argue that Augustine knew nothing of the unconscious, the similarity between the approach of Freud and that of Augustine continues to be recognised by others. Recent advocates of the latter view include Woolcott (1966) and Elledge (1988). For Gay (1986), the text of Freud's *Die Traumdeutung* operates much like the *Confessions*. By making public the author's internal world and particularly his dreams, it transforms what is an inherently private, personal story into authoritative wisdom.

> Freud's masterpiece *The Interpretation of Dreams* (1900) achieves
> authority precisely because it contains so many 'confessions'. It reveals
> Freud's jealousy, petty, sexualised, and hostile wishes, his grandiose
> ambitions, and his severe neuroticisms. In other words, it reveals a
> person much like ourselves, the difference being that Freud and
> Augustine created intellectual modes that permit confession but
> prevent narcissistic abasement.
>
> (Gay 1986: 64)

Indeed, in his *Écrits* (1977) Augustine was famously described by the French
psychoanalyst Jacques Lacan as foreshadowing psychoanalysis (Lacan 1977).

Psychoanalytic studies of the *Confessions*

Psychoanalytic studies of the *Confessions*, which was written for an educated
audience and demonstrated the author's exquisite literary sense and deep
immersion in the Latin classics, tend to take it for granted that the text is in
essence an autobiography (Brown 2000). But, in Marrou's words, *'ne sont pas
simplement une autobiographie'* (Marrou 1963: 43) but a theological work.
As such it is a text filled with allegory – that is, with things intentionally
hidden – and other literary devices, in which one scene after another takes on
a symbolic meaning. That is to say, it is not just a collection of recollections
but the work *'du rédacteur'* (Courcelle 1968: 159). As such it ought not to be
regarded merely as Augustine's autobiography 'for any period or section of his
life' (O'Meara 1954: 6). This was brought out in the masterful study, which
first appeared in 1950, by Pierre Courcelle (1968). He argued that, in order to
understand a text, one must interpret it in the light of the literary genre to
which it belongs.[3] By focusing on Augustine himself and his psychological
makeup, while taking an uncritical position on the nature of the text itself,
psychoanalytic studies have invariably been naive and limited, when not
directly misleading. For this reason scholars have generally shown little regard
for them. Solignac, following Labriolle (1926) and Zepf (1926), explicitly
argues against the *'psycho-psychanalytique'* explanation of Legewie (1925), in
which he describes Augustine as suffering from *'un désordre des fonctions
psychologiques de l'inconscient'* (Skutella 1998: 34 n.1, 1996: 541 respectively).

The psychoanalytic study of Augustine most often cited was made by
Kligerman in 1957. It became the model for subsequent studies and, like the
study by Legewie, took a naive view of the events described in the text and as
a result superimposed on that un-deconstructed symbolism, a further
interpretation.[4] For example, Kligerman argues that, where, in the *Confessions*,
we find Augustine identifying with Virgil's story of Dido and Aeneas, we see
an identification which contains the nuclear conflict of Augustine's infantile
neurosis and that this played 'a most decisive role in his subsequent career'
(Kligerman 1957: 472). This reading fails to take account of the fluctuating

use Augustine makes of the *Aeneid*, not just as literary modelling but as a reflection on the relationship between text and reader, which should at the very least put any psychological speculation into context (Bennett 1988).[5] For Kligerman, Augustine's conflict is explained in terms of his confused identifications with his parents, including a repressed erotic relationship with his mother, which he uses to explain Augustine's more general struggle with sexuality, his sibling relations, his bouts of illness and his flight from Rome (Kligerman 1957). On this view it was Augustine's fear of alienation from his mother due to sexual temptations which was the cause of the illness that affected Augustine's chest and throat.[6] Legewie (1931) had already suggested that there may have been a psychosomatic element in this period of ill health, which led to Augustine resigning the chair of rhetoric in Milan, but Legewie's conclusion was more tentative.

Kligerman did not rely on a scholarly analysis of the text of the *Confessions* and his assessment of Augustine's psychological makeup is largely based on conjecture. As a result it remains unconvincing. Nevertheless, his study, while not without its critics even within the world of psychoanalysis, has been relied upon by later commentators to a degree which is disproportionate to its true worth. Thus Woolcott writes that, despite the disadvantages inherent in the use of an historical document, Augustine's *Confessions* have certain outstanding advantages for psychoanalytic study 'as has been aptly demonstrated by Kligerman' (Woolcott 1966: 273). Elledge (1988) knew the scholarly background on Augustine. He had even read Courcelle, but strangely follows a similar line to Kligerman, suggesting that Augustine's conversion reconstitutes an ambivalence structured around a symbiotic relationship with his mother. He portrays Augustine constructing a defence against emotional betrayal in a deific embrace. Recently, more sophisticated versions of Kligerman's thesis have been developed, notably by Dittes (1965), Ziolkowski (1995), Barzilai (1997) and by Capps (2007).[7] All concur with Kligerman that Augustine was the best, if not the first, psychologist in the ancient world (Dittes 1965), because the *Confessions* exhibit 'a psychological astuteness centuries before some of its methods of self-examination and autobiography became institutionalised as legitimate scientific practice' (Elledge 1988: 72). Woolcott simply echoes Dittes' earlier assessment of Augustine as 'the greatest psychologist of his time and probably for many centuries to come' (Woolcott 1966: 273).[8]

In comparison to these studies of Augustine's psychology, the hermeneutic structure and allegorical exegesis which characterise Augustine's thought, and give the *Confessions* its unusual quality, has received relatively little attention in psychoanalytic literature. The exception should be the study by Rigby (1985). He attempted to take into account the theological and literary scholarship on the *Confessions* by explicitly mirroring the hermeneutic approach to Freud pioneered by Paul Ricoeur (1970). But in the end he has little to say that had not already been said by other analysts.

The deeper regions of the self

Although Augustine was first of all a theologian, he was ready to borrow from philosophy a conceptual framework for the purpose of theological argument. Indeed, according to the penetrating study made by Rist (1969), Augustine did not draw a clear boundary between philosophy and theology. The Neo-Platonism of Plotinus and Porphry had an independence that particularly suited Augustine's approach and provided a dynamic philosophical framework that Augustine was able to utilise in order to make sense of his experiences. As it was not a priori for or against Christian belief, it could be satisfactorily integrated into his theological project (Marrou 1963). Above all else Neo-Platonism gave Augustine the concept of an inner, psychological world (Brown 2000; also see Aubin 1963; O'Connell 1964) and he seems to have assumed that his readers shared this perspective (Theiler 1933).

In its style, the *Confessions* bears considerable resemblance to the *Enneads* of Plotinus. The *Enneads* are a collection of six groups of nine treatises arranged according to their subject matter. They follow a pedagogic path intended to lead the reader through various degrees of knowledge of virtue (Armstrong 1966). Plotinus developed the idea that our perceptual life is in some way unreal. This view, which would be mirrored in Freud's idea that the symptom could be interpreted like a dream,[9] had earlier been expressed in classical Greek poetry – we find it, for example, in Pindar (Pind. *Pyth.* VIII.95),[10] Aeschylus (Aesch. *Prom. Vinct.* 547ff.) and Aristophanes (Aristoph. *Birds* 685–7)[11] – and it was repeated vigorously by philosophers in late antiquity, on the basis of their reading of Plato. Prompted by this Werner Jaeger, in a study published in 1943, described Plato as the father of psychoanalysis.

> In order to understand [the character of our desires] we must descend into the subconscious. In dreams, says Plato, the soul casts off the restraining bonds put on it by reason, and the wild and bestial part of man awakens, revealing a part of his nature which he himself did not know. Plato was the father of psychoanalysis. He was the first to disclose that the horrible Oedipus-complex, the lewd desire to have sexual intercourse with one's own mother, was part of the unconscious personality. He disclosed it by analysing the experience of dreaming, and added a number of analogous wish-complexes . . . The unconscious, he says, thrusts upwards in dreams.[12]
>
> (Jaeger 1986: 343)

Plotinus, and to a lesser extent Albinus, Maximus of Tyre and Porphyry, insist that the inner man or interior experience is, within the hierarchy of the various degrees of selfhood, the true self (Dodds 1965).[13] 'The sum of things is within us' (Plot. *Enn.* 3, 8, 6, 40) and what is real in man is his inner world. Thus, if we wish to know what is real about ourselves we need to look within and reflect on our mental functioning, for what is within is better (*melius quod interius*).

> if we wish to know the Real, we have only to look in ourselves. This self-exploration is the heart of Plotinianism, and it is in the analysis of the Self that he made his most original discoveries . . . He was apparently the first to make the vital distinction between the total personality (ψυχή) and the ego-consciousness (ἡμεῖς); in the *Enneads*, as Stenzel observed, 'the ego' becomes for the first time a philosophical term. On this distinction between psyche and ego his whole psychology hinges.[14]
>
> Plotinus recognizes . . . that there are sensations which do not reach consciousness unless we specially direct attention to them (4,4,8; 5,1,12), and (anticipating Freud) that there are desires which 'remain in the appetitive part and are unknown to us' (4,8,8,9). The same is true of the permanent dispositions which result from past experiences or mental acts. Such dispositions, he says, can exert the strongest pull when we are least conscious of them.
>
> (Dodds 1960: 5–6)

According to Neo-Platonism the analytic withdrawal into the psyche demanded an examination of unconscious desire, which amounted to a therapeutic process. Plotinus described this withdrawal as a kind of catharsis – a breaking through the ego to get in touch with excluded, disassociated parts of the self. Hence Dodds considered Plotinus the first writer to recognise that the psyche includes dispositions 'of which the ego is normally unconscious' (Dodds 1965: 88 n.4; cf. also Schwyzer 1960). In this tradition of inwardness the notion of being turned-to-oneself became a paradigm of the philosophic life. Thus, Plotinus and Proclus urged their disciples to continually look within. This view also came to permeate Christian circles[15] and we find echoes of the Plotinian vocabulary in Greek patristic writers including Gregory of Nyssa, who refers to the illusion of the material world as a kind of sorcery (Daniélou 1944).[16] On this view the spiritual realm was not somewhere else but was to be found in the deepest level of the self – at a level that was deeper than rational thought; a region that, while normally remaining unconscious, periodically invades the field of consciousness. That is to say, for Plotinus, consciousness is a point of view, a perspective. What we are is something of which we are unconscious and we will not fully be who we are until we gain some understanding of the different levels of the self. By directing our attention within, to the interaction between the conscious and unconscious levels of the self, we become aware of the spiritual life we are somehow already unconsciously living. The reason this is thought to be therapeutic is because it amounts to a uniting of the self, a healing of the split between consciousness and the unconscious (Hadot 1973).

In one passage in the *Confessions* Augustine writes that there is something in man, something about himself that he does not know – *'tamen est aliquid hominis quod nec ipse scit spiritus hominis qui in ipso est'* (Aug. *Conf.* X.V.7). This hidden part is a psychic faculty but it is larger than consciousness.

> I cannot totally grasp all that I am. Thus the mind is not large enough to contain itself: but where can that part of it be which it does not contain? Is it outside itself and not within? How can it not contain itself? [How can there be any of itself that is not *in* itself]
>
> (Aug. *Conf.* X.VIII.15)

According to Dodds, in Augustine's description of the *abyssus humanae conscientiae* we get a glimpse of his notion of the unconscious – a notion that is fundamentally Gnostic in character (Dodds 1965), similar to the Valentinian mysterious primordial deep (*buthos*) where all things originally dwelt unknown, and to the *phragmos* (barrier) in Basileides, described by Origen in his *Contra Celsum*, where the world of conscious experience is cut off from unconscious inspirations (Dodds 1965; cf. also Blanchard 1954; Quispel 1947). Dodds was undoubtedly on to something, but Augustine's abyss may better be described as the ontological potentiality for consciousness. The psychic foundation of human subjectivity (Mills 2004).

According to Taylor (1989), although we already find the language of inwardness in Plotinus, Augustine gave it a more central place by introducing the idea that our inner world was not just unconscious but something fundamentally hidden (Cary 2000). This meant that we need to do more than just turn away from what is outside, but search within and disentangle various mechanisms that resist the process of bringing unconscious material into awareness (Taylor 1989: 537).[17] This idea led to what has been described as Augustine's invention of the inner self (Taylor 1989; cf. Cary 2000).[18]

> Let one very famous line stand for many: *'Noli foras ire, in teipsum redi; in interiore homine habitat veritas'* ('Do not go outward; return within yourself. In the inward man dwells truth'). Augustine is always calling us within. What we need lies *'intus'*, he tells us again and again.
>
> (Taylor 1989: 129)

The deceptive nature of consciousness

One of the reasons why Augustine thought that the depths of the personality were not to be found in consciousness was because he considered that one of the functions of rationality is to hide the truth of the personality. In this sense he saw consciousness as fundamentally deceptive, wrapped up in *figmenta* and therefore unreliable. A state in which 'the possibilities in me are hidden from myself' (Aug. *Conf.* X.XXXII.48). Thus he concludes, 'my [conscious] mind . . . feels that it cannot lightly trust its own report' (Aug. *Conf.* X.XXXII.48). In contrast, the hidden part of the mind, once accessed, reveals the truth and consequently enquiry into the unknown inner region of the mind was, he thought, one of the highest activities for man. At times Augustine describes the unconscious as the dead part of a person, a dark shadow encircling consciousness which, while belonging fully to the subject, nevertheless remains out of sight (Brown 2000; cf. also Holte 1962). On his view, knowledge of what is unconscious is equivalent to knowledge of one's feelings (*affectus*), particularly of one's desire which includes but is not synonymous with one's past desires (Aug. *Conf.* X.XIV.21). Although some hidden things, he observed, could be recalled immediately, other things took longer. Some, he said, are blurted out in slips of the tongue while we are looking for something else.[19] Speaking in a figurative way, he refers to the mind as a vast palace, a storehouse with different levels – some deeper, less accessible and some more secret. Indeed, some things are so repressed in its uttermost depths he considers them unreachable. They are, as it were, buried in a remote recess, thrust away so far back they are practically unsearchable, unless drawn forth by someone else. Without the Other, 'I might never have managed to think of them at all' (Aug. *Conf.* XI.21). Yet, even with the help of another, it may be that repressed material can only ever be penetrated as deeply as is possible at a specific moment. For researching the unconscious is a process that, for Augustine, had no end.

Bringing these hidden things back by remembering and thinking them out seemed to Augustine analogous to the way chewing the cud, for the cow, brings food up from the stomach. And yet, once repressed material is accessed, if we stop being aware of it, it quickly becomes repressed again and 'falls away into the more remote recesses of the memory' (Aug. *Conf.* X.XI.18). Should we want to re-access these things we need to 'think them out afresh' (Aug. *Conf.* X.XI.18).

> in other words they must be collected out of dispersion, and indeed the verb *to cogitate* is named from this drawing together. For *cogito* (I think) has the same relation to *cogo* (I put together) as *agito* to *ago* and *factito* to *facio*. But the mind of man has claimed the word *cogitate* completely for its own: not what is put together anywhere else but only what is put together in the mind is called cogitation.
>
> (Aug. *Conf.* X.XI.18)

This process of thinking out repressed material was described by Augustine as hard interior work, as 'toil within myself' (*laboro in me ipso*) (Aug. *Conf.* X.XVI.25). 'Who can analyse this?' he wrote, for 'I have become to myself a difficult soil and of heavy sweat' (Aug. *Conf.* X.XVI.25).

The unconscious as *memoria*

'Augustine had inherited from Plotinus a sense of the sheer size and dynamism of the inner world' and thought that 'knowledge of God could be found in the form of some "memory" in this inner world' (Brown 2000: 172). Butler (1951) had recognised that this corresponded in some way to the unconscious. For the memory was both a part of the mind but at the same time somehow beyond consciousness. It is 'beyond the power by which I am united to my body, and by which I fill its whole structure with life' (Aug. *Conf.* X.VII.11). In calling forth things from his memory, Augustine was convinced that somehow he would meet himself. For it is only by entering the memory that, he felt, genuine self-knowledge was possible. He was to compare this self-analysis with travel. 'Men', he said, 'go afar to marvel at the heights of mountains, the mighty waves of the sea, the long courses of great rivers, the vastness of the ocean, the movements of the stars, yet leaving themselves unnoticed' (Aug. *Conf.* X.VIII.15).

> And so I come to the fields and vast palaces of memory, where are stored the innumerable images of material things brought to it by the senses. Further there is stored in the memory the thoughts we think, by adding to or taking from or otherwise modifying the things that sense has made contact with, and all other things that have been entrusted to and laid up in memory . . . when I turn to memory, I ask it to bring forth what I want: and some things are produced immediately, some take longer as if they had to be brought out of some more secret place of storage; some pour out in a heap, and while we are actually wanting and looking for something quite different, they hurl themselves upon us in masses as though to say: 'May it not be me that you want?' I brush them from the face of my memory with the hand of my heart, until at last the thing I want is brought to light as from some hidden place. Some things are produced just as they are required, easily and in right order; and things that come first give place to those that follow, and given place are stored up again to be produced when I want them. This is what happens, when I say anything by heart.
>
> (Aug. *Conf.* X.VIII.12)

Here Augustine describes the memory as a hidden reservoir or inner receptacle where memories, thoughts and fantasies (*innumerabilium imaginum*) are put away as if in a limitless and secret place (*ex abditus*) within us (Margretts 1953; cf. also Winkler 1954). Thus Augustine describes the memory as an inner hidden container. Yet *memoria* for Augustine is more than a storehouse of concepts and fantasies, for it has an intimate dynamic relationship with the will, the emotions and interior experience in general. In fact, while describing the memory in spatial terms, he insists that it is not really a place at all. In fact, he says, the idea that it can be located inside a person is a ridiculous image.

> in my memory too I meet myself – I recall myself, what I have done, when and where and in what state of mind I was when I did it. In my memory are all the things I remember to have experienced myself or to have been told by others. From the same store I can weave into the past endless new likenesses of things either experienced by me or believed on the strength of things experienced . . . in the vast recess of my mind with its immeasurable store of images of things so great.
> (Aug. *Conf.* X.VIII.14)

For Augustine the memory is a mental faculty but is also synonymous with the mind.

> The mind (*animus*) and the memory (*memoria*) are not two separate things – for when we tell another to remember something we say: 'See that you have it in mind'; and when we forget something, we say: 'It was not in my mind' or 'It escaped my mind.' Thus we call the memory mind.
> (Aug. *Conf.* X.XIV.16–28)

And 'no one would say that the memory does not belong to the mind' (Aug. *Conf.* X.XIV.27–8). In fact, Augustine even describes the memory and the mind as the self: 'It is I who remember, I, my mind . . . [and] what could be closer to me than myself (*quid autem propinquius me ipso mihi*)' (Aug. *Conf.* X.XVI.25). In a very real sense, then, the subject is identical with the memory – '*et hoc animus est et hoc ego ipse sum*' (Aug. *Conf.* X.XVII.26, cf. X.XVII.21). 'Great is the power of memory, a thing . . . to be in awe of, a profound and immeasurable multiplicity; and this thing is my mind, this thing am I (*et hoc ego ipse sum*)' (Aug. *Conf.* X.XVII.12–14).

Augustine notes that the memory is full, not of things in themselves, but of images of things. These include images of material things that have come to us through the senses, as well as the thoughts we think and indeed everything we have experienced – all we have been told, everything we have learned, principles, laws and our feelings (*affectiones*). These *affectiones* include our desire (*cupiditas*), our regrets and our guilt. In fact, for Augustine, everything that a person is, is inwardly present in his memory including, so called, forgotten things: 'even the thing we remember that we forgot, we had not utterly forgotten. For if we had utterly forgotten it, we should not even be able to think of looking for it' (Aug. *Conf.* X.XIX.28). Augustine thus considers the memory as something dynamic. We can add to the thoughts we have stored there and modify them by somehow doing things inside ourselves. We can distinguish things found in the memory and weave into the past new experiences. And we can fantasise. For Augustine, one of the key dynamic aspects of the *memoria* is what Solignac calls totalisation (Skutella 1996: 559–60). This means bringing together and ordering interior experience. He describes this dynamic bringing together of things 'scattered and unarranged' (*quasi colligere atque animadvertendo*), collected out of dispersion, as a process central to the acquisition of self-awareness, characterised as it is by the integration of conscious and unconscious material. Without this dynamic process of integrating the unconscious part of the mind, we cannot, he argues, totally grasp 'all that I am' (*nec ego ipse capio totum, quod sum*; Aug. *Conf.* X.VIII.15.6–7). We may note here a similarity between Augustine and Lacan, who described the unconscious as a sort of register of memory (Lacan 1993). In fact, in his *Écrits* Lacan goes so far as to say that 'what we teach the subject to recognise as his unconscious is his memory' (Lacan 1977: 52).

Infirmitas, insania and discordia

Augustine diagnosed and described his conversion in psychological terms. The account he gives of himself comes to its climax in Book X of the *Confessions*. Here it is made clear that, far from being cured by his conversion, the author is still in mid-treatment (Dodds 1927–8). The medical image is drawn explicitly by Augustine himself (Brown 2000). He speaks of an inner crisis, akin to a fever in which he is somehow trapped in the past, in the habits of a lifetime (Brown 2000). Indeed, he considers that these habits are so ingrained in him that they have become compulsive. This leads him to conclude that his past – including his childhood – is very much alive in the present. It is something from which he cannot escape.

In Augustine's view a fundamental dislocation permeates the human subject. He described this as *discordia* (discordance) – a concept later to be introduced into psychiatry by Chaslin and into psychoanalysis by Lacan. It was Cicero, Augustine's 'chief informant' on Pre-Socratic philosophy (Hagendahl 1967: 588), who had first used the term to describe a state of being in which a person was in discord with his own self (*discordans secum*) (Lanteri-Laura and Gros 1992).[20] (According to Augustine each person seeks to restore, in some way, a balanced, undivided whole (*concordia*) within himself (Brown 2000). For the subject, Augustine considered, was made to be reunited with him or herself through a 'cure' (Brown 2000: 368). Augustine viewed sexuality as an outstanding example of *discordia*. This was due in part to the way he ties together his conception of the libido, which applies to many passions not just to sexuality, with that of the will. For Augustine the will (*voluntas*) is not the decision-making part of the psyche but the psyche itself. For this reason he considered it synonymous with the basic core of an individual. Thus, man 'is himself *voluntas*' (Rist 1969: 422) and cannot, therefore, claim he was not responsible for an action or behaviour because if he did it, in some way he must have willed it. Psychological compulsions are, for Augustine, not really compulsions at all, because to be compelled suggests that a person has not willed to act as he has. Augustine understood that desire was split off from his conscious intentions.

In keeping with the Neo-Platonic philosophy in which he framed his thought, Augustine saw the internal, mental world as fundamentally more significant than behaviour. As he looked back on his own sexual life, he was acutely aware of the frailty of sexual relationships, with their disturbing, compulsive and disruptive desires. Like Freud, he came to understand that sexuality, while being at the core of the personality was 'not fully available to consciousness' (Brown 2000: 422).[21] Augustine concluded that there was a profound disjunction between his understanding of the purpose of the sexual drive, as something harmonious and what he saw within himself, particularly in his dreams. Here a split (*discordia*) not harmony prevailed. The problem lay not in the existence of the erotic *per se*, but in the fact that sexual feelings can all too easily become uncontrollable and overwhelming. Exactly the same problem – namely, lack of control – he concluded, was the basis of impotence (Brown 2000). Unlike his contemporaries he viewed impotency and frigidity, quite logically as psychosomatic symptoms, the cause of which lay 'deep within the self' (Brown 2000: 418). In the fourth century this was a novel point of view. Rather than considering sexuality as primarily a physical thing, Augustine shifted it to the psychological level. In his exegesis of Genesis, he described the life of Adam and Eve in paradise as a fully sexual life, because in his view sexual desire indicated at its most basic that man was fundamentally enrolled in the symbolic, a subject continually driven towards intercourse with others (Brown 2000). This included sexual intercourse but also conversation and the bonds of friendship and intimacy, for the real importance of individual sexual pleasure lay, for Augustine, in its social nature (Brown 2000). Indeed, he saw that sex, when ordered, could drive a person towards harmony (*concordia*), not just at a physical level but more importantly at a psychological level.

Interpreting dreams is like reading scripture[22]

Augustine, like Freud, placed considerable emphasis on the interpretation of dreams. He saw dreams as a psychic mechanism of intricate signs which convey a powerful and direct meaning, capable of interpretation (Pépin, 1958; cf. Näf 2004). This view was not unusual in late antiquity and we find antecedents of it among pagan philosophers (Festugière 1975; also cf. Dodds 1951). But Augustine comes far closer than did his pagan predecessors to the views of Freud.[23] In fact, Peter Brown comments that Augustine takes up a position analogous to that of Freud in the way he assumes that 'the proliferation of [dream] images is due to some precise event, to the development of some geological fault across a hitherto undivided consciousness' (Brown 2000: 258), the difference being that the mythical story on which Augustine hangs the origins of the psychic mechanisms at work in repression was not Oedipus but Genesis. For Augustine it was the fall that made the symbolic the inevitable realm of human relationships (Duchrow 1961).

> For the Fall had been, among other things, a fall from direct knowledge into indirect knowledge through signs. The 'inner fountain' of awareness had dried up: Adam and Eve found that they could only communicate with one another by the clumsy artifice of language and gestures.
>
> (Brown 2000: 258)

Augustine's allegorical reading of the scriptures, with its runs of free association, formed the basis for an approach which amounts to an attempt at a self-analysis or self-examination.[24] He suggested that the person seriously intent upon grasping deeper levels of meaning could grapple with the text, which, he believed, had been veiled in order to exercise the reader. The philosopher was someone not content with the literal meaning of the text, but one who could grasp its deeper meaning in much the same way the disciples of Pythagoras sought to unravel the deeper meaning of his apophthegms or *symbola* (Dillon 1976).[25] This language of signs was made necessary by the dislocation (*discordia*) between our conscious and unconscious world. Progress in self-awareness was measured by his understanding of the scriptures and as he meditated on the text the effects of the therapy he had undergone was illustrated (Brown 2000). This perspective led Augustine to outline what amounts to a therapeutic methodology founded on the motif of *confiteri* (Verheijen 1949).[26] It was the act of confessing which was the dynamic form that this treatment took and in this act of opening up lay the possibility of generating psychological insight by descending into himself (Dodds 1927–8).

In the act of writing the *Confessions* and verbalising his memories, Augustine was consciously engaging in a process that he hoped would be curative. Drawing up into words his unconscious thoughts and feelings and analysing them was, he considered, an act of truth. Thus he opens Book X with the words 'he that *does the truth* [*facit veritatem*] is enlightened,'[27] I want to do it through confessing . . . in writing' (Aug. *Conf.* X.I.1).[28] He thinks that people may enjoy reading the *Confessions* in order to know what he was really like ('*ubi ego sum quicumque sum . . . quid ipse intus sum*'; Aug. *Conf.* X.III.4). For here he will not lie about himself but endeavour to be at his most transparent and most authentic. He described, for example, how it felt to end the relationship with his mistress and examined the complex unexpected emotions and the changes that had taken place within him when his mother died. He was surprised to find that he felt numbness, an unnatural self-control and shame at having wept so little (Brown 2000). Through this self-analysis of his present feelings the idealised figure of his mother, which had haunted his youth, was transformed into an ordinary human being.

Conclusion

'Turn your eyes inward, look into your own depths, learn first to know yourself!' (Freud SE 17: 144). These are Freud's words and they situate his work within the history of self-consciousness and spirituality. For Augustine, the way to a more spiritual life is precisely to turn inward (*in te redi*) and to attend to the self, for this is where truth lies. This reflexive position introduces into Western thought, the 'language of inwardness' (Taylor 1989: 131) that was previously associated with Plotinus.[29] In other words, for Augustine, the truth about ourselves is to be found, not just in the world, but more importantly in the intimacy of self-presence. It is hard not to see this inward turn foreshadowing Freud. This is particularly the case when we see that his understanding of memory (*memoria*) includes more than just past experiences. In memory he explores the paradox of the unconscious – the things about ourselves that can seem both known, and at the same time unknown and out of reach. As Taylor puts it:

> Deep within us is an implicit understanding, which we have to think hard to bring to explicit and conscious formulation. This is our *'memoria'*. And it is here that our implicit grasp of what we are resides, which guides us as we move from our original self-ignorance and grievous self-misdescription to true self-knowledge.
>
> (Taylor 1989: 135)

Neo-Platonism, with its insistence on spiritual exercises, orientated Augustine's thought inward. It was an inwardness that focused on mental conflict and his struggle with his own sanity, splitting (*discordia*) and sexuality; an analysis of his dreams and slips of the tongue which revealed hidden, complex and unconscious associations. But what makes the *Confessions* far more than autobiography is not so much Augustine's self-reflection but the tactic that he adopted for uncovering a new view of the subject. It is a hermeneutic methodology similar to that which was later to be adopted by Freud (Langs 1973). That is to say, it is a concerned introspection in which language is especially important (Burton 2007).[30] As such it is embedded in an exegetical tradition that has its roots in antiquity – specifically, as we learn from the *Questiones Homericae* of Pseudo Heraclitus, from the allegorical reading of Homer – and not just from Christian Greek writers like Origen or in the rabbinical tradition in Judaism, although both of these were to become important sources for psychoanalysis (Bakan 1958).[31] Both traditions, Greek and Jewish, favoured allegory and Augustine 'produced a singularly comprehensive explanation of why allegory should have been necessary in the first place. The need for such a language of "signs" was the result of a specific dislocation of human consciousness' (Brown 2000: 258; see also Vecchio 1994). In this tradition the biblical text was seen as a puzzle, a coded message, in which even the most bizarre incidents in the Old Testament could be taken as signs impregnated with a hidden meaning. A meaning of which one could only become fully conscious when it was verbalised (*confiteri*). This brings Augustine far closer to psychoanalysis than any other writer in antiquity. In his reading of Sophocles' *Oedipus Rex*, Freud was to treat the text in a manner similar to Augustine's treatment of biblical texts and particularly Genesis. No wonder, then, that Lacan, with his emphasis on the symbolic, and on language in particular, was to say to his students that 'everything I have been telling you' has been 'expounded with sensational lucidity . . . fifteen centuries earlier' by Augustine 'in one of the most glorious [texts] one could read' (Lacan 1988: 249).[32]

Notes

1 Freud's *Die Traumdeutung* was first published in November 1899, but an English translation did not appear until 1913.

2 This represented a key turning point in Augustine's intellectual development. From now on his thinking became more philosophical and his lasting interest in ancient philosophy was the outcome of the stimulus of reading the *Hortensius*. This is recalled 'in the preface to *De beata vita* . . . largely based on [the] themes of *tanto amore philosophiae successus sum, ut statim ad eam me ferre meditarer*' (Hagendahl 1967: vol. 2, 488). As well as Hagendahl's study of the influence of Cicero and of the *Hortensius* on the young Augustine, see C. Boyer (1920) *Christianisme et Néo-platonisme dans la formation de saint Augustin*, Paris: Beauchesne; and, by the same author (1937) Augustin *Dictionnaire de Spiritualité* vol. 1, 1102, Paris: Beauchesne. More broadly on the relationship between Cicero and Augustine, see the monograph by M. Testard (1958) *S. Augustin et Cicéron*, Paris: Études Augustiniennes.

3 Christine Mohrmann (1959) has written extensively on the *Confessions* as literature. See 'Le *Confessioni* come documento autobiografico and La lingua e lo stile delle', *Confessioni' Convivium* 3: 1–11 and 129–39. For an examination of the relationship between the literary form of biography and psychoanalysis in the *Confessions*, see J. Litchenberg (1978) 'Psychoanalysis and biography', *Annual of Psychoanalysis* 6: 397–427.

4 Labriolle, although critical of him, does admit that Legewie was very thoroughly versed in the opera of Augustine (Labriolle 1926: 39).

5 On Augustine's use of the *Aeneid*, cf. H. Hagendahl (1967) *Augustine and the Latin Classics. Studia Graeca et Latina Gothoburgensia*, 2 vols. Göteborg: Almquist and Wiksell; also see the bibliography in W. Hübner (1981) 'Die *praetorian memoriae* im zehnten Buch der *Confessiones*: Vergilisches bei Augustin', *Revue des Études Augustiniennes* 27: 245–63.

6 '*Quin etiam quod ipsa aestate litterario labori nimio pulmo meus cedere coeperat et difficulter trahere suspiria doloribusque pectoris testari se saucium vocemque clariorem productioremue recusare, primo perturbaverat me, quia magisterii illius sarinam paene jam necessitate deponere cogebat aut, si curai et convalescere potuissem, certe intermittere*' (Aug. *Conf.* IX.II.4–10).

7 Of these more recent attempts to read Augustine from the perspective of psychoanalysis, that of Barzilai (1997) is particularly interesting. He traces numerous references throughout Lacan's works to the *Confessions*, specifically to the scene in Book I, chapter 7 concerning sibling jealousy.

8 Referring to the attentions of modern psychological interpreters, Peter Brown comments shrewdly that it is 'as difficult as it is desirable to combine competence as an historian with sensitivity as a psychologist' (Brown 2000: 19).

9 The connection between Plotinus and Freud was discussed recently in a paper delivered by Jacques-Alain Miller at the 10th Congress of the New Lacanian School in London on 3 November 2011.

10 'Epameroi ti de tis; ti d' ou tis; skias onar anthrōpos'. Cf. Pind. Pyth. 8.94.

11 This is reminiscent of the words of the psalmist, 'To your eyes a thousand years are like yesterday, come and gone, no more than a watch in night'. Psalm 89: 4.'

12 It is likely that Freud would have been interested in one fact of Plotinus' childhood that has been preserved; namely, that he used to run to his nurse, even when he was going to grammar school, until the age of 8, 'uncovering her breasts and craving to suck them' (Edwards 2000: 5). Dodds suggests that the significance of this may fit with Freud's suggestion that mystical experience, with its sense of infinite extension and oneness with the Real, may represent a persistence of infantile feeling in which no distinction is yet drawn between self and other. A feeling which 'could co-exist as a sort of counterpart with the narrower and more sharply outlined ego-feeling of maturity' (Dodds 1965: 9–10; 91 n.2; cf. Freud SE 1930: 13–14). For a portrait of Plotinus and his thought see P. Hadot (1973) *Plotin ou la simplicité du regard*, Paris: Études Augustiniennes.

13 Cf. Aug. *Conf.* X.XXXIV.51. Also see Porphyry (Edwards 2000: 22).

14 Dodds argues that Plotinus is, with Alexander of Aphrodisias, the 'first writer to formulate clearly the general idea of self-consciousness (συναίσθησις or παρακολούθησις ἑαυτῶ), the ego's awareness of its own activity' (1960: 6). On the history of these terms, see Schwyzer (1960). The reference to Stenzel is to the final section of his book, see J. Stenzel (1931) *Metaphysik des Altertums*, München und Berlin: Druck/Verlag von R. Oldenbourg.

15 For a general review of the longevity of Neo-Platonism, see Edwards (2000: lv–lx).

16 On Gregory's anthropology, see von H. Balthasar (1942) *Présence et pensée. Essai sur la philosophie religieuse de Grégoire de Nysse*, Paris: Beauchesne, especially pp. 19–36 and 61–6, where he discusses Gregory's conception of the spiritual, the material (including the notion of desire) and the real (*du réel*) – the incomprehensible realm 'where understanding does not reach'; Grégoire de Nysse *La Vie de Moïse* 46: 8–10, ed. J. Daniélou (1968), Paris: Les Éditions du Cerf.

17 Brown points out that such a philosophical perspective may have suited Augustine temperamentally, for he was an extremely introverted and sensitive person, prone, as was Plotinus' biographer Porphyry, to bouts of depression (Brown 2000; Edwards 2000). For a discussion of the diagnosis of depression in antiquity, see P. Toohey (1990), 'Some ancient histories of literary melancholia', *Illinois Classical Studies* 15: 143–61.

18 For an alternative view, see G. Madec (1988) '*In te supra me*. Le sujet dans les *Confessions* de saint Augustin', *Revue de l'Institut Catholique de Paris* 28: 45–63. While it is undoubtedly true that Neo-Platonism was the foundation for his ideas on the unconscious, it is only when Augustine turned to Aristotle that he was able to formulate a fully coherent model for the psyche (Harrison 2006). In relation to Augustine's notion of the will, Harrison notes that the synthesis between Augustine and the Aristotelian philosophy of mind is the work of Thomas (Harrison 2006).

19 Quispel refers to 'Freudian slips' made by Augustine himself in relation to his use of the Diatessaron. See G. Quispel (1975) *Tatian and the Gospel of Thomas. Studies in the History of the Western Diatessaron* 60, Leiden: E.J. Brill.

20 Early on, in his doctoral thesis, in a translation of a passage from Spinoza's *Ethics,* Lacan had described one aspect of paranoia with the French word *discordance.* In French the term *discordance,* which was introduced in psychiatry by Philippe Chaslin (1857–1923), refers to a conflict between symptoms, particularly in cases of paranoia. As a result, *discordant* is closely associated with the introduction of the term 'schizophrenia'. The French term comes directly from the Latin *discordare* (Lanteri-Laura and Gros 1992) and translated as both 'splitting' and 'dissociation' (the German *Spaltung*) (Roudinesco 1993). What Lacan did was to equate the French term *discordance* with Freud's *Ichspaltung,* the 'splitting of the ego'.

21 In relation to Freud, Merkur (1994) and Bakan (1958) have demonstrated convincingly how this view of the sexual stems directly from the Jewish mystical tradition.

22 Freud was to say that interpreting dreams was like reading sacred scripture (*einen heiligen Text*) (Freud 1900 SE V: 514).

23 Here we see an example of Augustine sharing the ideas of his contemporary Evagrius Ponticus, who understood the dynamic influence exercised on dream activity, by the emotions a person experiences during the day and by the role of memory in mental life. See the excellent study by M. Dulaey (1973) *Le Rêve dans la vie et la pensée de saint Augustin,* Paris: Études Augustiniennes.

24 The unusual quality of Augustine's *Confessions* has led at least one scholar, Asmussen, to suggest that it was based on a Manichaean prototype of the examination of conscience but Hadot (1995) argues that the *Confessions* are an anti Manichaean theological polemic. Cf. Asmussen, *Xu ĀSTV ĀNIFT. Studies in Manichaeism. Acta Theologica Danica VII,* trans. N. Haislud, Prostant apud Munksgaard: Copenhagen; P. Hadot (1995) *Philosophy as a Way of Life. Spiritual Exercises from Socrates to Foucault,* Oxford: Blackwell. On the Manichaean background, see W.H.C. Frend (1953) 'The Gnostic-Manichaean Tradition in Roman North-Africa', *Journal of Ecclesiastical History* 4: 13–25; J. Ries (1957–8) 'Introduction aux études manichéennes', *Ephemerides Theologicae Lovanienses* 33: 453–82 and 35: 362–409; and A. Adam (1958) 'Das Fortwirken des Manichäismus bei Augustinus', *Zeitschrift für Kirchengeschichte,* 69: 1–25.

25 The strong similarity between the Christian examination of conscience and that of the Pythagoreans, which had a psychological and therapeutic character, has long been recognised. See the articles by H. Jaeger and J.-C. Guy (1961) 'Examen de conscience. Le monde gréco-romain and chez les pères de l'église', *Dictionnaire de Spiritualité* 32: 1792–94 and 1801–7.

26 As if to justify this, Augustine writes, '*An congratulari mihi cupiunt, cum audierint, quantum ad te accedam munere tuo, et orare pro me, cum audierint, quantum retarder pondere meo? indicabo me talibus*'; Augustine *Conf.* X.IV.5.

27 Lacan understood psychoanalysis in similar terms, and in Seminar I he refers to the subject finding the truth of himself in the process of the analysis (Lacan 1988).

28 For an alternative view, see G. Schmaltz (1952) 'Das "veritatem facere" des Augustinus als Wesen des Reinfungsvorganges', *Psyche* 6 (6/5): 304–19.

29 Tertullian may be the only earlier Latin writer to come near to Augustine in terms of his interest in the inner, subjective life of man. In his *De Anima* he stresses the importance of human psychology. Cf. J. Daniélou (1980), *A History of Early Christian Doctrine Before the Council of Nicaea,* trans. David Smith and John Austin Baker, vol. 3, p. 466, London and Philadelphia: Darton, Longman and Todd.

30 On Augustine's use of language and on his contribution to language theory, see Solignac in Skutella and Solignac (1998: 207–33, 264–5).

31 On the allegorical exegesis of texts Professor Jaeger, tracing the exegetical line from Homer and Hesiod through Virgil to Islamic commentaries on the Koran,

suggests that it is at the moment 'when the literal meaning of the sacred books had become questionable but when the giving up of those forms was out of the question' that allegory emerges, as the reason for the continuation of the literature was not primarily intellectual but sociological; W. Jaeger (1961) *Early Christianity and Greek Paideia,* Cambridge, MA: Belknap Press/Harvard University Press, pp. 127–8 n.6 (cf. pp. 47–52).

32 The text in question being the *De Magistro.*

Abbreviations

Works by ancient authors are cited as follows:

Aesch. *Prom Vinct.*	Aeschylus. *Prometheus Bound,* ed. and trans. A.H. Sommerstein. Loeb Classical Library 145. Cambridge and London: Harvard University Press.
Aug. *Conf.*	*Oeuvres de Saint Augustin,* vols 13 and 14, ed. M. Skutella, intro and notes A. Solignac, trans. E. Tréhorel and G. Bouissou (1996–8). Paris: Études Augustiniennes.
De Magistro	*Aureli Augustini Opera* II: 2. *Corpus Christianorum* 29: 155–203. Turnhout: Brepols, 1970.
Aristoph. *Birds.*	Aristophanes. *The Birds,* vol. 2, trans. B.B. Rogers (1924). Loeb Classical Library. London: William Heinemann.
Pind. *Pyth.*	Pindar. *Pythiques*, vol. 2, ed. and trans. A. Puech (1961). Collection des Universités de France. Paris: Société d'Édition Les Belles Lettres.
Plot. *Enn.*	Plotinus. *Enneades,* 7 vols, trans. A.H. Armstrong (1966–85). Loeb Classical Library. Cambridge, MA: Harvard University Press.

Bibliography

Armstrong, A.H. (1966). Preface to *Plotinus. Porphry on Plotinus. Ennead I,* trans. A.H. Armstrong. Cambridge, MA and London: Harvard University Press.

Aubin, P. (1963). *Le problème de la 'conversion': etude sur un terme commun à l'hellénisme et au christianisme des trois premiers siècles.* Paris: Beauchesne.

Bakan, D. (1958). *Sigmund Freud and the Jewish Mystical Tradition.* Toronto, New York and London: D. Van Nostrand.

Barzilai, S. (1997). Augustine in contexts: Lacan's repetition of a scene from the *Confessions. Literature and Theology* 11(2): 200–21.

Bennett, C. (1988). The conversion of Vergil: *The Aeneid* in Augustine's *Confessions. Revue des Études Augustiniennes* 34: 47–69.

Blanchard, P. (1954). L'Espace intérieur chez saint Augustin d'après le livre X des Confessions. *Augustinus Magister*, vol. 1, 536–42.

Brown, P. (2000). *Augustine of Hippo.* London: Faber and Faber.

Burton, P. (2007). *Language in the* Confessions *of Augustine.* Oxford: Oxford University Press.

Butler, C. (1951). *Western Mysticism* London: Arrow Books.

Capps, D. (2007). Augustine's *Confessions*: The story of a divided self and the process of its unification. *Pastoral Psychology* 55: 551–69.

Cary, P. (2000). *Augustine's Invention of the Inner Self*. Oxford: Oxford University Press.

Courcelle, P. (1968). *Recherches sur Les Confessions de Saint Augustin*. Paris: Éditions E. de Boccard.

Cross, F.L. (Ed.) (1963). *The Oxford Dictionary of the Christian Church*. London: Oxford University Press.

Daniélou, J. (1944). *Platonisme et théologie mystique*. Paris: Aubier.

Dillon, J. (1976). Image, symbol and analogy: Three basic concepts of neoplatonic exegesis. In *The Significance of Neoplatonism,* ed. R.B. Harris, pp. 247–62. New York: State University of New York Press.

Dittes, J.E. (1965). Continuities between the life and thought of Augustine. *Journal for the Scientific Study of Religion* 5(1): 130–40.

Dodds, E.R. (1927–8). Augustine's *Confessions*: A study of spiritual maladjustment. *Hibbert Journal* 26: 459–73.

Dodds, E.R. (1951). *The Greeks and the Irrational*. Berkeley, Los Angeles and London: University of California Press.

Dodds, E.R. (1960). Tradition and personal achievement in the philosophy of Plotinus. *Journal of Roman Studies* 50 (Parts 1 and 2): 1–17.

Dodds, E.R. (1965). *Pagan and Christian in an Age of Anxiety*. London: Cambridge University Press.

Duchrow, U. (1961). 'SIGNUM' und 'SUPERBIA' beim jungen Augustin. *Revue des études Augustiniennes* 7: 369–72.

Edwards, M. (2000). *Neoplatonic Saints: The Lives of Plotinus and Proclus by their Students*. Liverpool: Liverpool University Press.

Elledge, W.P. (1988). Embracing Augustine: Reach, restraint, and romantic resolution in the *Confessions*. *Journal for the Scientific Study of Religion* 27(1): 72–89.

Festugière, A.-J. (1975). *Artemidorus, The Interpretation of Dreams*, trans. R.J. White. New York: Noyes Press.

Freud, S. (1917). A difficulty in the path of psychoanalysis. In *The Standard Edition of the Complete Psychological Works of Sigmund Freud*, ed. and trans. J. Strachey, vol. 17. London: Hogarth Press/Institute of Psycho-Analysis.

Gay, V. (1986). Augustine: The reader as self object. *Journal for the Scientific Study of Religion* 25(1): 64–76.

Gibb, J. and Montgommery, W. (eds.) (1908). *The Confessions of Saint Augustine*. Cambridge Patristic Texts. Cambridge: Cambridge University Press.

Hadot, P. (1973). *Plotin ou la simplicité du regard*. Paris: Études Augustiniennes.

Hagendahl, H. (1967). *Augustine and the Latin Classics. Studia Graeca et Latina Gothoburgensia* 20, 2 vols. Göteborg: Elanders Boktryckeri Aktiebolag.

Harrison, S. (2006). *Augustine's Way into the Will*. Oxford: Oxford University Press.

Holte, K.R. (1962). *Béatitude et sagesse: Saint Augustin et le problème de la fin de l'homme dans le philosophie ancienne*. Paris: Études Augustiniennes.

Jaeger, W. (1986). *Paideia. The Ideals of Greek Culture* vol. 2, trans. G. Highet. Oxford: Oxford University Press.

Kligerman, C. (1957). A psychoanalytic study of the *Confessions* of St Augustine. *Journal of the American Psychoanalytic Association* 5: 469–84.

Labriolle, P. de (1926). Pourquoi Saint Augustin a-t-il rédigé des *Confessions*? *Bulletin de l'Association Guillaume Budé* 12: 30–47.

Lacan, J. (1977). *Écrits: A Selection,* trans. A. Sheridan. London: Routledge.

Lacan, J. (1988). *The Seminar of Jacques Lacan, Book I Freud's Papers on Technique 1953–1954*, ed. J.-A. Miller, trans. J. Forrester. Cambridge: Cambridge University Press.

Lacan, J. (1993). *The Psychoses. The Seminar of Jacques Lacan. Book III 1955–1956*, ed. J.-A. Miller, trans. R. Grigg. London: Routledge.

Langs, H. (1973). *Die Sprache und das Unbewußte. Jacques Lacans Grundlegung der Psychoanalyse*. Frankfurt am Main: Suhrkamp.

Lanteri-Laura, G. and Gros, M. (1992). *Essai sur la discordance dans psychiatrie contemporaine*. Paris: Les Editions Epel.

Legewie, B. (1925). *Augustinus. Eine Psychographie*. Bonn: Marcus and Weber.

Legewie, B. (1931). Die körperliche Konstitution und die Krankheiten Augustins. *Miscellanea Agostiniana* 2: 5–21.

Margretts, E.L. (1953). The concept of the unconscious in the history of medical psychology. *Psychiaric Quarterly* 27(1): 115–38.

Marrou, H.-I. (1963). Synesius of Cyrene and Alexandrian Neoplatonism. In *The Conflict Between Paganism and Christianity in the Fourth Century*, ed. A. Momigliano, pp. 126–50. Oxford: Clarendon Press.

Marrou, H.-I. (2003). *Saint Augustin et l'augustinisme*. Paris: Éditions du Seuil.

Merkur, D. (1994). Freud and Hasidism. In *The Psychoanalytic Study of Society*, ed. L.B. Boyer, R. M. Boyer and H.F. Stein, vol. 19, pp. 335–48. Hillsdale, NJ: The Analytic Press.

Meserve, H.C. (1965). Our hearts are restless *Journal of Religion and Health* 4(2): 115–18.

Mills, J. (2004). *Rereading Freud. Psychoanalysis through Philosophy*. New York: State University of New York Press.

Näf, B. (2004) *Traum und Traumdeutung im Altertum*. Darmstadt: Wissenschaftliche Buchgesellschaft.

O'Connell, R.J. (1964). The riddle of Augustine's 'Confessions': A Plotinian key. *International Philosophical Quarterly* 4: 327–72.

O'Meara, J. (1954). *The Young Augustine. The Growth of St. Augustine's Mind up to his Conversion*. London: Longmans, Green and Co.

Pépin, J. (1958). *Mythe et allégorie: les origines grecques et les contestations judéo-chrétiennes*. Paris: Éditions Montaigne.

Quispel, G. (1947). The original doctrine of Valentine. *Vigiliae Christianae* 1: 43–73.

Ricoeur, P. (1970). *Freud and Philosophy. An Essay on Interpretation*, trans. D. Savage. New Haven and London: Yale University Press.

Rigby, P. (1985). Paul Ricoeur, Freudianism, and Augustine's *Confessions*. *Journal of the American Academy of Religion* 53(1): 93–114.

Rist, R.A. (1969). Augustine on free will and predestination. *Journal of Theological Studies* n.s. 20: 420–47.

Roudinesco, E. (1993). *Jacques Lacan. Esquisse d'une vie, histoire d'un système de pensée*. Paris: Fayard.

Schmaltz, G. (1952). Das 'veritatem facere' des Augustinus als Wesen des Reinfungsvorganges. *Psyche* 6: 304–19.

Schwyzer, H.-R. (1960). 'Bewust' und 'Unbewust' bei Plotin. In *Les Sources de Plotin*, pp. 385–6. Geneva: Fondation Hardt.

Skutella, M. (ed.) (1998/1996). *Oeuvres de Saint Augustin*, intro. and notes A. Solignac, A., trans. E. Tréhorel and G. Bouissou, vols 13 and 14. Paris: Études Augustiniennes.

Taylor, C. (1989). *Sources of the Self*. Cambridge, MA: Harvard University Press.

Theiler, W. (1933). *Porphyrius und Augustin*. Halle: M. Niemeyer.

Vecchio, S. (1994). *Le parole come Segni. Introduzione alla linguistic agostiniana*. Palermo: Novecento.

Verheijen, M. (1949). *Eloquentia Pedisequa. Observations sur le style des Confessions de St. Augustin*. Nijmegen: Dekker and Van de Vegt N.V.

Winkler, K. (1954). La Théorie augustinienne de la mémoire à son point de depart *Augustinus Magister* 1: 491–509.

Woolcott, P. (1966). Creativity and religious experience in St Augustine. *Journal of the Scientific Study of Religion* 5: 273–83.

Zepf, M. (1926). *Augustinus Confessiones*. Tübingen: J.C.B. Mohr.

Ziolkowski, E.J. (1995). St Augustine: Aeneas' antitype, Monica's boy. *Literature and Theology* 9(1): 1–23.

8

MYSTICAL THEOLOGY, MYSTICISM AND MADNESS

Rodney Bomford

The popular understanding of mysticism is alien to the Christian mystical tradition. In particular, contemplation is not a means of inducing a changed state of consciousness, nor is union with God to be understood as an ecstatic absorption into him. I discuss this because meddling with one's state of consciousness might be seen as endangering mental health and the claim to be absorbed into God as a symptom of illness.

The patient who believes himself to be God figures in many a comic anecdote and embodies an identity between the divine and the insane. Theologians indeed use the word "deification" to describe the ultimate goal of Christian life. It figures particularly in works that are correctly described as mystical theology and, as I shall argue, incorrectly described as written by mystics. In this chapter I shall try to throw some light on how that tradition should be understood and upon the confusions that have gathered around the words 'mystic' and 'mystical'.

Mystics and mysticism

There is a popular notion of a category of people called mystics, people who have had some transcendent experience unlike the experience of more ordinary mortals. In this view there are mystics who have attained these experiences by prolonged religious or ascetic practices of varied kinds, and there are others who have simply received them out of the blue in the course of daily living. Mystics, particularly of the former sort, may be of any religious faith but their experiences are thought to be of fundamentally a similar nature, perhaps of some changed state of consciousness in which they experience intimacy with whatever is the fundamental ideal of their faith, or indeed absorption into God. It has been maintained that similar experiences can be induced by the use of a suitable drug.[1]

Such a view of mystics has indeed had some basis in the revival of interest in mysticism in Christianity that took place in the later nineteenth and early twentieth centuries. Theological writers from much earlier centuries were sometimes interpreted in ways that lend support to the caricatured notion of a mystic that I have described. While that popular view has become increasingly widespread, serious analysis of the notion of a mystic in Christian tradition has very largely undermined it. Indeed a number of recent publications have argued that those customarily understood as Christian mystics were actually opponents of mysticism in its modern sense.[2] Denys Turner writes:

> I have drawn the conclusion from my study that so far as the word mysticism has a contemporary meaning, and that in so far as that contemporary meaning links mysticism to the cultivation of certain kinds of experience – of inwardness, ascent and union – then the mediaeval mystic offers an anti-mysticism.[3]

'Inwardness', 'ascent' and 'union' are indeed terms frequently to be found in the writings of those described as mystical. Turner's point is that the medieval writers did not use them primarily to refer to spiritual experiences. The goal of union, for example, was not so much the achievement of an experience of God as the attainment of a conformity of the will with God's will. The classic writers expend few words on descriptions of their feelings, but many on the work of detaching the human will from worldly goals and aligning it with the divine. Union with God does not therefore result in new information about him such as one might expect would come from experiencing God directly. Claims to new information about God would have been treated with great suspicion by orthodox theologians, since it has always been held that God was fully revealed in Jesus Christ and to that revelation nothing could be added, and in fact the conclusions of the mystical writers are seldom particularly original and tend more to be affirmations of the shared faith of the church than new discoveries.

The originality of many mystical writers is in their descriptions of spiritual ascent through a number of stages. Some commentators have mistakenly taken these to be definitive, almost factual, as though expressing an already given topography of the human soul's progression towards God. Thus McIntosh writes:

> Mystical language is describing in a simple or direct sense neither God nor the mystic's experiences, but evoking an *interpretive framework* within which the readers of the text may come to recognize and participate in their own encounters with God.
>
> (McIntosh 1998: 124)

More generally, mystical texts may be seen as the writer's attempt to express something of the journey by which his or her own faith has appropriated beliefs that before were taken on trust. Thus St Anselm described this aspect of the journey of the Christian as 'faith seeking understanding',[4] which might be paraphrased as 'received belief transforming into a sense of knowledge'.

The words 'mystic' and 'mystical' derive originally from a Greek verb *muein*, 'to close' (usually the eyes), but which also meant 'to initiate'. The use of these words in classical Greek is generally linked to the Greek mysteries, a word from the same root. These words are used sparingly in the New Testament, but in the theology of the Fathers of the church (i.e. theologians roughly from the late second to the seventh centuries CE)[5] they are used much more. The primary meaning is always of something hidden.

Thus the sacraments of the church and particularly the Eucharist may be described as mysteries, because their meaning is hidden behind the outward form; the hidden reality of the Eucharistic bread, for example, is the body of Christ. Prevalent, also, was the belief that the true, or deepest, meaning of the Scriptures is a hidden meaning which only prolonged meditative attention could hope to disclose. A text bearing the fruit of such meditation might then be described as mystical theology. The crowning work of Dionysius the Areopagite, writing about the year 500, was indeed called *The Mystical Theology*, a work that became profoundly influential in the medieval Western church. When the anonymous fourteenth-century author of *The Cloud of Unknowing* translated it into English, he rendered the title *Hid Divinity*, thus accurately reflecting the original meaning of mystical.

In the earliest Christian centuries the noun mystic never designated a category of people within the church, but generally referred to an initiate of the pagan mysteries. Its application to those who in earlier centuries appeared to record spiritual experience is primarily a nineteenth-century development. Likewise, the term 'mysticism', or its equivalent in other languages, to denote a particular strand of Christian activity or reflection, is of recent origin. Bernard McGinn suggests that it is the invention of nineteenth-century scholars. He asserts that the term itself is first found in French in the seventeenth century (McGinn 1991), whereas the phrase 'mystical theology' precedes it by over a thousand years. The latter is concerned with the hidden meaning of texts and sacraments. The former has a quite different sense, accurately reflected in the definitions of the *Shorter Oxford English Dictionary*. A mystic in this sense is 'One who seeks by contemplation and self-surrender to obtain union with or absorption into the Deity, or who believes in the spiritual apprehension of truths inaccessible to the understanding'. The same dictionary defines mysticism as:

> the opinions, mental tendencies, or habits of thought and feeling, characteristic of mystics; belief in the possibility of union with the Divine nature by means of ecstatic contemplation; reliance on spiritual initiation as the means of acquiring knowledge of mysteries inaccessible to the understanding.

Over the course of the nineteenth century a canon of practitioners of mysticism in that dictionary sense came into being.[6] The members included in that canon were very diverse. Those who wrote about such themes as union with God and the vision of God dominate the early centuries. Those who recorded experiences of God in prayer come to the fore in the Middle Ages and the theme of spiritual marriage becomes important. At the head of the canon was the biblical St Paul, who claimed to have ascended to the third heaven: 'I know a person who was caught up to the third heaven . . . he was caught up into Paradise and heard things that are not to be told' (2 Cor. 12.2–4).

The influence of Platonism was seen as giving an impetus to the tradition starting with Clement of Alexandria in the late second century and continuing through a line of writers, first in the Greek-speaking church, and later in Latin and other languages as well. In most succeeding centuries there are representatives, including the women visionaries of the later Middle Ages and the famous Carmelites of sixteenth-century Spain, St John of the Cross and St Teresa of Avila. Some would include the increasingly bizarre writings – from the point of view of Christian orthodoxy – of such as William Blake.

Up to about the year 1200 the canon consists almost entirely of men, and moreover these men are all major theologians.[7] However, in the thirteenth-century Western church, there emerges a number of women mystics, many of whose mysticism in some degree rests upon visions.[8] After about 1350, there are almost no major theologians in the canon at all, and the men as well as the women have their place because they can be read as though they were specialists in religious experience.[9] There are several points to note about this evolution.

First of all, women, with few exceptions, had far less access to the learning of the time and could not compete with men in the traditional theological medium. Very often they had to use the services of a man, usually a monk in a male religious community with which they had some link, to publish, even to write down, their thoughts. Whereas the men had primarily expounded the meaning of biblical texts, the women reflected to a considerable extent on their own visions. Second, the men, too, included reports of their own experiences in prayer in texts that in earlier times were more likely to consist of direct commentary upon sections of the bible. This is doubtless connected with a third point: the beginnings of a modern interest in personal experience. Where, for example, early theologians would expound the Song of Songs (a love poem in the Hebrew scriptures) primarily as relating to the nuptials of Christ and the Church, St John of the Cross speaks of the engagement and marriage of the individual soul to Christ. Thus mystical theology became more individualistic and easier to misunderstand as mysticism in the dictionary sense.

Evelyn Underhill was a leading figure among those who might be said to have developed the canon and who popularised the writings of some of its major figures.[10] For her, the test of a mystic was whether or not he or she recounts a direct experience of God. McGinn writes:

> Evelyn Underhill, for instance, in differentiating true mystics from
> those philosophers (and, we may add, theologians) who reflect on

mystical experience said of the latter 'they are no more mystics than the milestones on the Dover Road are travellers to Calais'.

(McGinn 1991: xiii)

The suggestion implicit here is that some merely point the way to direct experience of God, or of union with him, while others have actually arrived at it. What is central, therefore, is personal experience and hence those with this understanding of mysticism proceeded to examine the writings of earlier centuries in search of 'autobiographical accounts of special visionary or unitive experiences of God' (McGinn 1991: xiv). At this point a problem arose, since such accounts are not to be found at all in some of those who were already accounted as leading figures in the mystical canon. Such accounts are rare in the whole of the first Christian millennium, become increasingly frequent from about the year 1200 and of supreme importance in the sixteenth century. Even St Augustine, whose *Confessions,* written probably in the year 400 CE, might be called a spiritual autobiography (indeed, the first in Christian history) and whose influence was enormous upon virtually all the Western writers who figure in the canon, gives no account of an experience of personal union with God.[11] The canon itself therefore subverted the preferred test for inclusion within it. Furthermore it has been widely recognised in more recent years that there is no definition of a mystic or even of a mystical writer that would encompass those to whom the terms have customarily been applied, such is their diversity. The whole notion of a category of Christian mystics is thus highly questionable.

Transformation by God

Nevertheless, the term 'mystical' at least has a long and honourable history in Christian discourse. I have already mentioned the sense in which it was originally used: the disclosing of the hidden significance of Christian sacraments, rites and texts. In the very first years of the Church, before the New Testament documents were written, the Jewish Scriptures (or the Christian Old Testament) were scrutinised to disclose prophecies believed to be fulfilled in the story of Jesus. This was held to be their hidden significance, their mystic meaning. While early Christianity is now generally believed to have been very diverse, apocalyptic expectation seems to have been a dominant theme: the Christ who had been taken up to heaven would shortly return, overturn the rulers of the earth and reward those who had been faithful to the call of the Gospel. This reward would include life with God in a transformed universe and communion with him there. Knowledge of God and the vision of God might, in such a view, primarily be an expectation in the life hereafter. In the meantime, faithful perseverance was the chief requirement.

In the writings of St Paul this relatively simple outlook begins to evolve into something more complex. Members of the early Christian communities while waiting for the end also expected themselves to avoid certain kinds of behaviour, such as are forbidden in the ten commandments of the Mosaic law. It was forced upon St Paul's attention that many in the churches that he founded or visited were not doing so. It was clear to him that it is not easy to be good – and elements of his own personal nature seem also to have been giving him the same message. He wrote: 'I do not understand my own actions. For I do not do what I want, but I do the very thing I hate' (Romans 7:15). To be good required not just obedience to rules, but a transformation of inner disposition, a renewal in the soul, the seat of motives and emotions. This transformation, for him at least, was to be effected by identification and indeed union with the risen Christ in heaven. To this point we might therefore trace one important beginning of an emphasis upon human subjectivity and hence of human experiences in the Christian path. St Paul himself mentions being taken up to the third heaven. While belief in the return of Jesus remained an expectation, increasingly as the years passed it became an expectation, no longer imminent, but of one (perhaps far-off) day in the future. In the meantime the desire to lead an ethical life – made possible by inner change and a desire to know the hidden God – began to be dominant themes in the Church.

Inner change is described by St Paul as 'having the mind of Christ' (1 Cor. 2.16), as being filled with the Spirit of God,[12] as one's true life being not one's own, but Christ's.[13] St John's Gospel, written perhaps thirty years after St Paul's letters, expresses a similar thought through the mouth of Jesus: 'Those who love me will keep my word, and my Father will love them, and we will come to them and make our home with them' (John 14.23).

Meditation on such texts inspired and expressed a longing for intimacy with God and this intimacy is an abiding presence transforming the will and thus making possible a life pleasing to God; it is not a description of momentary experiences of absorption into God.

At this point I need to break off my main line of argument to offer some explanation to any readers for whom talk of God is largely unintelligible. The traditional language of the Church about God is to a great extent metaphorical and it is by no means easy, indeed impossible, to dispense entirely with metaphor. For example, God is often spoken of as though he were a most powerful being outside the universe but given to intervention in its workings. Theologians who wrestled with the hidden (mystical) meaning of such metaphors, in contrast, describe God variously as Existence Itself (Thomas Aquinas), nothingness (John Scotus Erigena)[14] and as beyond both being and non-being (Pseudo Dionysius),[15] to give just three instances. Those readers to whom theism is alien may make some sense of this chapter if I suggest that the word 'God' may be understood as referring to the universe as a whole when apprehended as wholly coherent with itself and coherent in a benign way. Spinoza's famous phrase 'Deus sive natura' comes to mind – God or nature – and by nature he meant *natura naturans,* or self-generating nature.[16] The notion of the earth as Gaia might be seen as very loosely parallel, though Gaia refers to the unity of only planet earth, but the notion of Gaia is perhaps closer to that of the Christian God than is the image of the old man sitting on a cloud. Universal benign coherence is seen by Christians as expressed in the story of Christ, through his conscious and deliberate choice to live in concord with that benign coherence even to the point of losing his life to express it. Thus, when St Paul writes of Christ living within him, we might interpret this as a claim to be living in concord with all that is. To do this requires giving up our natural tendency to live in our own (apparently, but superficially) best interests by the furthering of our own desires and aspirations. It means a transformation from a self-centred life to a God-centred life, i.e. a life directed towards the wellbeing of the universe, what might be called replacing ego-centricity with theo-centricity (or even cosmo-centricity). Of course this account is not a wholly satisfactory translation of theological language, but perhaps it will give some hint of what a Christian understands from the metaphorical mythology of the faith.

St Paul's sense of the transforming of the self-directed life into the God-directed life remained a dominant influence on Christian faith. In time the early church took up (perhaps from Stoic sources) the word *apatheia* (literally, 'passionlessness') to describe one aspect of the inner change desired. The word is easily misunderstood. It does not demand the extinction of the passions or emotions, but their control, so that they do not minister to the satisfaction of the individual but to the purposes of God. The Christian was expected to progress, first by withdrawing from the selfish gratification of the passions and then by mastering them internally. This inner discipline is governed by ascetic theology and might include fasting, prayer, the recitation of psalms and the meditative reading of scripture. In principle, the whole of life came within this discipline, most notably perhaps in the lives of the hermits and monks of the Egyptian desert. Contemplation took place within this context and no firm line can be drawn between ascetic theology and what in time came to be called mystical theology, which is particularly linked with contemplation. Nor can either of these be separated from the desire for a truly ethical life, unattainable without the control of the passions but unattainable also by mere adherence to rules without inner transformation. The ascetic, the contemplative and the ethical aspects of life were essentially inseparable and directed to the single aim of God-directed living. Should a saint actually achieve this aim, then he or she could be described as divinised or deified,[17] a participant in the divine nature,[18] but not as absorbed into God. The term 'deification' was indeed sparingly used of the aim of faith, but not as the dictionary describes mysticism, as an absorption into the divine. The goal was not transformation into God, in its plainest sense, but transformation by God. Union was not a union of substantial nature, but a conformity of the will.

Knowledge of God

The desire for transformation and conformity of will cannot, however, be separated from a longing for intimacy with God, and such intimacy demands knowledge. Most particularly in the early centuries knowledge of God could be acquired through the scriptures by disclosing their inner meaning through allegorical interpretation. Philo (c. 20 BCE–50 CE), an Alexandrian Jew, was among the most prominent of those who used this method to expound the Jewish Scriptures. It was a method employed for centuries before by Greek philosophers examining Homer and other ancient texts (Winston 1981). In part from Philo, Origen, the greatest of the third-century Christian theologians, inherited this tradition and famously propounded as a principle that 'the Scriptures were written by the Spirit of God and have not just that sense that is evident, but another one hidden from most readers' (Trigg 1998: 20). This hidden sense was sought and categorised in a variety of ways by commentators until the reformation period. St Bonaventure (1217–74), for example, delineated, beside the literal meaning, a threefold spiritual interpretation: the topological, allegorical and anagogic. The topological sense might understand figures of scripture as representing different virtues, the allegorical discloses hidden doctrinal meanings and the anagogic raises the soul to God in ecstatic wisdom (Cousins 1978). This latter sense is the most relevant to the mystical tradition.

Knowledge of God was not primarily accessible to discursive reasoning. It was typically described through the metaphor of divine light, descending from God as a gift. This light was perceptible through the metaphorical eye of the mind, and the eye of the mind aspired to the vision of God. If we unpack the metaphor, then what the mind received may be described as intuitive wisdom, an understanding of the divine nature and will and purposes through which the whole of life could be attuned to God. This has very little in common with the modern notion of mystical experience as some overwhelming and transient event in which the individual feels absorbed into the divine.

The driving force in those who sought divine light is best expressed in English as a yearning for God, as Augustine wrote, 'The whole life of the good Christian is a holy longing' (Louth 1986: 140). The yearning of the Christian was inspired and reciprocated by the far greater yearning of God for the return of the world to its divinely created state. Human yearning in the early centuries led many to martyrdom. After the peace of the Church bestowed by the conversion of the Emperor Constantine, its clearest expression became life in the desert as a hermit or a monk, most prominently in Egypt. The search was not for some moment of ecstatic experience, but for a way of life that enacted human yearning for God and responded to the divine yearning for humankind.

For those in the desert tradition, and for many others, much time was given to the recitation of psalms and to slow, meditative reading of the scriptures. In the desert also developed a particular form of prayer that became of great significance and has features easily misunderstood as mystical in the modern and corrupt sense. This form of contemplation involved the emptying of the mind of thoughts, images and concepts in order to approach the God who is beyond all images and concepts. The constant repetition of a short phrase or single word as a means of helping the mind to remain empty has often been a feature of it. In later centuries this practice is continued in the Jesus prayer of the Greek Orthodox church and it was advocated in the fourteenth-century English treatise *The Cloud of Unknowing,* for example. This practice is to be found in most ages of the church and has been much revived in recent years. Since it is particularly open to misunderstanding in a false mystical sense, in part because of its similarity to the practices of other faiths, I shall discuss its history further.

The monastic and eremitic way of life was taken up also in the Western Church. It was influenced by the desert fathers of the East, particularly through John Cassian (c. 360–c. 432), a theologian who spent time in Egypt before travelling to the West. His writings encouraged the contemplative practice described above (McGinn 1994). Rules of life were adopted in the West. St Benedict's rule, in the sixth century, sets out an ordered way of life, emphasising charity between the brothers and a particular pattern of offices for the recitation of the psalms and of other readings from the scriptures. He encouraged his monks to read Cassian and there they will have found the self-emptying prayer recommended. Such prayer was therefore an optional addition to the monastic schedule.

Before turning to the medieval period in the Western church, it is worth noting that in the Eastern or Orthodox church all theology may be described as mystical. John Meyendorff writes:

> Indeed, the whole of Eastern Christian theology has often been called 'mystical'. The term is truly correct, provided one remember that in Byzantium 'mystical knowledge' does not imply emotional individualism, but quite the opposite: a continuous communion with the Spirit who dwells in the whole Church.
>
> (Meyendorff 1974: 14)

Meyendorff further asserts that a sense of the inadequacy of human intellect and language fully to express truth is implicit in the word 'mystical' and this implies that there is always a hidden aspect to theological statements.

It may appear that there is nothing said above that would not obviously be applicable to any theology. We may, however, contrast it with strains particularly of Protestant thinking that might be called anti-mystical.

An extreme example of this strain is to be found in the Glasite or Sandemanian church. This group began in the eighteenth century in Scotland and is now extinct. It is perhaps memorable most of all because the famous physicist Michael Faraday was a member. Its most distinctive tenet was the assertion that justifying faith is a simple assent to the divine testimony concerning Jesus Christ, differing in no way in its character from belief in any ordinary testimony. No doubt the church had strict standards of behaviour, but the transformation of the inner life seems to have been unnecessary for salvation, the overarching aim of the believer. Likewise, communion with the Spirit was doubtless desired, but would seem not to have been an essential mark of the Christian. The acceptance of a doctrine as mere fact, rather than as a starting point for a journey into deeper understanding, underlies these developments. There is no sense of the inadequacy of language or of human concepts. All lies clearly in the factual light of everyday information.

The mystical theology of the patristic age places great emphasis on the unknowability of God. God's words to Moses, 'you cannot see my face: for no one shall see me and live' (Exod. 33.20), were frequently quoted and God could at best be known in his acting, never in his essence. In the New Testament, the word *agapē* is used to mean 'love', and the love to which it refers is first of all the love of God for his Son and for his people, and second the love that there should be between people. The word is little, if at all, used to refer to the human response to God, which is one of faith and obedience. In the Greek fathers *agapē* is used much less of the human response to God than *erōs*, perhaps best translated as yearning. In the Western medieval church, however, where Latin was used, the distinction is less clear and *amor* is freely employed for both divine love and human response. The twelfth-century Cistercian monk St Bernard took a leading role in the developing devotion of a love for the humanity of Jesus and, along with this, he and other writers emphasise love (*amor*) for God. It is arguable that, thereby, the modelling of the human relation to God on the erotic attraction between humans was emphasised, a development that reached its highest point in St John of the Cross. This may be seen as one factor in the later misunderstanding of mysticism as ecstatic moments of absorption into the divine.

Contemplation and insight

I turn now to the practice of contemplation and in particular to Richard of St Victor,[19] one of the most influential writers in the history of mystical theology. A few years younger than St Bernard, and not a monk but an Augustinian canon in Paris, he wrote systematic and detailed works on the theory and practice of contemplation. Two particular aspects of his thought are especially relevant to this discussion. The first is his analysis, built upon earlier writers, of an ascending scale of modes of apprehension of reality. These were: a perception by the senses (of sight, hearing, etc.), imagination (in the sense of the forming of images or pictures) in memory or fantasy, conception (in the sense of forming concepts) and understanding (in the sense of grasping the deepest reality). The last of these was the faculty appropriate for apprehending spiritual realities, God, the angels, etc.

As the terms he used are unfamiliar today in the sense he used them, I will offer a very crude approximation to his use to illustrate them. Thus, it is possible to apprehend another person simply by sight, which gives knowledge of size, shape, colour, etc. This is sense perception. One may then form an image in memory of the person, and this Richard (and many others) called imagination. Then, one might describe a person in terms of concepts that today might be psychological or psycho-analytic or, indeed, sociological, economic, etc. This is the faculty of conception. Finally, one might have a personal understanding. This gives a deeper knowledge.[20] For example, if one had any amount of conceptual knowledge of another person, that would not necessarily enable one to predict their actions or understand their motives as well as might a close friend who had what Richard calls understanding. I emphasise that Richard would not have liked this description, since for him understanding was always to do with the apprehension of transcendent realities. There might be a case for arguing that the human person is indeed a transcendent reality, but that would not seem to have been his view. However, the insight that comes from personal knowledge is at least a rough approximation to what he meant by understanding. The word 'intuition' is also used to refer to this faculty and in this technical theological sense intuition has nothing to do with the popular use that refers it to a guess or a whim. Descriptions of this faculty of the mind, higher than conceptual reason, have a long history, and can be found in the pagan Hellenistic philosophers, such as Plotinus (MacKenna 1991) in the third century, as well as in Christian writers of all ages.[21]

Understanding is trained and developed by the work of contemplation. A commentator on Richard writes of this:

> The purpose of contemplation is not thinking of something, rational understanding, ferreting out new truths or any like mental operation. It is, rather, an *'adhering with wonder to the object that brings it joy'*. It enjoys rather than uses. It rests rather than acts.
>
> (Zinn 1979: 24)

Contemplation, which might be described as the highest form of Christian prayer in the tradition of mystical theology, has thus little in common with some modern notions of meditation as the achievement of an esoteric state of consciousness. Rather, it is a gazing with the eye of the mind in the direction of God.

The cultivation of religious experience

There is a second aspect of Richard's work relevant to my argument. He described in some detail the feelings that may accompany contemplation, and in his usual style these are carefully systematised. In ascending order, there may be an enlarging of the mind, an elevation of the mind and alienation of the mind. Alienation of the mind is also described as ecstasy, a state where the mind forgets the world around it and is filled with a joyful sense of the presence of God. He describes it as ascending to, taking possession of and occupying 'the supreme and innermost recess of the mind' (Zinn 1979: 43). Words like 'alienation' and 'ecstasy' may suggest states that today might be called states of altered consciousness. That would, however, be a mistake, unless one were to describe, for example, the intense joy a child may feel in a new toy as also a state of altered consciousness. In Richard's ecstasy there is nothing to suggest that the mind is not fully conscious in the normal sense; what is peculiar to the state is that it is conscious only of its own joy in the presence of God. This presence, it should be remembered, is not claimed to be a direct experience of God in himself, but primarily of his activity within the soul or mind. Further, the mind has prepared for this by emptying itself as far as possible of every thought, picture or concept, so that one who rejects theological language might well say that the mind is actually experiencing nothing but its own emptiness. It would be entirely mistaken to think that this is a kind of self-hypnosis or anything of the kind. In contemplation of this kind, the conscious mind is fully active, but is directed inwards to its own joyfulness by training and practice (and, Richard and others would add, by the working of God).

To the attention that Richard (and many others) gave to the experience of contemplative prayer we may trace the origin of the nineteenth-century misunderstanding of mystical theology. The vision of God which was desired was, as discussed above, not vision through the eyes, but the acquisition of intuitive understanding. This intuitive understanding was of God and of God's will for human life, something to be built into the whole life of the monk or other believer. In the writings of the desert Fathers and Mothers of the fourth and fifth centuries, there is very little said about the experiences of the contemplative. There is a great deal about the temptations of pride, lust and selfishness and there is subtle analysis of the way sin affects human relationships. The desert desire was for a life in total concord with God; it was not for specific experiences in prayer. However, once these experiences were described, as Richard and others did, misunderstanding is possible: the desire for God may become a desire for an experience of God. After that there may come a yet more serious error, when the desire for an experience of God becomes simply a desire for an experience, and the modern notion of mysticism as something for which faith and religion are merely an accidental setting is born. Mysticism becomes the pursuit of esoteric experience.

The increased attention to the humanity of Jesus that may be traced to St Bernard raised the sense of a personal relation to God. An emphasis on Jesus, the man, rather than on the Second Person of the Trinity incarnate in Jesus, naturally led to a sense of relationship to God more akin to human relationships. This accompanied a growing discussion of the experience of prayer, and the combination of these two influences can be clearly seen in the intense mystical writings of, for instance, St John of the Cross in the sixteenth century. The stages of relationship to God (or Christ) are described culminating in the engagement of the soul to marriage with Christ, and ultimately (though primarily post mortem) the spiritual marriage itself.[22] It is doubtless true that St John himself did not intend any sort of disconnection between such interior experience and the realities of daily living. However, subsequently, in the late seventeenth century among the Quietists and others, an intense interest in the individual's progress through stages of prayer, each marked by particular kinds of experience, dominated spirituality.[23] This development has been described as focusing upon the drama of the interior life: 'Mysticism is now understood as an inner drama enacted by the mystic's exquisitely refined feelings on the stage of the interior self' (McIntosh 1998: 69). It is very far from the practice of the earlier Christian centuries and prepares the ground for the modern notion of mysticism. A longing for the vision of God, as insight informing the whole of life, had gradually changed into a search for particular experiences of God in times of prayer. Thereafter it could easily degenerate into merely seeking experience for itself. Such experiences, particularly if understood as altered states of consciousness, might lead spirituality in the direction of psychosis.

The irrational and the supra-rational

I return now to the mystical nature of theology, the discovery and disclosure of what lies hidden in a text or a sacrament. I quoted Meyendorff's view that in the Orthodox church all theology can be described, in the proper sense, as mystical. As a wide generalisation in the Western church too there is no division apparent until the thirteenth century between theologians, who in the same sense may be described as mystical and spiritual writers who gave instruction in prayer, and accounts of experience in prayer. In referring to the Glasites, I gave an extreme case of a theology that is not mystical. For the Glasites merely accepting that Christ's death paid the price of sin thereby gives salvation to the sinner. This acceptance of a concept does not involve the mode of apprehension that I have called wise understanding or intuition. According to Richard of St Victor and to most mystical theologians, only wise understanding can at all apprehend God and spiritual realities (Zinn 1979: 24). Furthermore its apprehensions cannot be fully expressed in clear conceptual terms. If theology in the West became less mystical, it was in large part because it attempted to be wholly rational, that is to say expressed in concepts logically related to one another. This goal of complete rationality is at least hinted at in the writing of Thomas Aquinas and other scholastic theologians and recurred in as strong a form in Protestant theology when the first fervours of the reformation began to subside. While Thomas Aquinas himself remained firmly in the tradition of mystical theology, within a century of his death a divide begins to be detectable between academic theology and mystical experience. As mentioned earlier, the advent of a number of women theological writers in the thirteenth century emphasised this divide, for, while the men had a near monopoly of the traditional resources of biblical and traditional exposition, the women wrote more of their own experiences of contemplation and indeed of visions and voices. Thus a later age could misinterpret this divide as one between reason and the mystics.

If scholasticism is the attempt to express theology purely by concepts, then this passes easily into what is popularly called dogmatism, the attempt to enforce belief in such concepts. A dogma, properly speaking, is an item of teaching or belief and as such holds a proper place in any theological system. However, if theology aims to express the apprehensions of intuitive under-standing, then these cannot be fully reduced to conceptual thinking. Therefore if concepts are derived from intuitive insight – and they must be or else nothing can be said at all and theology lapses into eternal silence – then such concepts must be held in antithetic tension with other concepts. Mystical theology, arguably all theology, must therefore be, in a sense, irrational, counter to wholly rational thinking. Indeed, from an early period, this is an obvious feature of theological reasoning. The doctrine of the Trinity, that God is three and God is one, cannot be reduced to any rational account that avoids contradiction and I suggest that the same is true of all the fundamental doc-trines of the Church.

In my attempt to explain the meaning of the word 'God' in non-metaphorical terms, as expressing the benign coherence of the universe, I was obliged to offer a concept instead. Like any other concept it was quite inadequate to convey all that a believer would want conveyed by the word. If it has any theological acceptability it must immediately be qualified by paradoxical contradiction, for only in such a way do concepts begin to express the apprehensions of intuition. If intuition is irrational, then it is with the deliberate purpose of going beyond the limits of pure rationality and might better be described as supra-rational than irrational.

The self-contradictory aspect of theology is most clearly found and accepted in those theologians who are most likely to be described as mystical. It is prevalent, for example, in Pseudo Dionysus. Nearly a millennium later, perhaps in reaction to the scholasticism of the preceding two centuries, it comes to clearest expression of all in Nicholas of Cusa (1401–64). God is to be encountered only beyond the coincidence of opposites, that is to say, where opposing assertions are held simultaneously, for there conceptual reason fragments and truth may be elicited through the faculty of understanding. He wrote: 'when I am at the door of the coincidence of opposites, guarded by the angel stationed at the entrance of paradise, I begin to see you, O Lord' (Bond 1997: 252).

The self-contradictory nature of theology may make this seem like nonsense, even psychotic nonsense. I have suggested already that intuition is the mode of apprehension appropriate to our knowledge of people close to us. I now suggest that that knowledge also is not conceptual and indeed often leads to paradox or oxymoron. Consider the following:

- John and Jane are talking about their friend Michael. Jane knows him better than John.
- John says: 'I think Michael is rather mean – he never buys Remembrance poppies, and he never gives money to street collections.' Here, meanness is a conceptual description.
- Jane says: 'That may be so, but he is incredibly generous to his friends.' Generosity is another concept. 'I know two people he lent large sums of money and never wanted it back.'
- John: 'Did he? I am surprised. I suppose he only likes giving to friends then.' This is a refinement of his first conceptual description.
- Another friend, June, who knows Michael better still, joins the conversation.
- 'That's not really true. Didn't you know he has set up a private charity in a Third World country and gives half his income to it?'
- Jane: 'No, I am really surprised. It seems he likes to give when he feels personally involved. In a way that seems rather selfish.'
- June: 'I bet you don't give anything like as much to anyone. If Michael is selfish, it's a very unselfish kind of selfishness.'
- The conclusion is a paradox or oxymoron.

Psychoanalysis might be seen as attempting a conceptual description of the human personality but even the most deterministic of psychoanalysts would not claim to know everything about a person, however complete the analysis. The depths of humanity are indeed always paradoxical, where love and hate, arrogance and self-doubt, the longing for safety and the delight in danger, are intimately mixed. Readers familiar with the work of Ignacio Matte Blanco (who recognised his own kinship with Nicholas of Cusa) will remember his belief that in the unrepressed unconscious opposites are held together, ultimately in unity.[24] Referring back to the interpretation I offered of God as representing the unity of the cosmos, in which many opposites are at play, therefore the inmost depth of humankind may be seen as a microcosm of the macrocosm of the universe, a point that expresses the belief that humankind is made in the image of God.

Hence, disorder in the universe may be seen as arising from a failure of balance and harmony between opposites. Likewise, in psychosis, one of a pair of opposites may emerge from the inmost depths and dominate conscious thinking and behaviour. In contrast, in mystical theology, and in deep intuitive thinking in general, opposites are both allowed a voice and honoured as equal contributors to truth. Perhaps this is ultimately the most important distinction between psychotic thinking and genuine spirituality. Insanity may be irrational; divinity aims to be supra-rational.

Conclusion

To conclude, I have chosen to discuss mysticism because some of those who are today called mystics have manifested extreme behaviour, apparently irrational thinking and very often a sharp dislocation from the values and norms of the societies in which they lived. Such features may readily be taken as symptoms of mental disturbance and indeed of insanity. 'Insanity' and 'mysticism' are both words very hard to define adequately and, if insanity is defined only by exterior symptoms, some of the mystics of past ages might well be classified as insane by the criteria of our present age. However, I have argued that what is rightly valued in the mystics of the past is not their experiences, however abnormal, nor such matters as voices and visions and unusual states of mind, but their pursuit of an inner transformation. This transformation, which they too primarily regarded as important, is the subject matter of mystical theology and its aim is to conform the individual to what is seen as God's will for the flourishing of the whole creation. That, surely, is a very sane purpose.

Notes

1 Wulff (1997) has a section on drug-induced mysticism referring to experiments by Walter Pahnke in 1963 and Rick Doblin in 1987. He refers also to other attempts to induce mystical experiences.

2 I am referring particularly to Denys Turner, with whom I understand McIntosh (1998) to be in agreement. Much that McGinn (1991) writes supports the same position to a considerable degree.

3 Cf. Turner (1995: 4). My discussion of the modern meaning of mysticism and of the more ancient concept of mystical theology draws heavily on this book.

4 St Anselm (1033–1109). The phrase occurs as part of the name by which one of his works is known: *Proslogion Sive Fides Quaerens Intellectum*.

5 The Fathers of the church are those who, in the period mentioned after the composition of the New Testament, developed the tradition of the Christian Church, leading to the formulation of its beliefs and the endorsement of them in general councils, notionally of the whole church.

6 Jones, Wainwright and Yarnold (1986) give a brief but valuable account of the leading members of the canon.

7 Hildegard of Bingen (1098–1179) provides one important exception, but it would be hard to make a case for many others.

8 Angela of Folino (1248–1309), Hadewijch of Antwerp (floruit first half of thirteenth century), Mechthild of Madgeburg (1208–82) and Marguerite Porete (date of birth unknown, executed for heresy in 1310) are described by McGinn as the four female evangelists of thirteenth-century mysticism, because of the influence and often controversy that arose from them.

9 Nicholas of Cusa (1401–64) is the most important exception.

10 Evelyn Underhill (1875–1941). McGinn writes: 'her book *Mysticism*, first published in 1911 and many times reprinted, was the first of many that she dedicated to spreading knowledge of mysticism to a broad public' (1991: 273).

11 McGinn says that, 'in the case of the Bishop of Hippo [Augustine], union language seems to be deliberately excluded as a tool for the description of the consciousness of the divine presence in this life' (1991: 230).

12 'Do you not know that you are God's temple and that God's Spirit dwells in you?' (1 Cor. 3.16).

13 'I have been crucified with Christ; and it is no longer I who live, but Christ who lives in me' (Gal. 2.19–20).

14 A good summary of John Scottus Erigena's work is to be found in McGinn. He quotes John writing that God 'neither was nor shall be nor has become nor becomes nor shall become, nor indeed is' (McGinn 1994: 100).

15 In *The Mystical Theology*, Pseudo Dionysius writes that the supreme cause of all things 'falls neither within the predicate of nonbeing nor of being' (Luibheid 1987: 141).

16 Cf. Boyle (1959: 24). I do not intend to recommend the whole of Spinoza's metaphysics, simply the phrase in itself.

17 See Louth for a discussion of divinisation in mystical theology, especially: 'So, knowing God means divinization, *theopoiesis*. Knowing God is having the image of God . . . And contemplation is the means of this' (Louth 1981: 73).

18 'You may become participants in the divine nature' (2 Peter 1.4).

19 Richard of St Victor (c. 1130–73) (Zinn 1979).

20 In the course of writing this chapter I came across McGilchrist (2009). His account, based on neurological evidence, of the different ways in which the two hemispheres of the brain relate to the world, coheres remarkably with intuition (right hemisphere) and conception (left hemisphere) as Richard of St Victor and others describe them.

21 See particularly Plotinus' 5th Ennead.

22 See Kavanaugh (1987). The stages of prayer are implicit in the chapter headings of 'The Ascent of Mount Carmel' and are completed in 'The Spiritual Canticle', which treats more of the final stages of betrothal and spiritual marriage.

23 There is a brief account of the Quietists in Jones et al. (1986: 408–14).

24 Ignacio Matte Blanco (1908–95) was a psychoanalyst who claimed to have uncovered the paradoxical logic of the unconscious mind. Cf. I. Matte Blanco, *The Unconscious as Infinite Sets*, Duckworth, London, 1975 and *Thinking, Feeling and Being*, Routledge, 1988. The adaptation of Matte Blanco's ideas to mystical theology can be found in R. Bomford, *The Symmetry of God*, Free Association Books, 1999.

References

Bond, H.L. (trans.) (1997). *Nicholas of Cusa*. Mahwah, NJ: Paulist Press.

Boyle, A. (trans.) (1959). *Spinoza Ethics*. London: J.M. Dent.

Cousins, E. (trans.) (1978). *Bonaventure*. Mahwah, NJ: Paulist Press.

Jones, C., Wainwright, G. and Yarnold, E. (1986). *The Study of Spirituality.* London: SPCK.

Kavanaugh, K. (ed.) (1987). *John of the Cross.* Mahwah, NJ: Paulist Press.

Louth, A. (1981). *The Origins of the Christian Mystical Tradition.* Oxford: Oxford University Press.

Luibheid, C. (1987). *Pseudo-Dionysius. The Complete Works.* Mahwah, NJ: Paulist Press.

MacKenna, S. (trans.) (1981). *Plotinus. The Enneads.* London: Penguin Books.

Meyendorff, J. (1974). *Byzantine Theology.* Fordham: Fordham University Press.

McGilchrist, I. (2009). *The Master and his Emissary.* New Haven: Yale University Press.

McGinn, B. (1991). *The Foundations of Mysticism.* New York: Crossroad Publishing Co.

McGinn, B. (1994). *The Growth of Mysticism.* New York: Crossroad Publishing Co.

McIntosh, A. (1998). *Mystical Theology.* Oxford: Blackwell.

Trigg, J.W. (1998). *Origen.* London: Routledge.

Turner, D. (1995). *The Darkness of God.* Cambridge: Cambridge University Press.

Winston, D. (1981). *Philo of Alexandria.* Mahwah, NJ: Paulist Press.

Wulff, D. (1997). *Psychology of Religion, Classic and Contemporary.* New York: John Wiley and Sons.

Zinn, G.A. (trans.) (1979). *Richard of St Victor.* New York: Paulist Press.

Part 3

PSYCHOLOGY, PSYCHOSIS AND RELIGIOUS EXPERIENCE

Reality isn't at issue for him [for the person experiencing a psychosis], certainty is. Even when he expresses himself along the lines of saying that what he experiences is not of the order of reality, this does not affect his certainty that it concerns him. The certainty is radical. The very nature of what he is certain of can quite easily remain completely ambiguous, covering the entire range from malevolence to benevolence. But it means something unshakable for him.

(Lacan 1993:75)

INTRODUCTION TO PART 3

Religion, spirituality and the experience of psychosis

John Gale

Psychosis and the question of the real

Lacan's discussions of psychosis began with his doctoral thesis in 1932, where he attempted to apply post-Freudian conceptions to a case study of a young woman whom he called Aimée. Under the influence of structuralism his approach took a decisive turn in the 1950s, and this can be seen both in seminar 3 (1955–56), published as *Les Psychoses* (The Psychoses) (Lacan 1993) and which amounts to a detailed re-evaluation of the Schreber case, and in a paper he published in 1959 entitled 'On a Question Prior to any Possible Treatment of Psychosis'. In the latter Lacan argues that psychotic symptoms are the manifestation in the real of something that has been excluded from the symbolic through foreclosure. Lacan continued to revise and elaborate his notion of psychosis culminating in seminar 23 (1975–76). It is a conception derived from clinical experience working in his early years as a psychiatrist in a hospital in Paris and later as a psychoanalyst, as well as from a profound emersion into psychoanalytic theory and philosophy. The primary features of Lacan's approach include the idea that psychosis is structural and one that revolves around the notion of foreclosure. Foreclosure amounts to a 'malfunction in the Oedipus complex' or a reduction in the paternal function 'to the image of the father' (Evans 1996: 156). For Lacan, the structure of psychosis is quite distinct from psychotic phenomena like delusions and hallucinations, although they often have a stabilising function in a person's life (Leader 2011).

Autobiographical accounts of a religious psychosis

In Chapter 11, people who have experienced a psychotic breakdown, in which there was marked religious or spiritual content, give their own accounts of those experiences. We present these anonymously, in as unedited a form as possible. This is because of our wish to emphasise the need to pay careful attention to the subject's use of language and not to diminish its importance. Unusual capitalisation and emphasis, atypical punctuation, the repetition of words or phrases, seeming ambiguities and the introduction of neologisms may not be a question of poor syntax but may rather bear the weight of significance. As a result, these peculiar linguistic usages can provide important clues to our understanding of the inner landscape and determining elements of a psychosis.

This approach is in itself quite unusual, as most accounts of the experience of a psychosis come to us as case histories and as such aim at illustrating the therapeutic work that has been done with patients. Even the famous memoirs of Daniel Schreber are probably better known to most of us, second-hand as it were, from Freud's masterful study or possibly from the studies made by Niederland, Lothane, Steiner (Alanen 2009), Lacan (1981) or De Waelhens (De Waelhens and Ver Eecke 2001), none of whom ever met Schreber. However, while in this chapter, some of the authors do refer to various treatment interventions (e.g. seeing a psychiatrist, the effects of medication, being detained under a section of the Mental Health Act, etc.), but our intention in publishing these accounts is simply to provide a space to those who have suffered from a psychosis to give us their own description of what happened, what it felt like at the time and what sense they made of it. Above all, as the first account vividly illustrates, we acknowledge 'the central importance . . . [for] every patient, of *his own* story' (Conran 1999: 27; my emphasis).

These are records of moments of intense psychic pain, confusion and lack of coherence. The authors tell us of traumatic life experiences, such as being sexually abused, the death of a loved one and the gradual fragmentation of a marriage. They describe the feeling of being overwhelmed by a sense of guilt or of being punished, of despair and the struggle with evil forces; of prophetic dreams and revelations; as well as of moments of elation and joy, and the conviction that they were somehow inspired and chosen. Even on a cursory reading, it is hard not to notice some of the key themes that are discussed elsewhere in the book surfacing in these accounts – for example, the intimation in one of the accounts that a psychosis may always have been present before any hallucinations were triggered or any delusions surfaced; the centrality of death in the psychosis; an idiosyncratic use of language including, but by no means limited to, neologisms which makes some of the narratives hard to follow at times; familiar religious mythology (e.g. the Virgin) used in a singular way. Above all else, we get a sense of the way in which the authors clung to their religious delusions during periods of great distress. Indeed, in one case, it was prayer that strengthened a resolve to resist the impulse to self-harm and helped the person hold things together. In these examples, the religious and spiritual aspects only account for a small part of the psychotic phenomena that are described. The wider context is one in which more general features of the psychoses are present, including a loss of touch with reality, ideas of reference, feelings of grandiosity, visual and auditory hallucinations, disordered thought, paranoia and suicidal ideation. Together with these, we notice the often strained relationship with parents and other family members as they struggle desperately to try to understand and help the person concerned.

Religious practices, spirituality and psychosis

In the past spirituality was thought to be synonymous with religious belief and, unless it was pathological, as in the case of religious delusions, was thought to be outside the sphere of psychiatry. But we now find that many patients have a spirituality that is not attached to any religious belief or affiliation to institutional religion. Research shows that having a spirituality and practising spiritual techniques, like meditation, can have an influence on a person's mental health and can be useful because it may reduce stress and give hope to sufferers; therefore, psychiatry has begun to take account of spirituality and promote it. Raji (2009) emphasises the fact that health care professionals should help patients define their own spiritual approach, because the friendship and support that comes from belonging to a faith community benefits a person's mental health. Cook (2009) argues that spirituality has a protective function. As we might expect, the approach of health care professionals generally tends to be pragmatic and preoccupied with research methodologies that attempt to affirm that spiritual beliefs and practices can be helpful in contributing to the recovery of people diagnosed with a psychosis or other form of mental ill health.

References

Alanen, Y.O. (2009). The Schreber case and Freud's double-edged influence on the psychoanalytic approach to psychosis. In *Psychotherapeutic Approaches to Schizophrenic Psychoses. Past, Present and Future*, ed. Y.O. Alanen, M.G. de Chávez, A.-L.S. Silver and B. Martindale, pp. 23–37. London and New York: Routledge.

Conran, M. (1999). Sorrow, vulnerability and madness. In *Psychosis (Madness)*, ed. P. Williams, pp. 27–43. London: Institute of Psycho-Analysis.

Cook, C. (2009). Substance misuse. In *Spirituality and psychiatry*, ed. C. Cook, A. Powell and A. Sims, pp. 139–68. London: Royal College of Psychiatrists.

De Waelhens, A. and Ver Eecke, W. (2001). *Phenomenology and Lacan on Schizophrenia, after the Decade of the Brain*. Leuven: Leuven University Press.

Evans, D. (1996). *An Introductionary Dictionary of Lacanian Psychoanalysis*. London and New York: Routledge.

Lacan, J. (1981). *Le Séminaire de Jacques Lacan. Livre. 3, Les Psychoses 1955–1956*. Paris: Éditions du Seuil.

Lacan, J. (1993). *The Psychoses. The Seminar of Jacques Lacan*. Livre. 3, *1955–1956*, trans. R. Grigg. London: Routledge.

Leader, D. (2011). *What is Madness?* London: Hamish Hamilton.

Raji, O. (2009). Intellectual disability. In *Spirituality and Psychiatry*, ed. C. Cook, A. Powell and A. Sims, pp. 122–38. London: Royal College of Psychiatrists.

9

SPIRITUALITY AND THE PSYCHOTIC SUBJECT IN THE THOUGHT OF LACAN

Georgia Rapsomatioti

In this chapter I will outline some elements in Lacan's theory of the psychoses in order to help us make sense of the autobiographical accounts of religious psychosis described in the next chapter.

Introduction

Attempting to identify the function of religious belief in relation to the psychoses is an extremely complex task. The reason for this is partly because what lies behind religious beliefs and rituals is what we might call the unknown or more precisely, the unknowable. This is what Lacan called the real. The real refers to everything that *per se* escapes symbolisation, which is another way of saying that which cannot be put into words or even into thoughts. As such, it is part of the subject's confrontation with death. Because, for all of us, death is on the horizon there is a sense in which the unknown and unknowable is very present. But is it really a matter of the unknown when it comes to interpreting a psychotic belief or simply a failure on the part of the psychotic subject to communicate his or her experience to us within ordinary language or equally of our failure to really listen to the patient's speech? The two proto-psychoanalytic questions which confront everyone – 'Am I alone?' and 'Where did I come from?' (Sharpe 2006) – are questions associated with the desire to know and discover the meaning of life. The world as we experience it is an enigma, in the sense that the arrival of every human being into the world seems marked by absurdity, for we are all destined to die. Our inability to solve this riddle satisfactorily makes it difficult for us to make sense of life. This, in turn, pushes us all towards those forms of knowledge that appear to give a definitive answer to the mystery surrounding life and death. Yet, despite the various comprehensive systems of thought to which we turn, be they religious or scientific, death remains inevitable.

The controversial nature of the relationship between spirituality and psychosis derives, at least in part, from the divergences that exist between the philosophical assumptions which underpin the various clinical models of psychiatry, psychology and psychoanalysis. The psychotic subject may experience the mystical, spiritual and religious dimension of life in an exclusive way, refusing the fixed meaning which often is given by others (set doctrines or shared beliefs) and thus, in Lacanian terms, refusing castration – not in the literal sense of bodily mutilation, but as a denial of the lack or limit within oneself that castration signifies and which is implicitly reinforced by religions which ascribe omnipotence to God alone (Freud SE 1930). Both religion and psychiatry have failed to acknowledge the psychotic subject's beliefs in relation to the divine or the spiritual realms (Clarke 2001; Cook 2009). Simply put, for both systems those exclusive beliefs are considered false, valueless and in consequence a proof of madness. Lipsedge and Bhurga (1996) explores the scientific attempt in psychiatry for an interpretation of the psychotic subject's experience in relation to religion as witchcraft, possession by a spirit or pathology. This approach to religious experience can be understood within the more general history of madness, to use Foucault's famous expression (Foucault 2006). In psychiatry, psychotic beliefs related to religion have generally been considered not as part of a unique subjective experience but rather as a wrong belief. The use of the term pathological to describe experiences which do not meet the criteria of conformity to ordinary discourse and reason still remains very common and contributes to a reluctance to really engage with the patient. Trying to analyse or objectify a subject's experience is not easy, since it is a subjective and unique experience – an experience that comes from the subject. It has its own meaning, in a specific place and time determined by the subject. Nagel (1974) argues that it is never possible to learn from an objective third-person point of view what it is like to have a first-person experience. In other words, subjective experience always escapes scientific method. There is always a missing part and thus the spiritual easily gets forgotten at the moment of interpretation.

In contrast, psychoanalysis comes closer to the subject and his needs, but in a different way. Psychoanalysis is concerned with the subject in its singularity, including both pathological and normal behaviour. It is a talking cure about the subject's experience without any judgement, categorisation or any diagnostic aim. In this sense, psychoanalysis could be conceived of as an open ground where someone can talk about his experiences, beliefs and so on. Therefore we could say that the need for the psychotic subject to believe in something in order to deal with the suffering deriving from the unknown, is a need that he or she shares with the neurotic subject. The only difference is the process each employs to make the unknown tolerable. The first achieves this through the construction of a private belief and the second with a shared belief. In trying to understand the psychotic subject's relation to the sacred and his exclusive relation to spirituality through his symptom, it is essential to refer to the work of Ricoeur (1970), who addresses the issues of the sacred, guilt and consolation, and the psychoanalytic theory of Lacan in relation to the function of delusion in psychosis. These analyses attempt not so much to interpret the religious or spiritual experience as it is found in psychosis but to understand it as a unique manifestation of a turning away from the limits of certainty. Our aim here is to demonstrate the implication of psychotic beliefs and their importance, taking into account what is essential about spirituality in the care and treatment of someone experiencing a psychotic breakdown.

Ricoeur *avec* Freud: the different meaning of religious belief in psychosis and in neurosis

According to Ricoeur, the phenomenology of religion can be analysed 'as something intended in ritual actions, in mythical speech, in belief or mystical feeling' (Ricoeur 1970: 29). Religions have a particular relation to symbols and symbolism, and are constituted by symbols and refer to them. Religious experiences are expressed through symbols in a variety of ways and religion is made meaningful due to these symbols. In a broad sense, therefore, religious symbolism is meaningful if one considers it by analysing the experience which it expresses and from which it is derived. People believe in religion and its symbols in order to understand their inner world and the universe. And understanding any religious experience demands a familiarity with the specificity of the religious symbols in which the experience is formed. Religious symbols, which are, for Ricoeur, what is meant by the sacred, can be identified with various terms such as the awesome numinous (Otto 1924) or fundamental time (Eliade 1979: 29). According to Ricoeur, the sacred eludes being totally within language and thus has a linguistic and non-linguistic side. The symbols have a metaphorical function, which we need to attend to if we are to understand better the complex reality of religious experience as symbolism only works 'when its structure is interpreted' (Ricoeur 1970: 526). Ricoeur talks about the sacred as a form of symbols – a form of knowledge derived from the interplay of symbols, beliefs and myths. It is 'a signifying separation or otherness . . . the sign of that which does not belong to us, the sign of the wholly Other' (Ricoeur 1970: 531). He distinguishes between the sacred and the spirit. The former is teleological and thus directed towards an eschaton, whereas the latter is open and endless. He argues for this non-possibility of an end to the spirit, because it refuses interpretation and escapes every human attempt to give an absolute meaning or name to it. The spirit stands, therefore, for that which cannot be limited by human interpretations. It is something to be conceived of as beyond our existence. This corresponds, to a certain extent, to Aristotelian teleology. Spirit is that which refuses interpretation, because it remains unspoken something impossible to bring in to speech, an element beyond *logos* (reason) and therefore without meaning.

198

Freud had seen the idea of God as an expression of infantile longing for a protective father (Freud SE 1927a) and described religion as a universal obsessional neurosis (Freud SE 1907). He considered that religion creates guilt by setting high moral standards but also provides a number of techniques that maybe help alleviate guilt, e.g. confession, prayer and so on. From a psychoanalytic viewpoint Ricoeur sees guilt related to neurosis and the formation of the Oedipus complex and its dissolution. It functions as a preventive procedure with respect to anticipated punishment. In Freudian literature, he argues, guilt is consistently understood in the archaic sense and is related to myths built upon primal scene fantasies and subject to the anxiety of the super-ego. Freud saw religion as a form of consolation of which guilt is the primary cause. He argued that religions were an attempt to protect oneself against suffering by 'a delusional remoulding of reality' and thus concluded that they 'must be classed among the mass-delusions of human kind' (Freud SE 1930: 81).

Ricoeur, following a hermeneutic methodology, emphasises the role of language, and specifically of interpretation, as an essential tool to understand the truth of human experience. And yet something always escapes interpretation. Lacan sees religion as 'a denial of the truth as cause of the subject' (Lacan 2005: 872) and argues that the function of sacrificial rites is to seduce God, to arouse his desire (Lacan 1981). Thus, we must recognise the limitations imposed on everyone by religion. There is a lack of knowledge which causes in the subject the desire to know whether there is a God. Religion stands for something which is lost precisely because it cannot be symbolised in language. The absence of definitive truths within human experience means that the enjoyment of fullness is forever excluded.

According to Lacanian theory, the psychotic subject is free (Miller 2007) in the sense that he or she is not constricted by religious guilt or the need for consolation in the same way as the neurotic because psychosis is precisely an exclusion from a shared discourse. In a very literal sense psychosis is asocial (rather than anti-social) because in psychosis there is a withdrawal from shared language. According to Aristotle man is a political animal by nature, one who speaks and exists in *logos* (discourse).[1] Thus, according to Lacan (1993) psychotic thought is imprisoned in a private discourse of its own. While bearing a high degree of freedom, by not conforming to accepted standards of thought, it is not capable of being part of religious discourse precisely because it does not share the common ideas and beliefs of a particular religious community. In *Civilization and its Discontents*, Freud refers to psychosis as 'a desperate attempt at rebellion' (Freud 1930: 84). In relation to religious discourse, the psychotic rebellion situates the subject outside the shared language of belief. A shared language implies shared meaning and consequently equality along the path to the acquisition of happiness and protection from suffering. Yet it is not just the failure to engage in a shared discourse that acts as a barrier to participation in a community of religious thought but also the desire to exclude his belief from religious discourse. Thus, psychotic belief remains fundamentally excluded from religious discourse, as it refuses to compromise with the social belief that religious discourse annunciates.

In contrast to psychotic beliefs about religion, neurotic religious beliefs bear the character of agreed certainty. This agreed certainty in psychosis is experienced as unbearable and this drives the psychotic subject to create his or her own private belief. Of course, religious belief for the neurotic also functions in a similar way and provides a degree of certainty about existential questions, but these beliefs are characterised by a degree of ambiguity not found in psychosis. This stems precisely from the shared quality of the discourse. This does not mean that the psychotic subject does not have his or her own discourse which may include elements borrowed from neurotic religious language and rituals – symbols, myths, archetypes, belief in salvific events, the great myth of immortality and so on. But in psychosis those signifiers are detached from the signified and have their own meaning or what might be called an empty meaning, deriving from the imaginary of the subject and as such overshadowed by his or her experience and history. This problematic relation or disentanglement between signifiers and signified has the effect of making interpretation far more complex than it might otherwise be.

Lacan on the meaning of religious delusion in psychosis

In order for us to understand more fully the psychotic subject's non-relation to religion as a social discourse and the private nature of his or her religious beliefs, we need to understand how the subject functions in psychosis and the scope of psychotic delusions. Lacan discussed the delusional phenomena of psychosis in his seminar 3 (1955–56). He held that language and speech have a special function in psychosis and that the unconscious is somehow excluded or refused and appears in the real with the form of a delusion or hallucination.[2] In Lacanian terms psychosis is defined by the operation of foreclosure (*Verwerfung*): 'The foreclosure of the Names of the Father in the place of the Other is the defect in psychosis which gives it its essential condition that separates it from neurosis' (Lacan 2005: 575). The Name of the Father is the signifier – the signal that carries an idea to form a word – that stands for the phallus and foreclosure of the Name of the Father, at the point at which it is summoned, is a way of speaking about a failure in the Oedipus complex.

Delusions are usually defined in psychiatry as false beliefs, inconsistent with the other information that is available at the time. Sauvagnat (2000) discussed the elementary phenomena that appear in psychosis as an attempt to answer to the foreclosure of the Name of the Father. In Lacanian terms, the psychotic subject lacks the Name of the Father, as the master signifier which organises all the signifiers, and represses the possibility of *jouissance* (enjoyment), which is complete and immediate satisfaction. Instead, in psychosis the prohibited is not introduced as a social link or as the principle of coexistence (Apollon, Bergeron and Cantin 2002). In other words, there is a failure in psychosis to accept the Name of the Father and the symbolic loss caused by castration. Castration is the symbolic loss of an imaginary object, the phallus – which is not the same as the penis – which allows the subject to separate from the mother and thus realise her fundamental otherness – what Lacan calls *l'Autre* (the Other) – while at the same time allowing the subject to situate itself within the law and thus within society, by accepting that its own desire is not dominant and that it is not omnipotent (Bailly 2009). This separation is a loss for the subject that results in the birth of the neurotic subject, which is subjected to the Name of the Father. The psychotic subject, on the other hand, has not experienced the castration separation and fails to enter the symbolic order and language, which guarantee that complete and total satisfaction (*jouissance*) is impossible (Apollon et al. 2002). In psychosis, the subject continues living in the imaginary as a non-separated (uncastrated) object. This means that, in Lacan's terms, the mother is perceived as *l'autre* (the other) as opposed to *l'Autre* (the Other); that is to say, as a projection (Apollon et al. 2002).

In psychosis, the Name of the Father can be thought of as a lack or gap not filled by language but by the imaginary. 'In psychosis, reality itself contains a hole that the world of fantasy will subsequently fill' (Lacan 1993: 45). Thus, the psychotic subject having an open relation to the real-*jouissance* (enjoyment) tries to defend him- or herself, not within the unconscious but within the operation of the imaginary. Language in psychosis does not fill the gap left by the separation of mother and child, because the relation to the real and to language is marked by the failure of the paternal function. What remains is the imaginary as the area from which to perceive the world and to relate to the Other. From a Lacanian perspective, when there is a psychotic breakdown there is a collapse of the imaginary structure that has up to then ordered the way the subject perceives the world. Accompanied by hallucinations, delusions, paranoia and language disturbances, a psychotic break is followed by an attempt to restructure the world and the subject's relation to it. A delusion is this attempt to fill the hole left in the symbolic universe by the absence of the primordial signifier, The Name of the Father.[3]

Thus, the delusion does not equate with psychosis itself. On the contrary, it is an attempt at healing by means of a substitute formation. As Freud commented in his work on Schreber, '[t]he delusional formation, which we take to be the pathological product, is in reality an attempt at recovery, a process of reconstruction' (Freud SE 1911: 71). In other words, the delusion is an attempt by the subject to restructure the world and his or her relation to it. In relation to language, the psychotic experience is characterised by the use of holophrases and the use of neologisms. Due to foreclosure, the signifier is cut off from the signified that has been rejected rather than repressed as it has in neurosis, and it now returns in the real with the form of an unbearable bodily effect. The gap between signifier and signified is now filled by the establishment of a new link under a delusional metaphor. Thus, the delusion helps the subject to stabilise and find meaning between the empty signifiers.

The empty and full meaning of religious delusion

In order to come closer to the meaning of delusion in psychosis, Lacanian writers focus on what is happening before the production of a delusion. At the moment of the onset of a psychotic breakdown, the subject is confronted with perplexity, unbearable suffering and pain coming from the real. The subject experiences a kind of destruction of the world around him, a ravage of what until then has been perceived as truth or knowledge. In order to explain what happened the subject makes an effort to reconstruct all the fragmented pieces within a delusion. The delusion can take many different forms depending on the circumstances surrounding the event prior to the breakdown and the meaning that event has for the person.

One of the characteristics of delusion is certainty. Sauvagnat (2000) argues that the certainty about a delusional idea is in fact an attempt to respond to an enigma. Lacan says that 'even when he expresses himself along the lines of saying that what he experiences is not of the order of reality, this does not affect his certainty' (Lacan 1993: 75).

> What is the subject ultimately saying, specially at a certain period of his delusion? That there is meaning. What meaning he doesn't know, but it comes to the foreground, it asserts itself, and for him it's perfectly understandable. And it's precisely because it's situated at the level of understanding as an incomprehensible phenomenon, as it were, that paranoia is so difficult for us to grasp and, also, of such great interest.
>
> (Lacan 1993: 31)

In seminar 3, Lacan referred to Schreber's *Memoirs* and further explored religious delusions, as they had been experienced and written about by Schreber in 1903. Schreber was suffering from paranoia and 'believed that he had a mission to redeem the world and to restore it to its lost state of bliss' (Freud SE 1911: 112). He believed that he had a direct communication with God through nerves or rays. He thought that he was capable of expressing some ideas that had been revealed only to him. He thought he would succeed in this only if he was first miraculously transformed into a woman. He experienced these miracles physically and had confirmation of them by his voices. During the first year of his illness he believed that some of his bodily organs had suffered destructive injuries. Sometimes he believed he swallowed part of his larynx with his food. He had a feeling that enormous numbers of female nerves had already passed over into his body, and out of them a new race of men would proceed, through a process of direct impregnation by God. Not until then, it seemed, would he regain a state of bliss. In the meantime not only the sun, but trees and birds, which were in the nature of be-miracled residues of former human souls, spoke to him in human accents, and miraculous things happened everywhere around him.

> I cannot of course count upon being fully understood because these things are dealt with which cannot be expressed in human language; they exceed human understanding. Nor can I maintain that everything is irrefutably certain even for me: much remains only presumption and probability. After all I too am only a human being and therefore limited by the confines of human understanding; but one thing I am certain of, namely that I have come infinitely closer to the truth than human beings who have not received divine revelation.
>
> (Schreber 2000: 41)

According to Lacan, Schreber's delusion had an enigmatic element (transformation to a woman) that triggered the delusion (being pregnant) in order to give a solution to his enigma. Through his delusions, Schreber attempts to reconnect and reorganise the disconnected signifiers that resulted from his breakdown. He establishes a structure with signifiers that refer to him giving birth via the experience of contact with the divine (Alanen 2009). Schreber succeeds in this by transforming himself into a woman and having an erotic relation with God, as a living organism (Lacan 1993) and becoming pregnant. Laurent (2007), referring to Schreber, explains that in paranoia, the subject, through the production of a delusion, reconstructs her or his universe. When there is an experience of threat coming from the Other, causing a break in the imaginary, the person's world becomes obscure; it is at this moment that an enigma appears. At this point the delusion begins to be organised so as to reconstruct the person's broken world *more* meaningfully. Lacan notes that the psychotic subject, even if he is uncertain about the reality of his hallucinations, is convinced of an enigmatic element in the delusion, which is the essence of the delusional belief (Lacan 1993). In Lacanian psychoanalysis, linguistic disturbances related to delusions can be grouped into two opposing types: on the one hand are delusions with a fullness of signification and, on the other, delusions that emphasise empty formulas (Verhaeghe 2004). The former apply in cases of paranoia; the latter, in case of schizophrenia. In paranoia the delusional intuition is a 'full phenomenon that has an overflowing, inundating character for the subject' (Lacan 1993: 33). It reveals a new perspective to the subject and gives a solution to the enigma.

> *Paranoia is distinguished from the others because it is characterized by the gradual development of internal causes and according to a progressive evolution of a stable delusional system that is impossible to disturb and establishes itself with total preservation of clarity and order in thought, will, and action.*
>
> (Lacan 1993: 17; italics in original)

In seminar 3 Lacan emphasises that the enigma is 'the soul of the situation' (Lacan 1993: 33). But it is not just something obscure. It is that which can give a meaning that refers to another meaning. Thus, the enigmatic element is the opening of a moment where the subject can give a meaning to his experience. This is the full delusion found in paranoia. Thus Apollon et al. (2002) see delusion as an attempt to treat the real with signifiers, with representations where the psychotic subject is developing a *savoir* (an understanding) in the delusion. This new knowledge (*savoir*) means something to the subject. On the other hand, the delusion with empty meaning refers to anything when it is repeated, reiterated, drummed in with a stereotyped insistence; in other words, when it refers simply to itself and consequently remains irreducible.

Wachsberger (2007) sees the psychotic experience itself as something enigmatic, in which there is an attack of unlimited enjoyment from the real that highlights the emptiness of signification. This enigmatic experience is affected by a signification of death, when the subject fights *aphanisis* (disappearance). Thus, a delusion is fundamentally an effort of the psychotic subject to defend herself or himself against death. Delusions appear as revealed knowledge and an attempt to connect the signifiers, giving them a meaning (Apollon et al. 2002). They do not just provide a solution for the subject in despair, but can be considered as an attempt to escape from the position of being a victim of the *jouissance* (enjoyment) of the Other. Apollon et al. (2002) add that the psychotic's subject delusion demonstrates that what governs the universe is an Other who demands total and immediate satisfaction (*jouissance*).

Conclusion

Could a delusion be a description of an authentic spiritual experience? Certainly, the subject is not pretending or playing a game. While borrowing various religious or quasi-religious metaphors and incorporating these into the delusion, he or she also brings their own personal history, and particularly their suffering prior to the psychotic breakdown. The production of a religious delusion can be a protective mechanism, a defence against the suffering coming from what is known and well established, of not being able to accept God as a metaphor. In other words, in psychosis, the subject's experience in relation to divinity is an attempt to reduce the pain associated with castration. As we mentioned before, the psychotic subject having foreclosed the Names of the Father, remains under the threat of this returning signifier in the form of real castration (e.g. Schreber's bodily experiences), which is unbearable. A delusion, which has reference only to the subject and excludes others, can either bring happiness – even perhaps a sense of the numinous – or suffering and a feeling of being under constant attack from the Other, depending on whether the psychosis has paranoid features.

Many patients remain diminished through a failure to be able to talk about their experiences in sufficient depth. A thoughtful systematic exploration of many aspects of the complex problems associated with a psychotic illness is essential in order to understand the reasons and the causes of a person's beliefs and experiences in relation to spirituality. In paying attention to the patient's speech and patterns of thought, we can come to value her or his spirit. Apollon et al. (2002) note that, by approaching the person as a speaking subject and offering a place where she or he can speak his mind, we can begin to open the subject to her or his religious experiences. In this way the person's certainty remains unchallenged and this diminishes the possibility of a further relapse. Thus, the goal of treatment becomes the development of a new transference, in which the patient makes use of the analytic space to experiment with the reliability of the spoken word, the source of which, in the delusion, opens the patient to the truth of his or her history.

> When one looks for the triggering causes of a paranoia, one always observes, with the required question mark, an emotional element in the subject's life, a life crisis that in fact does involve his external relationships, and it would be astonishing were one not led to do this with respect to a delusion that is essentially characterized as a delusion of reference.
>
> (Lacan 1993: 17)

Psychoanalytic thinking can help us approach the content and meaning of psychotic symptoms in depth without risking increasing the patient's suffering, so long as the focus is more on the position we take up in relation to the patient, rather than on trying to categorise what is normal or pathological in the patient's experience when it comes to spiritual experiences. What we offer to the patient should be good listening (Fink 2007). Furthermore, we should be open to the spiritual needs of the subject. A humane and liberal approach to the care and treatment of people suffering from a psychotic illness, in which religious experiences predominate, is essential in order to respond effectively. Spirituality may be an important aspect of the life of someone who suffers from a psychosis.

The delusional system creates a special interior place in the world of the subject, which, in the case of a religious delusion, centres around prefabricated figures like Christ, or around quasi-religious figures like 'the wife of God'. Such a delusional system may provide stability and often gives the subject a purpose and mission in life.

> Throughout the seminar, Lacan returns to a comment Freud makes to Fliess in his early Draft H on paranoia, sent with a letter to Fliess in January 1885, a biblically allusive aphorism that seems to hold the

key to the truth about psychosis . . . 'They [paranoiacs] love their *delusions as they love themselves.* That is the secret.' (Sie lieben also den Wahn wie sich selbst. Das ist das Geheimnis.) . . . Hence it is not that the paranoiac 'has' a delusion; he *is* his delusion.

(Reinhard 2006: 28)

In the end, religion is all about castration. Castration is foreclosed in psychosis and when there is a threat of castration the psychotic experiences it as real. When the enigmatic element appears, it gives the opportunity for the establishment of a delusion which cannot be shared with others.

Notes

1 For Aristotle, anyone who is unable to live in society or who has no need of others because he is self-sufficient, he must be either a beast or a god! (Arist. *Politics* I.1253A). See H. Rackman (ed. and trans.) (1932) *Aristotle: Politics,* Loeb Classical Library. Cambridge, MA: Harvard University Press.

2 According to Lacan, the subject is positioned in relation to three fields or orders of experience – the real, the imaginary and the symbolic. The imaginary is the field of images and deception; the symbolic, the field of language; and the real, the field of that of which it is impossible to speak, for it escapes symbolisation. In the 1970s, Lacan reformulated his approach to psychosis around the image of the Borromean knot, the three rings in the knot representing the three orders. He considered that, while in neurosis these three rings are linked together in a particular way, in psychosis they become disconnected, because language, as a bond or a master signifier that connects the three rings, does not operate in psychosis.

3 Delusions are the central clinical feature of paranoia and can range from single ideas to complex networks of beliefs called delusional systems. Lacan insists on the significance of the delusion and stresses the importance of attending closely to the psychotic patient's own account of his delusion. The delusion is a form of discourse and must therefore be understood as a field of meaning (*signification*) that has organized a certain signifier.

4 In seminar 11, Lacan uses the notion of holophrases, when a single term takes on a wide range of grammatical functions, to explain the psychosomatic effect: 'I will go so far as to formulate that, when there is no interval between S_1 and S_2, when the first dyad of signifiers become solidified, holophrased, we have the model for a whole series of cases . . . This solidity, this mass seizure of the primitive signifying chain, is what forbids the dialectical opening that is manifested in the phenomenon of belief' (Lacan 1981: 237–8).

References

Alanen, Y. (2009). The Schreber case and Freud's double-edged influence on the psychoanalytic approach to psychosis. *Psychotherapeutic Approaches Schizophrenic Psychoses,* ed. Y. Alanen, M.G. de Chávez, A.-L.S. Silver and B. Martindale, pp. 23–37. London: Routledge.

Apollon, W., Bergeron, D. and Cantin, L. (2002). *After Lacan: Clinical Practice and the Subject of the Unconscious.* New York: State University of New York Press.

Bailly, L. (2009). *Lacan's Beginners Guide*. Oxford: Oneworld Publications.

Clarke, I. (2001). *Psychosis and Spirituality: Exploring the New Frontier*. London: Whurr Publishers.

Cook, C. (2009). *Spirituality and Psychiatry*. London: Royal College of Psychiatrists.

de Mijolla, A. (2010). *Freud et la France, 1885–1945*. Paris: Presses Universitaires de France.

Eliade, M. (1979). *Tratado de historia de las religiones*. Mexico: Biblioteca Era.

Evans, D. (1996). *An Introductory Dictionary of Lacanian Psychoanalysis*. London: Routledge.

Fink, B. (2007). *Fundamentals of Psychoanalytic Technique. A Lacanian Approach for Practitioners*. New York and London: W.W. Norton and Co.

Foucault, M. (2006). *History of Madness*. London: Routledge.

Freud, S. (1907). Obsessive actions and religious practices. In *The Standard Edition of the Complete Psychological Works of Sigmund Freud*, vol. 9, ed. and trans. J. Strachey. London: Hogarth Press/Institute of Psycho-Analysis.

Freud, S. (1911). Psycho-analytic notes on an autobiographical account of a case of paranoia. In *The Standard Edition of the Complete Psychological Works of Sigmund Freud*, vol. 12, ed. and trans. J. Strachey. London: Hogarth Press/Institute of Psycho-Analysis.

Freud, S. (1927a). The future of an illusion. In *The Standard Edition of the Complete Psychological Works of Sigmund Freud,* vol. 21, ed. and trans. J. Strachey. London: Hogarth Press/Institute of Psycho-Analysis.

Freud, S. (1927b). A religious experience. In *The Standard Edition of the Complete Psychological Works of Sigmund Freud*, vol. 21, ed. and trans. J. Strachey. London: Hogarth Press/Institute of Psycho-Analysis.

Freud, S. (1930). *Civilization and its Discontents*. In *The Standard Edition of the Complete Psychological Works of Sigmund Freud*, vol. 21, ed. and trans. J. Strachey. London: Hogarth Press/Institute of Psycho-Analysis.

Lacan, J. (1981). *The Seminar of Jacques Lacan. Book XI. The Four Fundamental Concepts of Psychoanalaysis*, trans. A. Sheridan. New York: W.W. Norton.

Lacan, J. (1993). *The Psychoses. The Seminar of Jacques Lacan. Book III 1955–1956*, ed. R. Grigg, trans. J.-A. Miller. London: Routledge.

Lacan, J. (2005). *Ecrits*, trans. B. Fink. New York and London: W.W. Norton and Co.

Lipsedge. M. and Bhurga, D. (1996). *Psychiatry and Religion. Context, Consensus and Controversies*. London: Routledge.

Miller, J.-A. (2007*). Lacanian Clinique of Psychoses,* trans. D. Bergetis. Athens: Patakis Publishers.

Nagel, T. (1974). What is it like to be a bat? *Philosophical Review* 83: 435–50.

Otto, R. (1923). *The Idea of the Holy*. Oxford: Oxford University Press.

Reinhard, K. (2006). Toward a political theology of the neighbor. In *The Neighbor: Three Inquiries in Political Theology*, ed. S. Žižek, E. Santner and K. Reinhard, pp. 11–75. Chicago: University of Chicago Press.

Ricoeur, P. (1970). *Freud and Philosophy: An Essay on Interpretation*. Yale: Yale University Press.

Sauvagnat, F. (2000). On the specificity of elementary phenomena. *Psychoanalytic Notebooks* 4.

Schreber, D. (2000). *Memoirs of my Nervous Illness*. New York: NYRB Classics.

Sharpe, M. (2006). In the name of the Father . . . Descartes, psychosis, God and 'reality'. *Journal of Lacanian Studies* 4(2): 214–32.

Verhaeghe, P. (2004). *On Being Normal and Other Disorders. A Manual for Clinical Psychodiagnostics.* London: Karnac Books.

Wachsberger, H. (2007). From the elementary phenomenon to the enigmatic experience. In *The Later Lacan: An Introduction*, ed. V. Voruz and B. Wolf, pp. 108–15. Albany: State University of New York Press.

10

AUTOBIOGRAPHICAL ACCOUNTS OF A RELIGIOUS PSYCHOSIS

Anonymous

When my mother died

My experience of psychosis was several years ago. Part of the difficulty in writing about it these many years later is because I have changed since then. I have found a means of understanding, interpreting and integrating my experience, although back then I had no such means of doing so. When my experience occurred, I had not known of a single human being in the history of the world who had ever had such an experience. I did not know what to call it, so I simply called it 'The Story'. In the course of my recovery I discovered other names: 'Dark Night of the Soul', 'The Night Sea Journey', 'Shamanic/Gnostic Initiation', 'Encounter with the Unconscious', 'Spiritual Emergency', 'Ego Collapse/Ego Death' and more. I also discovered that in this culture my experience was considered to be one of psychosis or schizophrenia.

To help provide the reader with a baseline, it might be useful to flesh out who I was before. Who I was then was a woman in midlife, mostly content, very much in love with my husband, my children, my family and friends, my life. I considered myself to be very fortunate. For the sake of this account, I think it's worth emphasising I was not a religious person. I had never identified with a formal religion, never attended church outside of a brief period in my childhood and the occasional wedding, never read the bible or any other piece of religious literature, although I did consider myself to be somewhat spiritual, in an earthy sort of way. I was drawn to nature, had a pack of tarot cards and a pretty rock collection that I had collected from a New Age bookshop. Somewhere in the back of my mind I must have believed in some form of God, too, because I recall the moment I no longer believed any kind of god could exist, along with my anguish and rage in those moments.

My experience began when my mother died. In the immediate aftermath of her death, two unusual things happened. The first was that I found I could not cry, even though I had been very close to my mother and loved her deeply. The second was that I became terribly frightened. This fear was not attached to mortality; rather, the world suddenly became a place that no longer felt safe.

I could not understand that fear nor find a rational source for it, so I pushed it away and pretended it was not there. A few short weeks after my mother's death, I lost my closest friend and confidante.

I understand those events now as three blows that came heavy and fast upon me. That was when I started to crack. Life began to get a bit odd from those points forward. The oddness persisted for several months and included a new fascination with specific pieces of music, prose and poetry that captured my attention for reasons I could not explain. It also included terrible nightmares, a growing obsession with someone I considered to be evil and a slow estrangement from my family and friends as they struggled to make sense of my new behaviours.

Ten months later, another series of blows would come, harder and heavier than the first. There was a tragedy, a travesty. People were dead. I connected this with my earlier fears and obsessions of evil. I felt responsible in some way. At the same time I lost my other most significant friend and confidante. I lost a role I had heavily invested in. I lost my larger community. I was horrified by those deaths. I felt I was sworn to a secrecy I could not keep and felt shamed, cast out, exiled and abandoned as a result of my transgressions. My husband was angry and at the end of his rope and refused to offer any form of comfort. That was the night I stopped believing there could be any form of God. That was the night I felt as if I was drowning over and over and over again. I felt there was no one I could talk to, save one casual friend known by the name of Kali.

The next day I got up and went through the motions of living. I did that for four months. During those months I also began to suspect I had died that night, but somehow managed to go on living. These were the events that brought me to the doorstep of The Story. It started like this: In the Beginning . . .

The opening credits of that story took me back to my maternal grandmother – a woman I had barely known except through family history. The setting placed me somewhere out in the darkness of the universe. That is where The Story took me – or most of me, anyway. There was another part of me that was sitting in my home office with the door locked, but that part was a broken, physical shell of me. Somehow, these two parts were connected. One part of me lived the experience that took place in that other world; the other part of me wrote it down to the best of my ability as it happened. To this day, I would never deny the reality of that experience. I cannot call it a delusion. I call it a different plane of reality. Every moment, everything that happened, in that space was entirely real to me.

In that new world I had entered, there was a residence of sorts. On the upper level lived a man whom I called Gallagher. I lived in a separate apartment beneath Gallagher's living quarters. My living quarters had seven rooms, including an outdoor garden. The entrance to my apartment was an opening in the floor, hidden under Gallagher's bed. A ladder connected the two levels.

Shortly after I settled in, a visitor arrived . . . A tiny pair of polished Mary Janes appeared at the top of the ladder that joined Room 311 with the apartment below. Next, leotard-covered legs could be seen. A lace-ruffled bottom appeared next and, finally, an upper torso complete with a head that bobbed Tess's way and sarcastically remarked, 'Y'know . . . I could've put you up at the Plaza.' Tess's face broke into a wide grin. 'Yo God! Long time no see.' Those were the first two characters that showed up – Gallagher and that little-girl god. There would be other characters, too, all of them related in some way to the people I had lost or been with through the course of those climactic events. My job was to tell the story and Gallagher's job was to listen. The other characters appeared in accordance with the telling: the devil, Kali, Limh, Five-Star-Woman. Christ also made several cameo appearances. A number of those earlier pieces of prose and music also re-emerged, with greater significance. Telling that story was akin to getting more naked than I had ever been. It was very painful but with each painful retelling; another piece of me would be stripped away. It was during the process of this stripping down that Christ imagery began to surface, sometimes in a very subtle manner . . .

Tess lay down on the couch. She crossed her arms over her chest and closed her eyes. 'Hey Gallagher, do I look dead? Woooooooo,' she wailed. 'I am the ghost of Elvis.' Crucifixion themes also crept in. She pressed her back to it and extended her arms out at the shoulders. 'It fits me.' Subtle. But I know where those places are. I also knew it was crazy, but it was all crazy. There came a point, the most painful point, when there was nothing left to strip away. I call that point 'The Place Where Time Melts'. I did not exist. There was no me left. This was the place of 'Dancing with God'. There was a death, then a birth; two sides of the same coin – life and death, black and white, night and day, love and hate, good and evil. The Story continued . . . Slowly, I came to the realisation that a new task had fallen upon me. I had to kill the devil and I had to do it in a way that involved no violence, no weaponry, no hatred. I had to do this so I could save my soul. I had to do it so I could save the world. But I did not know how I was going to do that. This was when I discovered that under my bed was another entrance to a deeper place. I thought it was hell. I thought I was going to hell. I thought that the devil was down there but I had to go. It was not hell. In that place God gave me a needle made of the purest love possible and this was how I killed the devil – by putting that needle into his heart. Love is the only poison that can kill a heart of darkness. By the time that point came, I had had my throat cut, my chest sliced open, my heart pierced. I was covered in blood, but I had also done what I had to do. Then, Gallagher had to undergo a similar process and I held his hand while he did, just like he had held mine when I was in so much pain and so frightened. When it was all done, Tess and Gallagher made love and that is where The Story ended. Later that day I lay down and slept for the first time in many days. That was when I heard the only voice that took place outside of that world I had been in. It was a little girl's voice and she spoke from underneath my real-life bed. She said only one word: 'Heart.'

More than a year later I would come across the work of Jungian-trained psychiatrist John Weir Perry and realise that every character in my experience could be mapped upon Jung's model of the psyche. A few months after that, I returned to work, initially in a part-time capacity only. I was never hospitalised during or after that experience of mine. Nor have I been medicated or received any degree of formal therapy. I have managed to hang onto my marriage and some of the same friends. I have also been able to hold a job for several years, save an extended period when one of my children underwent an experience similar to my own. I quit working then, so I could be a support to them. My birth father was also in and out of psychiatric hospitals, but I did not consider this to be an important detail until my child's experience. In terms of spirituality: I began to study various texts, because it was the only way I could try to understand what my experience was all about. I still do not follow a formal religious path, I still do not attend any sort of house of worship, but I do find solace in moments of silence. A new God image has arisen out of my experience and this centres around the dark, ancient, matriarchal feminine: Kali, Isis, Sophia, Binah, Shekinah, the Black Madonna, the Tao and the Unmanifest Absolute. This same imagery has fuelled an intense interest in quantum matters: dark matter, black holes, the universe itself. I still listen to the music . . . In the beginning . . . all was the void and all was black. God saw this and said: Let there be light. And there was.

Fear that God was punishing me

When I had my breakdown in 1999 it was at a time of acute stress and difficulties in my personal relationships. I was working in IT and my husband had had a stroke, and I was struggling to look after two young children and stay at work and keep everything going. I was not eating or sleeping and was becoming very obsessed and isolated, cutting myself off from all my usual activities and sources of support. My husband and I had a row and I got really upset, and eventually I became too stressed out to work, and then everything sort of spiralled . . . I had been using a self-hypnosis technique to help cope and I had had a session with a clinical psychologist where she had asked me about my childhood and that had all been very peculiar. Perhaps she had used hypnosis, or perhaps it had just been some dissociation on my part – I do not honestly know, but I was aware of a sort of splitting like as if I was in two parts, and that seemed to be the start of it really . . . I feel that that whole period had a sort of spiritual aspect to it as I felt I was in touch with something . . . something important . . . and out of touch with the normal material world. It is all very hard to describe, but I would say I had four main spiritual experiences which have remained especially significant for me ever since, and which I will now attempt to describe, although some of them are going to sound very strange.

212

The first of these was on a walk out to a local island, which is accessible on foot at low tide. I had gone there because I felt desperate and overwhelmed, and I needed time to think. With total disregard for the tide, I scrambled about through mud, cliffs and gullies and waded into the freezing January sea as far away from the land as I could get. It was a bizarre and dangerous thing to do. But out there in the sea I had the most amazing experience. The seabirds were wheeling and crying all around me, and I felt a wonderful sense of harmony, like I was at one with them, and that I knew all their names. It was like, 'Oh there's a redshank', as I suddenly recognised one for the first time. I felt free, and the sense of oneness was blissful and spiritual. There was a sense of openness and it was like I was somehow new. I did indeed feel different from this point on. From this experience, I learnt that I needed to escape my present difficulties and find a new direction for my life. Back then I did not care if I drowned. I felt I had lost myself already, and I had nothing else to lose. But what started out as despair turned out to be a mystic and brilliant experience, and one that enabled me to make some important adjustments to my life, and gave me strength for what lay ahead.

All sorts of things were going on at that time but it all got a lot worse when I had an out-of-body experience. This was my second spiritual experience and it was not at all pleasant. I had been having all sorts of strange and seemingly meaningful dreams, and had been waking up and writing things down in a notebook. One night this happened and I could not get back to sleep. I came downstairs and had the strange sensation of a roaring noise and the sound and feeling of two big planes or dimensions coming together – it seemed to be science and religion, and they were coming together and meeting, and I could really feel this and sense it as if I was literally somehow taking part. I thought I felt a sort of presence over the table that I thought might have been God, although I could not be certain because I was honestly too frightened to look. All this felt incredibly strange and powerful and I did not understand any of it. I had not had any interest in these subjects at all, and although I had been in a church choir as a child, and had taken my children to Sunday school, I would not have described myself as religious in any way. All I wanted at this point was just to sort my life out. As out-of-body experiences go, this was not an especially impressive one. I felt that I was just alongside myself, right by my left shoulder. It was as if I had been simply kicked out. Perhaps I was not properly out of my body at all, but the only thing I can say with any certainty is that I was definitely not in it. It seemed as if something awful must be happening to my soul and I found the whole experience too bizarre and terrifying to understand. I felt like I had somehow gained access to some forbidden knowledge, but it was all too vast, and in a format I was unable to understand. I thought that this must have been due to the self-hypnosis that I had been doing, as if I had unleashed something that was way beyond my understanding or control. Rather like in the Disney film *The Sorcerer's Apprentice*. I wished I had not done it, but it was too late now.

213

After this, something really horrible seemed to have happened to the thing that I had always thought of as myself. I had always in some way equated my self and soul together (although these were things I honestly never gave any thought to before). But instead of the definite entity that I felt had existed before, I had now become a vague and tenuous thing, which seemed to be drifting away like dust in the wind. I tried to concentrate very hard to hold it together, but it was impossible, like trying to catch hold of clouds. The fear of losing it was terrible, and sleep felt like extinction, like a candle guttering out. Worst of all was this terrible fear that God was punishing me for breaking his laws. I kept thinking of Jonah and the whale – that is, you cannot escape from God – and did not know who to turn to. I felt totally isolated, as I knew that no human being was going to be able to help with this. I went to church and saw a minister and told him about some of my troubles, but I did not dare to tell him that I was losing my soul.

A few days later, with little or no sleep, I was admitted to a psychiatric hospital, which initially was a relief because I was so scared of losing my soul and turning into some kind of zombie. I felt like I was hovering on the brink of oblivion and great iron shutters were coming down in my mind. But in hospital the drugs made me worse and the experiences became even more horrific, and it was at this time that I had my third and worst experience. At the time I did not consider this a spiritual experience and even now I am not sure that the term fits very well. It was basically a confrontation with my dead grandmother, who had turned into a terrifying monster, and I was promising her that the madness which had been in our family (my mother had been diagnosed with schizophrenia at one time and had longstanding intermittent mental health difficulties) would live on and on through me and my daughter for ever. In this vision or dream that seemed horribly real, I then stood up to this monster and refused to allow this to happen, and the vision ended. It was like a confrontation with evil, so not spiritual in the traditional sense, but I believe it was spiritual in its intensity and power.

Fortunately, after much begging and pleading, the staff allowed me to discontinue the medication I was on and things gradually improved, as I got some reassuring advice from a psychiatrist, support from other patients and friends, and gradually calmed down.

My fourth and perhaps most powerful spiritual experience of all happened the day before I was discharged. A group of us were having our evening meal, and we were all talking about the experiences that had brought us into the hospital. One man had been some sort of engineer. He had been in hospital for ages and spent all his time drawing complex technical diagrams. He once tried to explain them to me, but they were so complicated that they made my head spin. He described how he had been shopping in a busy city centre one Saturday afternoon with his family, when suddenly he felt hot and breathless, and the lighting in the shop made him dizzy. He found that he was shaking and sweating and he could not breathe. He ran out of the shop and, because of the dizziness, caught hold of a pillar for support. Then he felt he could not let go of the pillar. Someone called an ambulance and here he was, in a psychiatric hospital, several weeks later. This was amazing. I had had a similar experience while out shopping with my sister just a few hours earlier. Except I already knew it was just an anxiety attack, brought on by stress, and the heat and lighting in the shop, so I had not been bothered by it. This man had been on drugs for weeks. Maybe he would even lose his job. All for what? A panic attack? I suddenly felt the room was too small and I needed to be outside, so I made excuses and left. Being outside was not enough, though. I felt that I needed more space. So I walked over to the furthest perimeter fence and out into the field beyond. It was a beautiful February evening, clear and cold. The field was furrowed and crisp with patterned ice. It was dusk and the sky was full of stars. The field was empty. Here at last I had the space I needed, and here it was that the idea came. It was an idea that was so big that it needed all this space to happen in. It did not come in language. It came like a great burst of electricity that surged through me, arcing and crackling right down from the stars. It felt powerful and wonderful, as if the whole universe was powering through my veins. And then I understood it in words, like it was a great truth blazing across the sky. It felt so tremendous that I hardly dared think it. 'There is no mental illness. The doctors have got it wrong!!' And that was it. I feel it was a revelation and that madness gave me my greatest inspiration. It inspired me to study psychology and become involved in the voluntary sector and try to make a difference. Since then I have learned that many people have the same idea – for example, the famous anti-psychiatrist Thomas Szasz – but back then, as a vulnerable and confused psychiatric patient, I felt I was the only person in the world who thought that way.

So, to summarise what was spiritual about my experiences (all four of them), I gained some knowledge from each one. In the first I felt I knew the birds' names. In the second I somehow knew that science and religion were coming together, even though I did not understand it at all. Having studied transpersonal psychology, I now understand this a little more and that there are ways in which this can be said to be happening, such as Jungian ideas or quantum physics, to name just a couple. In fact, much of the discipline of transpersonal psychology is about bringing science and religion together, I would say. In the third experience there was the certainty of what was wrong and that I had to stand up to it. Although at the time this was possibly the worst, I now find this vision liberating, as it has set our family free of dubious genetic theories about madness being transmitted through the family, an idea that I feel is unscientific, cruel and damaging. The final experience gave me the clearest and most definite powerful revelation. All except the third experience were accompanied by a very strong feeling of knowing – especially the fourth one, which was really ecstatic.

All four experiences have been intensely meaningful and have guided my life since. I cannot say for certain whether I really did see a redshank, but the other insights I gained at that time seem to have been both powerful and true. Until then I did not know anything about psychology, but the experiences inspired me to learn, so I obtained a BSc in Psychology and a postgraduate diploma in Consciousness and Transpersonal Psychology from Liverpool John Moores University. I have now learnt a lot more about what happened to my mother, and how purely biological approaches in psychiatry are misguided. I have been active in the voluntary sector, and now, since being made redundant from IT, I am an independent mental health trainer and also work part-time as a clinical support worker in mental health.

Visions of the Virgin Mary

I have been religious all my life and I have been to church every Sunday and all holy days of obligation. The true miracles occurring commenced in 2005. I was aware of the miracle happening at work and at home. My mum was very ill at that time and then, after two falls she was admitted to hospital via an ambulance. I went with her. While she was in hospital my mum suffered a great deal because of her cancer, but she got regular visits from the priest and all through this process there was a guiding-in light. It was the Holy Spirit.

While my mum was in hospital, we had to negotiate with the medical profession, as a family. Then my mum was transferred to a medical centre for specialist cancer care. It was a truly holy place and the nurses were very kind. After an assessment process and many medical examinations, my mum was transferred to another hospice. She got wonderful care there and died on Easter Monday. That was significant in religious terms. Then I went back to work for a few months and after I was admitted to hospital under a Section. (I have been Sectioned a number of times in the past.) I suffered greatly, but all the time God was with me and, each time I felt sad, God would raise my spirits. It was a year later in 2006 that the true miracle happened. I went on home leave, still under a Section and I went to a local travel agency. I booked myself a package tour to Lourdes in France – people see a vision there of Our Lady. Prior to this, I received a magazine from the hospice. There was a photograph of the Chief Executive of the hospice and I kept that magazine, and I was constantly looking at his photo – I was enamoured by the photograph.

I slept in my house, and the following morning I took a taxi to the airport. God was with me and the flight went very smoothly. I really enjoyed it. When I arrived in France, I realised that I needed to get in a minicab to get me to my destination. It was the hand of God. I did not determine it. God wanted it. I arrived at the hotel and settled in, then went to visit Lourdes. It was a pilgrimage. What I suffered, I took as a great blessing.

I changed the hotels a couple of times (God was leading), but unfortunately I stopped taking my medication. But it was not that: it was a miracle and I went to stand in front of Our Lady, which was me. Because God had told me that I am the Blessed Virgin Mary. In paradise I would have baby Jesus and baby Madonna and my husband will be God, the chief executive of the hospice.

I visited the place (Lourdes) nearly every day and sometimes overnight I walked around the streets of Lourdes. It was raining. In the meantime, my family had been very concerned about me. I stayed in one hotel and I needed to go to another hotel to get my money to pay for it. So, the owner took me in the car to find the hotel. He was concerned about me, so he brought me to the police station. My family had been in contact with the police in England, who had alerted Interpol. They realised that I was a missing person. Arrangements were made for me to go to a psychiatric hospital in France. It was not easy, because I did not fully understand the language. The food was not good there. I was experiencing a down in my mental health because I went into spiral. The hospital phoned my family and my sister and sister-in-law came over to France to visit me at the hospital and brought me clothing. My mood was not good, because I was ill. Therefore my brother negotiated with the British Embassy and it was then arranged that staff from the hospital would come over to collect me and bring me back to England.

Over the last few years, the miracle continues and it is affecting the whole world. Not just me but the whole of the world. The miracle is about the end of this world and the beginning of a new world on earth in paradise, and I feel very privileged that God has chosen me, the mother of Jesus, to be the wife of the Holy One, the Chief Executive. Here, I need a lot of support, because it is so great that God said he gave it to the shoulders that can carry it. I sent a letter to the Chief Executive and I told him about my mental health history and I sent two photographs. One when I was young, and the other with my mum. Also, I spoke with him on the phone and I said, 'Do you say your rosary?' and he laughed. I feel a real connection with him. The connection is there.

I believe that God is three persons. God is the father, which is the Chief Executive; God is the Son, which is Jesus and is inside me, my baby; and God is the Holy Spirit. The Holy Spirit is in everyone and everywhere. I had never understood until God told me. I do not know too much about the bible. I had always had a simple faith. I believe strongly that this is a light. In another psychiatric hospital, I also had other mystical experiences: one when I was transfixed like a cross for eight hours in my room, and another when I was walking naked along a motorway. No car stopped, nobody stopped me and I went back to my mum's house and she bathed my feet. After this, I had a Catholic blessing, like exorcism for my mental health problems, and that made me feel better. The blessing helped me because I was not able to breathe at one point. This terrified me, but when I found the right medication and therapy I felt good. I thank God for what he had done for me, for the whole world. All the time God protected me and that is why I am still a virgin.

On the front of the bible there is a 'P' and an 'X'.[1] 'P' means 'peace' and 'X' means '10' (2010) in Latin. I know that this symbolises peace soon after 2010. That means paradise and there will be no wars, no pain, no suffering. Everybody will marry. If they are already married on earth, they will remarry again in paradise. God will find a husband or a wife for other single people. People will get married at Easter and then the twins will arrive for every married couple at Christmas. There will be great celebrations, honeymoons, hotels, beaches, big cars, mansions, for everyone. Everybody will be very rich and happy. I believe that the end of this world will happen soon and the beginning of the new world will happen at God's decree and a new social order.

This experience is a genuine religious one, because it highlights the beginning of a new world paradise and everybody will be there, even the bad people. They will have done their purgatory. It will also be beneficial, because the New Earth will be populated by perfect adults and children and we will all live in harmony. I believe that this will happen in the near future.

In conclusion, God will be the king, the Chief Executive. The Virgin Mary will be the Queen. I had visions of the Virgin Mary all through my childhood. In my room, above the wardrobe there was a bright light of the Madonna. In my junior school I saw a fairy in the gardens. I had also another mystical experience that took place when I was working in a bank. I was just 16 years old at that time. My father had died when I was 15 years old and I was going through a very serious breakdown. I was suffering greatly with all the symptoms of paranoid schizophrenia. I was at the computer at the bank when a power took me over and I started to write poetry that was centralised across the banking system. It was all about the world and what was going to happen to it. Due to my illness, I was admitted to hospital, where they made an analysis of the poetry. It was all centred on God's plan. There will be two people, Michael and I, who will be used for research purposes from the age of 16. The government wanted to study mental health and a satellite was going to film and cover every event throughout our life. In addition, God, the greatest power of all, meaning the Holy Spirit, will be a guiding light and this was a part of my religious experience, many of which I experienced throughout the whole of my life.

A black crow squawked at me – it was like the devil

Suddenly I felt a downward pull or rush of pure evil pour into my body and I knew it was of the devil, that he wanted me in his army, and would take my soul and do with it what he wanted. Humankind's ordeal had culminated in one moment. I felt I was surrounded by uncaring and devious darkness with no regard for fairness in the struggle of life, on the brink of the abyss, causing pain and agony to the innocent. I felt a great urgency to prove myself. I had a wayward comprehension of the magnitude of what was going on and what could have become of everyone if I had been taken to be bad. Whatever good is, it was not this, and I was not about to be ordered without question by an emperor who was only out to rule in darkness. I was fighting for humankind. Deep inside, a feeling of survival emerged and willed me to fight away this evil. There was no running from this mystical situation, I had to fight, but somehow I knew I could fight the evil away, that I was stronger than darkness, that deep down I was good and had no place for evil.

I fought like a mad dog to keep my soul. The vibrations of the devil made me struggle around on my bed. Sweating with fear and exhaustion I continued to resist. As the rush of evil subsided and I fought it away, I went into my mind's eye or pixelic mass, a spirit world inside my head, like a dream and pictured myself with the devil. I was in a boxing ring with the brown beast. He was a little larger than me, with defined big muscles. He had a tail like that of a dog. He had an ugly face with wide eyes full of mischief, and two curvy small spirally horns on his head. He had big blunt hoof-like things on his feet and hands with big claws on his fingers. He was grinning as though he was sure to beat me. I struck first and took him by surprise, throwing an overhand right that connected just above his left eye, knocking him off balance. As he rocked back I hooked him with a left uppercut to the right of his jaw. Sensing victory, making sure to finish him, I struck with another overhand right that landed bang on top of his left eye again. He toppled over and fell to the ground and, in a frenzy to show I was not scared, I kicked his gut several times – one too many. The ending bell sounded: 'Ding Ding Ding.'

I stood strong and left the spirit world. Lay on my bed in relief I knew I was good. I was not bad – how could I be? It seemed I had angered the balance of morality. The devil was not that bad. He controlled worse things than him in his hell; in a way he was the master of darkness that he could keep it in order so evil would not tear heaven apart. The truth was that, kicking him, when he was down, was wrong. I knew I would suffer for my weakness but I could not turn back time. Somehow he would want to avenge me. But I had made it clear that I was a warrior in God's army. My mind was free of guilt and filled to the brim with altruism in my quest to find the ideal personality so I could impress a woman. Still scared, I needed to meet God. He would come if I hoped enough, but I did not want to beg. I just needed him to come and meet me to give me the strength to fight against evil. If my religious friends spoke the truth, I would see the light. In the morning the sun shone through the window and God came to save me. A personified face of God showed in the light before me. He knew I suffered and that I was worried about my nose twitching aggressively. 'Show me respect,' he said. I stood there upright and still. 'Show me respect.' Again I was worried about my nose twitching. 'Salute me.' I saluted him. I stood there before him, praying he would be pleased. 'Put on your dinner suit to show your respect.' 'But I do not have a shirt.' 'Put it on, anyway.' So I put on my trousers and stood up like a soldier, and God said, 'Now, to prove your faith in me, go outside dressed like this for the whole world to see.' 'Yes, I will,' I thought. 'No, you do not have to do this,' he said. He gave me a rush and my whole body vibrated in ecstasy. I believed that these rushes strengthened me and made the universe as good and strong as possible. But I could hear the students getting jealous. 'How come he is getting so many rushes?' a neighbouring female said through the walls. 'I cannot take this rush with all these students around me.' 'Go to the park,' said God. So I went out into the sunny morning and walked five minutes to the park and to a patch of forest to continue there. A black crow squawked at me. It was like the devil. I waved my arms at it and it flew off. 'You must be a cool rock star,' said God. 'No, I will be a cool rock,' I replied.

I thought God was angry that people killed Jesus and I thought I had to save people from God's wrath by persuasion. I also thought God wanted me to go into the spirit world to fight, but I was scared I would become lost, so I refused. 'All people on earth are evil. I must destroy them,' God said. 'I am kind, so that's checkmate,' I replied. This meant there must be other kind people. God seemed happy with this, but I wondered if he was going to use me to destroy the earth. 'Go and be a tramp for the rest of your life to prove your faith in me,' God said. 'Yes I will.' 'You do not have to do this'. I waited. 'Stay in the wilderness for the rest of your life to prove your faith to me,' God said. After half an hour, which seemed like two hours, he let me go. 'He fits in,' the birds whistled as I walked back to my accommodation. 'Do not fear: I have passed all the tests from God and he will not destroy us,' I said aloud. 'I'm scared,' I heard the female neighbour say from her room. A storm was brewing outside. 'All you have to do is have faith in God and he will not destroy us,' I said aloud. I sensed vibes in my room that seemed to come from the other students' rooms. I cannot recall the vibes properly, but I felt like they were discussing me. I was walking around like a hero thinking I had saved the world, but worried about the Antichrist. I visited my religious friends, who I thought knew about what had happened through spiritual telepathy, but it seemed they had no idea when I told them. I went to the bathroom to be alone and to talk to God and the devil, and said, 'A man can choose his own destiny and hence checkmate.'

I thought the whole town knew about me. The spiritual voices drained my energy, but my guardian angel sometimes helped me to block the voices. My religious friends took me by car to a church with them, but I decided against it, as the church leaders might think I was Jesus. So I got out of the car at a garage and they decided to drive me back to my accommodation. I was exhausted from reading books, writing essays and theories, and now from the voices of birds, spirits and other people's vibes and body language, which bugged me, but occasionally my guardian angel managed to block the voices out when I called on her for help. That night I went to the park again, still on a mission to make everything as good and strong as possible. I walked a little into the forest but it was pitch black, so I ran the other way and did a star jump into the road and took a rush, and left all the voices behind. I was wandering around believing the whole town knew about me, and the people in the pubs seemed to be talking about me as I walked past. I went back to my small room to take another vibrating rush from God and leave the whole town behind. I played a music track called 'Leave Them All Behind' and succeeded in leaving the whole universe behind and becoming a unit in myself. I turned off the music track, and five minutes later there was a loud bang from the appliance. This made no sense to me. There seemed to be secret cameras in my room that the government was using to spy on me. In my room I detected vibes that seemed to be coming from neighbours in the building, whom I believed were talking about or with me, saying, among other things, that I was a dude. I walked to different places in the city – the train station, the civic centre – not knowing what to do, panicking about the voices, which seemed to be spirits or a female guide who was directing my journey. I thought the devil's recruits were after me. I was going to call for the dudes downstairs to help, but I decided against it. Not wanting to associate with the other students, I stayed outside to face the devil. I thought people were in great danger and I was shaking walking up the road, but I did not care. A security guard walked up the other side of the road. I was ready to fight or run like the wind. Suddenly the police pulled up. I turned and ran the other way. 'Stop, police!' a policewoman shouted. I ran straight at an officer and tried to go past him. He punched me in the leg. He was an experienced cop and I went down. They took me next to a police car and gathered round me to find out what was going on. 'What were you doing?' they asked. 'Some people were after me,' I replied. I was looking all around shaking, thinking I was in big trouble with the devil. A policewoman handcuffed me to her. 'Calm down. Who are you?' she said. 'Have you got any identification?' 'Yes,' I said, handing them my student card. 'Did you do that burglary in that garage across the road?' 'No,' I replied. In the end, two policemen took me back to my accommodation over the road. 'He's quite into it,' one of them said, talking about my studies. He also said sorry about the leg and then they left. I put my leg under the cold shower and it seemed to me that the devil healed it out of respect, so matters had been resolved with the devil. I cleaned my bathroom thoroughly and this had a therapeutic effect on me. Then I slept.

The next two days I mostly stayed in my room. I often heard the neighbours in the building and they seemed to be talking about me. It was not too stressful, but I thought I was finding out things that I should have already known. I was limping and everyone was talking about me, or so it seemed. In the refectory I overheard a beautiful ginger-haired older student say, 'It's exciting.' I was hearing the voices of angels and thought the birds were talking about me. I went to a seminar and the other students seemed happy I was OK, but walking out of the door I was practising acting like the Antichrist, and I sighed, and a girl saw me.

It was the Easter holidays. I had no money and no food, and took the train the hundred miles back to town. I believed that I had many followers, who now saw me as evil or did not understand what was happening. In this period I had a sense that the good people would have to hide, because I was the one who could tip the balance. I thought I was a dude and all the other dudes were giving me rushes out of respect, to strengthen me. I was worried about being an it-dude, and wanted to be normal. The train staff kicked me off the train at some town en route. Exhausted, I phoned my mum and she suggested I went to the police. They sent me to Social Services, but I could not find it and went back to the police, who gave me a special ticket home. This was a great relief, since in that town late at night some gang might have kicked me to death. At Waterloo there seemed to be more dudes giving me rushes. As the train pulled off, I had a fight with the devil in my head. I won but I did not kick him when he was down. I believed I had handled the situation perfectly. I had fought off the devil, befriended God, saved the earth and made the universe better. On the way, nearer to town, I sat opposite a friendly-looking man believing that he would protect me on the walk from the station back to my dad's flat, but he told me to leave him alone. It was a short walk from the station and, after arriving at my dad's flat, I talked to my brother at length about what had happened.

I fought all the evil spirits out of my body and made a small wooden cross and hung it round my neck. I got into bed. In my pixelic mass there were white balls of which the weaker ones the devil tried to find to destroy. Sometimes God or I would try to stop them being broken. Then my guardian angel became a fantasy for me and that night I slept for twelve hours.

The next day my dad took me to a psychiatrist and she listened to as much as I was prepared to tell her. She found it hard to believe I had slept well. My dad suggested that decent sleep was the answer and maybe sleeping pills would be useful, but she said they would only mask the problem, and she prescribed some antipsychotics. I only remember taking one of the pills. I seemed to be back to consensus reality and told my family and my old school friends what had happened with regard to my religious experiences. They were all amazed. After about three weeks, at the end of the holidays, my brother walked with me to the train station. He said to my dad that I looked very forlorn getting on the train. I told my theological student friends about the experience and they were excited by the news. I thought the Antichrist was after me and I was scared and very on edge. On the way back to my accommodation, a black man was standing next to a car that looked broken down. He started coming towards me and I thought he might be the Antichrist and so I ran off. Still worried by the Antichrist I went back to my small modern room and rang my dad for him to take me home. I thought there were government cameras in my room and I prepared discreetly for the dangerous night ahead by putting a cardboard box against the door and leaving a metal ornament on the desk to use as a weapon. The next day my dad and brother came. I was carrying a skateboarding tool ready to plunge it in the face of any aggressor. I hurried up my dad and brother to get my stuff in the car quickly and get on the journey home. But there seemed to be secret cameras in the car. When back home I watched television, thinking there was a camera in it and the whole world was watching me. The fans in a football stadium on television seemed to be cheering about me. It appeared everyone was pretending they did not know me, when really they all did, and people were not sure whether I was good or evil. I refused to go back to the psychiatrist and my dad and I went for a walk along the seafront. On the sea wall, a man who was shadowed by the sunlight looked like he might be a problem and I suggested we go a different way. Another time, out for a walk on my own, I saw a black car in front of me with flames on the bonnet. Thinking the driver was the devil, I ran across the road and past the side of the car, off across a park, where there was an old church tower. The driver got out, but the girl in the passenger street shouted 'No.'

Later I tried checking my dad's flat for bugs, but he would not allow me to, so when he was out of the room I took a light bulb out of the ceiling and carried it to the park and smashed it to see if there was a bug inside. But there was nothing there. In my dad's flat the sounds of people upstairs on the second floor worried me. I thought they were spies. I did not trust anyone, not even my own family. That night I fantasised about a beautiful angel and went to sleep. The next morning I thought the government had put a bug in my nose during my sleep.

I felt I was on the verge of complete insanity

When I became ill, I wanted to treat my condition holistically. Having never accessed mental health services before, I wondered what the outcome would be. Perhaps I had been suffering from aspects of mental illness for a long time but I had never attributed my difficulties to that before. The words I had used were 'heartbroken' or 'stressed and traumatised'. I was simply reacting to life's events and doing the best I could in the circumstances. I felt that life had dealt me a series of blows and that each time it took a little bit longer to recover. I was one of those optimist types who kept going, but in the end I felt the stuffing had been knocked out of me and I began to lose hope. I had used up all my reserves. There were various factors that led to my illness.

I was victim of incest and sexual abuse as a child, and the perpetrator of child abuse, of which I was convicted and jailed in my late teens. I was a victim of bullying at school, which left me suicidal at one point. My first husband dealt with my abuse by asking me to recount my experiences of abuse and previous boyfriends in great detail. He was possessive and obsessive, and left me for another woman. This led to an episode of self-harm and feeling suicidal. But I had three kids under school age and realised that my death would not help them, so I survived. I suffered from postnatal depression after the birth of my second child. I felt suicidal, then but controlled it and came out of it without drugs. Others were also affected, my partner worse than me. All affected parties lost their housing, their jobs and became financially crippled for years. I lived with, and eventually married, the other affected partner. We have had trouble with debts and the poor job climate, with mergers and redundancy. My next partner reacted to my history of sexual abuse by finding it exciting.

I am a fighter and I use knowledge to help me understand what was happening in my life. I am a nurse and involved in Christian healing, so I can see things from a physical, psychological and spiritual outlook. In the last two or three years, I have experienced visions with a beginning, middle and end, and for a specific purpose – for example, just before a healing conference. In this vision I became depressed, withdrawn, stopped opening mail, finding it difficult to concentrate, experiencing blind rage, oppressive fear, violence, down to self-harm and feeling suicidal. But, although I thought about self-harming all day, I could control it, and with the help of others I prayed my way out of it. Within two days I was having prophetic dreams and experiencing complete joy and a sound mind. (The whole experience from beginning to end lasted about a month.) The last two visions have been terrorist-related: I am the victim – drugged, raped, tortured – but the end result is a moderately long bible study, which is used in church.

My relationship became more stressful as a result of a threat to my new job because of drink-related, previous sex abuse-related things. My life is in layers and they are all interlinked. The last layer has impacted on all the others, even though I thought I had processed them and fought through them. My husband and I had a big argument that seemed to blow me apart. I was in vision mode and I was shown different aspects of myself: the little girl (who is in charge), the suicidal teenager, the nurse, the Christian warrior, and another woman, who is slightly aggressive and wants to be left alone, and two or three baddies created by terrorism (the whole thing is incorporated into the terrorist vision). After four days I felt together again and my husband and I have resolved our differences. Since then, I have tried to wrestle with this and hope to get counselling – I am on a waiting list. I can now look from a clearer perspective. I am not in the middle of it any more, but I have had trouble sleeping and eating, and I call out in my sleep and wake up shaking. After telling this to a counsellor, I began to want to self-harm but I wrestled with this for a few days and overcame it. Then I felt suicidal for several days and overcame that, too. Now, if I confront my past in any way, I instantly get a thought in my head that I should kill myself. I resist, of course, but I have been doing this for years. It appears now that I can feel suicidal and happy at the same time. Part of me is over all this and happy, but another part thinks of death all the time. I find it hard to motivate myself to do anything – pay bills, tidy the house, be sociable with friends and relatives, or get excited about things. If I focus on one side I can be completely normal, such as in work situations.

But if I focus on the other side, I find it hard to function, and at one point I felt I was on the verge of complete insanity and would soon lose touch with reality.

I now have what appears to be suicide programmes playing in my head – something like 'The secret's out' and 'You've got to kill yourself'. I do things like call the Samaritans, or ring my doctor. This helps, but does not stop it. Creative problem-solving cures it. For example, my mind tells my mind that it will not stand for it! I have told the doctor that psychotherapy looks like a good option. The logical part of me will not stand for a suicide programme that is deliberately set to cause the mind distress and to control issues. When the other part of my mind, that is badly affected by the programme, realises that the logical part refuses to be threatened, controlled or distressed because the psychologist is going to reprogramme it for me, the programme is neutralised! Still I need help with the other programme, although I know it's a Satanic programme, though not necessarily my diagnosis – could it be stress or witchcraft? Once, when assisting in a healing service, I asked for anointing with oil after experiencing violent feelings in my gut, which is better than my head! They disappeared, only for me to realise I had anxiety in there, too. It was a shame I did not realise this earlier, as I could have asked for both to be healed! Am I dissociated? I score less than thirty on a self-test. Are the visions partially created by others trying to get their story heard? Normally I am well-known for my cheerfulness, sociability and relaxed manner. Only those closest to me can pick up what's going on in the inside.

The thoughts of suicide, self-harm and anxiousness have gone for now, but I still feel a bit post-traumatic. The feeling is not of worry and resulting anxiety – more of panic in the middle of my being – and does not seem related to any particular event. Sometimes it is there and sometimes not. I wake up with bizarre dreams. Here is an extract from a dream.

I've been involved in a car crash and we arrive at Mum and Dad's house. My head is cut and bleeding but when they check more closely they find a deeper wound which is more serious. My mind is bleeding. (I wonder if this is repressed memories.) As the thoughts at the surface of the mind are scratched away, the deeper thoughts come to the surface. There may be more to come. I am woken an hour later with another dream. I go home from church but I realise something is different. This time there is no light. I am in complete darkness, no street lights and completely alone. It is going to be more difficult to make it back and much easier for people to attack me. I am rung in the evening to see if I can work in the Burns Unit tomorrow. I say, 'Yes.'

In the night, I am awoken with a start. Perhaps I have been thinking about things in my sleep. It feels like one of my legs has been kicked with a great intensity. My lower half is lifted off the bed. One or two hours later I have another dream.

I am in church; as we worship I feel myself getting heavier and heavier. I can barely stand and then I collapse. The next thing I know was that someone is sitting by my side. I have been out for a time. She says that when I collapsed, it was like I was having full-blown sex with someone. (These things can be seen as demonic manifestations, e.g. hissing, writhing like a snake, animal noises and claw-like movements.) She is in the middle of explaining things further when, unfortunately, I wake up shaking like a leaf.

I feel completely different when I wake up and I am so glad that I am in my bed, not in church! Has Jesus been ministering to me? I feel clearer in my head and body. The image I have is of me standing at the edge of a cliff with my box of sex abuse. Jesus promises he will catch me and that I can trust him. He is faithful. Together we can sort out the box, but he will never force me to open the box. It has to be something that I do of my own free will.

There was a strong spiritual theme running through my illness. I felt that God was prompting me to give over another area of my life to him. I had to face my childhood trauma. This had to be an act of will; it was not forced on me. I had also noticed a pattern developing. My emotions were connected to the spiritual. When things heated up spiritually, part of me would descend into despair. When a spiritual breakthrough came, I would improve. I have had more visions since then. It is exhausting, but exciting. The last two have been different. They are very fast-paced thriller-type visions about terrorism, rape, kidnap, assault, etc. where good and evil play a game of cat and mouse, but in the end evil is vanquished completely. I get to be one of the victims, fatally drugged and have to jump from burning ships, plan miraculous escapes from the perpetrators, etc. I end up in hospital on my last legs and get treated. These pictures come in loops. I have a very small piece of the huge scenario playing in my head all the time. I take it to work, but ram it right to the back of my mind. I take it to Tesco's, I take it to church and it is with me when I sleep, and my sleep patterns are disturbed or I sleep lightly. My mind never switches off – that is why you get tired. After the loop has played one or two days, you get a revelation and I vigorously scribble down notes any time, day or night. Then I get the next loop. The worst thing I faced, mentally, was over Christmas and New Year. Before this, I was working as a nurse part-time and I was probably sinking into a depression. I found there was so much happening in my psyche that I had less and less energy to live and work. Financially I was under pressure to work and this endless financial burden got me down. There were staff shortages, so I could work lots of shifts, which was great financially but not good for your general wellbeing. For months my husband had been threatened with redundancy and had also experienced a family bereavement, which meant a trip abroad and funeral expenses when we could least afford it. I remained calm and motivated at work, but I felt different. I functioned, but when I came home I turned into an emotional wreck. Part of my experience was that I had being blown apart – as if my soul had been broken. Maybe that was why the nurse could be independent from other parts of me.

Note

1 The Chi Rho is one of the earliest forms of Christogram and is usually thought to be formed by the first two capital letters of the Greek word *ΧΡΙΣΤΟΣ* (Christ). However, not all scholars are in agreement. The fullest treatment is by Henri Leclercq in *Dictionnaire d'Archéologie Chrétienne et de Liturgie* 3(1): 1481–1534.

11

DIMENSIONS OF RELIGIOUS/ SPIRITUAL WELLBEING AND THE PSYCHOTIC EXPERIENCE

Empirical results and perspectives

Human-Friedrich Unterrainer

Studies indicate that religious and spiritual dimensions are positively related to all forms of mental health, including indicators of subjective wellbeing and personality factors. It has also been suggested that religious/spiritual wellbeing might play an important role in the development, course and recovery of mental illness. However, despite such claims, there have been numerous recordings of delusions and hallucinations adopting a religious nature. Furthermore, there is some evidence that religion and spirituality can be harmful for patients experiencing psychosis. Currently, relevant empirical evidence is sparse and more research is needed in order to delineate the role of religious/spiritual issues, as religion and spirituality may be part of the disease as well as part of the cure. Thus patients with a severe mental disorder might use different religiously/spiritually based strategies to cope with their disease effectively. Religion and spirituality were found to protect against addictive behaviours and suicide attempts. Furthermore, religion and spirituality enable the experience of personal growth and might be considered as important topics within in-patient treatment. Based on empirical results, we will discuss the question of religious/spiritual needs among patients diagnosed with a psychotic disorder.

A bio-psycho-socio-spiritual model of mental health and illness

The bio-psycho-social model of health and disease, first proposed by Engel (1977) includes different aspects of health and illness such as biological (e.g. cancer, heart attack), psycho-social (e.g. depressive/anxiety disorders) and socioeconomic (e.g. financial problems, divorce) factors. The basic idea of this model is an ongoing interaction between these dimensions within the process of health and disease. This bio-psycho-social model has to date been established on a theoretical level, as empirical research on this topic is comparatively rare (Unterrainer 2010). Specifically, on evaluating relevant literature in this field of research, it can be concluded that this model – though comprehensive in principle – disregards a variety of facets that may also play a crucial role in health and illness. For instance, this model does not consider religiosity and spirituality, which can be assumed to be important in health and subjective wellbeing (Unterrainer 2006). Mostly, religiosity has been defined as being more related to institutions or traditions, whereas spirituality often has been described as a broader concept or belief system, without any institutional bindings (Miller and Thoresen 1999). Furthermore, there has been extensive research about the consideration of religiosity/spirituality as an independent factor to those usually included in the bio-psycho-social model, and is most prominently related to the concept of the Big Five personality dimensions: extraversion, neuroticism, openness to experience, conscientiousness and agreeableness (Piedmont 1999, 2004; Saroglou 2002).

What do we mean when we talk about spirituality or religiosity? What is religion or a religious/spiritual belief system? For more than a hundred years, these questions have been a key problem for psychologists of religion who try to define their research object (James 1902/1979; Pargament 1999; Wulff 1997; Zinnbauer et al. 1997), and there is still an ongoing discussion in the field. Both religiosity and spirituality relate to the realm of transcendence: while religiosity has often been described as being more oriented to institutions and traditions, spirituality has been conceptualised as a broader construct, without confessional bonds (Unterrainer 2007). Religious coping, for instance, has been found to play an important role in the process of dealing with a serious disease (Huber 2008; Pargament 1997, 2007). Moreover, Pargament (1999) provided one of the most influential attempts to define religiosity/spirituality from a clinical psychological perspective. Accordingly, religiosity/spirituality can be viewed as a search for meaning in ways related to the sacred.

Furthermore, religiosity and spirituality has attracted a lot of interest from psychoanalysis over its history. Beginning with Freud (1907, 1913, 1923, 1927, 1939), who could be named as the most famous psychologist of religion – *wider Willen* – religion and spirituality have been addressed by highly established authors like Erik Erikson, Donald W. Winnicott or Heinz Kohut, to name but a few (see also Black 2006; Capps 2001; Corveleyn and Luyten 2005; Jones 2001; Kernberg 2000; Wulff 1997). More recently, Ana Maria Rizzuto (1998) asked, 'Why did Freud reject God?', and succeeded in giving an adequate answer from the very perspective of a psychoanalyst (see also Rizzuto 1996).

In general, there is a huge amount of research emphasising the beneficial effects of religiosity and spirituality on mental health and/or subjective wellbeing. Religiosity and spirituality have also been found to play an important role in clinical settings (Koenig, McCullough and Larson 2001; Miller and Thoresen 1999; Smith, McCollough and Poll 2003). There is substantial evidence for religiosity and spirituality being an efficient suicide buffer, especially among psychiatric patients, as, for instance, Dervic et al. (2004) demonstrated that religious affiliation was substantially associated with less suicidal behaviour in depressed inpatients. After other factors were controlled, it was found that greater moral objections to suicide and lower aggression level in religiously affiliated subjects may function as protective factors against suicide attempts. This result is in line with our own findings, as the affiliation to a religious community consistently turned out to be negatively related to suicide attempts or even suicidal ideations. These findings may be considered significant, as the rate of suicidal tendencies is substantially increased among psychiatric patients (see also Coghlan and Ali 2009).

There is also substantial evidence for a negative association between religiosity/spirituality and nearly all kinds of addictive diseases. In a study by Kendler et al. (2003), different dimensions of religiosity and relations with God were found to be negatively related to lifetime substance misuse disorders. An extensive meta-analytical review of 263 papers supports this negative correlation between spirituality and addiction (Cook 2004). Although religion and spirituality are positively related with nearly every indicator of mental health (Koenig et al. 2001), the working mechanisms behind these findings remain unexplained, which challenges those engaged in neuroscience and brain research (Fenwick 2009, 2010; Newberg and Newberg 2005). Sloan, Bagiella and Powell (1999) criticised what they called a sometimes hasty overinterpretation of the positive connection between religiosity/spirituality and mental health. So, why does it still make sense to consider religious/ spiritual as an important topic in clinical and health research?

As described by Ernest Becker (1973) in *The Denial of Death*, as human beings we confront our own mortality every second of our lives. Accordingly, religion and spirituality could be taken as an important means to transcend this kind of existential fear or the dilemma of mortality through facilitating a feeling of heroism and, therefore, being part of something eternal (see Hartley 2010). Along the lines of thought of Ernest Becker, mental illness is extrapolated as a failing in one's hero system(s), such as in depression. Depressed individuals are being consistently reminded of their mortality, resulting in a feeling of insignificance. Within this picture, schizophrenia might be taken as a step further than depression, in which one's identity is falling apart, making it impossible to engender sufficient defence mechanisms against mortality. Thus, people diagnosed with a psychosis have to create their own reality or inner world in which they can continue to exist as heroes. However, as Julian Jaynes noted, we have to be careful by expanding our theories, especially in the field of schizophrenia research, as 'recent decades have watched with gratitude a strong and accelerating improvement in the way this illness [schizophrenia] is treated. But this has come about not under the banners of new and sometimes flamboyant theories . . ., but rather in down-to-earth practical aspects of day-to-day therapy' (Jaynes 1976: 431).

Psychoticism as the dark side of spirituality – or spirituality as benign psychoticism?

In this chapter psychosis is not being regarded as necessarily the same as schizophrenia. Schizophrenia might be conceived as a specific form of psychiatric diagnosis (e.g. paranoid schizophrenia), while the term 'psychosis' is used here to refer to a broader group of psychotic disorders, such as schizophreniform disorder, schizoaffective disorder, delusional disorder or brief psychotic disorder (Huguelet and Mohr 2009; see also Mitchell and Roberts 2009). Furthermore, according to the *Diagnostic and Statistical Manual of Mental Disorders-IV* (DSM-IV; Saß, Wittchen and Zaudig et al. 1996) delusions can be described as false beliefs based on incorrect inference about external reality that is firmly sustained and contrary to normal beliefs of that person's culture of and despite incontrovertible proof or evidence to the contrary of the belief . . . According to Peters (2010: 129) there are several problems with this definition. These problems range from plainly false assumptions to points of vagueness and ambiguity, as well as several unjustified theoretical conjectures. Thus, several authors pointed out that delusions need to be understood against a background of thorough knowledge of the psychology of beliefs (Freeman 2006; Peters 2010).

Hallucinations may be manifested in a variety of forms, as the *American Psychiatric Association's Psychiatric Glossary* describes it simply as 'a sensory perception in the absence of an actual external stimulus' (Chen and Berrios 1996: 54). Hallucination comprises a common symptom in both medicine and psychiatry. According to Chiu (1989), the frequencies of auditory hallucinations in schizophrenia and acute organic brain syndrome are about 50% and 15% respectively, while the frequencies of visual hallucinations in these two disorders are about 10% and 30% respectively. Thus, doctors of any speciality are likely to encounter some patients presenting with hallucinations in their practice. An alternative definition was given by Mullen (see Chiu 1989: 293), who excluded dreams explicitly and argued that 'hallucinations are involuntary false perceptions occurring concurrently with real perceptions (thus excluding dreams), and having qualities of real perceptions, i.e. vividness, substantiality'.

Furthermore, hallucinations might be taken as normal phenomena, as very common experiences, but can occur in neuropsychiatric disorders like narcolepsy syndrome, chronic alcoholism and delirium. Unlike hallucinations, an illusion is a real (e.g. having actual external stimulus) perception distorted in some way. It can be a normal (e.g. misperceiving the outline of a bush as that of a man at dusk) or a morbid phenomenon (e.g. a delirious patient mistaking inanimate objects for people). In the latter case, it frequently coexists with hallucinations.

According to Mohr and Pfeiffer (2009; see also Getz, Fleck and Strakowski 2001; Mohr et al. 2010; Pfeiffer 2007; Siddle et al. 2002), hallucinations and delusions with religious content are not restricted to schizophrenia, as they were described in nearly all kinds of mental disorders. Furthermore, they argue that the term 'religious delusion' is often a confusing category for clinicians, as well as a stigmatising category for patients, and there is evidence that religious delusions might be associated with poorer prognosis and may lead to violent behaviour (e.g. Reeves and Liberto 2006). In general, biological, psychological, sociological and spiritual factors are thought to account for schizophrenia and to mediate the effects of various treatments (Mohr and Huguelet 2004; Mohr et al. 2006, 2007). Delusions, especially, have long been considered as a hallmark of psychotic disorders such as schizophrenia. However, as has been noted, delusions may not only be observable in individuals with psychotic conditions and could also occur in non-clinical groups. Approximately 1% to 3% of the non-clinical populations have delusions of a level of severity comparable to clinical cases of psychosis. About 5% of the non-clinical population have a delusion, but not of such severity. Although less severe, these beliefs are associated with a range of social and emotional difficulties. A further 10% to 15% of the non-clinical population has fairly regular delusional ideations. There is convincing evidence that delusions in clinical and non-clinical populations are related and may lie on a continuum (see Claridge 2010). Therefore it may be possible to obtain information about delusions seen in clinical settings by studying delusional ideation in nonclinical populations.

Excursus: measurement of religious/spiritual wellbeing – a multidimensional approach

Based on varying theoretical backgrounds and different forms of religiosity/ spirituality, some scales have been also constructed or translated for German-speaking people (e.g. Huber 2003; Murken 1998; Unterrainer 2007). The Spiritual Well-Being Scale (Ellison 1983) became particularly popular in this field (translated into German by Unterrainer 2006). The instrument was originally developed by Ellison and Paloutzian (Ellison 1983; Ellison and Smith 1991; Hill and Hood 1999) and aimed at measuring the quality of one's spiritual health. In this context, spiritual wellbeing is conceptualised as a two-dimensional construct. On the one hand, religious wellbeing describes, on a vertical dimension, wellbeing as it relates to God or even to a transcendent dimension. On the other hand, existential wellbeing addresses, on a horizontal dimension, our wellbeing as it relates to a sense of life purpose and life satisfaction, without any specific reference to a higher power (Ledbetter et al. 1991).

Empirical research on this instrument is comparatively rare. Existing studies suggest that it displays a rather poor psychometric quality (ceiling effects), especially when applied in non-clinical samples (e.g. Ledbetter et al. 1991). In the German adaptation of this scale, such problems did not occur (Unterrainer 2006). Motivated by our positive experience with these scales in several research projects, we developed a multidimensional version by adding a new concept of religious/spiritual wellbeing (Unterrainer and Fink 2010; Unterrainer et al. 2010a, 2010b, 2010c, 2010d) covering several aspects of psychological wellbeing concerning an immanent/transcendent area of perception. Religious/spiritual wellbeing is defined as the 'ability to experience and integrate meaning and purpose in existence through a connectedness with self, others or a power greater than oneself' (Unterrainer et al. 2010c). In the following paragraph, different dimensions of religious/spiritual wellbeing are discussed on a theoretical level in order to explain the meaning of the whole scale more thoroughly. Furthermore, item examples are given for each subscale to explain each dimension more precisely. The scale measures six dimensions of religious wellbeing: General religiosity, Forgiveness, Hope-immanent, Hope-transcendent, Connectedness, and Experience of sense and meaning. Each dimension comprises eight items, creating a total of forty-eight items for each scale. These dimensions could be broadly described as follows:

- *General religiosity*: This dimension includes the belief in God, who is merciful, with whom one is able to converse with a feeling of closeness, and thus experience contentment, security and trust in God's help. It also presupposes attendance in communitarian religious events and the recognition of the presence of God in nature. Item example: 'My faith gives me a feeling of security.'
- *Forgiveness*: The items here are straightforward; they measure the willingness to forgive, absence of hate, avoidance of revenge and wishing well of enemies (see McCullough et al. 2000). Item example: 'There are things which I cannot forgive' (coded reversely).
- *Hope-immanent*: Being optimistic that the future is going to be exciting. This dimension includes a sense that life is moving in the right direction; if this is not the case, to be certain that at least things will improve in the future. Hope-immanent implies also having a clear picture of the future and to expect positive experiences and the possibility to live as one envisages life. Item example: 'I view the future with optimism.'
- *Hope-transcendent*: While hope-immanent is focused on this life, even if it is about the future, hope-transcendence is about the afterlife. It consists in the recognition of the transience of this life, together with the hopeful acceptance of a life after death as well as an experience of hope that emerges from the possibility of being remembered after death. Item example: 'I often think about the fact that I will have to leave behind' (coded reversely).

- *Connectedness*: This dimension refers to the experience of the feeling of being absorbed into something greater. For instance, being reborn after death, a feeling of supernatural connection with some people, the experience of the ineffable, and a strong belief in an existence after death. Item example: 'I have experienced the feeling of being absorbed into something greater.'
- *Experience of sense and meaning*: This dimension is about the experience of authentic feelings, including deep affection and true friendship. It also takes into account a sufficient grasp of meaning of life. This also includes meaningful experiences of openness and honesty, as well as occasions of getting absorbed in something to the point of forgetting everything around. Item example: 'I have experienced true (authentic) feelings.'[1]

The MI-RSWB has been employed in several research projects concerning the role of religiosity and spirituality in the process of mental health and illness (Unterrainer 2010). Dimensions of religious/spiritual wellbeing (RSWB) were found to be substantially associated with indicators of subjective wellbeing and personality, like a sense of coherence, as the core concept in the *salutogenesis* approach (Antonovsky 1987). Dimensions of RSWB have been also discussed in the context of varying indicators of psychiatric illness. Unterrainer (2010) reports substantial negative correlations with, for example, depression and anxiety, as well as with psychoticism. Furthermore, dimensions of RSWB have been linked, especially in German regions, with the very established concept of the structure and centrality of religiosity (Huber 2003). Different profiles of RSWB were found depending on the amount of centrality of religiosity. A more in-depth analysis showed positive and negative god representations (e.g. Rizzuto 1998; Rudolf 2006) to be substantially connected (especially in psychiatric patients) to different indicators of mental health and mental illness, even after controlling for the general amount of religiosity.

Dimensions of religious/spiritual wellbeing among psychotic and schizophrenic patients

Magical thinking as an indicator of schizotypy

According to Meehl (1990; see also Eckblad and Chapman 1983), magical ideation might be described as 'belief, quasi-belief, or semi-serious entertainment of the possibility that events which, according to the causal concept of this culture, cannot have a causal relation with each other, might somehow nevertheless do so'. An increased amount of magical ideation was found among persons prone to schizophrenia or schizotypy (Chapman et al. 1994; Eckblad and Chapman 1983).

Schizotypy

The term 'schizotypy' (as a short form of 'schizophreny phenotype') was first coined by Rado (1953) to characterise persons showing eccentric personality traits, similar to symptoms of schizophrenia. Meanwhile, there is substantial evidence that schizotypy might be best described as a multifactorial continuous construct, as three or even four factors (paranormal experiences and beliefs, cognitive failures, introvertive anhedonia, asocial behaviour) that can be identified consistently in this context (Claridge 2010; Goulding 2004; Peters 2010). Along with this, numerous scales have been developed to assess the various aspects of the schizotypy concept and its multifactorial structure (Farias, Claridge and Lalljee 2005; Feldman and Rust 1989; Fisher et al. 2004; Raine and Benishay 1995; Vollema and van den Bosch 1995; White, Joseph and Alastair 1995).

Schizotaxy

There might be a neuronal or biochemical defect – namely schizotaxy, which was found to be increased among family members of people suffering from schizophrenia and might lead to schizotypy depending on specific developmental circumstances (Ameen, Praharaj and Sinha 2004). Very recently, Raballo and Parnas (2010) reported anomalous subjective experiences as an expression of schizotaxic vulnerability.

Schizotypal (personality) disorder

According to the DSM-IV personality disorders are pervasive, inflexible, maladaptive collections of traits that impair individuals and interfere with their ability to function productively (Saß et al. 1996). Raine and Benishay (1995) describe schizotypal personality disorder (SPD) as representing a serious personality disturbance that borders on the major psychoses and might be closely related to schizophrenia. Based on International Classification of Diseases (ICD 10; see Dilling et al. 1994), a 'schizotypal disorder' is characterised by eccentric behaviour, anomalies of thinking and affect which resemble those seen in schizophrenia, though no definite and characteristic schizophrenic anomalies have occurred at any stage. No dominant or typical disturbance can be described, but McGlashan (1987; see also Raine and Benishay 1995) has noted that odd communication, paranoid ideation and social isolation might be taken as the core symptoms.

The relationship between religiosity/spirituality, magical thinking and personality traits

Eysenck's model of personality (Eysenck and Eysenck 1975) consists of three factors: psychoticism (solitary, troublesome, cruel, inhumane personality traits), extraversion (sociable, carefree, optimistic, sensation seeking personality traits) and neuroticism (anxious, worrying, moody and depressive personality traits). There is a large body of evidence that higher religiosity scores are associated with lower psychoticism scores in adults (Francis 1993; Kay 1981; Smith, Riley and Peters 2009; White et al. 1995) as well as in children and adolescents (Francis 1993), whereas no relevant associations were found with neuroticism or extraversion. According to Eysenck (1992), this association might be taken as a function of conditioning, as religiosity belongs to the domain of tender-minded attitudes. People who score low on psychoticism are known to condition more readily. Furthermore, Eysenck (1992; see also Corr 2010) described psychoticism as representing a dimension of personality defined at the far ends of schizophrenia. Thus, higher scores on religiosity should be linked to lower levels on schizophrenic-relevant measures. Maltby and Day (2001) noted a 'wealth of information, that suggests that low psychoticism is fundamental to religiosity across a number of cultures' (2001: 187; see also Diduca and Joseph 1997).

Religiosity and spirituality among psychotic patients: cult or cure?

Menezes and Moreira-Almeida (2010) discuss the relationships between religion, spirituality and psychosis. They argued that, although religious/ spiritual problems may appear to be synonymous with psychotic problems, this might also be taken to be a manifestation of non-pathological religious/ spiritual experiences. This was based on the result of empirical evidence demonstrating that hallucinations also occur in the non-clinical populations, and thus are not exclusive to psychotic/schizophrenic patients. Other studies are pointing out the strong presence of religious content in psychotic patients, as spirituality and religiousness have been shown to be highly prevalent in this patient group. Furthermore, several questions arise concerning the relationship between religion and mental illness among patients with psychotic disorders. The first question asks whether religion affects the development of psychosis and, what's more, whether it could have a harmful influence for psychotic/schizophrenic patients? According to Huguelet and Mohr (2009), there is some evidence that religion and spirituality can be harmful for patients with psychosis, for example, patients who have delusions with religious content may experience a worse long-term prognosis (see Huguelet and Mohr 2009).

Are patients more prone to engage in religious activities and is there a positive effect of religious coping? Mohr et al. (2006) studied the function of religious coping among 115 stabilised patients with schizophrenia or schizoaffective disorder. It was found that for 45% of the patients religion was an important part in their lives. Furthermore, 62% of the patients used positive religious coping strategies (e.g. meaning, purpose, hope) to deal with their illness, and only 14% reported negative religious coping strategies (guilt, shame). In addition, the authors of this study were able to replicate these findings in 123 patients living in Quebec (see also Huguelet et al. 2010).

The last question (also from the perspective of a clinician) might reference how to deal with delusions with religious content presented by psychotic patients? Huguelet and Mohr (2009) list three ways in which religiosity/spirituality might help psychotic patients in a way that could be addressed by the clinician: (1) religion and spirituality could be used to cope with current symptoms as well as social and interpersonal problems; (2) religion and spirituality might help to prevent potentially harmful behaviours, this includes substance abuse as well as suicidal and par-suicidal attempts; and (3) religion and spirituality might even allow patients with severe forms of schizophrenia to experience personal growth.

We might conclude that religious delusions, as an expression of a psychiatric disorder, on the one hand, and dimensions of religious/spiritual wellbeing as well as positive religious coping strategies, on the other hand, may interact in a very complex manner among psychotic patients. Thus, it is a challenging task for the clinician to separate between them, as religion and spirituality might, at the same time, be part of the cure as well as part of the disease.

Acknowledgement

The author wants to thank Sahaya G. Selvam for his substantial contribution to the further development of the concept of dimensions of religious/spiritual wellbeing.

Note

1 For details about the items of the English version of the scale, together with a short manual, please contact the author of this chapter

References

Ameen, S., Praharaj, S. and Sinha, V.K. (2004). Schizotaxia: A review. *Indian Journal of Social Psychiatry* 20: 27–34.

Antonovsky, A. (1987). *Salutogenese: Zur Entmystifizierung der Gesundheit.* Tübingen: DGVT.

Becker, E. (1973). *The Denial of Death.* New York: Free Press Paperbacks.

Black, D.M. (2006). (Ed.) *Psychoanalysis and Religion in the 21st Century. Competitors or Collaborators?* London: Routledge.

Capps, D. (2001). *Freud and the Freudians on Religion. A Reader.* Yale: Yale University Press.

Chapman, L.J., Chapman, J.P., Kwapil, T.R., Eckblad, M. and Zinser, M.C. (1994). Putatively psychosis-prone subjects 10 years later. *Journal of Abnormal Psychology* 103: 171–83.

Chen, E. and Berrios, G.E. (1996). Recognition of hallucinations: A multidimensional model and methodology. *Psychopathology* 29: 54–63.

Chiu, L.P.W. (1989). Differential diagnosis and management of hallucinations. *Journal of the Hong Kong Medical Association* 41: 292–7.

Claridge, G. (2010). Spiritual experience: Healthy psychoticism? In *Psychosis and Spirituality. Consolidating the New Paradigm*, ed. I. Clarke, pp. 75–88. Oxford: Wiley-Blackwell.

Coghlan, C. and Ali, I. (2009). Suicide. In *Spirituality and Psychiatry*, ed. C. Cook, A. Powell and A. Sims, pp. 60–80. London: Royal College of Psychiatrists.

Cook, C. (2004). Spirituality and addiction. *Addiction* 99: 539–51.

Corr, P.J. (2010). The psychoticism–psychopathy continuum: A neuropsychological model of core deficits. *Personality and Individual Differences* 48: 695–705.

Corveleyn, J. and Luyten, P. (2005). Psychodynamic psychologies and religion: Past, present, future. In *Handbook of Religion and Spirituality*, ed. R.F. Paloutzian and C.L. Park, pp. 80–101. New York and London: Guilford Press.

Dervic, K., Oquendo, M.A., Grunebaum, M.F., Ellis, S., Burke, A.K. and Mann, J.J. (2004). Religious affiliation and suicide attempt. *American Journal of Psychiatry* 161: 2303–8.

Diduca, D. and Joseph, S. (1997). Schizotypal traits and dimensions of religiosity. *British Journal of Clinical Psychology* 36: 635–8.

Dilling, H., Mombour, W., Schmidt, M.H. and Schulte-Markwort, E. (eds) (1994). *Internationale Klassifikation Psychischer Störungen: ICD 10* [Tenth Revision of the *International Classification of Diseases*: *ICD 10*]. Bern, Göttingen, Toronto and Seattle: Hans Huber.

Eckblad, M. and Chapman, L.J. (1983). Magical ideation as an Indicator of schizotypy. *Journal of Consulting and Clinical Psychology* 51: 215–22.

Ellison, C.W. (1983). Spiritual well-being: Conceptualization and measurement. *Journal of Psychology and Theology* 11: 330–40.

Ellison, C.W. and Smith, J. (1991). Toward an integrative measure of health and well-being. *Journal of Psychology and Theology. Special Issue: Spirituality: Perspectives in Theory and Research* 19: 35–48.

Engel, G.L. (1977). The need for a new medical model: A challenge for biomedicine. *Science* 196: 129–36.

Eysenck, H.J. (1992). The definition and measurement of psychoticism *Personality and Individual Differences* 13: 757–85.

Eysenck, H.J. and Eysenck, S.B. (1975). *Manual of the Eysenck Personality Questionnaire.* London: Hodder and Stoughton.

Farias, M., Claridge, G. and Lalljee, M. (2005). Personality and cognitive predictors of New Age practices and beliefs. *Personality and Individual Differences* 39: 979–89.

Feldman, J. and Rust, J. (1989). Religiosity, schizotypal thinking, and schizophrenia. *Psychological Reports* 65: 587–93.

Fenwick, P. (2009). Neuroscience of the spirit. In *Spirituality and Psychiatry*, ed. C. Cook, A. Powell and A. Sims, pp. 169–89. London: Royal College of Psychiatrists.

Fenwick, P. (2010). The neurophysiology of religious experience. In *Psychosis and Spirituality. Consolidating the New Paradigm*, ed. I. Clarke, pp. 9–18. Chichester: Wiley-Blackwell.

Fisher, J.E., Mohanty, A., Herrington, J.D., Koven, N.S., Miller, G.A. and Heller, W. (2004). Neuropsychological evidence for dimensional schizotypy: Implications for creativity and psychopathology. *Journal of Research in Personality* 38: 24–31.

Francis, L.J. (1993). Personality and religion among college students in the UK. *Personality and Individual Differences* 14: 619–22.

Freeman, D. (2006). Delusions in the nonclinical population. *Current Psychiatry Reports* 8: 191–204.

Freud, S. (1907). Obsessive actions and religious practices. In *The Standard Edition of the Complete Psychological Works of Sigmund Freud*, ed. and trans. J. Strachey, vol. 9. London: Hogarth Press/Institute of Psycho-Analysis.

Freud, S. (1913). Totem and taboo. In *The Standard Edition of the Complete Psychological Works of Sigmund Freud*, ed. and trans. J. Strachey, vol. 12. London: Hogarth Press/Institute of Psycho-Analysis.

Freud, S. (1923). A seventeenth-century demonological neurosis. In *The Standard Edition of the Complete Psychological Works of Sigmund Freud*, ed. and trans. J. Strachey, vol. 19. London: Hogarth Press/Institute of Psycho-Analysis.

Freud, S. (1927). The future of an illusion. In *The Standard Edition of the Complete Psychological Works of Sigmund Freud*, ed. and trans. J. Strachey, vol. 21. London: Hogarth Press/Institute of Psycho-Analysis.

Freud, S. (1939). Moses and monotheism. In *The Standard Edition of the Complete Psychological Works of Sigmund Freud*, trans. and ed. J. Strachey, vol. 23. London: Hogarth Press/Institute of Psycho-Analysis.

Getz, G.E., Fleck, D.E. and Strakowski, S.M. (2001). Frequency and severity of religious delusions in Christian patients with psychosis. *Psychiatry Research* 103: 87–91.

Goulding, A. (2004). Schizotypy models in relation to subjective health and paranormal beliefs and experiences. *Personality and Individual Differences* 37: 157–67.

Hartley, J. (2010). Mapping our madness: The hero's journey as a therapeutic approach. In *Psychosis and Spirituality. Consolidating the New Paradigm*, ed. I. Clarke, pp. 227–38. Chichester: Wiley-Blackwell.

Hill, P.C. and Hood, R.W. (eds) (1999). *Measures of Religiosity*. Birmingham: Religious Education Press.

Huber, H.P. (2008). *Allgemeine Klinische Psychologie*. In *Lehr- und Forschungstexte Psychologie: Neue Folge* 14, ed. D. Albert, M. Oswald, K. Pawlik and K.-H. Stapf (Hrsg.). Göttingen: Hogrefe.

Huber, S. (2003). *Zentralität und Inhalt. Ein multidimensionales Messmodell der Religiosität*. Opladen: Leske and Budrich.

Huguelet, P. and Mohr, S. (2009). Religion/spirituality and psychosis. In *Religion and Spirituality in Psychiatry*, ed. P. Huguelet and H.G. Koenig, pp. 65–81. Cambridge: University Press.

Huguelet, P., Mohr, S., Gilliéron, C., Brandt, P.Y. and Borras, L. (2010). Religious explanatory models in patients with psychosis: A three-year follow-up study. *Psychopathology* 43: 230–9.

James, W. (1979). *Die Vielfalt der religiösen Erfahrung*, ed. W. Olten. New York: Longman. (Original edition published by Longmans, Green and Co. in 1902 as *The Varieties of Religious Experience*. German edition published in Olden by Walter.)

Jaynes, J. (1976). *The Origin of Consciousness in the Breakdown of the Bicameral Mind.* Boston and New York: Mariner Books.

Jones, J.W. (2001). *Contemporary Psychoanalysis and Religion: Transference and Transcendence.* New Haven, CT: Yale University Press.

Kay, W.K. (1981). Psychoticism and attitude to religion. *Personality and Individual Differences* 2: 249–52.

Kendler, K.S., Liu, X.Q., Gardner, C.O., McCullough, M.E., Larson, D. and Prescott, C.A. (2003). Dimensions of religiosity and their relationship to lifetime psychiatric and substance use disorders *American Journal of Psychiatry* 160: 496–503.

Kernberg, O.F. (2000). Psychoanalytic perspectives on the religious experience. *American Journal of Psychotherapy* 54: 452–74.

Koenig, H.G., McCullough, M.E. and Larson, D.B. (2001). *Handbook of Religion and Health.* Oxford: University Press.

Ledbetter, M.F., Smith, L.A., Vosler-Hunter, W.L. and Fischer, J.D. (1991). An evaluation of the research and clinical usefulness of the Spiritual Well-Being Scale. *Journal of Psychology and Theology* 19: 49–55.

Maltby, J. and Day, L. (2001). Spiritual involvement and belief: the relationship between spirituality and Eysenck's personality dimensions. *Personality and Individual Differences* 30: 187–92.

McCullough, M.E., Pargament, K.I. and Thoresen, C.E. (2000). The psychology of forgiveness: History, conceptual issues, and overview. In *Forgiveness – Theory, Research, and Practice*, ed. M.E. McCullough, K.I. Pargament and C.E. Thoresen, pp. 1–16. New York and London: Guilford Press.

McGlashan, T.H. (1987). Testing DSM-III symptom criteria for schizotypal and borderline personality disorders. *Archives of General Psychiatry* 44: 143–8.

Meehl, P.E. (1990). Toward an integrated theory of schizotaxia, schizotypy, and schizophrenia. *Journal of Personality Disorders* 4: 1–99.

Menezes, A. Jr, and Moreira-Almeida, A. (2010). Religion, spirituality, and psychosis. *Current Psychiatry Reports* 12: 174–9.

Miller, W.R. and Thoresen, C.E. (1999). Spirituality and health. In *Integrating Spirituality into Treatment. Resources for Practitioners*, ed. W.R. Miller, pp. 3–19. Washington: American Psychological Association.

Mitchell, S. and Roberts, G. (2009). Psychosis. In *Spirituality and Psychiatry,* ed. C. Cook, A. Powell and A. Sims, pp. 39–60. London: Royal College of Psychiatrists.

Mohr, S. and Huguelet, P. (2004). The relationship between schizophrenia and religion and its implications for care. *Swiss Medical Weekly* 134: 369–76.

Mohr, S. and Pfeiffer, S. (2009). Delusions and hallucinations with religious content. In *Religion and Spirituality in Psychiatry*, ed. P. Huguelet and H.G. Koenig, pp. 81–96. Cambridge: Cambridge University Press.

Mohr, S., Borras, L., Betrisey, C., Pierre-Yves, B., Gilliéron, C. and Huguelet, P. (2010). Delusions with religious content in patients with psychosis: How they interact with spiritual coping. *Psychiatry* 73: 158–72.

Mohr, S., Brandt, P.Y., Borras, L., Gilliéron, C. and Huguelet P. (2006). Toward an integration of spirituality and religiousness into the psychosocial dimension of schizophrenia. *American Journal of Psychiatry* 163: 1952–9.

Mohr, S., Brandt, P.Y., Borras, L., Gilliéron, C. and Huguelet P. (2007). The assessment of spirituality and religiousness in schizophrenia. *Journal of Nervous and Mental Diseases* 195: 247–53.

Murken, S. (1998). *Gottesbeziehung und psychische Gesundheit. Die Entwicklung eines Modells und seine empirische Überprüfung.* Münster, New York, Munich and Berlin: Waxmann.

Newberg, A.B. and Newberg, S.K. (2005). The neuropsychology of religious and spiritual experience. In *Handbook of Religion and Spirituality*, ed. R.F. Paloutzian and C.L. Park, pp. 199–216. New York and London: Guilford Press.

Pargament, K.I. (1997). *The Psychology of Religion and Coping. Theory, Research, Practice.* New York and London: Guilford Press.

Pargament, K.I. (1999). The psychology of religion and spirituality? Yes and no. *International Journal for the Psychology of Religion* 9: 3–16.

Pargament, K.I. (2007). *Spiritually Integrated Psychotherapy: Understanding and Addressing the Sacred.* New York: Guilford Press.

Peters, E. (2010). Are delusions on a continuum? The case of religious and delusional beliefs. In *Psychosis and Spirituality. Consolidating the New Paradigm*, ed. I. Clarke, pp. 127–38. Chichester: Wiley-Blackwell.

Pfeiffer, S. (2007). *Phänomenologie und Psychodynamik des religiösen Wahns.* Paper presented at the RPP (Institute for Religion in Psychiatry and Psychotherapy) Congress – Religiosity in Psychiatry and Psychotherapy held in Gras, Austria in 2007.

Piedmont, R.L. (1999). Does spirituality represent the sixth factor of personality? Spiritual transcendence and the five-factor model. *Journal of Personality* 67: 985–1013.

Piedmont, R.L. (2004). Spiritual transcendence as a predictor of psychosocial outcome from an outpatient substance abuse. *Psychology of Addictive Behaviors* 18: 213–22.

Raballo, A. and Parnas, J. (2010). The silent side of the spectrum: Schizotypy and the schizotaxic self. *Schizophrenia Bulletin* 37(5): 1017–26.

Rado, S. (1953). Dynamics and classification of disordered behavior. *American Journal of Psychiatry* 110: 406–16.

Raine, A. and Benishay, D. (1995). The SPQ-B: A brief screening Instrument for schizotypal personality disorder. *Journal of Personality Disorders* 9: 346–55.

Reeves, R.R. and Liberto, V. (2006). Suicide associated with the Antichrist delusion. *Journal of Forensic Sciences* 51: 411–12.

Rizzuto, A.M. (1996). Psychoanalytic treatment and the religious person. In *Religion and the Clinical Practice of Psychology*, ed. E.P. Shafranske, pp. 409–32. Washington, DC: American Psychological Association.

Rizzuto, A.M. (1998). *Why did Freud reject God? A psychodynamic interpretation.* New Haven, CN and London: London University Press.

Rudolf, G. (2006). *Strukturbezogene Psychotherapie. Leitfaden zur psychodynamischen Therapie struktureller Störungen.* Stuttgart and New York: Schattauer.

Saroglou, V. (2002). Religion and the five factors of personality: A meta-analytic review. *Personality and Individual Differences* 32: 15–25.

Saß, H., Wittchen, H.-U. and Zaudig, M. (eds) (1996). *DSM-IV: Diagnostisches und statistisches Manual psychischer Störungen.* Göttingen: Hogrefe.

Siddle, R., Haddock, G., Tarrier, N. and Faragher, E.B. (2002). Religious delusions in patients admitted to hospital with schizophrenia. *Social Psychiatry and Psychiatric Epidemiology* 37: 130–8.

Sloan, R.P., Bagiella, E. and Powell, T. (1999). Religion, spirituality, and medicine. *Lancet* 353: 664–7.

Smith, L., Riley, S. and Peters, E.R. (2009). Schizotypy, delusional ideation and well-being in an American new religious movement population. *Clinical Psychology and Psychotherapy* 16: 479–84.

Smith, T.B., McCullough, M.E. and Poll, J. (2003). Religiousness and depression: Evidence for a main effect and the moderating influence of stressful life events. *Psychological Bulletin* 129: 614–36.

Unterrainer, H.-F. (2006). *Spiritualität & Sucht. Glaube als Ressource in der Alkoholismustherapie.* Saarbrücken: VDM.

Unterrainer, H.-F. (2007). *Spiritualität und psychische Gesundheit. Glaube als Ressource in der Krankheitsverarbeitung.* Saarbrücken: VDM.

Unterrainer, H.-F. (2010). *Seelenfinsternis? Struktur und Inhalt der Gottesbeziehung im klinisch-psychiatrischen Feld.* Münster, New York, Munich and Berlin: Waxmann.

Unterrainer, H.-F. and Fink, A. (2013). Das Multidimensionale Inventar zum Religiös-Spirituellen Befinden (MI-RSB): Normwerte für die Österreichische Allgemeinbevölkerung. *Diagnostica* 59: 33–44.

Unterrainer, H.-F., Huber, H.P., Ladenhauf, K.H., Wallner, S.J. and Liebmann, P.M. (2010a). MI-RSB 48: Die Entwicklung eines multidimensionalen Inventars zum religiös-spirituellen Befinden [MI-RSWB 48: The development of a Multidimensional Inventory for Religious/Spiritual Well-Being]. *Diagnostica* 2: 82–93.

Unterrainer, H.-F., Ladenhauf, K.H., Wallner-Liebmann, S.J. and Fink, A. (2010b). Dimensions of religious/spiritual well-being: A comparison study between addicts and healthy controls. [Submitted to *Personality and Individual Differences.*]

Unterrainer, H.-F., Ladenhauf, K.H., Wallner-Liebmann, S.J. and Fink, A. (2010c). Dimensions of religious/spiritual well-being and their relation to personality and psychological well-being. *Personality and Individual Differences*, 49: 192–7.

Vollema, M.G. and van den Bosch, R.J. (1995). The multidimensionality of schizotypy. *Schizophrenia Bulletin* 21: 19–31.

White, J., Joseph, S. and Alastair, N. (1995). Religiosity, psychoticism, and schizotypal personality. *Personality and Individual Differences* 19: 847–51.

Wulff, D.M. (1997). *The Psychology of Religion: Classic and Contemporary.* New York: John Wiley.

Zinnbauer, B.J., Pargament, K.I., Cole, B., Rye, M.S., Butter, E.M., Belavich, T.G., Hipp, K.M., Scott, A.B. and Kadar, J.L. (1997). Religion and spirituality: Unfuzzying the fuzzy. *Journal for the Scientific Study of Religion* 36: 549–64.

GLOSSARY OF LACANIAN TERMS

Daniel Lagache, writing almost forty years ago, pointed out that aversion to psychoanalysis sometimes takes the form of disparaging comments about its terminology (Laplanche and Pontalis 1980). Evans (1996) noted that the various psychoanalytic languages, rather than being dialects of the same language, are languages themselves, each with their own lexis and syntax. Since the 1950s a number of glossaries, lexicons and dictionaries of psychoanalysis have attempted to help readers grapple with analytic texts. Below we give a brief description – based, for the most part, on Evans (1996) and Bailly (2009) – of some of the key Lacanian terms used in this book. But, for those seeking an in-depth discussion of psychoanalytic terms, we direct them to more specialised dictionaries (e.g. Evans 1996; Hinshelwood 1989; Laplanche and Pontalis 1980; Rycroft 1968; Samuels, Shorter and Plant 1986).

Castration   In Lacan's thought, this refers to the symbolic loss of the imaginary phallus. He links it to fantasies of bodily mutilation that originate during the mirror stage of development. Castration is crucial to our understanding of the Oedipus complex, where it represents the dissolution of the complex. As a result, symbolic castration is at the root of psychopathology. In psychosis, the subject fundamentally refuses to limit *jouissance* (pleasure) through a denial of castration. This rejection then generates hallucinations of dismemberment (e.g. the Wolf-Man).

Foreclosure   This term was originally introduced into psychology in 1928, when Edouard Pichon published an article on the psychological significance of negation, borrowing the legal term *forclusif* to indicate things that the speaker no longer sees as part of reality. The publication appeared against the background of the dispute between Freud and René Laforgue concerning scotomisation (Mijolla 2010). Lacan first translates *Verwerfung* as 'foreclosure' in seminar 3. In 'On a question prior to any possible treatment of psychosis' (2006) he defines *Verwerfung* as a foreclosure 'of the signifier': 'at the point at which the Name of the Father is summoned . . . a pure and simple hole may thus answer in the Other; due to the lack of the metaphoric effect, this hole will give rise to a corresponding hole in the place of phallic signification' (Lacan 2006: 558). He specifies that it is the Name of the Father that is foreclosed. If the Name of the Father is foreclosed and the symbolic function of castration is refused by the subject, the signifiers of the father and of castration reappear in reality, in the form of hallucinations. Thus, in developing the concept of foreclosure, Lacan was able to declare, 'What does not come to light in the symbolic appears in the real' (Lacan 2006: 388). Lacan reconceived Freud's hypothesis of an original affirmation as a symbolic operation in which the subject emerges from an already present real and recognises the signifying stroke that engages the subject in a world symbolically ordered by the Name of the Father and castration. In his seminar 'The Four Fundamental Concepts of Psychoanalysis' (1977), Lacan took up Freud's *Beyond the Pleasure Principle* (Freud SE 1920) and approached the real in terms of compulsion and repetition. He proposed distinguishing between two different aspects of repetition: a symbolic aspect that depends on the compulsion of signifiers (automaton), and a real aspect that he called *tuché*, the interruption of the automaton by trauma or a bad encounter that the subject is unable to avoid. Engendered by the real of trauma, repetition is perpetuated by the failure of symbolisation. From this point on, Lacan defined the real as 'that which always returns to the same place' (Lacan 1977: 49). Trauma, which Freud situated within the framework of the death drive, Lacan conceptualised as the impossible-to-symbolise real.

Imaginary This term is one of the three orders of the psyche and has the characteristics of illusion and seduction. It is set in motion during the mirror stage of infantile development and refers to the formation of the ego, which is rooted in the subject's relationship to the image of his or her body in the mirror. The principal illusions of the imaginary are those of completeness, autonomy.

Jouissance This term, which has a sexual connotation, means pleasure or enjoyment and comes close to Freud's notion of libido. It is a word usually left untranslated in Lacanian literature. It is related to the notion of the pleasure principle in Freud, who argues that is achieved when excitation is reduced. Lacan uses the term *jouissance* to indicate an excessive quantity of excitation or the desire to transgress the prohibition against incest. Thus Lacan describes it as the paradoxical pleasure derived from the symptom. Entry into the symbolic order, through symbolic castration, amounts to a renunciation of (an already impossible) *jouissance*.

Name of the Father The Name of the Father is the fundamental signifier which permits signification to proceed normally. Lacan used this concept to redress what he perceived was an overemphasis of object relations theory on the dual relationship between child and mother. Instead, Lacan stressed the importance of the third party in the Oedipus constellation and of the father in the promulgation of the law that enables the child to engage in a shared intersubjective world, in language and culture (the symbolic). In psychosis the Name of the Father is foreclosed and thus there can be no paternal metaphor and hence no phallic signification.

Oedipus complex The Oedipus complex is the passage, through a complex sexual dialectic, from the imaginary to the symbolic, which occurs between the third and fifth year of life. It is the paradigmatic triangular structure in which the father transforms the dual relationship between the mother and child. Lacan follows Freud in attributing all psychopathological structures to a malfunction in the Oedipus complex. In other words, access to the symbolic order is achieved through confronting sexual difference. Central to this is the child's realisation that the mother is incomplete (because she lacks the phallus) and his or her wish to become the phallus and satisfy the mother's desire. Lacan argues that this is true regardless of the sex of the child. Partial resolution comes through the mother's behaviour and words, which somehow make it clear to the child that there is a law forbidding it to have sexual access to his or her mother. Later, the child becomes aware of the father and his role in relation to the mother's desire. The child realises there is no point in competing with the father and consequently feels castrated. This liberates the child from the impossible task of fulfilling the mother and allows it to identify with the father.

Other According to Evans (1996), the introduction of the term other (*autre* in French) by Lacan is dependent on his reading of Hegel. Lacan distinguishes between what he calls the big Other (designated by a capital 'A' for *Autre*) and the little other (designated by a small '*a*', which is always italicised). The term *objet* (*petit*) *a* (object little *a*) or just *objet a* (object *a*), which Lacan insists should not be translated, appears in Lacan's work from 1955. Unlike the big Other, which denotes a radical and irreducible alterity, the little other is coupled with the ego. See the recent discussion by Vanheule (2011: 125–48).

Real The notion of the real (*réel*) is one of the most complex – some would say incoherent – concepts in Lacan's entire *oeuvre*, as the notion of a lack-within-the-real perhaps suggests. In fact, he uses the term in countless different ways and at times in contradictory senses. Most often it does not correspond to reality (*réalité*), but to what cannot be symbolised (put into language) and which stretches all representations and is outside all systems of thought. As such, it is only in its traces that it is glimpsed or, perhaps more accurately, that its implicit absence is suggested. This has particular relevance in psychosis for two reasons at least: first, because psychosis is described by Lacan as a failure to enter into the symbolic (which includes language and therefore social relations); and second because, he argues, what is not symbolised appears in the real (e.g. as hallucinations).

Symbolic The symbolic, in Lacan's oeuvre, refers to one of the three orders of the psyche. It is a term largely derived from the structural anthropology of Lévi-Strauss, with its emphasis on the exchange of gifts. Lacan describes it as crucial to psychoanalysis, as the most fundamental form of exchange is that of communication and because speech functions in analysis to shift the subject's identification away from the analyst. It is also the realm of the Other (radical alterity), of the Law (the universal principles that underpin social interaction – importantly, the regulation or limiting of desire through the law against incest) and of the unconscious, which is made up of repressed signifiers.

References

Bailly, L. (2009). *Lacan. A Beginner's Guide*. Oxford: Oneworld.

Evans, D. (1996). *An Introductory Dictionary of Lacanian Psychoanalysis*. London: Routledge.

Freud, S. (1920). Beyond the pleasure principle. *The Standard Edition of the Complete Psychological Works of Sigmund Freud,* ed. and trans. J. Strachey, vol. 18. London: Hogarth Press/Institute of Psycho-Analysis.

Hinshelwood, R.D. (1989). *A Dictionary of Kleinian Thought*. London: Free Association Books.

Lacan, J. (1977). *The Seminar of Jacques Lacan,* Book 11, *The Four Fundamental Concepts of Psychoanalysis*, trans. A. Sheridan. London: Hogarth Press/Institute of Psycho-Analysis.

Lacan, J. (2006). *Ecrits. The First Complete Edition in English*, trans. B. Fink. New York and London: W.W. Norton.

Laplanche, J. and Pontalis, J.-B. (1980). *The Language of Psycho-Analysis,* trans. D. Nicholson-Smith. London: Hogarth Press/Institute of Psycho-Analysis.

Mijolla, A. de (2010). *Freud et la France 1885–1945*. Paris: Presses Universitaires de France.

Rycroft, C. (1968). *A Critical Dictionary of Psychoanalysis*. Harmondsworth: Penguin.

Samuels, A., Shorter, B. and Plant, F. (1986). *A Critical Dictionary of Jungian Analysis*. London and New York: Routledge.

Vanheule, S. (2011). *The Subject of Psychosis: A Lacanian Perspective*. London and New York: Palgrave Macmillan.

INDEX